Introduction to Operating System Design

Introduction to Operating System Design

A. N. Habermann

Carnegie-Mellon University

SRA

SCIENCE RESEARCH ASSOCIATES, INC.
Chicago, Palo Alto, Toronto
Henley-on-Thames, Sydney, Paris, Stuttgart

A Subsidiary of IBM

The SRA Computer Science Series

Mark Elson, *Concepts of Programming Languages*
Mark Elson, *Data Structures*
Peter Freeman, *Software Systems Principles: A Survey*
C. W. Gear, *Introduction to Computer Science*
A. N. Habermann, *Introduction to Operating System Design*
Harry Katzan, Jr., *Computer Systems Organization and Programming*
Stephen M. Pizer, *Numerical Computing and Mathematical Analysis*
Harold S. Stone, *Discrete Mathematical Structures*
Harold S. Stone, editor, *Introduction to Computer Architecture*

Library of Congress Cataloging in Publication Data

Habermann, Arie Nicolaas, date
Introduction to Operating System Design

(SRA computer science series)
1. Electronic digital computers—Programming.
I. Title.
QA76.6.H28 001.6'42 75-34073
ISBN 0-574-21075-X

Printed in the United States of America.

PREFACE

The study of operating systems became a respectable computer science topic after the introduction of timesharing and multiprogramming—features that revolutionized the use of computers. Without them, only one programmer at a time can use a computer, and programs must be executed one after the other. With them, systems can serve a number of concurrent users and execute several programs in parallel.

Operating systems are worth studying because of the interesting problems that arise when several users share computer facilities. These problems concern the interaction and communication of the various concurrent activities, the allocation and reservation of resources, scheduling disciplines and the sharing of data bases.

This textbook introduces topics relevant to the design of an operating system. It is primarily designed for undergraduate students in their junior or senior year and beginning graduate students who have entered computer science from another discipline. The text functions best if used in the fourth or fifth course of a computer science curriculum in which programming and programming languages, data structures, the design of large programs and compiling techniques have already been covered. More important than the specific contents of preceding courses is programming experience, since the program abstractions and outlines presented in this book will be better understood if the student has had the opportunity to work with large programs.

This book is not oriented toward any particular operating system or machine. Instead, it presents major concepts that apply to a variety of systems. It is the author's belief that concepts are far more important than implementation. Moreover, presenting any particular system has two serious drawbacks. First, one tends to put too much emphasis on a particular implementation and therefore to overlook alternatives. Second, discussing an implementation answers *how* the system works, but fails to answer *why* the system has been designed in a particular way.

Another major concern in writing this book has been the level of detail at which programs are presented. It is of the utmost importance to separate basic ideas from details of implementation. This is one of the reasons why the programs in this book have not been written in one of the established programming languages. Such a language is, on the one hand, too demanding and, on the other, not flexible enough. It is too demanding because it requires that programs be written in detail, including declarations and punctuation symbols. This is not only a nuisance at times, but diverts the student's attention from the real issue. Programming languages are not flexible enough to easily represent any kind of object. If we use the term *stack*, a programmer understands that we wish to apply the operations *push* and *pop* to this object. Most programming language systems are not smart enough to understand this; the programmer must represent the object as an array or linked list and must define the operations push and pop as part of the program. The programming language suitable for this textbook would contain all the data structures we need as primitive types similar to the types *real* and *integer.* Such a programming language does not exist.

It is sometimes argued that writing programs in an existing language is an advantage because the programs can then be run on a machine. If this were a convincing argument, the programs should undoubtedly be written in FORTRAN, because this is the only language which is generally available. Any other language either is no better than FORTRAN or needs so much explanation that a substantial part of this book would have to be dedicated to a tutorial on that language. There are strong arguments against this approach, the least of which is the fact that FORTRAN is simply not adequate for the design description. The strongest argument is that it is much easier to encode a well-described design specification in the programming language of your choice than to derive the design specification from a given program. In addition, a specific programming language obscures the real issues because of the coding detail it requires. Since we are concerned with the design concepts of operating systems, the choice of a particular programming language would be a poor start.

The book is organized to suit three types of readers. The reader who wishes to be informed about the basic ideas of operating systems, and some of the best-known types of systems, should read chapters 1 and 2, skipping the problems. The reader who wants to know how systems are organized and how various problems have been solved should read, in addition, chapters 3, 7, 8 and 9. However, the book is primarily written for students who wish to work actively on the subject matter, not merely read and listen. For these students there is a set of problems at the end of every section. The problems are not merely exercises based on the presented material but an extension of (and an elaboration on) the text. Since it is impossible to discuss all the variations or modifications of the basic ideas in the text, some alternatives and special cases are discussed in the problems. Therefore, the student should at least read the problems.

The difficulty of the problems ranges from simple variations on the text that can be programmed in an hour to large projects that require a substantial amount of time. It is not recommended that the instructor assign the problems as homework without any comment. The problems are written in narrative style so that the instructor can use them as the basis for assignments in the programming language of his choice.

Those readers who do not have time to work through the whole book should note the sections that are starred in the table of contents. These sections should not be skipped. The sections that are not starred are also useful: they deal with a variety of important issues and provide background information for the material in the starred sections. Therefore, the reader should at least scan the unstarred sections.

Each chapter ends with a short reading list. Most of the papers or books are listed only once, but some relate to the topics of several chapters. The reading lists are by no means exhaustive. The items listed are directly relevant to the text, show a different viewpoint, or are useful as an example or survey. The reader will find in them many references to additional relevant literature.

No effort has been made to design a class project in which the students are supposed to implement some kind of operating system during the course. My experience with such projects is not favorable. A substantial amount of time is wasted in programming all kinds of irrelevant support programs. Also, it is not possible on most machines to run programs in parallel without going all the way down to the hardware-interrupt level. Time is better spent if problems are staked out so that the solution does not critically depend on the implementation of support programs.

This textbook is an introduction to the design of operating systems. At the same time it is an adequate introduction to more theoretical work in design methodology, system validation, and queueing theory. These areas often use abstract models, which in many cases apply to some aspect of an operating system. This book provides the proper background for such studies.

Realizing that it can offer not more than an introduction to such a vast topic as operating systems, it is my hope that this textbook will encourage many students to do some interesting work in a fascinating area.

ACKNOWLEDGMENTS: Many of my friends and students helped me by correcting the text and the problems. I wish to thank in particular Anita Jones, Forest Baskett, and Jim Eve for carefully reading the whole manuscript, my wife Marta for preparing the sketches for the artwork, and Dorothy Josephson for her excellent typing. Finally, the implementers of the XGP hardcopy-printing system deserve my gratitude. Their work enabled me to prepare the manuscript as a set of files and get nicely printed copies whenever needed. This greatly improved the correction process.

Pittsburgh
March, 1976

A. N. Habermann

CONTENTS

Introduction to
Operating System Design

1. Introduction

1.1 ON WRITING PROGRAMS

1.1.1 An operating system consists of a large number of programs, varying from small to large. It is not uncommon for the code of an operating system to require between 32K and 128K 32-bit words of storage as compared to between 8K and 40K for an ordinary programming language compiler. (K is an abbreviation for kilo, which means a thousand. In the context of computing machinery, K stands for 1024).

In this book the study of operating systems is approached from the designer's point of view. This means that we will analyze and synthesize the various functions performed by an operating system. Emphasis is placed on the synthesis, the discussion of how various functions of a system can be realized in given circumstances. In this respect this book prepares for other books emphasizing systems analysis. The student who works through the material presented in this book is well prepared for an in-depth analysis of system performance and topics such as queueing theory. A design study provides the proper background for the mathematical analysis of system models. The analysis in this book is restricted to comparing some alternative designs and implementations.

Operating system design is based on a collection of fundamental ideas which have emerged during the last two decades. Our first task is to find an adequate representation of these ideas. The assembly language or programming language in which the programs of a system are encoded is not the right vehicle to communicate these ideas. Written in one of these languages, the programs contain the tremendous amount of information necessary for execution. However, all this information (names of fast registers, memory locations or declarations and semicolons) makes it difficult to extract the basic idea behind a program.

On the other hand, a description in plain English is also not adequate. The most serious drawback of a description in day-to-day language is the lack of control flow representation (the order in which the steps of an algorithm are executed). Therefore, this book uses a programming style which does not require the detail of a programming language, but shows the control flow of an algorithm as much as is relevant to the idea being discussed.

1.1.2 The three most frequently used control structures are

if condition *then* command* {*else* command*} *fi*
repeat command* *until* condition
while condition *do* command* *od*

The form "command*" represents a sequence of zero or more commands. The bracket pair { } indicates that the *else* part is optional. The closing brackets *fi* and *od* indicate where a control structure ends. Several commands can be placed between the control brackets without an extra enclosing bracket pair.

The semantics of the three control structures are the same as in many programming languages. If the condition in the *if* clause is true, the commands following *then* are executed; if false, the commands following *else* are executed, or, if there is no *else* part, control is immediately passed to the point following *fi*. The conditions in the *repeat* and *while* command determine when execution of the controlled commands is terminated. The *repeat* command terminates when the condition evaluates to true and the *while* command when the condition is false. This means that the controlled commands in the *repeat* command are executed at least once, whereas those in the *while* command are not executed at all if the condition is false when execution of the *while* command begins.

The use of the *repeat* command is a matter of programming convenience. It can easily be replaced by a *while* command provided that some initialization commands are added to make the first-time evaluation of the termination condition possible. For example, let P[1:n] be a permutation of the numbers 1 through n ($n > 1$). A permutation can be uniquely partitioned into a number of disjoint cycles. A cycle is a subset of index numbers permuted onto itself; this subset itself cannot be split into smaller cycles. For instance, the permutation

$$i = 1\,2\,3\,4\,5\,6\,7$$
$$P[i] = 4\,7\,3\,1\,2\,5\,6$$

has the cycles (14), (2765) and (3). The cycle to which a given index k belongs is printed by the commands

x ← k; *repeat* PRINT(x); x ← P[x] *until* x = k

Using a *while* command, the first element of the cycle must be printed separately before the test can be applied.

PRINT(k); x ← P[k]; *while* x ≠ k *do* PRINT(x) *od*

In addition to the three most important control structures, the following three are occasionally used.

if condition *then* expression *else* expression *fi*
for variable *in* range *do* command* *od*
repeat command* *until* condition *do* command* *od*

The first of these four is the conditional expression. Note that here the *else* part is not optional. The second is the well-known *for* command. The iteration variable steps through all the elements of the given range and executes the controlled commands once for every value of the iteration variable.

The third structure is an extension of the *repeat* command. The termination condition is this time somewhere in the middle. The extended *repeat* command is typically used if the outcome of the termination test depends on input or the value of an expression which is computed in the iteration, while the test must be applied before the controlled commands are executed. Some examples follow.

Example 1: An input data set of positive numbers terminated by a zero is processed by the command

repeat READ(x) *until* x = 0 *do* ⟨process input x⟩ *od*

Example 2: Given array A[0:n], n > 1, A[n] = 0. The pairs (index, square of element) are printed in ascending index order up to, but not including, the first element whose square is less than a given positive number "max" by the commands

i ← 0; *repeat* x ← A[i]*A[i] *until* x < max *do* PRINT(i,x); i ← i+1 *od*

Commands on one line are separated by a semicolon. The end-of-line is used as a separator of commands on successive lines. It can easily be derived from the context whether an end-of-line is used as a command separator or as a blank. A single quoted character stands for the numeric machine representation of that character.

1.1.3 The most frequently used data structures are array, list, and record. Arrays are well known in FORTRAN and ALGOL-like languages. A list consists of a number of linked elements. Every element has a link field which points to the next element in the list. The link field of the last element has the value *nil* or points to the first element. In the latter case the list is called a *circular list*. Access to a list is through a variable list header pointing to the first element (to the last in case of a circular list) or having the value *nil* if the list is empty.

A record consists of a set of variable fields distinguished by their names. A field q of a record r is represented by r.q. A list element is a record; one of its fields is the link field pointing to the next list element.

Example: The records of a list L are records consisting of two fields, "val" and "link". The header of L is the variable HEAD. The following program finds the first element whose val field is greater than a given number size if there is such an element; otherwise, the result is *nil*. The result is stored in the variable ptr.

```
ptr ← nil
if HEAD ≠ nil then
   local x = HEAD
   repeat if x.val > size then ptr ← x else x ← x.link fi
   until x = ptr
```

The local variable x is initialized at the value of HEAD so that it points to the first element of list L if the list is not empty. The *repeat* command terminates as soon as an element is found whose val field is large enough or, if there is no such element, when the last element is inspected and x is set to *nil*. Lists play an important role in operating systems.

1.1.4 The programs in this book should not be studied independently of the text in which they are placed. The term *program* means in this context a structured description of an algorithm accompanied by an explanation of its composition and function. Because of this tight connection between program and surrounding text, it is often unnecessary to explain the meaning of names in the program by a declaration if the object of that name is accurately specified in the text. A general rule is, then, that names used in a program, but not defined in that program, are considered global objects of that program. Local objects, in particular names of dummy variables, will be declared in the programs.

In addition to the control structures introduced above, two Boolean expressions are used in a few places representing predicates with a single quantifier. The expressions are

some variable *in* range *sat* condition
all variable *in* range *sat* condition

The keyword *sat* is an abbreviation of "such that" or "satisfies" or "satisfy." The first expression is the equivalent of the logical expression prefixed by "there exists"; the second expression corresponds to the logical expression prefixed by "for all." The variable steps through the whole range of the *some* (*all*) expression if the resulting value of that expression is false (true). If the resulting value of the *some* (*all*) expression is true (false), the variable has the value of the leftmost range element for which the condition is (not) satisfied. For example, the expression

all x *in* [1:n] *sat* (*some* y *in* [1:n] *sat* A[x,y] = 0)

is true if every row of array A has at least one element equal to zero. With regard to efficiency, some logical expressions should not be literally transcribed into *some* and *all* expressions. For example, the mathematical notation for the predicate stating that all elements of a given array A[1:n] are different is

$$(x)(y)\ A[x] = A[y] \rightarrow x = y \qquad \text{for } x,y \in [1:n]$$

The Boolean expression corresponding to this predicate is

all x *in* [1:n−1] *sat* (*all* y *in* [x+1:n] *sat* A[y] ≠ A[x])

More than half the work is saved by restricting y to values greater than x. This is irrelevant where the mathematical notation is used, because it merely states a fact. Because the Boolean expressions represent an executable piece of program, efficiency becomes an issue.

The *some* expression is useful in linear search algorithms. Let *array* BLOCK[1:p] be used for recording the allocation of storage blocks to user tasks. If BLOCK[i] is in use, it points to the task using it. If it is free, its value is zero. If a free block exists, it is found by the command

if some x *in* [1:p] *sat* BLOCK[x] = 0 *then* RETURN(x) *else* RETURN(−1) *fi*

1.1.5 This section concludes with a more elaborate example of the programming style and the tight connection between a program and the explanatory text. The reader who already is familiar with abstract programs may skip this example and proceed with section 1.2.

A compiler keeps a record of all the names (identifiers) of program objects such as variables, arrays and procedures. The set of all these records is called the symbol table. First, the routine that reads a name character by character from the source converts it to an internal representation. Next, the symbol table is searched for the occurrence of this name. If found, the routine returns the index of the location in the table holding the name. If not found and there is a free slot in the symbol table, the routine places the assembled name in a free table location and returns the index of that location. If there is no free location in the symbol table, the routine reports failure by returning the value −1.

We assume that only up to 15 characters of a name are significant. If a name is longer than 15 characters, the remaining characters are ignored. A name consists of small and capital letters, digits or the concatenation character "_" (underscore). The permissible characters are mapped onto the numbers 1 through 63. The number zero is used to fill up unused character positions. Assuming a 32-bit word machine, the routine can pack five characters per word. The routine is called when its calling environment finds the first letter of a name.

Once the internal representation of a name has been created, the routine applies a linear hash function to the internal representation of the name. This function yields a number in the range [1:p] where p is the maximum number of records in the symbol table. The number is used as the starting point for a search through the symbol table. As long as no match or free location is found, the routine proceeds to the next entry in the symbol table. (This is why the method is called the *linear hash* method.) If the routine returns to the starting point, the search was unsuccessful. A comment in a program is opened by a dollar sign and terminated by the end of the line.

```
procedure ENTERNAME = result integer
begin local name = array[0:2] of integer(0)
local i, char, hash, count = integer(0)      $ all variables are initialized to
                                             $ zero
repeat char ← LOOKAHEAD                      $ the read pointer is not
                                             $ advanced
    char ←
      if 'a' ≤ char and char ≤ 'z' then READCHAR-'a'+11
      else if 'A' ≤ char and char ≤ 'Z' then READCHAR-'A'+37
      else if '0' ≤ char and char ≤ '9' then READCHAR-'0'+1
      else if char = '_' then READCHAR = '_'+63
      else 0      fi fi fi fi
  until char = 0 do
    count ← count+1
    if count ≤ 15 then i ← count%3; name[i] ← name[i]*64+char fi
  od                     $ the symbol % represents the remainder function
  hash ← if name[1] > p then name[1] else name[0] fi
  count ← 0
repeat hash ← (hash+count) % p
until count = p or ST[hash] = 0 or
    all i in[0:2] sat ST[hash+i*p] = name[i] do
      count ← count+1
  od
  if ST[hash] = 0 then for i in[0:2] do ST[hash+i*p] ← name[i] od fi
  if count = p then RETURN(−1) else RETURN(hash) fi
end
```

A name is not stored in three contiguous locations of ST, but in locations which are distance p apart. The LOOKAHEAD procedure allows us to look at the next character of the input without advancing the read pointer. The procedure READCHAR returns the numeric value representing the next character and moves the read pointer one character position ahead.

This program with its explanation is a typical example of the size and style of the programs to come. An attempt has been made to split the material into small pieces that can be handled more or less independently from each other. The relationship between these various parts is clarified in the text.

PROBLEMS

1. The *repeat* command can always be replaced by a *while* command provided that the variables used in the termination condition are properly initialized before the iteration starts. It is not always possible to replace a *while* command by a *repeat* command. Try, for instance, to program a *while* command and an equivalent *repeat* command printing out the elements of a given array A[1:n] up to, but not including, the first array element that is equal to zero. Formulate the condition that must hold to be sure that a *while* command can be replaced by a *repeat* command. The example shows that a *while* command is more universal than a *repeat* command.

2. The elements of a list consist of two fields, a value field "val" and a link field "link." The latter points to the next element in the list, the last has the value *nil.* The variable HEAD points to first element of the list. (This variable is of the same type as the link fields.) If e is an element of the list, its fields are accessed by e.val and e.link. Write a program that searches for an element with a given value and then deletes this element. Assume that the list is sorted by ascending value of the value field. Write a program that inserts a given new element in the list such that the order is maintained.

3. One of the most significant features of operating systems is the parallel execution of several programs. The computer may not be able to execute simultaneously all the programs that can run. Moreover, a program cannot always run. It may, for instance, need more input. Because the operating system must keep track of what is happening, the programs are recorded in various circular lists: one list for executable programs, and several lists for programs waiting for various events. There is an efficient way of representing and manipulating the lists if the maximum number of programs is fixed and every program is given a unique number in the range [1:n] (where n is that maximum number). A program record is then in not more than one list at a time. Define the arrays PRED[1:n] and SUCC[1:n]. Element PRED[i] (SUCC[i]) is the index of the predecessor (successor) of program C_i in the list in which it is recorded. If C_i is not in one of the circular lists, PRED[i] = SUCC[i] = i (C_i points to itself). The kth list header is stored in the variable LIST[k] whose value is the index of the *last* program in that list. If the kth list is empty, LIST[k] = 0.

Write the procedures for removing a program record from a list, appending one at the end of a list, inserting one at the top of a list and transferring a program record from one list to the end of another list.

4. Instead of placing program records in a list, we could have one table of program records in which their state is described. In this case it will not be necessary to insert or delete a program into—or from—a list. On the other hand, now it will often be necessary to find a record matching some given state. Let the table be implemented as an array CR[1:n]. A field f of a record is accessed by CR[i].f. Write the command that finds the index of a program whose f field matches a given state s. Write various versions of the command using the *while* command, the *repeat* command and the *some* expression.

5. Arrays A[1:m] and B[1:n] are both sorted in ascending order ($1 < m < n$). There are several ways in which the elements of A and B can be merged into array C[1:m+n] such that C is also sorted in ascending order. It is easy to write a program which, for every element placed in C, tests whether A has been exhausted, B has been exhausted and if not, compares the next two elements of A and B. This means that three tests are applied for every element placed in C. However, it is possible to reduce the repeated tests considerably. Write a program that merges arrays A and B into C such that C is sorted in ascending order, but in such a manner that not more than one test is needed per element placed in C. (Hint: one single test reveals whether or not all elements of B are larger than all elements of A. If not, transfer the top elements of B until an element smaller than the largest element of A is found. Now we can be sure that the largest remaining element is the top element of A.)

1.2 THE FUNCTION OF AN OPERATING SYSTEM

1.2.1 An operating system is a set of programs that monitor the execution of user programs and the use of resources. The major reason for having an operating system is that contemporary operating systems allow several programs to run at the same time. This has the tremendous advantage that one user does not have to delay starting his program until some other users have finished their programs. Another useful task of an operating system is the support of user programs with standard routines driving the input and output devices (I/O for short). These routines are the same for every user program. It would be a waste of time and effort if every user had to write his own I/O routines.

This section briefly describes the nature of the common parts of a computer system, the basic functions of an operating system, and additional functions of somewhat more advanced systems. The remainder of the chapter concerns a primitive model for a uniprogramming system (handling one program at a time). The fundamental ideas of interrupt, process, multiprogramming and timesharing are discussed in chapter 2. Since the motivation for incorporating the various monitor functions into an operating system is primarily determined by the multiprogramming concept, discussed in section 2.4, the order in which the various topics are presented in chapters 3 through 10 is explained in that section.

1.2.2 The central part of a computer system consists of one or more central processing units (CPU) and a main store (Ms) in which programs and data can be stored. The real work, such as addition, multiplications or activating the I/O devices, is done by a CPU. All an Ms can do is produce the value of a storage cell, or place a given value in a storage cell. These actions are invoked by a CPU when it executes a LOAD or STORE command. A storage cell carries a unique number (called its address) which is used in all references to that cell. The LOAD and STORE commands use an address as a parameter in order to single out a particular storage cell.

A CPU consists of a number of fast registers referred to by name. Two of these registers are the program counter PC and the instruction register IR. A CPU considers a program to be a set of contiguous storage cells. The program counter PC points to one of those cells. A program is executed by letting PC step through this set and executing the instruction stored in the cell pointed at by PC. The heart of the computer is the FETCH-EXECUTE cycle. If M[0:n] represents the main store (for a medium-size machine, n is a number in the range 64K to 256K), the FETCH-EXECUTE cycle is represented by the program

```
repeat
   IR ← M[PC]
   PC ← PC+1
   ⟨EXECUTE(instruction in IR)⟩
until CPU halt
```

This program is part of the hardware, that is, these actions are performed by the electronic equipment. The term *FETCH-EXECUTE cycle* is explained by the fact that an instruction is retrieved from Ms and subsequently executed. The CPU hardware repeats these actions until it encounters the halt state. A CPU is transferred to this state by a special HALT instruction. The program counter is advanced in the second command of the cycle so as to prepare the fetch of the next instruction. If the executed instruction is a JUMP or subroutine call, the PC value is overwritten by the target address or subroutine starting address. In the latter case the PC value is saved before it is overwritten. The value saved is the address of the storage cell following the one that contains the subroutine call.

Input and output data is handled through the I/O devices. The most common type of I/O devices are the card reader, the line printer and the keyboard terminal. Terminals come in several varieties, ranging from teleprinters to displays. Other common I/O devices are the paper tape reader, the cardpunch, the paper tape punch and the graph plotter. Each has a specialized processor capable of executing a small set of relevant commands. These devices are described in many machine handbooks. Commands for bulk input devices, such as card readers or paper tape readers, specify the size and location of an area in the main store to which the input data should be transferred. Similarly, commands for bulk output devices, such as line printers or punch devices, specify the size and location of a main store area from which the output should be fetched. A keyboard terminal is an input and output device at the same time. Its commands are even simpler. It specifies that the next character must be transferred to a special fixed location or must be fetched from a special fixed location and printed.

Another major difference between a CPU and a specialized device processor is the fact that a device processor does not automatically fetch its instructions from storage as does a CPU. A device command must be placed from outside into the device command buffer (corresponding to IR in the CPU). After the command has been placed in the command buffer, its execution does not automatically begin. The device is activated by setting the BUSY flag. While it is not executing a command, the device is continually inspecting the BUSY flag. As soon as it finds the flag set, it resets (clears) the flag and starts executing the command in its command buffer. When it finishes the execution of a command, the device processor sets the DONE flag to inform its user that the command has been obeyed. The device user clears the DONE flag before placing another command in the command buffer.

The term READY is often used instead of DONE. Handbooks reflect a slight preference for using READY for input devices and DONE for output devices. However, because the function of the DONE flag and READY flag is exactly the same, no distinction is made between these two terms in subsequent chapters. We use whichever term is more meaningful in given circumstances.

Most computer facilities are equipped with several auxiliary storage devices. The major types of auxiliary storage devices are magnetic tape units, rotating drums and rotating disks. Disks come in two varieties, movable-head disks or fixed-head disks. The latter has a read/write head for every track on the disk. This has the advantage that no time is lost going from one track to another. The time lost in moving the head of a movable-head disk is proportional to the distance the head must travel. The storage capacity of these devices is an order of magnitude greater than that of the main store. The data transfer rate of a magnetic tape is somewhat lower than that of a disk or drum, but the equipment is cheaper. All three devices are discussed in more detail in following sections of this chapter.

Magnetic tapes are typically used as archive storage media. Information that must be retained over long periods of time while infrequently accessed is kept on magnetic tape. Dismountable disks share with magnetic tapes the advantage that these objects can easily be replaced. Because this is not true for a drum, a drum is typically used as backup storage of the main store. This means that if there is too much data for the main store, the excess is transferred to the backup store device and retrieved when needed. One of the major tasks of the operating system is to support a continuous data flow between the main store and the backup store. Since a disk is almost as fast as a drum, but also has the flexibility of magnetic tapes, disks are used for either backup storage or archive storage.

Auxiliary storage devices and I/O devices do not automatically fetch commands from the store. A command must be placed in the device command buffer by an outside authority. Execution of a command does not start until the BUSY flag is set and command completion is indicated when the device sets the DONE flag. A command for an auxiliary storage device indicates, in addition to the area in the main store, the area on that device from which (or to which) data must be transferred.

1.2.3 One of the primary tasks of an operating system is to control the use of the system's resources. The physical resources consist of one or more CPUs, the storage space and the I/O devices. A machine may have several CPUs. If so, it is called a *multiprocessor*, otherwise it is called a *uniprocessor*. The operating system is responsible for allocating CPUs to executable programs for some period of time. In early operating systems, a CPU was allocated to a program until the program terminated. Contemporary systems allocate a CPU for a short while to one program, then for a while to another program. This technique is known as *CPU multiplexing*. If the CPU is allocated for a fixed period of time to each program, we speak of *timeslicing*. The effect is that it seems to the user as if several programs run simultaneously. (Multiplexing is discussed in detail in chapter 2.)

CPU multiplexing requires two activities of a system: bookkeeping and scheduling. Bookkeeping consists of recording which program is ready to run, which CPU is allocated to which program, how many CPU timeslices were used by a program, etc. Scheduling is the term for deciding in which order a CPU is allocated if there are several executable programs. In more general terms, scheduling is the activity of deciding in which order a sequential resource will be allocated if several programs want to use it. (The term *sequential* means that the resource can be used by only one user at a time.) A CPU, storage space and I/O devices all are sequential devices.

Both bookkeeping and scheduling depend on the chosen strategy or policy which underlies the implementation. A scheduling strategy is often called a scheduling discipline. An example of a bookkeeping policy follows. Assume that all the uncompleted programs are recorded in a single list containing one record for each program. The relevant state information, which conveys matters such as *executable* and amount of CPU time used, is described in various fields of a program record. To find a program in a given state, the list must be searched for a record matching this given state. Alternatively, the records can be sorted by program state. That is done by keeping separate lists for all executable programs, for programs presently being executed and several lists for programs waiting for I/O operations. Circumstances determine which policy is the most efficient. A change of state is a trivial operation if the first strategy is adopted, but involves removal from, and insertion in, a list if the second strategy is adopted. On the other hand, if a change of state is a rare event compared to finding a program in a given state, the second strategy is more efficient.

The most elementary scheduling strategy is the first-come first-serve discipline (FCFS). This discipline schedules requests by arrival time. If $request_i$ for a sequential resource came before $request_j$, then $request_i$ will be honored before $request_j$. This discipline does not take into account the possibility that one program may be more important than another (for example, execution of an operating system routine is more important than execution of a user program) and does not take into account the history of resource utilization. It allocates resources independently of how many resources a program is already using or has been using in the past and independently of how long it used other resources. The FCFS discipline is in fact the default scheduling strategy if there is no other criterion upon which a priority rule can be based. Scheduling strategies for allocating CPU time and storage space are discussed in chapters 6 and 8. Some logical aspects of resource allocation are considered at the end of chapter 3 and in the first section of chapter 10.

1.2.4 Numeric and combinatorial problems long ago lost their monopoly of computer use. Now, the function of a computer as storage and retrieval medium of large data bases is as important as its computing capabilities. It is very convenient to have information permanently accessible in the auxiliary store. It saves manual bookkeeping and physical storage space. In addition, permanent program utilities, such as editors, greatly facilitate the modification process.

Support programs such as editors and language compilers are not considered part of an operating system. These programs use the system facilities in the same manner as user programs do; however, information kept on auxiliary storage devices is not immediately accessible. This information can be made available in the main store through commands placed in the command buffer of the auxiliary storage device. This aspect of manipulating data bases, location of information on the various store devices and the transfer from one storage device to another, belongs to the realm of an operating system, because it concerns the allocation of resources (in this case storage space). Moreover, the operating system can make life easier for the user if it provides a convenient set of programs for information storage and retrieval. Such a program package enables a user to name a data set and access the data through this name. Such a named data set is called a *file*, and the set of programs that manipulate files is the *file system*. This topic is discussed in chapter 9.

We mentioned that the first major task of an operating system is the monitoring of user programs. This means that the operating system must protect one program against malfunctioning of another program. For instance, it must not be possible for a program to overwrite data belonging to another program. Other ways in which programs may affect each other are discussed in chapter 3.

The use of a computer as data base storage and manipulation medium has added another dimension to the protection problem. It is often useful for users to share data bases. However, it is unlikely that one user would be willing to grant file access rights to every other user. The principal user may wish to grant access to some files to one set of users and access to other files to another set of users. Also, the kind of access granted to one user may not be the same as that granted to another user (for example, user A is allowed to execute file f, whereas user B gets the right to copy file f).

In recent years this aspect of protection has received much attention. Its purpose is to allow users to share files in such a way that the access rights to a file can be specified separately for each user. Protection is discussed in general terms in chapter 9.

After this brief introduction to the nature of an operating system we begin a systematic study of operating system issues in the next section with a very simple system model. This model will be extended and modified in subsequent sections resulting in some realistic examples of operating systems.

PROBLEMS

1. Look up in a machine handbook the set of commands which apply to a card reader, a line printer and a teletype. The names for the flags which activate a device and indicate command completion vary from one machine to another. In this text we use the names BUSY and DONE (or READY) for these flags. List for these devices the transfer rate expressed in characters per second or cards per second or lines per second. Finally, list their storage capacity.

2. Bookkeeping strategy S_1 calls for one uniform list in which all programs are recorded. A program record has three fields: state, CPU time, and priority class. The value of state is either running, or ready-to-run, or not-executable. Write a search routine which finds the record of the program which is ready-to-run and in the lowest priority class; if there are more than one, the program with the smallest CPU time must be chosen. If this still leads to a tie, any may be chosen.

3. Bookkeeping strategy S_2 records programs by index in three different lists based on the computation state which is either running, ready to run, or not executable. A program record has three fields, one for the program number, one for the total CPU time used and one for the priority class. The ready-to-run list is ordered by priority class; within one class by increasing CPU time used. Write the routine which selects the program which is ready to run and in the lowest priority class; within this class the program with the smallest CPU time should be selected. The routine returns the program index if a program with the desired properties exists.

4. Assume that a CPU is allocated to the program selected by strategy S_1 of problem 2 or by strategy S_2 of problem 3. In any case, the state of this program changes from ready-to-run to running. Write the commands for changing the state of a program in either strategy from ready-to-run to running and also for the change from running to ready-to-run. The latter transition occurs when the CPU is deallocated at the end of a fixed time interval (at the end of a time slice). Assume that for every search for a ready-to-run program in the lowest priority class with minimal CPU time the state of two programs changes (the state of the program from which the CPU is deallocated and the selected program itself). Discuss the efficiency of both strategies S_1 and S_2 with respect to this assumption.

5. The first-come first-serve discipline is appealing for its simplicity and ease of maintenance. The proper data structure for an FCFS discipline is a queue. This is a linear data structure to which elements are added at one end and from which elements are removed at the other end. A queue can be implemented as a linked list or as an array. Assume the FCFS queue is implemented as an array Q[1:n] where n is the maximum number of programs that can run at the same time. Write the commands for appending an element to the queue and for removing the first element from the queue.

1.3 A SIMPLE OPERATING SYSTEM

1.3.1 We begin with a simple computer configuration as represented in figure 1.3a. The central machine consists of a central processing unit, the CPU, and a main storage box, Ms, large enough to hold some control programs and a user program with its input and output data. A card reader, CR, is attached to the machine as an input device and a line printer, LP, serves as an output device.

When the CPU places a command in CR's command buffer and sets the BUSY flag, CR copies the characters from the card into an area of Ms as specified in the command. When the CPU places a command into LP's command buffer and sets the BUSY flag, LP prints a line which it finds in an area in Ms as indicated in the command. Thus, a storage address is passed as an argument of a read or print command.

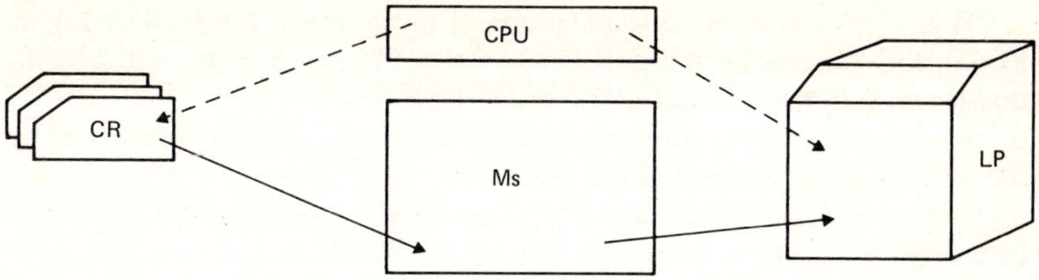

Figure 1.3a Simple computer configuration

A straightforward strategy for running programs on this machine would be this sequence of steps:

repeat read card deck
compile
load
execute
print results
until machine halt

However, there is no built-in hardware to carry out these steps, nor is there a hardware mechanism that activates these steps in sequence. A program must be stored in the machine to control the sequencing of steps. That program is exactly the one above, if we read the steps as procedure calls. It is the framework of an operating system for the given machine. It transforms the hardware system into a machine able to compile and execute a sequence of user programs.

In addition to the control program, the programs for the individual steps must also be stored in the machine before the system can operate successfully. It is customary to consider programs that "read card deck" and "print results" as part of the operating system, because both involve control and management of resources. The programs compile, load, and execute are part of a separate language processing system independent of the operating system except for a small interface. (It would be perfectly feasible to replace the language system by another one, even one for a vastly different language, without changing the operating system.) The input interface consists of the information which tells the compiler where to find the source program. The output interface comprises a set of formatting procedures which arrange the output as a string of LP lines. Another part of the output interface is the indication where to find the output lines. This information is needed by "print result."

1.3.2 Our next task is to design programs for read card deck and print results, since these are part of the operating system. Before writing the programs, we need to know how the hardware of CR and LP works.

CR and LP are at any instant in one of three states: IDLE, READY or BUSY. Both devices have a start/stop switch. When the start switch is off, the device is in the idle state. The state of LP depends further on whether there is a command pending (this means that a command has been given by the CPU, but the device has not finished it yet). The state of CR depends upon the start/stop switch, whether a command is pending, and whether a card deck is actually in the reader. State tables for the two devices are given in figures 1.3b and 1.3c. Start switch on, command pending and card deck in reader are represented by the number 1; the negation of these conditions is represented by the number 0.

LP	start	com	STATE
0	0	0	IDLE
1	0	1	IDLE
2	1	0	READY
3	1	1	BUSY

Figure 1.3b LP state table

CR	start	deck	com	STATE
0 . . . 3	0	0,1	0,1	IDLE
4	1	0	0	IDLE
5	1	0	1	IDLE
6	1	1	0	READY
7	1	1	1	BUSY

Figure 1.3c CR state table

The possible state transitions can easily be derived from the state tables. For instance, the ready state of LP is (1,0); this state can be reached as a result of one change from either states (0,0) or (1,1), from either IDLE or BUSY. The state transition diagrams are given in figure 1.3d and figure 1.3e.

The cause of a particular state transition can be found by looking up the begin and end state in the state tables. For instance,

IDLE → BUSY in figure 1.3d: push start button of LP while print command is pending

BUSY → IDLE in figure 1.3e: push the stop button while CR is reading (7 → 3) or after reading the last card of a deck (7 → 5)

Reading can start only when a card deck has been placed in the reader and the start switch is in the on position. Pushing the stop button while a device is busy does not have an immediate effect. The device completes the command it is working on (reads the whole card, prints the whole line), but at completion the state changes from BUSY to IDLE instead of to READY. Such stopping of the device is advisable if something goes wrong (a card gets stuck or is upside down) or to tear off preceding output from the printer. Both devices normally alternate between the states READY and BUSY. When a command is given in the ready state (to read a card or print a line), the device becomes BUSY. When the device is finished with the command, the state normally changes back to READY. However, we see in the state table of figure 1.3c that after reading the last card of a deck and emptying the reader, the state of CR changes to IDLE.

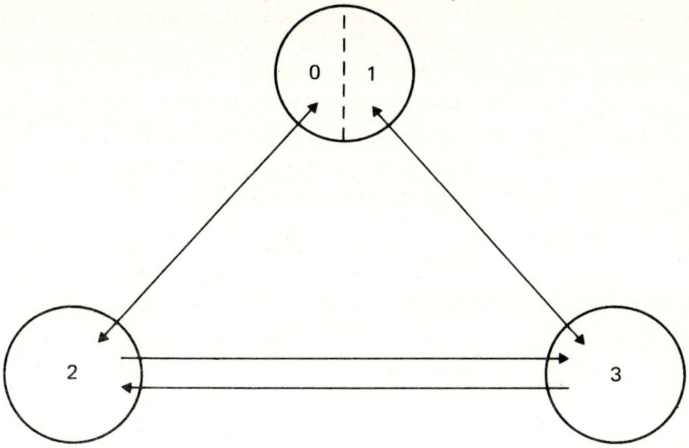

Figure 1.3d State transition diagram of LP

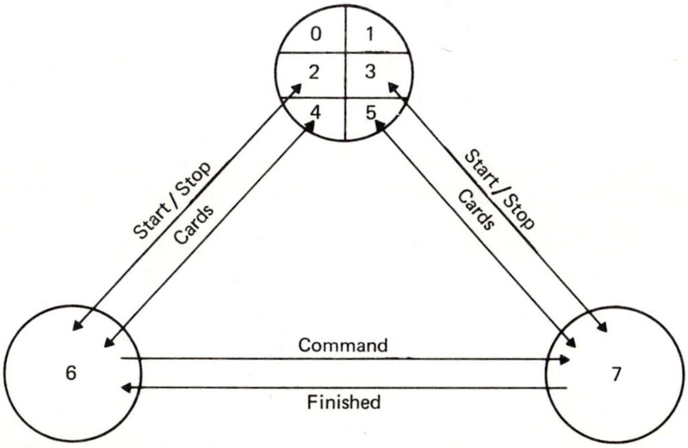

Figure 1.3e State transition diagram of CR

1.3.3 The CPU must initiate all reading and printing by sending the proper commands. Hence, the primary task of "read card deck" and "print results" is to control the devices by sending commands to the I/O devices at the right moments.

Before reading can be started, a free area in the main store Ms must be reserved for the input. We call the address of the first location of this area the *starting address*. We also need a variable "cc" to keep track of the number of cards read. Actual reading cannot start until CR is in the ready state. Once CR is READY, successive cards can be read. We call the begin address of the area reserved for the next card image the *input address*. The input address and card count must be updated with each card. The process must stop when CR returns to the idle state. A program for "read card-deck" is

```
CR Control: select starting address sam
            initialize input address ain to sam
            initialize card count cc
            wait until CR READY
   repeat   select input address ain
            command read card (ain)
            increment card count cc
            wait while CR BUSY
   until    CR IDLE
```

This program is written to read all cards in a card deck. Its reaction to pushing the stop button is rather simplistic; it terminates after completing the current command. The first wait statement prevents the procedure from starting until CR is READY; that is, when the start switch is on and a deck is in the reader. Without that wait statement, the repetition would terminate immediately if the reader is still IDLE. The repetition terminates after reading all the cards of a card deck. The place and size of the input are indicated in the variables sam and cc.

The command "print results" gets as input parameters a starting address of the output lines (sa) and a count (lc) of the number of output lines. Its program differs slightly from the card reader control program:

```
LP Control: initialize output address aout to sa
   repeat   select output address aout
            wait until LP READY
            command print line (aout)
            decrement line count lc
   until    lc = 0
```

We programmed a potential delay (the commands beginning with wait) in the loops of both control programs. These commands are essential because without them the control program may be too fast in comparison to the device and overwrite a previous device command before it is finished. The CPU and devices work at their own processing speeds. There is no hardware mechanism that synchronizes the processors of these devices; they carry out *asynchronous processes*. The wait commands force some degree of synchronization on the asynchronous processes. A detailed discussion of synchronization follows in chapter 4.

PROBLEMS

1. The card reader control program has two commands beginning with "wait...". The line printer has only one such command. Could the first wait

command in the card reader control program be removed and could the other wait command be replaced by one similar to the one in the line printer control program? Why or why not?

2. An alternative policy of identifying "end of program" is to indicate the end of the program by a special-purpose control card which carries a code uniquely distinguishable from any other program or data card. It is then not necessary to place exactly one program in the reader. A large program can be loaded as successive parts; several small programs can be loaded consecutively. Program card reading for this policy. Note that the read control loop should not terminate on the idle state.

3. Suppose that the stop button is pushed while cards are being read only if something goes wrong so that further reading or compiling is useless. The manufacturer of card readers took notice of this case and added a state ESCAPE with the additional transitions:

BUSY → ESCAPE when the stop button is pressed while BUSY
ESCAPE → IDLE when card deck is removed, or when the CPU explicitly changes the state from ESCAPE to IDLE

Program control of the card reader taking advantage of this new state. You can start either with the original program or use your solution of problem 2.

4. Show that no harm is done if the stop and start buttons of the line printer are pressed in this order while printing is in progress.

5. Suppose a system supports two different programming languages, and hence, two compilers. How would the operating system control program change and how would the interface change between the operating system and the two language processing systems?

1.4 THE PERFORMANCE OF THE SIMPLE OPERATING SYSTEM

1.4.1 So far we have not paid attention to the efficiency of the simple operating system of the preceding section. We will soon find out that the system must be radically changed, because, even on a small contemporary computer, the system will be very inefficient. The major reason is that the peripheral devices CR and LP are no match for the CPU in processing speed. Processing speeds of devices can be compared by looking at the amount of information handled by each of them during a time unit. Information can be measured in number of storage words or bytes. In most machines the term *byte* means a fixed-size bit string of eight bits. A *word*, on the other hand, is the unit of information that can be retrieved or stored in one reference to storage. The time it takes to retrieve a word from storage is known as the cycle time of the machine. Typical figures for word length and cycle time are:

word length	*no. bits*	*speed*	*cycle time*
very small	8	very slow	10 microsecond
small	12–16	normal	1
medium	24–36	fast	0.8
large	48–128	very fast	0.1

Practice has shown that the need for a high processing speed often goes together with the need for a large store. If no specification of word size or cycle time is given in the text, we will assume a medium scale computer with a word size of 32 bits (equivalent to 4 bytes or 4 characters) and a cycle time of 1 microsecond. Here we first look at a very small computer with a word length of 8 bits or 1 byte and a cycle time of 10 microseconds. A fast card reader can read at a speed of 20 cards/second and the speed of a high speed line printer is 20 lines/second. Let us assume that a card has 80 character positions and that a line printer has 120 character positions per line. Character transfer from CR to Ms or from Ms to LP is controlled by the hardware processors of CR and LP. However, the device processors of a small and cheap machine test and update a command control word which is stored in Ms. This control word is decremented for every word loaded by CR or fetched by LP.

The number of storage references for transferring one word is estimated at three; one for loading or storing the transfer word, and two for a decrement and test of a control word. This means that CR will reference storage $20*80*3 = 4800$ per second. The LP will reference storage in the order of $20*120*3 = 7200$ per second. (These figures would be one-fourth as large on a 32-bit machine because four characters are packed in a word.) With a 10 microsecond cycle time, the number of cycles available in one second is 100,000. The cycles used for reading cards and printing lines account for only 4.8% and 7.2% of the available capacity. These figures are 0.12% and 0.18% for a medium scale machine with a 1 microsecond cycle time. The demand for storage operations is apparently small for a very small machine and negligible for a medium scale machine.

The tremendous discrepancy between the CPU and the peripheral devices causes the control programs to spend most of their time waiting. Let us look at the LP control program and assume that the number of machine instructions that must be coded for each command is as follows:

initialization	2
select next aout	5
wait until LP ready	?
command (aout)	5
decrement lc	2
test lc = 0	2

The average execution time of an instruction on a machine with a 1 microsecond cycle time is typically 2.5–3 microseconds. Most of that time is spent in storage access; two cycles are required, one for fetching the instruction, and one for fetching the memory operand. Ignoring the initialization (which is negligible compared to the contribution of the repeatedly executed commands), roughly $15*3 = 45$ microseconds are needed to control the printing of one line. Processing one line takes 1/20 second = 50,000 microseconds. The control program has to wait a very long time for both. In fact, it spends most of its time waiting. It could have handled over 1000 lines (close to 20 printer pages!) instead of one line. The waste of CPU time is even greater for the card reader.

PROBLEMS

1. One can argue that a much slower (but also much cheaper) storage device suffices for the simple operating system. That is certainty true. Core storage in the machines of the late Fifties provided only enough space for some small control programs and part of a user program in addition to buffer space for input and output. Its size was 100–500 words. Moreover, device commands of CR and LP did not include a storage address as parameter. Instead, data was read into and transferred from buffers fixed in size and in a fixed set of Ms locations.

Consider a configuration like the one in figure 1.4a (on the following page). CR deposits (for each device command) a card image of 80 characters in a 20-word read-in buffer, RIB, and LP unloads a 30-word print out buffer, POB.

The bulk of storage is on a drum D with the following specifications:

200 tracks of 256 words each
speed: 40 revolutions/second
reading does not slow down the drum
drum states while in operation: READY, BUSY
two kinds of commands: drum read (D ⟶ DTB) (explanation of DTB follows) and drum write (DTB ⟶ D).
command has two parameters: first parameter is a drum address; the second parameter is the number of words to be transferred.

DTB is the drum transfer buffer. Data can be directly transferred from one buffer to another, because all are located in Ms. CPU must load (or unload) a buffer before sending a next command to ensure that a buffer is not read twice or overwritten. Assume a cycle time of 12 microseconds (IBM 704) or 2 microseconds (IBM 7094). The total space available for the three buffers is 100 32-bit words in Ms.

Write an operating system control program for this machine and write programs for input and output control, but realize that Ms will be too small

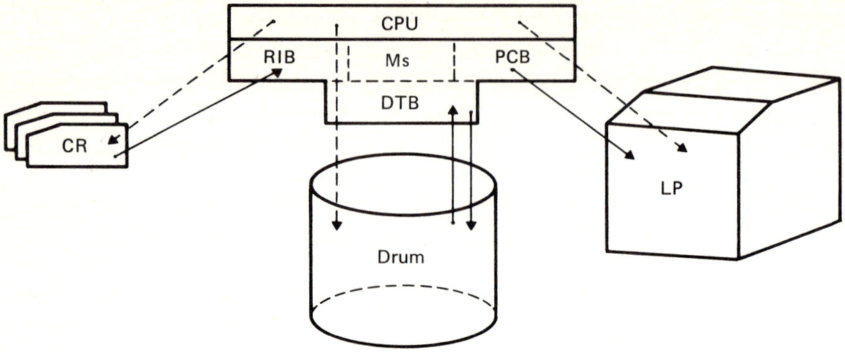

Figure 1.4a System with small main store and drum

to hold the information of a card deck or a set of printer lines. Evaluate the demand for storage access per second of the devices. (Note: drum devices are often used as backup storage. A size of 1 million words and a transfer rate of 75,000 words/second is normal.)

2. Given the control programs for a system as described in problem 1, verify that no extra time is needed to store and retrieve information onto and from drum D in addition to the time needed for the input and output phases.

3. Another variation on our simple system of section 3 would be to add another card reader and read in card decks from both readers in one phase. Two programs are then run in succession and, after printing their output, the card decks of two new programs are read.

Write the modified input control program and check whether the input phase requires any more time than before.

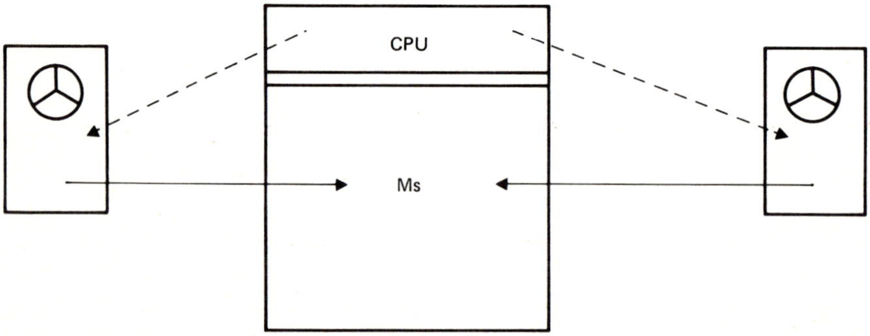

Figure 1.4b Dual magnetic tape system

4. A batch of source programs is prepared externally and stored on a tape. The machine that will execute the programs uses a tape drive as an input device instead of a card reader and another tape drive as an output device instead of a printer. (See figure 1.4b.) The specifications of a tape drive are as follows:

reading or writing: 10,000 words/second
start and stop time: 10 milliseconds
blocksize: 250 words (of 32 bits each)
three states: state transition diagram as for the line printer (see figure 1.3d)
three types of blocks: program/data block, end (of program) block and end of tape block. Each of these types is recognizable by reading the beginning of a block.
six commands: START, STOP, SKIP, REWIND, READ and WRITE (forward only). The latter two take as an argument the starting address in the main store and process exactly one block (thus, there are no read-in or print-out buffers of the types RIB and POB). SKIP and REWIND take as parameter the number of blocks to skip or spool backwards. STOP causes the transition READY → IDLE and START the transition IDLE → READY.

The most commonly used method of writing on a tape has the nasty property that all information following the place of writing gets lost. This implies that it is impossible to READ and WRITE a tape in such a way that WRITE overwrites the block already read. This could be done if the tape is preformatted.

Assume that blocks are stored sufficiently far apart to allow for a STOP and START between any two blocks.

Program input and output control for this system and estimate the demand on the storage device if a small machine with a cycle time of 4 microseconds is used.

5. The performance of the device control programs in problem 1 critically depends on the type of storage device used. If the cycle time is on the order of milliseconds rather than microseconds, the time it takes to load or unload a buffer could be so long that the next command cannot be transmitted to the device in time to keep the device going at full speed. The devices are modified to cope with this problem in the following way: instead of one read card command, two commands of that kind are provided, read1 and read2 (likewise print1 and print2). Read1 loads characters in a fixed area RIB1 in storage, but read2 loads characters in another, nonoverlapping buffer, RIB2, in storage. Likewise, print1 and print2 unload two nonintersecting buffers, POB1 and POB2 in Ms.

Reprogram the device control programs taking advantage of the command extensions and show that the new versions depend less critically on the cycle time than the earlier ones.

Historical Note

The performance of hardware systems was vastly different when the first magnetic drum computers were developed around 1953. A drum access time of 5–25 milliseconds was considered very fast. The size was also quite different. Early versions of the IBM 650, for instance, used a drum of only 2000 10-bit words and a core storage of 60 words. The drum size was increased to 4000 words in later models. Its drum speed of 200 revolutions per minute (rpm) was high compared to a speed of only 50–60 rpm for other drums at that time. Contemporary drums have a storage capacity in the order of a million words and a speed in the order of 3000 rpm.

The use of an assembly language, but more importantly the first working version of a FORTRAN system in 1957, spurred the development of a simple batch operating system that would take over the irrelevant coding of I/O procedures and increase the throughput. Another factor that greatly stimulated the development of operating systems (sometimes called supervisory systems or executive systems) was the advent of the second computer generation. The second generation used transistors instead of vacuum tubes. The average time between hardware crashes changed from minutes, or hours at best, to days and weeks. It then became feasible to run a series of programs without experiencing a hardware failure and without the ensuing problems associated with recovering from such an event.

1.5 IMPROVEMENT OF THE PERFORMANCE

1.5.1 The example discussed below shows that the processing of input and output constitutes a considerable fraction of the total runtime of a program. (The runtime of a program is the time interval between starting to read in a program and printing its last output.) For a program of, say, 200 lines, in which each statement is executed 400 times, and which produces 100 lines of output data, the figures look something like this:

input 200 cards	200∗1/20∗1000 msec.	= 10,000 msec.
compiling	200∗5∗500∗0.003 msec.	= 1,500 msec.
loading	200∗5∗100∗0.003 msec.	= 300 msec.
execution	200∗5∗400∗0.003 msec.	= 1,200 msec.
listing	200∗1/20∗1000 msec.	= 10,000 msec.
output	100∗1/20∗1000 msec.	= 5,000 msec.
total input and output processing		25,000 msec.
total runtime		28,000 msec.

The number 5 in the second, third and fourth lines is an estimate of the average number of machine instructions generated for one line of source program. The number 500 in the second line and the number 100 in the third line are based on an estimate of 500 compiler instructions and 100 loader instructions per generated object code instruction.*

This example may not be representative of an average program, but shows that input and output processing account for a considerable fraction of the runtime. Thus, the performance of the simple operating system can be greatly improved by a reduction of the input and output processing time.

One gets an idea of how bad the performance of the present version is by looking at the throughput and at some improvements which can be achieved without any additional effort. (The term *throughput* means the average number of programs that can be executed per time unit.) The throughput of our simple system can be improved only through making the card reader and line printer work much faster. However, because the speed of input and output devices depends on mechanically moving parts, it seems to have been pushed to its limits. So, device speeds must be considered as given quantities. Modern I/O devices are much faster than they used to be but the example shows that even a factor of ten does not help much.

1.5.2 The time needed to process n programs is I+CLE+O, where

I = the sum of the input processing times
CLE = the sum of the compile, load and execute time
O = the sum of the output processing times.

The throughput is n/t = n/(I+CLE+O).

The fact that the three devices CPU, CR, and LP operate almost independently makes an important improvement possible. We get a much more efficient system if the input and output phases overlap in time. An even better result is obtained if all three phases overlap. We investigate first how the simple operating system can be modified so that the input and output phases overlap in time.

Let the operating system distinguish between an I/O phase for processing input and output and a COMPUTE phase for compilation, loading and execution. Once started, the I/O phase control program, IOC, will issue commands to any ready device and will wait only when both devices are BUSY. The I/O phase is terminated when all output lines are printed and

*The estimate is based on a sample of 39 programs written in PL/1, and some in Fortran, compiled on an IBM 360/67 running under OS (MFTII and MVT) or MTS at the University of Newcastle upon Tyne, England.

the card reader is IDLE. The input of IOC is the number of output lines, lc, and the location, saout, where the output starts.

```
IOC: select start address for input sain
        initialize {input address ain to sain, output address aout to saout, card
          count cc to zero}
repeat wait while LP and CR BUSY
  if CR READY then
      select input address ain; command read card (ain); increment cc
  fi
  if LP READY and lc > 0 then
      select next output address aout; command print line (aout)
      decrement lc
  fi
until lc = 0 and CR IDLE
```

Note that IOC does not wait if either CR or LP is idle. IOC processes the input correctly if there is no output to be processed, provided that the line count lc is properly initialized to zero. IOC is also able to handle the output of a program when there is no new input. If the COMPUTE phase follows the I/O phase, the former should not have any effect when the output of the last program has been processed. The value of the input count cc indicates whether or not a new source program was read in. The new version of the operating system control program is:

```
         set line count lc to zero
repeat   I/O phase
         COMPUTE phase
until    machine halt
```

where COMPUTE phase is controlled by the program:

if cc > 0 *then* compile; load; execute *fi*

The throughout has improved significantly. Let i_k and o_k represent the processing time of input and output of the kth program, and let $m_k = \text{MAX}(i_{k+1}, o_k)$ for $k = 1, \ldots, n-1$. Input and output processing for n programs using the new version of the operating system can be as low as

$$M = i_1 + \sum_{k=1}^{n-1} m_k + o_n$$

with a throughput of

$$\frac{n}{t} = \frac{n}{\text{CLE}+M}$$

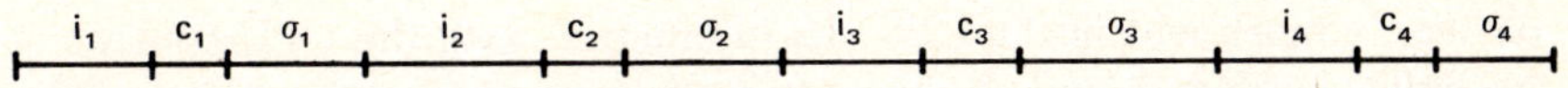

Figure 1.5a Throughput of a serial system

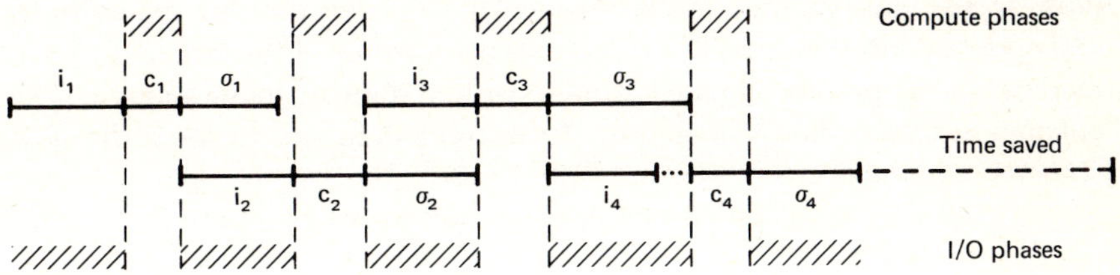

Figure 1.5b Throughput of overlapped system

instead of, as in the earlier version,

$$I+O = \sum_{k=1}^{n} (i_k + o_k)$$

with

$$\frac{n}{t} = \frac{n}{I+CLE+O}$$

Figures 1.5a and 1.5b give an idea of the difference in throughput between the simple operating system and its improved version. Notice how much earlier input i_3 and i_4 of the third and fourth program are started.

Historical Note

Overlap of input and output as just described was impossible in computers manufactured before 1960 because the CPU acted as a device processor for all devices in addition to its function of central processor and was involved in every action. The first step towards autonomous devices was the design of device processors that could load or unload a buffer in a fixed area of main storage. The CPU had to start data transfer by giving a command, and had to load or unload a buffer before passing the next command (IBM 650, UNIVAC I).

The most significant step was the development of data channels (IBM 7090) in the early 1960s. A data channel is a specialized processor containing local control and buffer registers. It has direct access to the storage device, independent of the CPU. Its interaction with the CPU consists of receiving commands and sending notifications when commands have been obeyed. A channel eliminates the need for CPU involvement by unloading buffers. Channels of various manufacturers may differ in their demand for storage cycles. In the UNIVAC 1108 and the low models of the IBM 360 series the control words of a channel are kept in main storage; the channel must access main storage rather frequently to check transfer space limits and update control words. The transfer control words of the larger IBM 370 models are in private channel storage rather than in main storage. The channel accesses main storage only to transfer data and to fetch the next channel command.

PROBLEMS

1. Consider a configuration as in figure 1.4a with a main store which is not large enough to hold a complete card deck or set of output lines. Because the commands to the devices contain a main storage address, data can be loaded into, or fetched from, an arbitrary area in Ms without needing fixed buffers. The specifications of the devices are described in section 1.3 and problem 1 of section 1.4 (except for the buffer DTB).

An attempt to overlap card reading with the transfer of card images from main storage Ms to drum D (called card dump) led to this control program:

```
select starting address sain in M
select starting address sad on D
initialize {card count cc and dump count dc to zero
   input address ain in Ms to sain, input address ad on D to sad, dump
   address dam in Ms to sain, card coming to false}
repeat wait while CR and D busy
         if CR not busy then
            if card coming then card coming ← false; increment cc fi
            if CR ready then card coming ← true
               ain ← NEXT (ain); command read card (ain) fi
         fi
         if D ready and dc < cc then
            dam ← NEXT (dam); command write (dam, ad, 20); add 20 to ad;
               increment dc
         fi
until    dc = cc and CR idle
```

A card image should be transferred to D if D is ready to accept a command and a complete card image is present in main storage. The latter condition is true if and only if the number of dumps is less than the number of cards read (dc < cc). Hence the test in the last if statement. (The function

NEXT(x) has no side effects. It could, for instance, simply compute the value x+20.) However, we must be careful not to change card count cc before CR has completed the transfer of a whole card. The proper moment is when the state of the CR changes from BUSY to either READY or IDLE. The Boolean variable "card coming" assures that card count cc is changed exactly once after CR leaves the busy state.

a. Prove that the program uses the Boolean variable "card coming" correctly by showing that variable cc counts exactly the number of completed card inputs.
b. What could go wrong if the line "*if* CR not BUSY *then*" and the matching delimiter *fi* were deleted, but not the lines in between? (It has to do with the problem of CR leaving the BUSY state at an unpredictable moment.)
c. What could go wrong if the compound *if* statement were replaced by two separate *if* statements:
if CR not busy *and* card coming *then* card coming ← *false*; increment cc *fi*
if CR ready *then* card coming ← *true*; ain ← NEXT (ain); command read card (ain) *fi*

(The root of the trouble is the same as mentioned under (b).)

2. Write a control program for output processing, given the configuration for problem 1. Let the output lines be stored on drum D. The values of two global variables "sadout" and "lc" are respectively the starting address on the drum and the number of output lines.

3. Investigate the possibility of combining input and output processing as developed in problems 1 and 2 into one phase such that throughput is improved through time overlap. Be careful when programming the drum transfers because D can only handle one command at a time, either a dump or a fetch, but main storage is not large enough to hold an arbitrary number of card images or output lines.

4. Suppose main storage Ms in the configuration of problem 1 is large enough to hold at least a card deck, a set of output lines, or a compiled program. Furthermore, suppose it can almost hold two of these. A system with two phases is proposed: an I/O phase and a COMPUTE phase. The I/O phase is designed in three subphases: (a) first drum phase FD; (b) pure I/O phase PP; (c) second drum phase SD. In phase FD the set of output lines is transferred from D to M; in phase PP the card deck is loaded and lines are shipped to LP at the same time. Phase SD starts as soon as a card deck has been transferred from CR to Ms and it takes care of the transfer Ms → D, while any remaining output lines are shipped from Ms to LP.

Compare an estimate of the throughput of such a system with one of the systems developed in problems 1 and 2.

5. The system designed in problems 1 and 2 ignored the possibility that main storage Ms could be so full that no more information could be brought into Ms. This problem is particularly relevant if I/O overlap is implemented as studied in problem 3. It would be unwise, however, to limit input and output space separately because space that becomes available after dumping input or printing output can be used for either purpose. Incorporate special checks and actions to account for limited I/O space in main storage. For instance, the function NEXT of problem 1 can be defined such that areas are reused by rotating the input address ain.

READING LIST

Some excellent ideas on program construction are presented in [1, 2]. General concepts of programming languages are found in [3]. An example of advanced ideas in programming is [5]. A survey on machinery [6] is useful for understanding the task of an operating system. The survey in [4] discusses a variety of programming systems; it is recommended as a general reference text for understanding the relationship between all sorts of systems implemented on one machine.

1. Dahl, O.J., and C. A. R. Hoare, "Hierarchical Programming Structures," in *Structured Programming*, Academic Press, 1972.
2. Dijkstra, E.W., "Notes on Structured Programming," in *Structured Programming*, Academic Press, 1972.
3. Elson, M., *Concepts of Programming Languages*, Science Research Associates, 1973.
4. Freeman, P., *Software Systems Principles: A Survey*, Science Research Associates, 1975.
5. Liskov, B. H., and S. Zilles, "Programming with Abstract Data Types," *SIGPLAN Notices* 9, 4 (April 1974).
6. Rosen, S., "Electronic Computers: A Historical Survey," *Computing Surveys* 1 (1969).

2. Basic Operating System Concepts

2.1 SWITCHING CPU CONTROL

2.1.1 The transfer of input and output data leaves many storage cycles unused as we saw in section 1.4. The involvement of the CPU in I/O operations is so minor that it could do other useful work while the devices transfer data. In the model of the preceding section either the CPU is active in a COMPUTE phase, or CR and LP are simultaneously active in an I/O phase. The next step is to aim for parallel activity in all three processors: CPU, CR, and LP.

One problem is that CR and LP cannot work without a little help from the CPU. The CPU must send the commands to the devices. If the two phases are merged, some CPU time must be allocated to the control of the device processors. How do we force the CPU to switch from the program it is executing to a device control program and back?

The problem cannot be solved by programming alone. If the program that controls a computation must cause a switch of control, statements to that effect must be inserted at regular intervals in the program. However, the programmer cannot be expected to insert such statements, because these are in no way related to the logic of his program. Moreover, a programmer should not be trusted with a responsibility for a task which clearly belongs in the realm of an operating system.

A workable solution for switching control has been built into the hardware. This concept, known as *hardware interrupt*, is explained below.

The CPU hardware loops through the FETCH-EXECUTE cycle which is described by the iterative command

```
repeat  IR ← M[PC]
        PC ← PC+1
        EXECUTE(IR)
until   IR = halt instruction
```

where the notation M[x] means the location in main storage Ms whose address is the value of x. (Thus, if PC = 256, IR is loaded with the storage word M[256], PC is incremented to 257 and the contents of IR is decoded and executed as an instruction.)

The rigid execution cycle is broken by a timer interrupt. A timer interrupt works like an alarm clock. The CPU is extended with a count, AK, which is decremented every time through the instruction cycle. When AK reaches the value zero, IR is loaded with the value of a fixed location in Ms, say M[0], instead of with M[PC]. The modified instruction cycle is

$$
\begin{array}{ll}
\textit{repeat} & \textit{if}\ \mathrm{AK} \neq 0\ \textit{then}\ \mathrm{IR} \leftarrow \mathrm{M[PC]};\ \mathrm{PC} \leftarrow \mathrm{PC}+1 \\
 & \textit{else}\ \mathrm{IR} \leftarrow \mathrm{M[0]}\ \textit{fi} \\
 & \mathrm{AK} \leftarrow \mathrm{AK}-1 \\
 & \mathrm{EXECUTE(IR)} \\
\textit{until} & \mathrm{IR} = \text{halt instruction}
\end{array}
$$

The value of AK can be set in a program. If, for instance, AK has been initialized to 1024 the alarm will go off after 1024 instructions. M[0] contains an instruction which changes the value of PC while saving the current value of PC so that the central processor can return to the interrupted program. The mechanism can be viewed as an externally forced procedure call or, more precisely, as a coroutine call, for both the timer procedure and the interrupted program will be resumed in the state in which they were suspended; neither is restarted at its beginning.

2.1.2 The alarm clock interrupt mechanism can be used to achieve the desired overlap in time of computation, input and output. It can also simplify some of the complexity built into the I/O phase of the model of section 1.5 as explained below.

Consider a generalized model of a computer configuration as shown in figure 2.1a. The nature of the peripheral devices and the number of devices has no impact on the use of the alarm clock.

The CPU must send commands to the peripheral devices. These devices are capable of autonomously transferring information to or from Ms after accepting a command from the CPU. We now investigate how the devices are kept busy while most of the CPU time is used for executing user programs.

We saw in the preceding sections that control programs $CP_1, CP_2, \ldots, CP_n$ are needed to manage the devices. There is for each control program CP_i a condition, $\mathrm{cond.}_i$, which determines whether it is useful to run program CP_i or not. In case of the line printer LP, for instance, the condition is

$$\mathrm{cond.}_{LP}\text{: LP READY } \textit{and}\ \mathrm{lc} > 0$$

These conditions should be evaluated by the operating system, because a device control program should not be allowed to make decisions which might affect other control programs. It is as in city traffic: no driver has the

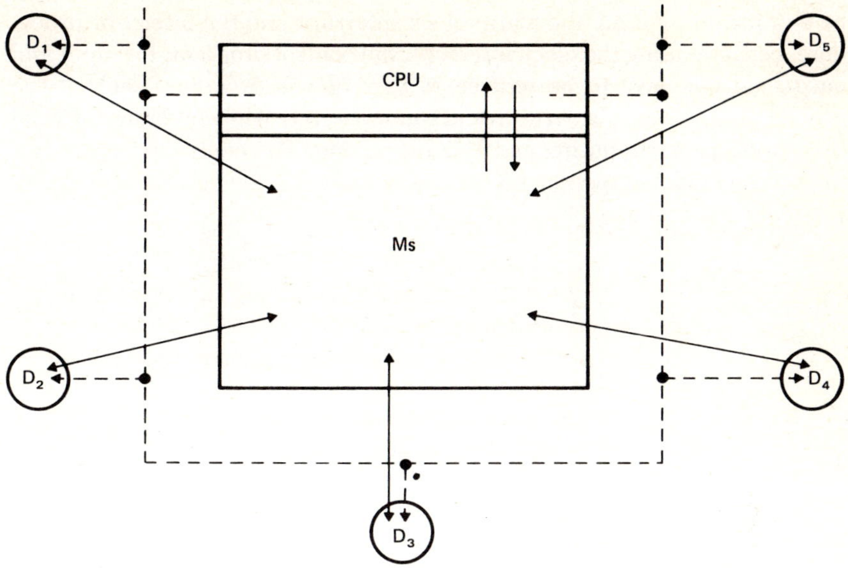

Figure 2.1a Schematic representation of a computer configuration

right to set all traffic lights to green along his way to work. Instead, an independent supervisory system regulates the lights to the best interests of all motorists. When the alarm clock goes off the proper thing to do is to investigate whether any of the devices needs the assistance of its control program. This leads to the following design for the interrupt procedure (activated by executing M[0]):

begin
save status of interrupted program
if cond.$_1$ *then* call CP_1 *fi*
if cond.$_2$ *then* call CP_2 *fi*
.
.
.
if cond.$_n$ *then* call CP_n *fi*
reset AK, restore status and continue interrupted program
end

The variables belonging to a control program are not initialized every time the program is activated. These variables are treated as global variables. For instance, the card count cc is such a global variable. When the CR control program is started it uses the current value of cc.

2.1.3 Much complexity was added to the simple model of section 1.3 by merging input and output into one phase in section 1.5. Most of this complexity can be eliminated by using the alarm clock interrupt and the interrupt procedure, because, using the clock interrupt, the control programs for input and output do not have to be written as part of one program. Each of the control programs can be written and run separately while maintaining total time overlap of computing and I/O processing. The control programs for the simple model of section 1.3 become:

```
interrupt control: begin save status of interrupted program
                      if CR READY then call CR control fi
                      if LP READY and lc > 0 then call LP control fi
                      reset AK
                      restore status and continue interrupted program
                   end
CR control:        begin ain ← NEXT(ain)
                      command read card (ain); cc ← cc+1
                   end
LP control:        begin aout ← NEXT(aout)
                      command print line (aout); lc ← lc−1
                   end
```

When the operating system is started, it must initialize AK, ain, aout, cc, and lc. Then it starts the compiler, which does nothing until there is some input. If a card deck is placed in CR and the start button is pushed, the compiler will receive input after the interrupt system has called CR control (see the problems).

2.1.4 Another type of interrupt system, called *device interrupt*, is actually more popular than a time interrupt system. As its name suggests, it causes an interrupt when a device needs assistance. A disadvantage of the alarm clock is that the interrupt procedure may be activated when none of the control programs can run. The waste in running the interrupt procedure is not so much in checking the conditions $\text{cond.}_1, \ldots, \text{cond.}_n$ but more in saving the state of the interrupted program and its resumption later on. The basic idea of device interrupt is to cause an interrupt of the normal instruction sequence only if there is a device that needs help from its control program. A bit vector, called the interrupt vector, in the CPU records interrupts. Conceptually, the bit position in the interrupt vector corresponds to a particular device. A more detailed discussion of such interrupt systems follows in chapter 3.

The instruction cycle and interrupt procedure for a device interrupt system are basically:

```
cycle: repeat  if interrupt vector = 0 then IR ← M[PC]; PC ← PC+1
               else IR ← M[0] fi
               EXECUTE(IR)
       until   IR = halt instruction
```

```
interrupt procedure:
  begin
    save status of interrupted program
    x ← index of bit that caused interrupt
    turn off x-th bit of interrupt vector
    call the x-th control program
    restore status and continue interrupted program
  end
```

A major difference between the two interrupt systems is that a clock interrupt is planned in advance under program control (by setting AK), whereas a device interrupt cannot be programmed. A device interrupt can be caused by a device only. Later on we will see how the occurrence of a device interrupt can be postponed under program control. Another difference between the two systems is that the interrupt routine of a device interrupt system can get interrupted! Therefore a single fixed location to save the PC value of the interrupted computation is not sufficient. We postpone further discussion of these problems until chapter 4. We assume here that the probability that the interrupt vector has more than one 1 is zero.

The distinction between the two types of interrupt systems is rather superficial because a device interrupt system can easily be designed to provide a timer interrupt and vice versa. Given a device interrupt system, a special device can be added to make it behave as a timer interrupt system. This device is a clock which performs exactly the function of the count AK. The clock can be set by a CPU command. When it reaches a certain value, it sets a bit in the appropriate position of the interrupt vector. On the other hand, given a timer interrupt system, the effect of a device interrupt system is practically achieved by inspecting which device is ready when the alarm goes off. A disadvantage of the timer interrupt system is that a device may remain in the ready state for up to one timer interval before receiving a command. Since device interrupt systems are most common, this type is assumed throughout the text unless explicitly specified otherwise.

The slight disadvantage of the timer interrupt system is that a device may remain in the ready state for up to one timer interval before receiving a command.

PROBLEMS

1. The operating system control program can be improved. The compiler waits until there is source program to read, but the compiler may process the source more rapidly than the CR can input it. Therefore, the reading of input should be continued after the end of a program. The compiler should be designed so that it maintains a private pointer indicating up to how far it has seen the input, and the compiler should idle while waiting for more

source to arrive. Moreover, the compiler must be able to detect the end of a program, since this is no longer indicated by the idle state of CR. Each program will be terminated with a special control card EOP (end of program), uniquely distinguishable from all other source cards. The compiler must be able to detect this special card. The first phase of the compiler is a lexical scan of the source. The lexical scan looks at the source program as one long string of symbols terminated by EOP. Suppose the compiler reads the source character by character using *procedure* NEXTCHAR(x) which deposits the next character of the source in variable x. The main body of the lexical scan deals with characters only, and other matters, such as cards or absence of source, are hidden from it and buried in NEXTCHAR. Program procedure NEXTCHAR to use two buffers in alternating fashion for storing cards in order to get as much time overlap of computation and card reading as possible.

2. If input from CR is stored in buffers as in problem 1, CR will not work at full speed if successive read requests are issued too far apart in time. One way to keep CR busy while watching for overloading Ms with input is to dump input on a drum D. Procedure NEXTCHAR will then function in the same way as designed in problem 1, but it will get its input from D rather than from CR. CR control continues as long as there is a card to read and asks D control to dump the input on the drum.

Write the control programs for CR and D in this operating system assuming a machine with a device interrupt system.

3. Suppose a computer has the following peripheral equipment running at full speed: two card readers, a line printer, two magnetic tape units, and a drum. Choose reasonable specifications for computer and peripheral devices and, assuming a device interrupt system, estimate the fraction of CPU time left for computations. Do the same for a time interrupt system and try to determine an optimum value for resetting the timer AK. A reasonable solution of this problem will justify the choice of a device interrupt system in preference to a timer interrupt system.

4. A dual reader and drum configuration is used to correct programs. One card reader has the original card deck, which includes some incorrect cards. The other card reader has the correction card deck. The corrected card sequence is dumped on the drum. Each card contains a number in the last eight positions. The correction rules are as follows:

a. Cards in the original deck with numbers less than or equal to that of an earlier card in the deck are discarded.
b. A similar rule holds for cards in the correction card deck. The card sequences resulting from the application of rules a and b are subject to the further rules.
c. If a correction card contains a number that also occurs in the original

deck, the correction card should replace the first occurrence of the original card with the same number.

d. If a correction card contains a number that does not occur in the original deck, this card should be inserted in sequence in the original deck.

Rules c and d apply to cards which are not deleted by rules a and b.

Write one control program for the card readers and one for a drum to which the result of the correction is shipped. The programs should not allow more than six card images to be in main storage Ms at any one time. Assume a device interrupt system.

5. An operating system supporting the three different language systems A, B, and C, runs on a machine with device interrupts. Cards are read from one card reader, and programs written in languages A, B, or C may follow in arbitrary order. Each program starts with a special card, called a program control card, PCD (in other popular systems, called a job control card). The PCD card is distinguished from any non-PCD card by the first four characters.

The operating system is designed to read programs from the card reader, transfer them to the drum as soon as possible and build program queues for each language on the drum. Information about the three queues is kept in three queue tables, one for each drum queue (thus for each language). An entry in the table consists of two fields. The first field points to the starting address of the source program on the drum, and the second field indicates the number of cards in the program. Each table is fixed in main storage and cannot contain more than 10 entries.

Write the control programs to handle the input from the card reader. Do not permit more than 10 card images in main storage at any time.

2.2 BATCH SYSTEMS

2.2.1 The techniques and ideas discussed thus far are sufficient to design quite interesting systems. One such system is a *batch system* which has complete time overlap of I/O and computation phase. Source programs are assembled in a queue prior to successive execution. Some interesting aspects of such systems are relevant to a wide class of operating systems. Consider a configuration as shown in figure 2.2a.

The operating system is designed for a 32-bit word machine with device interrupts. Cards are read and stored in units of 240 words as an input stream on the drum. The compile, load, execute system, CLE, reads 240-word units from the input stream and produces 240-word units of output lines, also stored on the drum. The output line printing program fetches lines in units of 240 words from the drum. The CLE system detects program boundaries internally and takes care of the formatting of output.

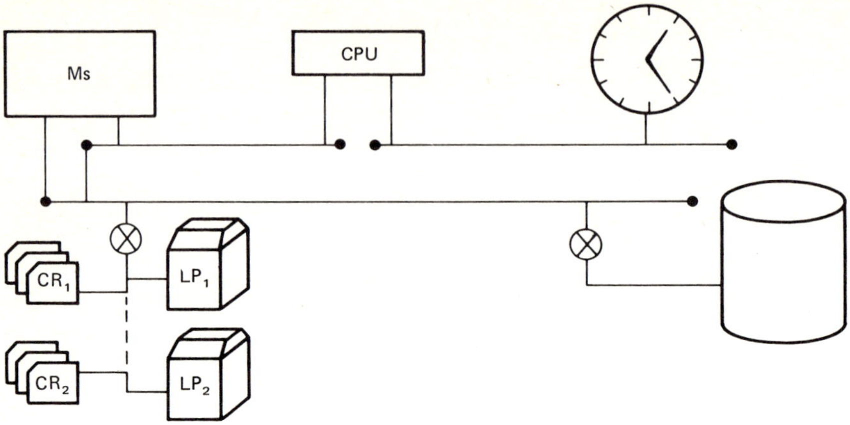

Figure 2.2a A host machine for a batch system

Consequently, the operating system control programs do not have to look at the information contained on cards or output lines. The interface between CLE and the operating system consists of two procedures: READBUF(x) and WRITEBUF(x), where x is an address in main storage Ms. When CLE calls READBUF(base), the operating system must fetch the next 240-word source unit from the input stream on the drum and deposit them in locations M[base] through M[base + 239]. CLE can dump 240 contiguous words of Ms onto the drum by calling WRITEBUF(bbb), where bbb is the starting address in Ms. The flow of information is represented in figure 2.2b.

We use the device interrupt program of the preceding section. The batch operating system consists of control programs for the card reader CR, line printer LP and drum D, and the programs for READBUF(x) and WRITE-BUF(x). The control programs for CR or LP are activated by an interrupt; this occurs when a device leaves the busy state (see figures 1.3d and 1.3e).

2.2.2 The completion of a command is the proper time (and the earliest moment) when two things can be done:

a. Record the progress of loading (unloading) a 240-word buffer. It is particularly important that a control program detects a full (empty) buffer, because then another unit can be added to the input stream (taken from the output stream).
b. Send the next command to the device. However, if we set aside a limited area for buffer space, it could be that the next command cannot be started until a buffer has been dumped onto (or fetched from) the drum. Once the space becomes available a command will be issued whether the state is READY or IDLE. In the latter case, the

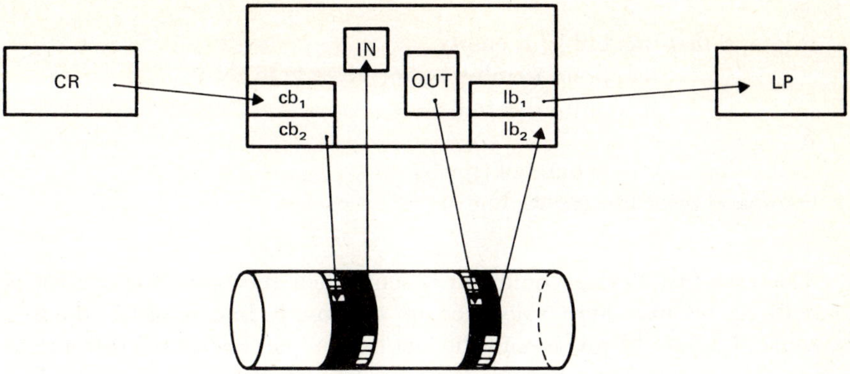

Figure 2.2b Information flow in a batch system

pending command serves as an initialization which gets the device started as soon as it leaves the idle state. We have seen before that it is not wise to use a buffer of exactly the unit size, because CR and D (or D and LP) cannot be allowed to work on the same buffer simultaneously. Therefore, we assign two card buffers and two line buffers of 240 words each (12 cards or 8 lines). Such dual buffer systems resemble the working of a seesaw; when one buffer is being loaded the other is being unloaded.

The initializations at the beginning of the programs are carried out when the operating system is started.

CR control: initialize {i = 0, base address of card buf [1] and [2]
card buf [1] and [2] empty; issue the first command,
cc = 0}

begin
  if cc = 12 *then* card buf [i] is full
    let i point to other buffer
    reset cc to one
    wait until card buf [i] empty
  fi
  ain ← base address card but [i] + 20*cc
  command read card (ain); cc ← cc + 1
end

LP control: initialize { j = 1, base address of line buf [1] and [2]
line buf [1] and [2] empty, wait until line buf [1]
full, issue first command, lc = 0}

```
begin
  if lc = 8 then line buf [j] is empty
                let j point to other buffer; reset lc to zero
                wait until line buf[j]full
  fi
  aout ← base address line buf [j]+30*lc
  command print line (aout); lc ← lc−1
end
```

The very first device command is sent when the operating system is initialized, because there is no interrupt to cause it. In case of LP, the first command cannot be given until the first line buf has been loaded from the drum. The *if* statement in both programs records the state of the buffers and indicates when a buffer is ready for drum processing. A next command is issued in the remaining statements.

2.2.3 Let the auxiliary store device be a drum D. When drum D causes an interrupt, it signals the completion of one of four different types of transfer (see figure 2.2c). A card buffer might have been added to the input stream or a line buffer might have been fetched from the output stream. It could also be that the CLE system fetched part of the input stream by calling READBUF, or dumped output in the output stream by calling WRITEBUF. Moreover, the drum control program must remember which buffer it handled so that the state, empty or full, is correctly recorded. The possible causes of a request for drum control are listed in figure 2.2c.

	IN	OUT
input stream	CR control from card buf [i]	READBUF(x)
output stream	WRITEBUF(y)	LP control to line buf [j]

Figure 2.2c Causes for drum control

Many important issues involving drum control are not discussed here. In this section, we restrict ourselves to a simple policy for drum control. Possible variations, relevant considerations for modifications and other problems will be discussed in later chapters.

Data transfer requests will be recorded in a code vector consisting of six elements. The six elements represent respectively the addresses of card buf [1] and card buf [2], the parameter x of READBUF, the parameter y of WRITEBUF, and the addresses of line buf [1] and line buf [2]. We avoid unnecessary complexity by assuming that READBUF and WRITEBUF also operate in units of 240 words per transfer. We adopt the policy that the program in which a drum transfer request originates will place the main storage address in the appropriate field of the code vector. When drum control completes a data transfer, it will clear the field in which the request was indicated. Drum control will use an internal flag to remember which of the six possible transfers it is dealing with. The major task of drum control consists of two parts, similar to the other control programs. The occurrence of a drum interrupt is the proper moment (and the earliest possible one) for doing two things:

a. Recording the completion of the latest transfer. (The flag indicates what kind of transfer took place.)
b. Issuing a next drum command if there is a request.

Drum control: {flag = *0*, codevector = 0, start drum control at statement, "wait until codevector ≠ *0*"}

begin
  if flag ≤ 2 *then* card buf [flag] is empty
  else if flag ≥ 5 *then* line buf [flag] is full *fi fi*
  clear codevector[flag]
  wait until codevector ≠ 0
  repeat flag ← *if* flag = 7 *then* 1 *else* flag+1 *fi*
  until codevector[flag] ≠ *nil*
goto L[flag]
  L[1]: DUMP (base address card buf [1], end of input stream)
    record growth of input stream
  L[2]: DUMP (base address card buf [2], end of input stream)
    record growth of input stream
  L[3]: FETCH (x, beginning of input stream)
    record shrinking of input stream
  L[4]: DUMP (y, end of output stream)
    record growth of output stream
  L[5]: FETCH (base address line buf [1], beginning of output stream)
    record shrinking of output stream
  L[6]: FETCH (base address line buf [2], beginning of output stream)
    record shrinking of output stream
end

The code vector may contain more than one request at any given time. So, we must decide in which order the requests will be processed. The worst policy is the one that always starts searching the code vector at field 1 because it fixes a preference for each of the six possible transfers, attaching the highest preference to dumping card buf [1] and the lowest preference to fetching output lines for line buf [2]. This policy seems bad for at least one reason: the lowest preference is given to an operation that will release overall storage space by sending output lines to LP. On the other hand, it is debatable whether or not preference should always be given to fetching from the output stream, because this policy may cause READBUF to wait, with the result that the CLE system cannot continue. The policy implemented in the drum control program tries to give each type of request an equal chance by cyclically scanning the code vector and selecting the first request following the most recent one (see also problem 1).

2.2.4 The buffer states (empty or full) are implemented by the fields of the code vector. For instance, the statement "card buf [n] is full" means that CR control requests a dump; hence the proper action is to place the buffer address in code vector field [i]. The condition "card buf [i] empty," on which CR may have to wait, can be checked by inspecting code vector field [i]. Consistent replacement of these statements and conditions by operations on code vector fields makes the first *if* statement in the drum control program superfluous.

READBUF(x) and WRITEBUF(y) indicate the transfer request in the appropriate code vector field. The CLE system determines where input should be placed in Ms (from where output should be fetched) and passes this information on to the drum control through the parameter x (parameter y). The specification of our system restricted the interface to the functions READBUF(x) and WRITEBUF(y). The compute phase must be suspended until a request has been granted for two reasons. First, if CLE continues after calling READBUF(x), it may operate too fast on the incoming buffer and get ahead of information which has yet to arrive. Second, if the call of READBUF(x) is followed by a second call READBUF(z), the second request gets lost if the code vector field for READBUF has not yet been cleared. This second point is a matter of implementation. It can be handled by replacing the single code vector field by a request queue. We will discuss this implementation in later chapters. However, the first problem cannot be solved by a mere change of implementation; it would be a bad decision to give CLE access to the code vector, because it would seriously alter the specified interface and give CLE an almost unlimited ability to interfere with the control of data transmissions. CLE should not be allowed to operate freely in the domain of the operating system for many reasons: reliability, added complexity, difficulties in understanding or changing either the operating system or the CLE system. The more functions an operating system is asked to perform, the more important become the issues of reliability, complexity, management and understanding.

The programs for READBUF(x) and WRITEBUF(y) are:

```
READBUF(x)  = begin place x in codeword field [3]
                  wait until codeword field [3] has been cleared
              end
WRITEBUF(y) = begin place y in codeword field [4]
                  wait until codeword field [4] has been cleared
              end
```

PROBLEMS

1. The policy adopted for the order in which drum transfer requests are granted in the drum control program is based on the idea that all types of requests are equally probable. Investigate whether or not (and if so, how) the policy should be changed if, on the average, three times as much output is processed as input.

2. The control programs do not account for any restriction on the amount of space available either in main storage Ms or on the drum D. There is, for instance, no check on how many times in a row the CLE system may call READBUF without deleting any of the buffers read in previously. Construct modified control programs which take account of the additional restrictions.
   a. The number of calls on READBUF should never exceed by more than two the number of calls on WRITEBUF.
   b. Space on the drum is limited, so the total space available for input stream and output stream is together restricted to a certain fixed amount.

3. The specification of the interface does not allow the use of a seesaw buffer for source input to the CLE system or for output that it produces. As a result, CLE idles whenever input is entered from the drum or output is dumped onto the drum. To avoid this inefficiency of CPU utilization a change of the interface is considered. The new proposal is to change the specification of the functions READBUF and WRITEBUF and to add a function DONE. The functions READBUF and WRITEBUF will only initiate a drum transfer and will do this only if the total number of times that READBUF and WRITEBUF were called never exceeds the number of times DONE was called by more than four. The advantage is that the CLE system can continue its operations after initiating a drum transfer. The function DONE waits for the least recent transfer to be completed.

Program the functions READBUF(x), WRITEBUF(y) and DONE and modify the drum control program.

4. Users of the one-reader, one-printer batch system would soon discover that the turnaround time (this is the time from the moment a program is submitted by a user until he gets the results) for short programs is adversely affected by the presence of long computing programs in the same batch. The problem is cured by extending the machine with another card reader and another printer. Short programs use the second card reader and print their results on the second line printer.

Modify the batch system to handle the extension. In many cases it is desirable to give priority to short programs, but the larger programs should not be neglected, or they may never be completed.

5. The buffer size of 240 words was rather arbitrarily chosen. An argument in favor of a block size this large compared to, say, 20 or 30 words is that the number of drum transfers is much lower than with smaller buffers. But an argument in favor of the small size is that less space in main storage is required. The disadvantage of a larger number of drum transfers may well be compensated for by the time overlap with card reading and line printing, although more CPU time is needed for drum control.

Investigate the effect of lowering the buffer size and try to estimate the change in throughput (the number of programs executed per time unit).

In problems 6 and 7 we discuss two alternatives for the machinery that supports the batch system.

6. Traffic along the data paths for input and output to and from drum D is competing for access to D. It might be worth considering replacing drum D by two less expensive devices that will handle one path of each pair and, although slower than the drum, can operate simultaneously. Such a configuration is shown schematically in figure 2.2d.

Drum D is replaced by two magnetic tape devices (see section 1.4, problem 4). It looks as if the REWIND and SKIP operations kill the whole idea. Every time a new buffer is read from the tape it must be spooled backwards to locate the spot where reading stopped last time.

Choose reasonable specifications for the devices involved and investigate the difference in performance of this machine and the one with the drum.

7. Another approach with the advantage that the separate data paths can be used simultaneously, but without the disadvantage of REWIND and SKIP, is a machine configuration with a satellite computer. Four magnetic tape devices and two separate central processors are used. Two of these devices are connected to one CPU, and two to the other. From time to time, the connections are switched. Figure 2.2e shows a schematic representation.

CPU_2 with Ms_2 is a very small machine which controls CR, LP and 2 MTs. The larger machine has only two MTs as I/O devices, one for input and one for output. This system is truly a batch system: the small machine prepares a batch of programs on MT_2 or MT_1 while the large machine processes a batch of programs on the other tape. Output is treated likewise.

The two machines can directly interrupt one another (each appears to the other as a peripheral device). The rules to implement are these:

a. When the small machine receives an interrupt from the large one, it should read until end of program and then switch the connections of MT_1 and MT_2 such that the new batch becomes available.
b. When the large machine receives an interrupt from the small one, it must complete the dump of the current output until end of program and then switch the connections of MT_3 and MT_4 such that a new batch of output becomes available for the small machine.

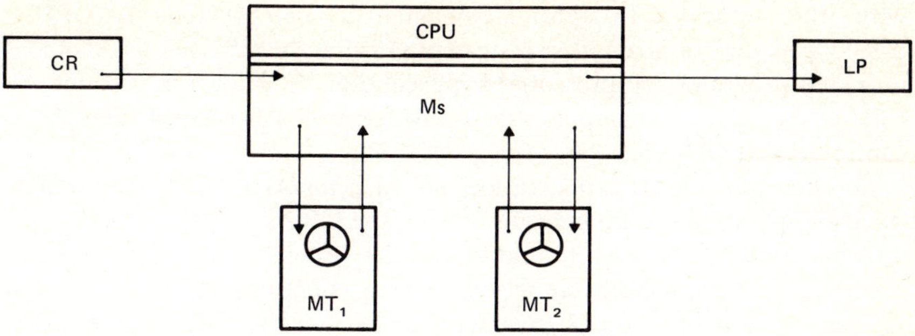

Figure 2.2d Batch system with two magnetic tape devices

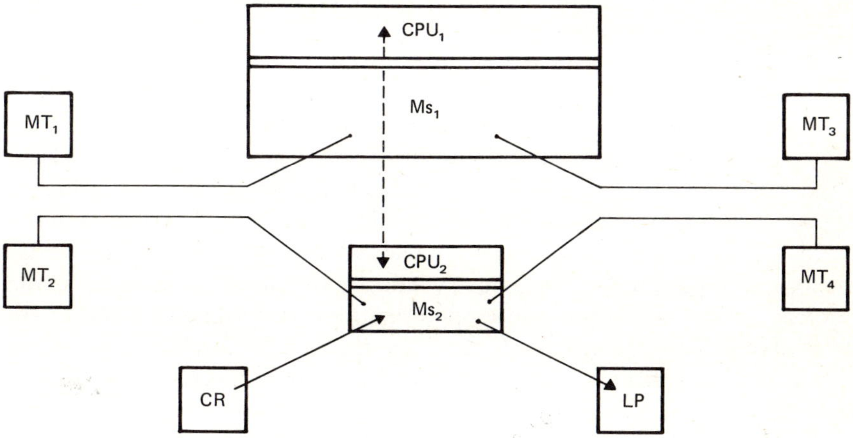

Figure 2.2e Satellite computer for I/O

Investigate whether or not this is a sound design; if not, modify or complete it. Write the control programs which are activated upon the occurrence of the two newly introduced interrupts.

2.3 PROCESSES

2.3.1 At this point we are ready for a change of our conceptual view. The first step toward a wider view is the observation that the control programs in the preceding examples are related to each other in much the same way as the hardware devices. Each of them is largely independent of the others, except for some necessary activation (corresponding to the CPU commands to devices). The drum control program of section 2.1 can be viewed as an independent process controlling the traffic between main storage Ms and drum D. It interacts only rarely and at well defined points in its program with other activities. In addition, we might as well say that the CPU is passed from one job to another instead of viewing the CPU as a fixed object to which programs are presented for execution. In the batch system, the CPU is passed from computation to CR control, LP control, and drum control, and then back.

Another observation is that it does not help much to design and understand an operating system in terms of what the CPU is doing at a particular moment. Instead, we wish to understand the system in terms of the functions it executes and their mutual relationship. Relating this observation to the batch system of section 2.1, we see that the successive states of the CPU are rather irrelevant, even unpredictable at times, because interrupts may change its state in a manner outside of CPU control. But the system can be clearly understood in terms of the functional specification of computation and various forms of device control with their common data structures for exchange of information.

The term *process* is generally used for such a functional unit in an operating system (a task in OS/370). A process is controlled by a program and needs a processor to carry out this program. We will resist the challenge to give a precise definition of the term because various attempts to do so have not, so far, led to a generally accepted definition. Instead, we will rely upon our intuitive feeling for what constitutes a functional unit and use the term for the activity invoked by it. (The closest description in the terminology of programming languages would be to consider a process as the execution of a closed procedure operating in a well-defined execution environment.) Taking a pragmatic view, the main characteristics of a process are that it is controlled by a program and it needs a processor on which it can run.

Some processes have processors permanently associated with them. A typical example of such a process is a peripheral device with its control unit. The device performs a well-defined task in the system (printing lines on paper, for instance). It has its own processor and the commands sent to it are the input to the hardwired program that controls it.

Other processes do not own private processors. An example of such a process is the drum control process. It has its control program but shares the use of a processor (the CPU) with user programs and other control processes. A processor is a piece of equipment able to carry out a set of instructions or commands. A processor understands an instruction through a fixed interpretation mechanism. Instructions must therefore be written according to those interpretation rules. We call such a set of rules a programming language. If a process does not own a processor, we associate with it a *virtual processor*. This is a hypothetical piece of equipment which is able to interpret the language in which the control program of this process is written. In some cases it is easy to realize such a virtual processor by means of a real one; in other cases it requires a substantial programming effort to simulate it. For instance, in case of the control processes of the batch system, the virtual processors are an exact model of the CPU which can realize these virtual processors. However, if the control program is written in APL, the real processor must be a complete programming system in the form of an APL interpreter.

2.3.2 Two ways of classifying processes are relevant to our subject. The first is a distinction between deterministic and non-deterministic processes. The second distinguishes between sequential and parallel processes. A deterministic process is one for which the sequence of successive data transformations (caused by executing the program instructions) is fixed for given input. Such a deterministic process satisfies the most stringent requirement of reproducibility. A weaker form of determinism is of more interest for our purposes: a process is input/output deterministic if the resulting output is fixed by given input. This property guarantees a functional behavior of a process: the result is a function of the given argument. It also guarantees a form of reproducibility, one in which we are highly interested. For example, suppose a program were written in such a way that it could make the choice to either use very little storage space but take a rather long time to run, or to run very fast at the cost of a considerable increase of space. The program has the choice when it starts according to the space that is available at that moment. This feature is useless if the result of the program depends on this choice. We demand that the execution of a program is input/output deterministic.

A sequential process is one in which the instructions are executed strictly in order, one after the other. The order of execution is often mandatory in the sense that the result of a computation depends on it. There are other cases in which instructions have to be placed in order because the processor can execute only one instruction at a time, but the order is in fact irrelevant to the logic of the program.

A comparison with human activities may clarify this situation: after waking up in the morning I may have breakfast first and then shave, or the other way around. Although the order does not really matter, I am forced to choose one because I (the processor) cannot do these things at the same time. But I do not always have a choice of ordering my activities; it would be totally impossible for me to shave first and then wake up.

Examples of mandatory and arbitrary ordering are shown in a program below. Given are a constant stop, two variables, x and y, and two functions, l and s, which have no side effects (a possible interpretation for l(x) and s(x) would be length of x and successor of x in a list).

```
repeat  y ← s(x)
        if x+l(x) = y then l(x) ← l(x)+l(y); s(x) ← s(y)
        else x ← y fi
until   x = stop
```

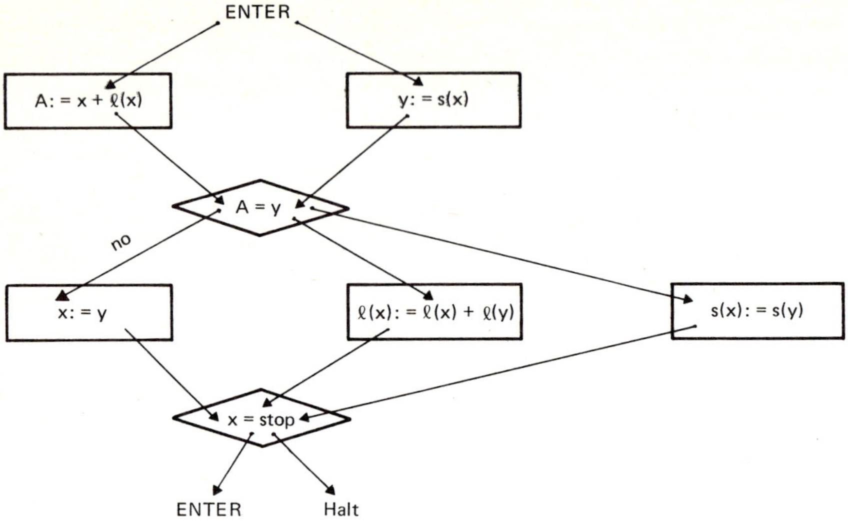

Figure 2.3a Program represented as partially ordered set of commands

Note that it is necessary to assign the value of s(x) to y and to compute the sum x+1(x) before the equality test in the *if* clause can be carried out. But the decision to perform the assignment before evaluating the sum is arbitrary. If all unnecessary decisions of ordering are removed, we come to a representation which shows the program as a partially ordered set of instructions as in figure 2.3a.

If we had a parallel processor, it could concurrently execute the instructions for which the order of execution is immaterial. A process which can execute commands in parallel is called a *parallel process*.

The batch system of section 2.2 can be viewed as a parallel process if we think of it as one unit that handles user processes, because it reads cards, computes and prints lines at the same time. However, it is customary (and from the designer's point of view more useful), to consider such a system as a collection of processes rather than as one monolithic process. The term *concurrent processes* is generally used to indicate a collection of processes that have some form of connection and operate simultaneously. The terms *parallel* and *concurrent* are not clearly distinguished in the literature.

Historical Note

The concept of a process was used extensively for the first time by the designers of the MULTICS system and, independently, by the group that designed the T.H.E system The task concept of OS/370 is essentially the same idea. The term *process* must not be confused with terms such as *job*, *computation*, and *virtual machine*. Job and computation are generally used to indicate a unit of work which must be carried out for a user, including input/output, compilation, etc. Thus, the processing of a job may require the activity of many processes. The term virtual machine differs from process in that no activity is associated with it. Given a virtual processor and a control program, one must push the start button, so to speak, to start a process. Where confusion is unlikely, the term *process* is often used to mean either process in the active sense or virtual machine.

The idea of parallelism has been around for a long time and has found useful applications, particularly in hardware design. We find applications not only in the device control units, but also in the design of central processors. An instruction placed in the instruction register of a contemporary machine is handled by a parallel operation which decodes the instruction code and computes the address of the memory operand(s) at the same time that the program counter is incremented. Another speed-up of the instruction cycle is achieved by a time overlap of instruction execution and the next couple of instruction fetches. Although a problem arises with branch instructions, the success of large fast machines such as the CDC 6600 and IBM 360/91 proves that this kind of speed-up can pay off. It is almost inevitably associated with another kind of speed-up known as *interleaved memory*. Here the idea is to reduce the competition for storage access among the asynchronous devices by distributing storage over a number of separate banks. There is competition if devices attempt to access one bank at the same time, but the probability that this will occur decreases as the number of banks increases. The number of banks is usually two to four. The CDC 6600, however, has fixed size banks of 4096 words. Thus, a medium-size main store may have as many as 20 to 30 banks. A division into two banks separates the even addresses from the odd addresses; all the storage locations with an odd address are in one bank, those with even address in the other one. Instead of selecting on the low-order address bits, a bank could be selected on the high-order address bit. An example of a machine that does both is the UNIVAC 1108.

An interesting application of parallelism is found in the ILLIAC IV machine. Each of 64 identical processors has private storage and can operate directly on some fast registers of other processes. One central control process broadcasts instructions (one at a time) to all 64 processors, and processors that are not masked off to accept the instruction execute it simultaneously. Such a machine is extremely useful for parallel operations on arrays.

The latest developments in hardware and programs that employ parallelism look promising and a study of this topic from other sources is recommended.

PROBLEMS

1. A process can be represented in several ways. The most precise representation is a control program written in the language of the processor on which it is to run. This representation is often hard to work with: first, because one has to interpret the coding while reading, and second, because one is usually not interested in all details at one time. It is therefore good practice to represent a process also in readable language and various global descriptions that deal with particular aspects of the process. As a matter of fact, we have seen various ways of representing a process, by a state table or a transition diagram (see section 1.3) and by abstract programs.

   a. Represent the drum control process of section 2.2 by a state table and a transition diagram.
   b. Represent the card reader hardware, as specified by its state table and transition diagram, by a program written in a readable language like the control programs in section 2.2.

2. A variation of the state table representation is the state transition table which represents a process as a finite state machine. Such a table lists all possible actions of the process and is therefore useful only if the number of possible actions is small. The table below (see figure 2.3b) represents a binary adder. It is assumed, for simplicity, that the input strings are equal in length such that "end of bitstring" appears on both input lines at the same moment. The initial state is S_0, and the elements in the table list the output and successor state.

   A number is negated in a two's complement machine by taking the one's complement and adding one to it. Thus, figure 2.3c represents a machine that will subtract two binary numbers (of equal bit length).

   Design the state transition tables for the complement box, the increment one box, and design one for the machine as a whole.

State / Input	S_0	S_1
00	$0S_0$	$1S_0$
01	$1S_0$	$0S_1$
10	$1S_0$	$0S_1$
11	$0S_0$	$1S_1$
End	Halt	Overflow

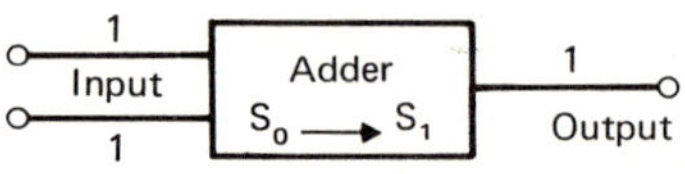

Figure 2.3b State transition table representing a binary adder

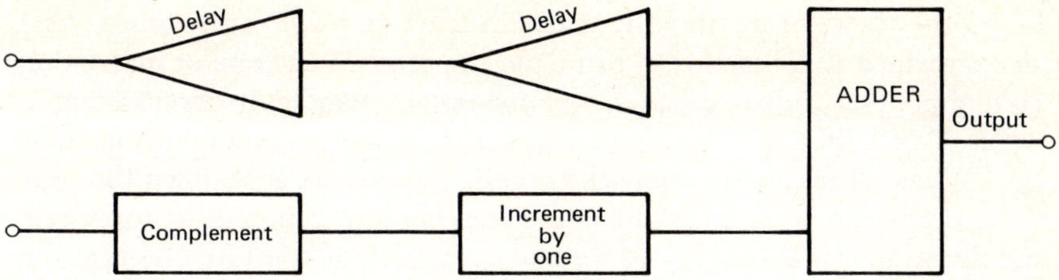

Figure 2.3c Subtraction in a two's complement machine

3. Figure 2.3d represents a parallel machine with 8 identical processors. Instructions of the machine are of the form (OPC, OPR, MASK) where OPC is the operation code, OPR the operand and MASK a mask that indicates which of the processors are supposed to perform (listen to) the instruction that is broadcasted. For instance, ADD m[1](11110000) means that the first four processors must add the contents of location 1 in their local storage to their function register. An operand OPR is either an operand in local memory or the function register itself or of its right or left neighbor (if any). The set of operation codes is as usual; the solution of this problem requires, among others, an instruction of the type LOAD left neighbor (01010101) which would copy the values of the function registers in processors 0, 2, 4 and 6 in those of processors 1, 3, 5 and 7.

Suppose the function registers and local storage location Mem have been initialized with numbers as indicated in figure 2.3c. Write a parallel program that computes

$$a_7x^7 + a_6s^6 + a_5x^5 + \ldots + a_1x + a_0$$

and delivers the result in one of the function registers. The program should not include more than five multiplication instructions.

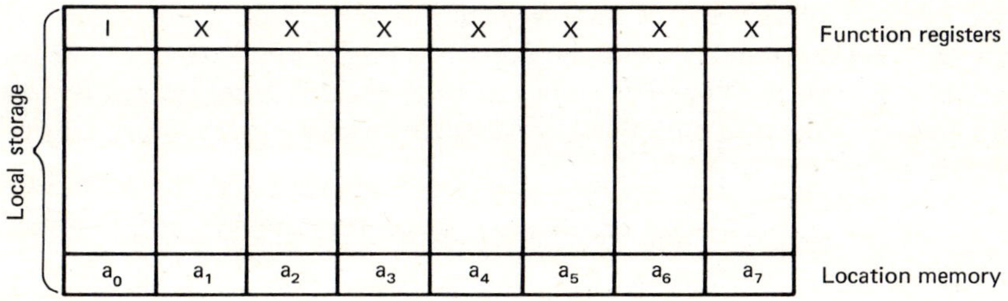

Figure 2.3d Parallel machine with 8 processors

4. Another form of parallelism at the instruction level is *pipelining*. The idea on which it is based is in principle the same as the one of improving throughput by a time overlap. A pipeline process handles its input string in stages. While item i_k is in stage s_p, item i_{k+1} is in s_{p+1} and i_{k-1} is in stage s_{p-1}. When all stages are done, the modified items are sent down the pipe to the next stage. Such an organization does not have a broadcasting system and the various processors may well be executing different functions at the same time. Figure 2.3e represents a compiler organized as a pipeline. The stages are the successive functions of the compiler and suitable items might be subsequent statements of the source program.

Stage 1	Lexical scan
Stage 2	Syntax scan
Stage 3	Code optimizer
Stage 4	Code generator
Stage 5	Loader preparation

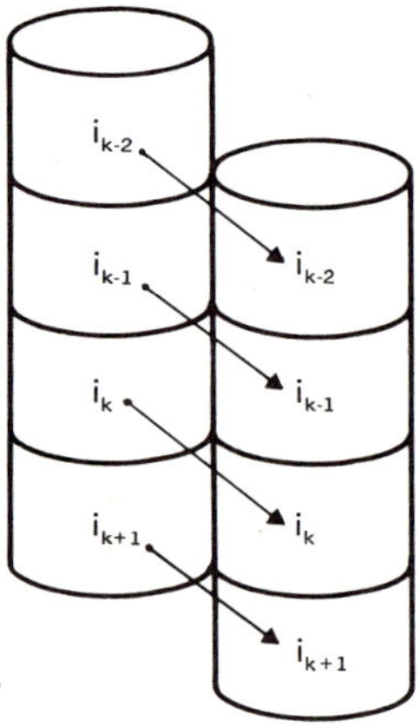

Figure 2.3e Pipeline process for compiling

Suppose we have a pipeline machine with n states (for our purposes, n = 3). One can assign an operation (LOAD, ADD or MUL, etc.) to a stage; each stage has two operand registers and a result register. A central control unit CC can address any of those registers as well as the main store. CC presents, going around in a circular fashion, a pair of operands to the stages in rapid succession. When CC comes to a stage which is not yet ready, it is automatically delayed until the stage operation is finished. Program for this machine a process which computes the vector operation

$$a_1 * (b_1 + c_1) + a_2 * (b_2 + c_2) + \ldots + a_n * (b_n + c_n)$$

assuming that the arrays $A = (a_1, \ldots, a_n)$, $B = (b_1, \ldots, b_n)$ and $C = (c_1, \ldots, c_n)$ and the number n are in the main store.

2.4 MULTIPROGRAMMING

2.4.1 There is a significant difference in the way CPU time is allocated to processes in the model of section 1.3 and in the one of section 2.2. In the former, a process is run to completion before another one is able to start, but in the latter model, a process may be interrupted during its run and another process continued from where it was suspended earlier. CPU time is distributed among several processes in the batch system of section 2.2 to permit each of them to execute for a while. We say that CPU time is multiplexed between a set of processes and that the processes are interleaved in time.

Once we discover the idea of interleaving the execution of processes, we wonder how many processes can share a CPU. We saw in chapter 1 that only very little CPU time is required to control the devices. The programs running on one of the systems discussed in this chapter may have to wait for data transfers. This means that a program may not be able to use the CPU continually. Since data transfer operations are relatively slow, the CPU is idle for long periods of time. It is therefore worthwhile to bring several user programs in the main store so that if some of them have to wait for data transfers, others can run for a while. A particularly suitable mix consists of more programs which frequently require I/O operations (we say that such a program is *I/O bound*) and one or more programs with few I/O operations but with extensive computations (we say that such a program is *compute bound*, since the speed of this program primarily depends on how much CPU time is allocated to it). The compute bound programs receive most of the CPU time, but when an I/O operation is completed for an I/O bound program, the latter is allowed to run until it requests another I/O operation.

The limitation on how many programs should share the CPU is primarily determined by the size of the main store. If too many programs share the use of the main store, each of them has too little space in the store. This

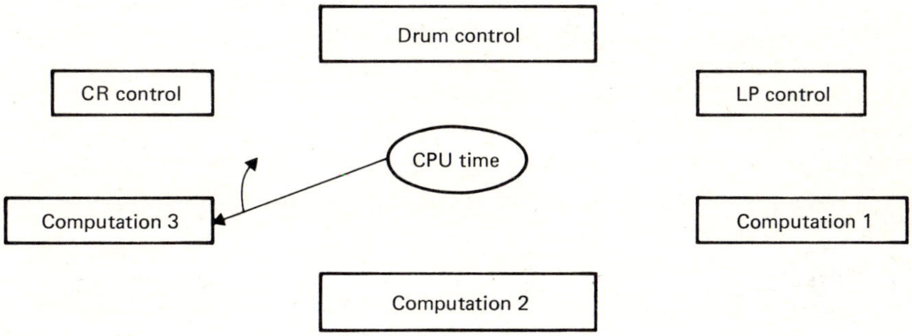

Figure 2.4a CPU miltiplexing

results in frequent requests for data from the auxiliary store. The data transfers can bring the programs almost to a halt. This phenomenon is called *thrashing*. It is discussed in detail in chapters 7 and 8.

If the CPU is multiplexed, it is no longer necessary to run user programs in a strict order as in the batch system model. The small programs will particularly benefit from this technique. *Multiprogramming* describes a system in which several computations are executed by concurrent processes which use parts of the main store and part of the CPU time.

2.4.2 There are in fact two types of concurrency in a multiprogramming system. First is the type of concurrency where several processes run at the same time. The second type interleaves several program executions. This distinction is important with regard to systems design insofar as a mechanism must be implemented for multiplexing the CPU among the interleaved processes. However, the logical problems of organizing a suitable environment in which concurrent processes can operate is independent of the distinction. There is no difference between the two types of processes for the computer user. Control switches from one process to another take place in milliseconds, but the smallest unit of time suitable for a user is measured in seconds. The rapid switches of control give the user the impression that the interleaved processes operate simultaneously.

The interrupt program as developed in section 2.1 is not adequate to distribute CPU time among all processes in a multiprogramming system. CPU time is allocated to device control processes when a device interrupts, but there is no such external signal to activate any of the programs. We may consider a slight change in the interrupt program of section 2.1: instead of returning automatically to the interrupted program after running a device control process, a scheduling routine is implemented which decides to which process the CPU will be allocated next. User processes are now activated by the external device interrupts. However, device interrupts occur at unpredictable moments, so CPU time will not be evenly distributed among the user processes. That is, compute bound programs which may not issue any I/O commands (causing device interrupts) retain the services of the CPU for disproportionately long periods of time, whereas I/O bound jobs result in many device interrupts causing frequent executions of the CPU scheduling routine.

The problem is solved by a timer interrupt. We add to our machine a timer device programmed to interrupt at regular intervals. At the end of a time slice control can be switched to another process.

It is possible to add one or more CPUs to the machine and multiplex several CPUs among a group of processes. We have seen specific examples of multiprocessor machines in sections 2.2 and 2.3; here we observe that a machine could have several identical CPUs which operate the same as the single one does in a uniprocessor machine.

2.4.3 We have now reached a point at which some reflection is appropriate. The environment in which a program executes is radically different from a simple operating system, where a program had all of the CPU time and storage space. It has changed into a multiprogramming environment in which it shares the facilities with others. We discovered step by step the feasibility of some programming techniques, but did not question the desirability of applying such techniques and whether or not the cost of their implementation and maintenance is justified.

Generally speaking, there is evidence that it is worth the effort and cost to design and maintain a multiprogramming system which allows programmers to share the computer features dynamically and to run their programs simultaneously under certain restrictions. The evidence is based on the success of several systems which are still operational or which have served as a model for more advanced systems (CTSS, ATLAS, MULTICS, THE, RC4000, B5500, OS/360, CP67, MTS, TSS8). There are cases where the nature of the computing work to be done justifies a simpler operating system at a much lower cost (the system on the UNIVAC 1108 at Case Western Reserve University is an example).

Implementation of multiprogramming adds a substantial amount of work to an operating system. The ultimate cause of this expansion is the conflict of interest that arises among the processes by the mere fact that they coexist and share the use of resources. Competition exists without multiprogramming (every programmer wants his program to run immediately and have access to all the facilities he needs), but it is resolved by human management. Rules for submitting and running programs are established which classify programs based on information such as length, expected runtime and the nature and importance of the program.

A closer look at the implications of multiprogramming gives insight into the kind of functions which an operating system must perform in addition to device control and interrupt handling in order to monitor concurrent user jobs. This survey also gives an idea of the topics which are discussed in subsequent chapters.

a. Delays: when a process attempts to access common data or one of the devices, it may not be allowed to do so until that data or device is released when another process finishes using it. An operating system provides the environment in which processes are coordinated in this manner. The basis for such an environment is discussed in chapters 3 and 4.

b. Waiting times: if several processes are competing for a resource, the decision on which process the resource will be allocated must not depend on incidental causes. The operating system must follow a fair policy for selecting the next process to run. Short term and long range decision policies of this nature are discussed in chapters 6 and 8.

c. Overhead: if concurrent processes are supposed to obey certain traffic rules restricting their rights, the operating system must enforce these rules through monitor programs. This costs execution time and storage space for bookkeeping purposes. We should be continually concerned about finding the right compromise between providing elaborate bookkeeping and slowing down user programs. This aspect is associated with every subject discussed and is therefore not treated separately.

d. Run time increase: the number of programs executed in a fixed time interval actually decreases when the CPU is multiplexed between several processes rather than allocated sequentially, because CPU time is spent in frequent control switches from one process to another. Another substantial cause of runtime increase is that of data transfer times. The more processes that share the use of main storage, the less space is allocated to each of them. This results automatically in more data traffic to and from main storage. This justifies a separate discussion which is found in chapter 7.

e. Malfunctioning: The errors of one program must not affect another program. For instance, a program must not write outside the storage area allocated to it. Such mistakes can be prevented by regulating the exchange of data by communication rules, discussed in chapter 5, and by regulating the creation and use of names, discussed in chapters 7 and 9. Malfunctioning may have internal or external causes. Incorrect input may bring a program into an infinite loop so that it does not release a resource. Or concurrent processes may be by accident waiting for one another to release one of a pair of devices. Such problems are discussed at the end of chapter 3 and in chapter 10.

f. Shared data: users like to share their programs and data, but a user must have the ability to specify who is permitted to use his information. The right to access some object may be different for various users. For instance, a compiler writer has the right to modify his codes and may grant this right also to some other programmers, but will deny it to most users. A multiprogramming system has the inherent capability of letting programmers use each other's programs. The operating system must provide the means to regulate the degree of access authorization to data which users wish to share.

g. Modularity: multiprogramming gives us an opportunity to structure an operating system as a set of interconnected functional units. This is not just a local issue at the design phase. It is crucial to be able to verify, explain, modify or tune the system in accordance with reasonable demands of performance and service. Although it is applied in all our discussions, this topic is discussed separately in chapter 10.

PROBLEMS

1. Write a modified version of the interrupt program presented in section 2.1 for a multiprogramming system. Assume that the interrupt program will resume one of the other programs rather than return to the interrupted program.

2. It is obvious that a multiprogramming system must record the status of a program when it is interrupted so that it can resume the program at a later time. A small storage area is permanently reserved for this purpose and a process control block (PCB) of fixed size is assigned to every process. Design a format for PCBs, then investigate when the information in a PCB is used and when it is changed.

3. The drum control program of section 1.5 contains the statement "wait until codevector ≠ *0*". It would be a waste of CPU time to let the drum control process wait by repeatedly inspecting the codevector. Moreover, such an implementation with only one CPU prevents the activity that could help it to get out of the wait state, because it inhibits the programs which need the CPU. The routines READBUF and WRITEBUF cannot run and set the codevector. Specify an action which does not waste CPU time. It transfers control to the drum control program when READBUF or WRITEBUF sets the codevector unequal to zero.

4. An attractive policy for multiplexing a CPU among interleaved processes is the round robin schedule which allocates CPU time to the processes in a circular fashion. The policy is particularly suitable if little information is available to classify processes, and is attractive because of its simplicity, fairness and minimal overhead. We discuss here a variation of a round robin schedule based on an idea which was implemented in CTSS. Suppose the operating system is able to detect whether or not a process is working on the same program as when it last looked at the process. The system keeps a steady count for each process. The longer a program runs, the higher the steady count gets. This count can be used predictively by postulating: if the steady count is getting high, the process is apparently working on a long program. Processes are classified according to how long they run. We define for that purpose two threshold values t_1 and t_2 (the choice of two is arbitrary). Whenever a steady count passes t_i, the process moves from class i–1 to class i. The significant difference between the classes is that, when CPU time is allocated to a process in class i, it will get twice as much CPU time as a process of class i–1 gets. On the other hand, the programs in class 1 have the highest priority and those in class 3 the lowest priority. That is to say, the CPU is allocated to a program in class 3 only if both classes 1 and 2 are empty and it is allocated to a program in class 2 only

if class 1 is empty. This policy favors the short programs at the expense of the compute bound programs.

The classification is brought into effect by an alarmclock interrupt (see section 1.4). The value of AK is set depending on the class of the process that is resumed. Describe an implementation of such an allocation policy, including the bookkeeping of class and steady count and the programming of the selection algorithm. Describe also where and how the descriptive variables of the policy are updated.

5. Let f be the ratio of the average runtime between two I/O requests of an I/O bound program and the average duration of an I/O operation. The operating system allows so many I/O bound programs to run concurrently that all n I/O devices are kept busy. Express the percentage of CPU time spent in controlling the I/O devices in f and n. Use this expression to plot n as a function of f in the interval $0.002 \leq f \leq 0.1$, while the percentage of CPU time allocated to controlling the I/O devices is fixed at 20%. The result shows that having a large number of I/O devices does not cause a particular hardship for the CPU. It also shows that a program mix should consist of several I/O bound programs and one or two compute bound programs.

2.5 TIMESHARING

2.5.1 The basic idea of a timesharing system is to use a machine as a sophisticated multiple desk calculator. Users have immediate access to their programs and data and interact directly with the operating system which provides the timesharing facilities. Equipment is multiplexed between users so that many of them can work at the same time. Contemporary timesharing systems are, almost without exception, multiprogramming systems. Timesharing systems have introduced additional problems of interest, the major ones being user/machine interaction and the management of user data (files) which reside semipermanently on a secondary storage device (usually a disk).

A timesharing system does not have to be a multiprogramming system. It is easier to discuss the basic idea of timesharing without adding the complexity inherent to multiprogramming. The early timesharing system did not have multiprogramming. The model presented in this section resembles those systems more than contemporary timesharing systems.

Figure 2.5a presents a schematic view of a machine on which a timesharing system can be implemented. There are n terminals connected to the machine through p low speed data channels.

Terminals transfer data on a character-by-character basis. When the user strikes a key, the corresponding character is placed in the data transmission buffer of the keyboard and an interrupt is caused. The character must be

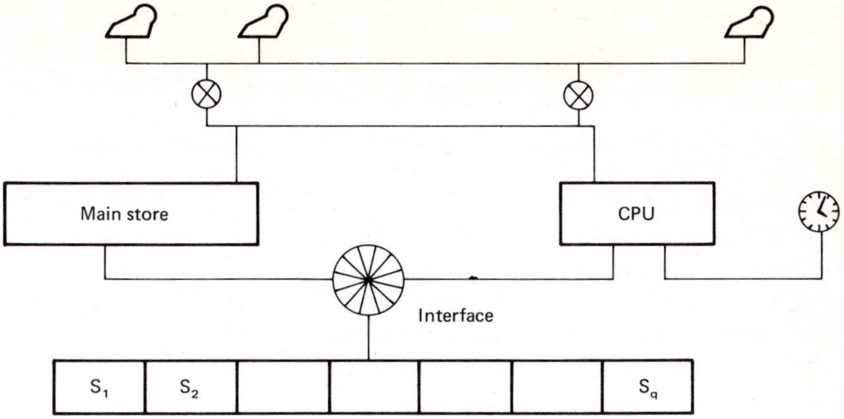

Figure 2.5a Machine configuration for timesharing system

removed from the transmission buffer before the user strikes another key, or else the first character is overwritten by the next character.

The main store is divided into two parts, one for the operating system and the buffer space, the other part for the user jobs. A large backup store (a drum or disk) is divided into q slices $s_1, \ldots, s_q$, where each slice is of the same size as the user area in the main store. Programs and data of user reside either in the user area of Ms, or in one of the slices on the auxiliary store D. Let the user area in Ms be s_0.

The operating system performs two functions: it transmits characters to and from the terminals, and it loads and unloads (called *swapping*) slice s_0. The programming of these two functions is discussed below.

Every user sitting at a terminal is connected with his own user area through two fixed buffers. The user area resides in one of the slices, the buffers reside in the operating system area of Ms. There is a pair of buffers for each terminal. The buffers are fixed in size and place. Their capacity is one line. Character transmission takes place solely between terminals and buffers; slices cannot directly communicate with terminals.

A terminal is a combination of two devices in one unit: a keyboard and a printer (or visual display). When a key is struck, the terminal acts as input device and places the character in its data transmission buffer. When the terminal receives a character from the computer, it acts as output device. It prints the character on paper (or displays it on the scope).

A terminal may be operated in one of two modes: half duplex or full duplex. Older types of terminals can be operated only in half duplex mode. A terminal in half duplex mode is at any one instant either input device or output device, but is never both at the same time. While the machine is printing characters on the teleprinter, typing by the user is inhibited (we say that the keyboard is *LOCKed*). The state of the terminal is changed from input device to output device and vice versa by LOCKing and UN-LOCKing the keyboard. This can be done under control of an operating system program. It is general practice to LOCK the keyboard not only during printing, but also after the user has finished typing a line. The keyboard is then UNLOCKed when the user's program has accepted the input line.

If a terminal is operated in full duplex mode, keyboard and printer are completely independent of each other. The user can type input while output is printed. It seems that the output would get mixed with the characters the user is typing. This is not the case. A terminal does not work like a typewriter. The characters which the user types are not automatically printed on (or displayed on) the user's terminal. The typed character is only transmitted to the machine as input. However, the operating system shows what the user is typing. It generates an output character identical to the input character it receives and it transmits this character to the output buffer for printing. We say the operating system *echoes* every input character. This technique is applied to both terminal modes, half duplex and full duplex. Unless explicitly stated otherwise, we assume that a terminal is operated in full duplex mode.

2.5.2 A terminal causes an interrupt each time a key is struck and each time a character has been printed (assuming interrupts are not inhibited). Typing and printing on a terminal operated in full duplex mode can be controlled by two separate control processes. Process KCP controls the input which must be transferred from the data transmission buffer of the keyboard to the input buffer. Process PCP controls the output which must be transferred from the output buffer to the data transmission buffer of the printer. Process KCP is activated when a character has been typed and the terminal causes an interrupt. A program for KCP is

Keyboard Control Process KCP: initialize {all input buffers and echo buffers empty}
begin local i ← index of keyboard causing the interrupt
  take character out of keyboard transmission buffer_i
  add this character to input buffer_i
  add this character also to echo buffer_i
  if input buffer_i full *then* wait until input buffer_i is empty *fi*
end

Process PCP is activated when a character has been printed and the teleprinter interrupts. It transfers a character either from the output buffer or from the echo buffer, giving preference to the former. PCP adds an extra new line character to the output when it switches from the echo buffer to the output buffer in order not to confuse a string of echo characters with output characters.

Printing Control Process PCP: initialize {all echomodes to *false*, all output buffers empty}

begin local j ← index of teleprinter causing the interrupt
  wait until output buffer_j or echo buffer_j is not empty
  if output buffer_j full *then*
    if echomode_j *then*
      echomode_j ← *false*; output character ← ⟨new line⟩
    else take next character from output buffer_j
    if no more characters in output buffer_j *then*
      mark output buffer_j empty *fi*
    fi
  else echomode_j ← *true*; take next character from echo buffer_j *fi*
  place character in transmission buffer of teleprinter_j
end

The output buffer remains full until PCP has transmitted all the characters one by one to the transmission buffer of the teleprinter. The user program does not start filling the buffer again until PCP has marked it empty. The user program marks the output buffer full when it wants the contents to be printed. When the input buffer is full, its contents are copied into the user's storage area.

The interface between a user program and the character transmission system consists of a procedure COPY(direction, address). The first parameter indicates whether the input buffer must be copied into the user's area, or whether data must be copied from the user's area into the output buffer. The second parameter points to the area in Ms into which (or from which) data must be copied. COPY(in,a) cannot proceed as long as the input buffer is not full. The input buffer is marked empty at the end of this procedure. Likewise, COPY(out,a) must wait until the output buffer is empty. It marks the output buffer full at the end of its program.

The CPU can execute a great number of instructions while a terminal fills an input buffer or while the content of an output buffer is being printed. Therefore, if a user program calls COPY and the buffer in question is not available, the user program is swapped out. That is, this program is removed from s_0 and another user program (which is ready to run) is loaded into s_0. The ready to run programs are placed in the ready list in the order in which their buffers become available. Maintaining the order implies a policy decision. The designer makes such a decision, because he expects a certain benefit from it (better service for the users). Practice has shown that such expectations are often not at all justified. Therefore, when the system becomes operative, it is mandatory that the expectation be checked through simulation or measurement.

Swapping a process out of slice s_0 pays in particular if a program frequently calls COPY (an I/O bound program). However, it is not sufficient to swap user programs only when COPY is called. A timer interrupt is still needed, because this is the only way to interrupt a user program that continually needs CPU time without calling COPY (a compute bound program).

Contemporary timesharing systems have the basic idea in common with this very simple model. A considerable amount of CPU time is wasted in this model during swapping (hundreds of milliseconds). If Ms is divided into more slices, one user program can execute while another pair is being swapped. This works if a user job can be loaded into an arbitrary slice of Ms. (This technique is called *relocation*). Several methods for saving considerable amounts of swaptime (and space) have been devised. One approach is to load only that part of a user program which will be relevant in the near future. Another approach is to let users share code (a compiler for instance) and have only one copy of the code in main storage by several users. These ideas are discussed in chapters 6 and 8.

Two significant aspects of current timesharing systems which have not been discussed here are the structure of a file system and the function of a control language. A file system enables a user to store and retrieve his programs and data over long periods of time (months). The user can build a private programming system to eliminate having to read in programs and data as new input at the beginning of every session. The major function of a command language is to serve as a convenient tool for requesting services of the system. File systems are discussed in chapter 9.

PROBLEMS

1. An obvious interpretation of the *buffer full* state is that all character positions of the buffer have been filled. But a more useful interpretation commonly used in timesharing systems is to define *full* as: the symbol nl (for new line) was just added to the buffer. This is well defined for input typed by a user, because the lines end with an nl and the input buffer is large enough for a line. But output may be generated without new line symbols. Therefore, COPY(out,a) should fit an appropriate number of characters in the output buffer, and if no nl is found, it should automatically append one.

Write a program for COPY(out,a) which fits the model of the timesharing system of this section. Your procedure should use the latter definition of buffer full and insert an nl automatically if necessary.

2. The operating system of a real timesharing system does not transmit the input characters unseen to the input buffer. Several characters have a special meaning and trigger a special action by the operating system. One such character is the RUBOUT. If the user strikes the RUBOUT key, the character preceding the RUBOUT must be deleted from the input buffer. (What do you propose to do if the preceding character was the one which

made the buffer full, or how do you propose to make sure that this situation cannot occur?) The RUBOUT character is deleted and not placed in the input buffer. It is also not echoed. Instead, the character which is deleted from the input buffer is once more echoed to show the user which character is deleted.

Write a modified version of the keyboard control program which handles the RUBOUT feature.

3. If a terminal is operated in half duplex mode, the user cannot strike a key while the keyboard is LOCKed. This implies that no keyboard interrupt can take place unless the keyboard is UNLOCKed. The PCP process keeps the keyboard LOCKed while it takes characters from the output buffer. However, the keyboard must not remain LOCKed after printing an echo character or else further typing is impossible.

Program the control of keyboards and teleprinters for a system in which all terminals are operated in half duplex mode.

4. The example system works in two phases: a compute phase and a swap phase. A considerable amount of CPU time is wasted while programs are swapped. Compare the following proposals to mitigate the situation.

Proposal 1. Extend main storage with another slice so as to switch to a program in one slice while the other slice is being swapped. How could the relocation problem be avoided in this system?

Proposal 2. Build a special hardware interface that accepts a command SWAP(i) which not only loads s_0, but at the same time, and one step ahead, dumps the contents of s_0 back in the slice where it came from. The drum transfer time is reduced to half of the time without this interface.

5. Suppose the main store has room for two slices as proposed in problem 4. Choose one of the swapping policies and write a program for the operating system process which takes care of the swapping.

READING LIST

The basic ideas of timesharing are described in [1, 4]. Critical sections and P and V are introduced in [2]. A good treatment on parallelism, particularly on parallelism in central processors, is found in [3]. The various types of operating systems are reviewed in [5].

1. Corbato, F.J., et al., "An Experimental Time-Sharing System," *Proceedings of the AFIPS SJCC* 21 (1962).

2. Dijkstra, E. W., "Cooperating Sequential Processes," *Programming Languages* (F. Genuys, ed.), Academic Press, 1968, 43–112.

3. Lorin, H., *Parallelism in Hardware and Software: Real and Apparent Concurrency*, Prentice-Hall, 1972.

4. McCarthy, J., "A Time-Sharing Debugging System for a Small Computer," *Proceedings of the AFIPS SJCC* 23 (1963).

5. Rosin, R. F., "Supervisory and Monitor Systems," *Computing Surveys* 1 (1969).

3. Concurrent Processes

3.1 ACCESS TO SHARED DATA

3.1.1 We concluded in section 2.3 that effective use of a computer is impossible if there exists only one version of a program to direct that computer, coded in the language of the processor on which it is to run. It is good practice to work with various representations of a program, each of which exhibits a particular aspect abstracting from details which are irrelevant to the particular aspect being represented. All of the programs in chapter 1 are such abstract models.

For each representation of an algorithm we can imagine a virtual processor able to execute the program in this form. The virtual processors each have their own language and differ in the unit of action they carry out. For instance, we can imagine a virtual processor which is able to execute the command

increment x by 1

as one action. The same statement is written as

$$x \leftarrow x+1$$

for a processor which considers this operation as two successive actions: add and assign. The representation

```
LOAD  A,x
ADDI  A,1
STORE A,x
```

is accepted by the processor of a machine code assembler.

A description of this code sequence as executed by a hardware processor with its instruction decoder, arithmetic units and registers requires a more detailed representation (as in section 2.1 where the fetch-execute cycle was discussed).

We say that the first representation is an *abstraction* of the Algol-like command. This one is an abstraction of the assembly code version, etc. An abstraction is obtained when a group of related, but separate, actions are considered as one action. In our discussions it is not necessary to go into more detail than can be expressed in assembly code, and we will consider such a representation of a program as the most detailed one.

3.1.2 A natural way of constructing a program is to start with an abstract version that reflects only its overall structure. When a more detailed version is written, we must make sure that all the characteristics of the abstract version are preserved. Unfortunately, when processes run concurrently, this is not always so. This important fact is demonstrated in the following example.

Suppose an operating system shares the use of main storage with three computations. Storage is divided into three areas: one for the system, one for the three computations, and one used as a pool of data blocks. Data blocks are equal in size and a block is either in use or free. The system keeps track of the free blocks in a stack S: when a free block is requested, the top element is handed out; when a block is released its address is placed on top of stack S.

A program can request a free block by calling the procedure "getspace." It can release a block by calling "release(ad)," where ad is the address of the block to be released. This abstract representation of the actions to acquire or release a data block is sufficiently detailed as far as the logic of the programs is concerned. Only the result of either action is relevant to the programs. Suppose the processor executing getspace or release is multiplexed between the three programs in the main store. A series of space requests and releases can be performed in arbitrary order provided that

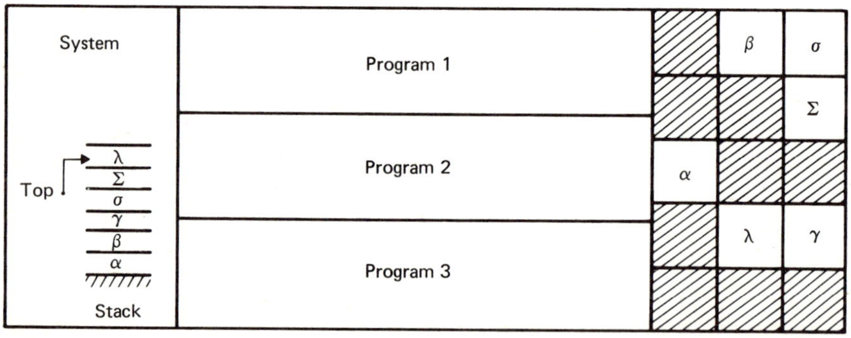

Figure 3.1a Storage shared by three computations

stack S does not become empty (see figure 3.1a). Since data blocks are identical, any permutation of S is as good as any other.

3.1.3 An important characteristic of the abstract version is lost if the procedures are coded in more detail. A more detailed (Algol-like) description is

getspace = *begin* getspace ← Stack[top]; top − 1 *end*
release(ad) = *begin* top + 1; Stack[top] ← ad *end*

If the processor which executes these actions is multiplexed between the three processes, getspace and release may be executed in interleaved time intervals. The result of such interleaving may be disastrous. Let top = h_0 at time t_0. The following sequence of events is possible

t_0: top + 1	→ top = $h_0 + 1$
t_1: getspace ← Stack[top]	→ getspace = Stack[$h_0 + 1$]
t_2: top − 1	→ top = h_0
t_3: Stack[top] ← ad	→ Stack[h_0] = ad

The result is that an undefined value is taken from a location above stack S, and the released block address is written over a valid free block address on top!

The interleaving may cause an incorrect system state. We must find a way to make sure that getspace and release are not executed in interleaved time intervals, but strictly in sequence. It does not matter in which order the procedures are executed as long as stack S is not empty. There is no problem in the abstract version, because getspace and release are considered in that version as single actions. In the more detailed representation we must find a way to treat getspace and release each as a single action although both consist in fact of more than one action. Such action sequences, which must be executed as units without interleaving, are called *critical sections* or *critical regions*.

The processor in this example was shared by several processes. However, if each process had its own processor, the problem of accessing shared data would be exactly the same. The necessity to build critical sections is a logical problem inherent to sharing data and concurrent execution of processes; it cannot be avoided by adding equipment.

When programs for concurrent processes are designed in detail, critical sections will be needed in several places in the programs. Suppose, for instance, that the three processes of the given example also share the use of some magnetic tape drives with identical specifications. These can be handled in a manner analogous to that used for the free blocks of storage space. A critical section is needed to reserve a magnetic tape drive or to release one, but no harm is done if a critical section for free blocks and one for magnetic tape drives are concurrently executed. Thus, critical sections can be partitioned in nonintersecting sets, where each set operates on a different shared data object. In this particular example, we need two classes of critical sections with two operations each: {getspace, release} and {reserve MT, release MT}. Classes are easily distinguished by associating a unique name with each of them. A critical section will be indicated in a program using the associated class name in a standard form:

when ⟨classname⟩ *do* ⟨critical section⟩ *od*

Let sp be the name of class {getspace, release}; the programs for getspace and release look like this using the new notation:

getspace = *when* sp *do* getspace ← Stack[top]; top − 1 *od*
release(ad) = *when* sp *do* top + 1; Stack[top]; ad *od*

The notation indicates that only one critical section can be active at a time. Several mechanisms to implement critical sections will be discussed.

PROBLEMS

1. The stack discipline for keeping track of the free blocks (see figure 3.1a) is an arbitrary choice because the free blocks are identical. It does not matter which one is given in response to a request. Let us therefore consider a maintenance policy using a queue. We might as well use the free data space to store the queue of free blocks because the queue is proportional to the number of free blocks. Therefore, we propose to have two fixed pointers, FIRST and LAST, in the system area, and link the free blocks by storing the address of the next free block in the first location of a free block. FIRST points to the least recently entered free block in the queue, which will be used when a request is granted. A newly released block will be appended following the one pointed at by LAST.

Program the procedures getspace and release using this queue discipline, assuming that the queue is never empty. Would it be necessary to program the procedures as critical sections?

2. At a first glance it seems as if the mistakes in stack maintenance are due to a mixup of getspace and release, but that interleaving two or more executions of releases or of two or more executions of getspace does not matter. Find timing sequences of two concurrent executions of getspace which show that such interleaving is not permitted. Do the same for two or more interleaved executions of release.

3. Suppose an accounting system which determines the cost of running a program is partly based on the CPU fraction of a program. The CPU fraction of a program is the ratio of the CPU time allocated to this program and the total CPU time allocated to all programs. The latter is not the total elapsed time because it does not include CPU idle time. This part of the accounting system is implemented by a global variable TT (=total CPU

time used) and a table of local variables LT[i], each representing the local amount of CPU time used by a particular program. If a program runs from moment t_0 until moment t_k, its runtime cost factor is computed as

$$\frac{LT[i]}{TT(t_k) - TT(t_0)}$$

Discuss at which points the time variables must be updated in a multiprogramming system. Program the update statements and the computation of the runtime cost factor. Real time can be read from a timer device t.

4. Another variation on the data block management policy is this one: data blocks are not equal in size, but are made available according to size requests passed as parameters of getspace. When a block is released, its size is passed as a parameter of procedure release. If the free blocks are arranged in a queue as discussed in problem 2, the queue must be searched when a request arrives (by means of the call getspace(s)) for a free block that is large enough. A free block has not only a pointer to the next free block, but also a variable that indicates the size of this block.

When a block is released, it may be adjacent on either (or both) sides to another free block. If so, this block should not just be appended onto the queue; instead, it should be merged with its neighbor(s) into one large free block.

Write new versions of the programs for the procedures getspace and release for this policy.

5. It was observed that the implementation of the policy discussed in problem 4 could probably be improved by using a sort of hash coding to speed up the search for a block of a particular size. The proposal is to replace the pair FIRST, LAST by a table with an entry for a fixed set of block size ranges (first entry for blocks of size 16 through 127, second entry for blocks of size 128 through 256, etc.). An entry in this table points to the first block of a queue in which the blocks are ordered either by ascending size or by ascending storage address.

Investigate the merits of these two alternatives for programmaing getspace and release to determine whether or not the use of the size-hash table yields an improvement over the solution of problem 4. Investigate whether or not it would be possible to associate a separate class of critical sections for each table entry with its associated queue.

3.2 LOCK OPERATIONS

3.2.1 In the preceding section we introduced a notation to indicate a critical section in a program, but we have not yet discussed how critical sections can be implemented and realized at runtime. It may seem as if the problem could be resolved by timing the execution of programs such that critical sections are always executed in separate time intervals. Such a solution must be rejected because it implies that programs can acquire information about their mutual behavior, or that an outside agent is able to gather such information. This is counter to the idea that a system must be viewed as a collection of functional units which know nothing of one another other than their mutual external specifications. It must be possible to modify or replace a functional unit without affecting the rest of the system as long as the external specifications of that function remain the same. Hence, we must find programming tools to form compound units inside a program that behave as critical sections independently of how many, and where, corresponding critical sections occur in other programs.

Any implementation of critical sections must be based on a smallest unit of execution which does not have to be programmed as a critical section, or else the problem recurs indefinitely. Such a smallest unit is provided in hardware by the read-write cycle to main storage. If one of the devices acquires access to a storage box, no other device is able to get read-write access to that same box. No matter how many CPUs or devices there are, a particular word in main storage can be accessed by only one of the devices at a time. Hence, assembly instructions that involve only one storage operation such as

```
LOAD A,x
```

or

```
STORE A,x
```

where x represents the address of a storage location, cannot be executed more than one at a time and need not be programmed as a critical section with a sequence of more detailed instructions inside.

The following model clarifies the requirements for programming arbitrary critical sections. Let s be a class of critical sections, only one of which may be executed at a time. Associate with class s a key which is carried along by a process that executes a critical section of class s. During that time, no other process can pick up the key and enter a critical section of class s. If no process is executing a critical section of class s, the key is available and can be grabbed by any process that is lucky enough to get at it. This implies, of course, that the key must be returned when a critical section is finished.

The programming structure of this model is

```
LOCK (key[s])
⟨statements of critical section⟩
UNLOCK (key[s])
```

where key[s] is the key attached to the class of critical sections named s.

3.2.2 Assume key[s] = 1 means the key is available and key[s] = 0 means that it is not. The statement UNLOCK (key[s]) can be implemented as

$$\text{key[s]} \leftarrow 1$$

However, implementation of LOCK (key[s]) is somewhat more difficult because it must assure that no process gets through when key[s] = 0 and that only one process can get through when key[s] = 1. An implementation such as

```
LOCK(x) = begin local v
              repeat v ← x until v = 1
              x ← 0
          end
```

is not satisfactory. If several processes call LOCK (key[s]), more than one may find the value 1 before one of them reaches the assignment x ← 0. All those processes will complete their LOCK operation and enter their critical section. One result of finding the key available must be that no one else can find it available later. This effect can be achieved only if inspection of the key sets it to zero. When the designers of the IBM/360 series recognized the need for such an instruction, the instruction set of those machines was extended with a test and set instruction. The statement

$$\text{v} \leftarrow \text{test and set(x)}$$

has the effect that the value of x is copied into v, while the value zero is assigned to x within the same read-write cycle. LOCK(x) can be correctly implemented with the aid of this instruction:

```
LOCK(x) = begin local v
              repeat v ← test and set(x) until v = 1
          end
```

A similar effect can be achieved in other machines with an instruction of the sort

EXCH A,x

where A is a local register in a processor and x a location in main storage. The instruction exchanges the contents of A and x within one read-write cycle.

PROBLEMS

1. Suppose two processes call LOCK (key[s]) to enter a critical section of a class s. Investigate possible timings of the two executions of LOCK and show that the first attempt to program LOCK is incorrect.

2. Write a program that implements LOCK by means of the instruction EXCH A,x. Show that, when two processes call LOCK, exactly one of the two will be able to pass LOCK for all possible timings of the execution of the two LOCK operations.

3. It is often said that this implementation of critical sections with LOCK and UNLOCK is not fair because if two processes frequently try to execute critical sections of a class s, one of the two may get the key every time and the other never gets a chance. This problem is known as *permanent blocking* or by the colorful name *starvation*. Show a possible timing of LOCK and UNLOCK executions by two processes such that one of them can never enter its critical section. Describe the characteristics of process behavior that would make the use of LOCK and UNLOCK an acceptable policy.

4. Suppose a system has six magnetic tape devices $MT_1, \ldots, MT_6$. Each MT_i has a key[i] which a process must possess in order to use MT_i. An MT_i can be used by only one process at a time. This rule can be enforced by critical sections. Don't let a process wait to enter a critical section for a particular MT while other MTs are idle. Show that the MT allocation can be adequately regulated using the exchange instruction or the test and set instruction.

5. The following is a proposal to deal with the empty stack of free data blocks. Before calling getspace, a process should enter a critical section for stack inspection, for which purpose a global count stacklength records the current number of free blocks. A process should not call getspace until stacklength > 0. Write the piece of program that implements this strategy. Should repeated inspection of stacklength $= 0$ take place inside or outside this critical section for stacklength inspection? At which points in the programs must stacklength be updated?

3.3 CRITICAL SECTIONS WITHOUT SPECIAL INSTRUCTIONS

3.3.1 There is a way of programming critical sections without the aid of special instructions such as exchange or test and set. This solution does not have the drawback of starvation (see problem 3 of the preceding section). It assures that a process, once it tries to enter a critical section, will definitely get a chance to do so. A solution for two processes A and B uses a priority indicator which is set to point to the other process when a process finishes a critical section. The priority indicator is not sufficient to allow a process to enter a critical section. If process A wishes to enter while the indicator points to B, but process B is not trying to execute a critical section, process

A should not be forced to wait until it pleases process B to execute a critical section and set the indicator to A. On the other hand, if both processes try to enter, the indicator can be used to give preference to the process it points at. The other one apparently was the last one which executed a critical section, because it was responsible for the current value of the priority indicator.

The state IN[A] = 1 in the program below means that process A attempts to enter a critical section, but it will do so only if it found IN[B] = 0.

```
A: IN[A] ← 1
while IN[B] = 1 do
   while priority ≠ A do IN[A] ← 0 od
   IN[A] ← 1
od
⟨statements of critical section⟩
   priority ← B; IN[A] ← 0
```

The program for B is derived from this program by interchanging A and B.

It is obvious that process A can enter its critical section only if the outer loop terminates in the state IN[A] = 1 *and* IN[B] = 0. Thus, process A can proceed without delay if B is not interested or if priority = A and process B is in its inner loop. If process B is in its inner loop, it will remain there until process A sets the priority indicator to point to B. It remains to be verified that, if B tries to enter while A does, and the indicator points to A, process B will end up in its inner loop. This will happen when B enters its outer loop while IN[A] = 1 and priority = A. So, this program implements critical sections correctly; it uses storage access as smallest instruction unit; and, if there is competition, it treats the processes fairly in that it gives access permission to the process that has had the least recent chance.

3.3.2 We now turn to the case of n processes $P_1, \ldots, P_n$ ($n \geq 2$) trying to enter critical sections of a class s. An immediate extension of the program for two processes does not work, because, with at least three processes, the priority indicator may point to one process which does not try to enter a critical section while two other processes are both waiting in the inner loop. A modified generalization makes the processes compete for the priority pointer. One process will try to get the priority indicator to point to itself, but will succeed in doing so only if none of the processes between the one pointed at by the priority indicator and itself is eager to enter a critical section of class s. This situation will ultimately arise because the priority indicator is moved to the right every time that a critical section is completed (see figure 3.3a and the program below). The program uses the fact that the expression "*all* j *in* ⟨range⟩ *sat* ⟨condition⟩" is *true* if the range is empty.

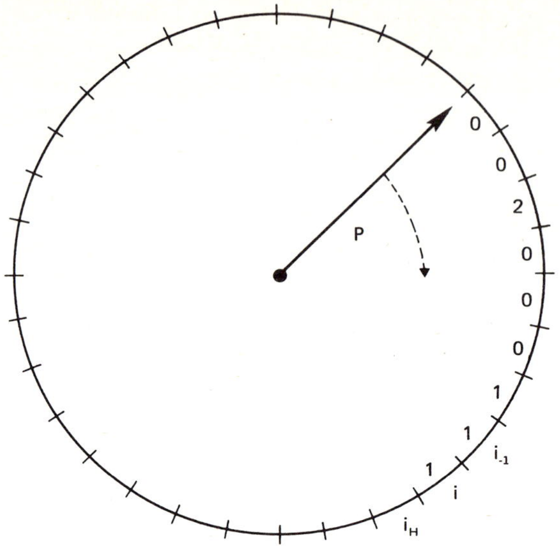

Figure 3.3a P_{i-1} and P_i try to enter the critical section

```
begin
  local x, y, j; x ← p
     $ the priority pointer p, array IN, the process index i
     $ and the number of processes n, are global objects.
  repeat
     IN[i] ← 1; y ← i−1+(if x > i then n else 0 fi)
     if all j in [x:y] sat IN[j%n] = 0 then IN[i] ← 2 fi
  until (IN[p] = 0 or p = i) and (all j in [i+1:n+i−1] sat IN[j%n] ≠ 2)
  p ← i
  ⟨statements of critical section⟩
  if some j in [i+1:n+i−1] sat IN[j] ≠ 0 then p ← j fi
  IN[i] ← 0
end
```

An interesting case to verify is the one in which process p_{i-1} starts the *if* command in the loop at the moment that process P_i successfully completes that statement. If P_{i-1} also finds the *if* clause *true*, one of the two processes will be the first to set its IN to 2 in the next statement. This action is sufficient to prevent the other from terminating its loop. Both will inevitably set their IN variable to 2. We must verify that the two processes will not indefinitely prevent each other from entering the critical section. If both find that the other process reached state 2, both will execute the loop again. In the second round, P_i finds the condition *false*, whereas P_{i-1} finds it *true*. If process P_i acts very quickly in the first round, it may be able to beat P_{i-1} and slip through, but will not be able to do this another time. The priority indicator may skip over a process once, because it was too late to be noticed, but will catch this process the next time around.

PROBLEMS

1. The representation of the critical section program for n processes may not be suitable for execution on a computer in this form, because of the use of the *some* and *all* expressions. Write a machine-executable version of this program.

2. If only two processes (A and B) are involved, the *all* and *some* expressions can be expressed as conditions in the state variables of those processes and the priority indicator. Write this simplified version of the critical section program for two processes and compare it with the one presented earlier in this section. What could go wrong if the outer *while* statement in the earlier version is replaced by a *repeat* statement of the form

```
repeat
   while priority ≠ A do IN[A] ← 0 od
   IN[A] ← 1
until IN[B] = 0
```

3. The programs of this section are an improvement over LOCK and UNLOCK discussed in the preceding section. Here, we succeeded in building in a guarantee that a process, once it indicates that it is eager to enter a critical section, will get a chance to do so. Investigate whether or not LOCK and UNLOCK could be modified to contain the same guarantee but still use the more powerful instructions test and set or exchange. If so, write the programs for LOCK and UNLOCK; if not, explain why not.

4. A machine has the nice instruction

SOS A,x

where A is a fast register in the processor and x a storage operand. The instruction subtracts one from the storage operand within one read-write cycle to storage and also records the result in register A. Investigate whether or not this instruction can be used to program critical sections, preferably with the properties discussed in this section. Use a shared variable count(s) (initialized to zero) for a class s of critical sections. The problem is easier to solve if the machine also has the instruction

AOS A,x

which adds one to storage cell x within one read-write cycle and records the result in the fast register A.

5. Consider two alternatives for the repeat statement in the critical section program structure for n processes.

a. *local* x,y,j; x ← p; y i − 1 + (*if* p > x *then* n *else* 0 *fi*)
repeat
repeat IN[i] ← 1 *until all* j *in* [x:y] *sat* IN[j%n] = 0
repeat IN[i] ← 2 *until all* j *in* [i+1:n+i−1] *sat* IN[j%n] ≠ 2
until IN[p] = 0 *or* p = i

b. ⟨the same initialization as in (a)⟩
repeat IN[i] ← 1 *until all* j *in* [x:y] *sat* IN[j%n] = 0
repeat IN[i] ← 2 *until all* j *in* [i+1:n+1−1] *sat* IN[j%n] ≠ 2) *and*
(IN[p] = 0 *or* p = i).

If the alternative programming is correct, describe a verification of its correctness. If it is not correct, indicate what can go wrong and when the problem can occur.

3.4 P AND V OPERATIONS

3.4.1 In the two methods discussed in the preceding sections, the responsibility for testing whether or not a critical section can be safely entered resides with the processes. This is wrong. The decision as to which process is allowed to enter a critical section when there is competition should be taken by the operating system monitoring the concurrent processes. Taking this point of view, a critical section should be built into a process by marking it as we did in section 2.1. Execution of the critical section construct ought to be implemented in the shared environment in which concurrency is monitored. Under such an organization, all that matters to a process is the specification of how to build a critical section, but not how to enter it.

The shared environment regards the construct

when s *do* ⟨statement list⟩ *od*

(where s is the name of a class of critical sections) as a pair of function calls for which the names P and V traditionally are used. The operation P(s) acts as the open bracket of a critical section and its function is to acquire permission to enter. The operation V(s) is the matching close bracket which records the termination of a critical section.

The P,V operations were invented by E. W. Dijkstra. He called the single argument of a P or V operation a *semaphore,* in analogy to the railroad traffic light which indicates whether a train can enter the next railroad section. Passing the semaphore implies that it changes so that another train cannot also pass.

The name which we associated with a class of critical sections is the semaphore for that class. The semaphore has a value which indicates whether or not a critical section in the class can be entered. The operation P(sem) cannot be completed if one of the critical sections in class sem is being executed. If some processes were not able to pass P(sem) and another process executes V(sem), one of the suspended processes will be enabled to enter a critical section of class sem, but others must still wait.

Placing the implementation of the critical section construct in the shared environment in which it naturally belongs also has an advantage from a practical point of view. If a process has to do the testing, it must continually inspect the semaphore until it finds that it can enter safely. If the processor is multiplexed among several processes, waiting is a waste of processor time. If, on the other hand, the shared environment executes the permission request P(sem), it can avoid such a waste: it can mark the process that asked access permission as waiting (if access permission cannot be granted) and allocate the processor to another process. Such an implementation for P(sem) implies, of course, that, when a critical section is terminated by V(sem), one of the waiting processes (if any) must be reactivated. The operation P(sem) may block a process with the result that it goes to sleep. Execution of V(sem) has the effect of waking up a process (if there were any asleep). The function of P(sem) and V(sem) is described by

P(sem) = *if* sem = 1 *then* sem ← 0
    else block calling process; switch to another process *fi*
V(sem) = *if* there is a process waiting on sem *then*
    i ← select waiting process; wake up (process[i])
    else sem ← 1 *fi*

P and V must be implemented as critical sections, because concurrent execution of P and V causes problems. It does not suffice to use a test and set or exchange instruction, because blocking must not be separated from the semaphore test. If these two are separated, a V operation can come in between, not find a waiting process, and set sem to 1. The result is that a process goes to sleep while sem = 1. This should never happen.

3.4.2 P and V can be programmed as critical sections using LOCK and UNLOCK. Because their action is short, the probability of an access conflict is much smaller than for the class of critical section protected by it. Implementation details are discussed in chapter 4. It does not make sense to switch to another process which is blocked. It is useful to distinguish between *blocked* (or *waiting* or *asleep*) and *ready to run* processes. Control will be switched only to a process that is ready to run, but such switching can be done only if there is always a process ready to run. Many a system assures that the control switch can always succeed by means of a programming technique which is also useful for dynamic adjustment of system performance. The trick is to associate with each processor a null process which is always ready to run. This process is activated only if none of the other processes which can run on the processor is ready to run. This null process is usually disregarded when processor allocation policies are discussed.

The transition ready to run → blocked is the result of the action block current process. The action wake up (process[i]) within the V operation causes the transition blocked → ready to run. This transition does not necessarily imply that the selected process will get a physical processor and run! It merely changes the state of the selected process. These and related questions are discussed in chapter 4. The only place where a ready to run process is promoted to running is in the P operation when the CPU is allocated to another process.

The P operation and LOCK have in common that finding the semaphore available prevents subsequent callers from entering, but they differ vastly in the way waiting processes are treated. LOCK is similar to calling from a telephone on a shared line; if the other telephone on the line is busy, the caller has to try again and again until the other party hangs up. P and V, however, treat the waiting processes as people queueing for a window in a bank. No activity is required until the process blocked in a P can proceed and is made ready to run in a V operation. The use of P and V makes the programming of critical sections trivial.

Arbitrarily large critical sections can be built by placing small standard critical sections at the beginning and the end. Each standard critical section can be implemented with even more primitive means which can be applied to small well-defined pieces of code. These rely eventually on the indivisible storage access cycle.

PROBLEMS

1. It was observed and argued that the P operation must be implemented as a critical section. Show that the V operation also must be a critical section and find a timing which demonstrates what can go wrong if it is not implemented as a critical section.

2. Suppose a process has in its process control block (PCB) a link field which contains a pointer to the next process in the queue in which it resides (the link field of the last element is *nil*). A process is at any one moment in exactly one queue: either in the ready to run queue or in one of the semaphore queues. Suppose all the queues are handled in FIFO order. Program P and V in more detail and estimate the time needed on a 1-microsecond cycle time machine to execute a P operation when it blocks its caller and to execute a V operation when it wakes up a waiting process.

3. Suppose two processors are multiplexed between k processes ($k \geq 2$). P and V operations are implemented as critical sections with a key[PV].

Verify that the operations LOCK and UNLOCK are sufficient to program P and V on these processors. Another approach would be to attach a key and a LOCK, UNLOCK pair to each semaphore. The key is exclusively used to implement P and V as critical sections. The advantage is that P and V operating on different semaphores can be concurrently executed. Verify the validity of the second approach and compare the two methods. (Interrupts on the processor should be disregarded.)

4. Suppose a system has six identical magnetic tape devices $MT_1, \ldots,$ MT_6. When a process is using a tape drive, no other process should have access to it. However, it is unwise to program a separate critical section for each MT_i, because a process may be waiting for a particular MT_i to become free, while others were idle. A slight modification of the semaphore concept is desirable: the range of the semaphore value is defined as [0:m], where m is the maximum number of processes allowed to execute a critical section of class s simultaneously. In this particular example, 6 would be the appropriate upper limit for m, so that up to six processes at a time are allowed to use the MTs.

```
P(MT)
   i ← free MT
   ⟨use MT[i]⟩
   release MT[i]
V(MT)
```

Program the selection of a free tape drive and of releasing one. Is it necessary to program these operations as critical sections?

5. The structure *when* s *do* ⟨statement list⟩ *od* assures that critical sections can be programmed in a nested form or in sequence. That is not true for the implementation with P and V. Errors which can occur if P, V operations are used are demonstrated by a variation on the use of the six MTs. Suppose a separate semaphore s[i] was associated with each MT[i] and a separate sem with searching for a free MT and releasing one. To avoid the situation mentioned in problem 4 (a process waiting for a particular MT while others are idle), a process searches first for a free MT and uses the one for which it finds the lowest demand. Investigate whether the following programs work correctly or contain the problem of waiting for the wrong MT.

a. P(sem); i ← MIN(MT); MT[i] ← MT[i] + 1; P(s[i]); V(sem); ⟨use MT_i⟩
   P(sem); MT[i] ← MT[i] − 1; V(s[i]); V(sem)
b. P(sem); i ← MIN(MT); MT[i] ← MT[i] + 1; V(sem); P(s[i]);
      ⟨use MT_i⟩; V(s[i])
   P(sem); MT[i] ← MT[i] − 1; V(sem)

The demand is recorded in a vector MT[1 . . . 6], where the value of MT[i] indicates the number of users of MT[3].

3.5 DEADLOCKS

3.5.1 If each process needs several resources (for example, I/O devices) the system must be careful not to reach a deadlock state. This happens if all the processes ask for more resources while all the resources are in use and no process is willing to give up some of its resources. We demonstrate this problem in this section with an example of magnetic tape device allocation.

Suppose a system has six magnetic tape devices $MT_1, \ldots, MT_6$ and suppose there are three groups of processes: $P_1, \ldots, P_k$, $Q_1, \ldots, Q_m$ and $R_1, \ldots, R_n$. A process P_i may use several MTs, but will use only one at a time. A process Q_i uses two MTs (for copying, for instance) and a process R_i uses three MTs (for correction, for instance). To finish its work, a process Q (or R) must acquire two (three) MTs at some time.

Since all MTs are identical, it is better to attach a semaphore to the pool of six MTs initialized to the value 6 (see problem 4 of section 3.4). The operation P(sem) decreases sem by one if sem is positive but otherwise blocks the calling process. The operation V(sem) wakes up a process if one was waiting, or increments sem by one.

Matching pairs P(sem), V(sem) are not nested in a P-type process, but are nested up to one level (two levels) in a Q-type (R-type) process. The relevant structure of a Q-type process is basically:

```
type Q: P(sem); seize free MT
        ____________________
        ____________________
          P(sem); seize another free MT
          ____________________
          ____________________
          release MT; V(sem)
        ____________________
        ____________________
        release MT; V(sem)
```

The relevant structure of P-type or R-type processes is now obvious.

Certain combinations of P-, Q- and R-type processes may want more than six MTs. Strange things can happen if these processes are allowed to compete freely for the use of the MTs. Suppose three R processes start looking for MTs almost simultaneously. Each one finds a pair of MTs as shown in figure 3.5a, but none will ever find a third one! Such a situation is known as a *deadlock*. Other examples of deadlocks are: two R-type processes holding two MTs each and two Q-type processes holding one MT each; or, five R-type processes holding one MT each and a P-type process using the remaining MT. Releasing that MT will not satisfy any of the R processes.

3.5.2 Interestingly enough, a slightly different allocation state does not cause any problem. For example, if one of the three R processes in figure 3.5a is replaced by a Q process, the problem vanishes entirely. The Q process finds two MTs and is able to run. When it finishes, it releases two MTs, enough to satisfy the two R processes. But don't let two Q-type processes both seize one of the released MTs.

Observe that a deadlock is not caused by programming errors. Each of the programs is correct. The concurrency of the processes causes the trouble.

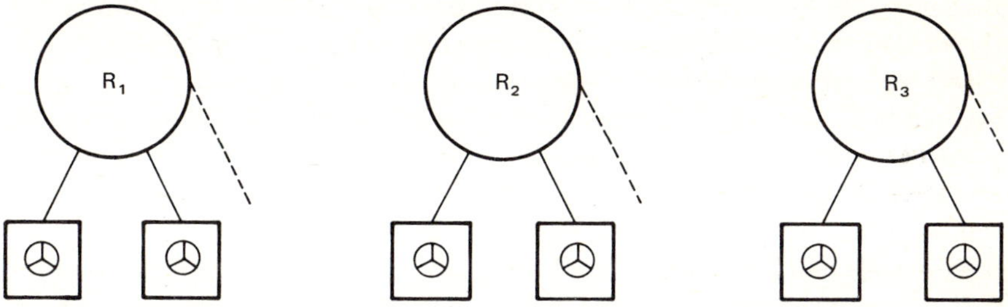

Figure 3.5a Three R-type processes competing for six magnetic tape devices

Deadlocks may be caused by a combination of circumstances. Suppose the processes Q, R and R' have the following programs:

Q: —P(A);—P(B);—V(B);—V(A)
R: —P(B);—P(A);—V(A);—V(B)
R': —P(B);—P(A);—V(B);—V(A)

If the initial value of both A and B is one, concurrent execution of Q and R, or Q and R', may cause a deadlock, because each process can pass a P operation and then be forced to wait for the other (which will never be released).

Generally speaking, a deadlock occurs when some processes are waiting for each other's resources, but, since all are waiting, none is able to release a resource. We must look for methods of preventing deadlocks or rules for timing processes that will avoid deadlock situations. A rigorous rule to prevent deadlocks is: the set of processes allowed to run concurrently is restricted to such a collection that their total demand for resources does not exceed the total number initially available. This rule is very strict. It implies that a process might as well reserve the resources it needs right away and keep them until it does not need them anymore. This means that the resources which a process may need at some time are all tied up during its entire run. This is bad, because it is unlikely that a process continually needs all its resources.

The strict rule can easily lead to a degradation of device utilization, because resources are left idle. In the six MTs example, two R processes can start with two MTs each while a Q process has the two remaining MTs. These two can be allocated to the R processes as soon as Q is finished. The total demand of the processes is for eight MTs, but not more than six are in use at any one instant.

In certain cases it is necessary to apply the strict resource sharing rule. For instance, if real-time processes are involved, we can not afford a delay. A resource must be available when requested. In some cases we can apply the strict rule, because not much is lost if a resource is permanently allocated. This is particularly so if the resource is cheap or if plenty of resources are available. An example is a small amount of storage space; instead of releasing and requesting some minimal amount of storage space, a process might as well own this space during its lifetime. Deadlocks cannot occur in the allocation of preemptive resources: processes compete for the use of these resources, but a process is willing to release a resource instantaneously at any time that this may become necessary. (A CPU is an example of a preemptive resource.)

An alternative to the strict rule is to devise a strategy for allocating resources in such a way that deadlock situations are avoided. An algorithm which decides whether or not a given situation is deadlock-free must find in which order resources could be allocated to ensure that each process can acquire the combination of resources it needs at some time. It will find, for instance, that the situation: "four R-type and one Q-type process are holding one MT each" is deadlock-free, because the remaining MT can be allocated to the Q-type process; when this one finishes, the two released resources can be given to any one of the four R-type processes. When that one finishes, another can get the resources it wants, and so on. If in the given situation one of the four R-type processes asks for the remaining MTs, the algorithm will decide that this may cause a deadlock, because the transformed state will be: "three R-type and one Q-type process holding one MT each and one R-type process holding the remaining two MTs." If the algorithm decides that a new situation is not deadlock-free, it is better not to grant the request and to play it safe by staying within deadlock-free situations. The result of applying such a deadlock algorithm is that processes cannot grab any free resource and a resource may not be allocated when requested, even if one is free.

Such a deadlock avoidance algorithm is feasible if the combination of resources a process may need at some time is known in advance. Each process must supply this information in advance, because, without it, any situation (with non-preemptive resources) may develop into a deadlock.

PROBLEMS

1. Consider the three predicates below which relate to the example system of the three types of processes sharing six MTs.
   a. A P-type process is holding an MT, or at least one MT is free.
   b. A Q-type process is holding two MTs, or a Q-type process is holding one MT and condition (a).
   c. An R-type process is holding three MTs, or an R-type process is holding two MTs and condition (a), or an R-type process is holding one MT and condition (b).

   Formulate a necessary and sufficient condition in terms of predicates (a), (b), and (c) that describes when a situation is deadlock-free. Program a deadlock avoidance algorithm based on this condition of process is a small constant (for example, 5).

2. In the example of sharing data space in the form of blocks of storage (see section 3.1 and figure 3.1a) the problem of empty stack was not discussed. A simpleminded solution associates a semaphore DS with the data space and initializes it at the number of data blocks initially available. Processes use a data block within a critical section:

   P(DS); getspace; . . . ; release(ad); V(DS)

   This strategy is correct with respect to counting the number of available blocks and having processes wait when the stack is empty. But the possible nesting of these P, V pairs causes the same deadlock problem as the six MTs system. Therefore, when a process starts, it must announce the nesting depth (that is the maximum number of data blocks it will need at one time), and we assume it is programmed to do so. A record of this information is kept in a claim vector, cv, while the amount of data blocks a process T is using at a particular moment is recorded in an allocation vector, av. Write a program that decides whether or not a given situation is deadlock-free.

3. The group of processes competing for the use of data space gradually changes: processes terminate and new processes are created. When a process terminates, its entries in the claim vector and allocation vector are reset to zero. A process starts when it announces its claim. At that time, an index is associated with it and its claim is booked in the proper entry of the claim vector, cv. Show that a deadlock-free situation remains deadlock-free when a new process is added. If this is true, it seems that it does not matter how many processes are contending for resources. Investigate what difference it makes by comparing the case of 10 processes competing for the use of the six MTs with the case of 100 competing processes.

4. It is likely that an operating system must cope with deadlock problems

for more than one kind of a resource, for example, for the use of MTs and at the same time for data space. Show that the problems cannot be solved separately by using two independent deadlock avoidance algorithms. This fact contributes to the phenomenon of permanent blocking, encountered in section 3.2 where the LOCK operations were discussed. Suppose three types of processes P, Q, and R use resources A and B: a P-type process only needs resource A, a Q-type process only needs resource B, an R-type process needs resources of both kinds. Applying one monolithic deadlock avoidance algorithm can have the effect that a request of an R-type process is never granted, while P-type and Q-type processes continually use the resources. Devise a policy that must be applied in addition to a deadlock avoidance algorithm to avoid permanent blocking. Could permanent blocking also occur if there were only one kind of resource to worry about (as in the six MTs example)?

5. A vastly different approach to the problem of deadlock and permanent blocking is presented below. Investigate whether or not it works and try to extend it to handle more than one kind of resource. The method is explained in terms of the six MTs example. The six MTs are not considered identical; instead, a hierarchy is superimposed. Two MTs belong to the lowest class, c_1, two others form class c_2, and the highest class, c_3, is formed by the remaining two MTs. A process gets assigned a certain rank $r \in \{1,2,3\}$. When rank r is assigned to it, it may request an MT of class c_r or higher. A P-type process (as defined earlier, not as in problem 4) is always of rank 1; a Q-type process starts with rank 2 and gets promoted to rank 1 as soon as it has one MT; an R-type process starts at rank 3 and gets promoted twice: to rank 2 when it acquires one MT and to rank 1 when it gets a second MT. So, a P process is allowed to request any MT, but a Q-type process can initially not request an MT of class c_1 and an R-type can initially request only an MT of class c_3. Investigate if a degradation of the utilization of MTs is to be expected, because of the possibility that the two MTs of class c_3 could be in use by P-type or Q-type processes while an R-type process requests its first MT, while several MTs of class c_2 or c_1 are idle. Is it possible to define the classes dynamically instead of the fixed assignment suggested above?

READING LIST

Several systems that made history are described in [1, 2, 3, 4]. These papers discuss not only processes synchronization but also scheduling and storage management. Thus, much of the material in these papers also relates to chapters 6 through 8. Synchronization solely based on exclusive access to a storage cell is presented in [5]. The process concept is discussed in [6].

1. Betourne, C., et al., "Process Management and Resource Sharing in the Multiaccess System ESOPE," *Comm. ACM* 13, 12 (December 1970).

2. Bobrow, D. G., et al., "TENEX, a Paged Time Sharing System for the PDP-10," *Comm. ACM* 15, 3 (March 1972).

3. Corbato, F. J., and V. A. Vyssotsky, "Introduction and Overview of the Multics System," in *Programming Systems and Languages* (S. Rosen, ed.), McGraw-Hill, 1967.

4. Dijkstra, E. W., "The Structure of the 'THE' Multiprogramming System," *Comm. ACM* 11, 5 (May 1968).

5. Dijkstra, E. W., "Solution to a Problem in Concurrent Programming Control," *Comm. ACM* 8, 9 (September 1965).

6. Horning, J. J., and B. Randell, "Process Structuring," *Computing Surveys* 5, 1 (March 1973).

4. Cooperating Processes

4.1 SYNCHRONIZATION

4.1.1 In the preceding chapter we studied the restrictions imposed on concurrent operations applied to shared objects. Not more than one operation modifying a shared data object must be performed at a time. Operations on shared data objects are therefore programmed as critical sections. The order in which two critical sections are executed is immaterial; all that matters is that the two program sections are not executed in overlapping time intervals.

In this chapter we discuss the programming of another timing rule known as *synchronization*. This timing is necessary when a process P_1 must wait until another process P_2 has caused a certain event. For instance, the card reader control process in the batch system model of section 2.2 must not send another command until the card reader has finished reading the current card. The event caused by the CR is the state transition of the card reader from BUSY → READY. Another example is the user program calling COPY(dir,a) in the timesharing system of section 2.5. The program must wait until the input buffer is full if it wants new input and it must wait until the output buffer is empty if it wants to generate more output. The events are in this case caused by the character transmission processes KCP and PCP.

The processes P_1 and P_2 are *cooperating processes*. This term describes the relationship between two processes if one of them waits at a certain point in its program until the other has caused a certain event. Process P_1 depends on the cooperation of process P_2.

It is necessary to put a potential delay in the program of process P_1 at the point where it must not continue unless a particular event E has happened.

We attach to a particular event an event name and we indicate a potential delay in a program by

wait(⟨event name⟩)

The occurrence of an event is programmed by the statement

signal(⟨event name⟩)

The batch system of section 2.2 contains several examples of cooperating processes. The control processes for card reader and line printer request the drum control process to transfer data. The control processes must wait as long as its buffer is still involved in a drum transfer. Synchronization is also needed for an I/O device and its control process. The latter sends data transfer commands to the device it controls, but must wait to send the next command until the device has changed its state from BUSY to READY. Using the wait and signal statements, the programs of the control processes are:

```
CR control:
  wait(CR READY)
  repeat
    for cc in [0:11] do
      send read command to CR
      signal(CR BUSY)
      wait(CR READY)
    od
    set(flag to i)
    signal(Drum Request)
    let i point to the other buffer
    wait(buf[i] available)
  until CR halt

LP control: ⟨can be derived from CR control by making the obvious
  substitutions⟩
Drum control:
  repeat wait(Drum control request)
         flag ← next request
         prepare drum command(flag)
         signal(drum BUSY)
         wait(drum READY)
         signal(buf[flag] available)
  until  machine halt
```

4.1.2 This program for CR control differs from the one given in section 2.2 in two respects: the statement "wait(CR READY)" is added, and the program is written as a *repeat* statement to reflect its repeated execution. The two representations are in fact the same, because the repetition is realized in section 2.1 by activating the program each time the card reader interrupts and waiting until CR ready is implemented by ending the program, which has the effect that CR control is suspended until the next card reader interrupt. This program shows more clearly the cyclic character of CR control. A cyclic rearrangement of the statements in the repeat statement changes nothing except the specification of how the programs must be initialized. Except for the cyclic transformation, the representation of drum control given here is merely a generalization of the one in section 2.2.

The programming of wait and signal statements does not bring about such a natural nested structure as critical sections do. Normally one process waits for an event occurring in the program of another process. On the other hand, critical sections can be constructed using wait and signal statements where the associated event name is the semaphore of the critical section class. The critical section is opened with the statement wait(s) and it is closed with the statement signal(s).

It is often useful to use an integer as event name and not just a Boolean indicating whether the event has happened or not. A useful demonstration of this point is the storage management example of section 3.1. The functions getspace and release were designed assuming that the stack would never get empty. If this restriction is removed, we consider filling the stack as an event that is represented by the event name "stacklength". This event name can be seen as a special integer which is initialized to the number of data blocks in storage. The only operations defined for event integers are wait and signal. The effect of signal(stacklength) must be to postpone the occurrence of an empty stack by one more step, while execution of wait-(stacklength) brings this occurrence one step closer. This is naturally achieved by adding or subtracting one from stacklength. On the other hand, stacklength should never become negative. Thus, when the stack is empty, wait(stacklength) must cause a delay of its caller, whereas signal(stack-length) should reactivate one of the delayed processes if one is waiting. This, by the way, makes the wait and signal operations logically equivalent to P and V (see section 3.4). Therefore, wait and signal can be implemented as P and V operations. Programs for getspace and release which take the possibility of an empty stack into account are:

```
function getspace =
  begin wait(stacklength)
    when stackfree do getspace ← stack[top]; top−1 od
  end
function release(ad) =
  begin
    when stackfree do top+1; stack[top] ← ad od
    signal(stacklength)
  end
```

Implementing wait as a P-operation has the advantage that a waste of CPU time can be avoided by allocating the CPU to another process.

PROBLEMS

1. A group of processes $P_1, \ldots, P_n$ ($n \geq 4$) shares three line printers LP_1, LP_2, and LP_3. In order not to mix output lines coming from different processes, a process P_i must reserve a line printer before using it. A variable current is attached to each printer. Its value is either the index of the process currently using this line printer, or zero. Write the program for requesting and releasing a line printer using critical sections, wait and signal operations, and event names where necessary.

2. The line printer control process, LPC, has two output buffers which have a capacity of one printer line each. Once a process P_i succeeds in reserving an LP (see problem 1), it starts interacting with LPC to get its output printed. When P_i finds one of the two output buffers empty, it fills that one in a series of machine word transfers and, when the buffer is full, it notifies LPC that there is another line ready to be printed. LPC notifies P_i when it finished printing a line that the output buffer is available to P_i again. Write cooperating programs for P_i and LPC using event names where necessary.

3. Collisions at an intersection of two one-way streets can be avoided if cars are only allowed to pass one by one. This is represented in a program by a critical section

when intersection free *do* cross *od*

If it frequently happens that cars from both directions almost simultaneously arrive at the intersection, it is fair to place STOP signs in both streets and require that cars pass from alternating directions. On the other hand, if a car approaches the intersection and there is no car visible in the cross street, it should be able to pass independently of recent history. Assume that it is not possible for two cars to arrive at the intersection at exactly the same moment. Represent in abstract program form the rules a car driver should observe. The programs must assure that, when a car crosses while cars are waiting in both streets, a car from the other street will move next. (The ordering of cars within one street can be left out of the problem; the only thing that matters in that respect is the fact that just one car per street can inspect the intersection at a time.)

4. Suppose, similarly to problem 3, Wall Street, a one-way street running west-east, intersects with Broadway, a two-way street running north-south. The traffic rules for passing the intersection are the same as in problem 3 except for one additional rule: if a car travels along Broadway and spots a

car traveling in the other direction crossing the intersection, then it is allowed to cross irrespective of the cars in Wall Street. This arrangement has the theoretical danger that traffic along Broadway can bring traffic on Wall Street to a complete stop, but this is indeed realistic in traffic situations. Write a program which represents the car drivers on Broadway. Would it be hard to extend your program to four lane traffic on Broadway and two lane traffic on Wall Street?

5. Write programs for the cooperating processes of timesharing system of section 2.5. Attach to the interrupt vector the event name "TTY interrupt" with initial value zero. It counts the number of non-zero elements in the interrupt vector. It is assumed that a terminal indicates its request for attention in the interrupt vector as before, but it also performs signal(TTY interrupt). Write the programs for KCP, PCP and for the procedure COPY.

4.2 PRIVATE SEMAPHORES

4.2.1 The possibility of a deadlock state was demonstrated in section 3.5 by the example of an allocation policy for six magnetic tape devices. A deadlock is possible if the MTs are used in a critical section

P(sem); release MT; V(sem)

where sem is a semaphore initialized to 6. Executing P(sem) is in fact a request for an MT, so it would be necessary to implement one of the various strategies to prevent or avoid deadlocks in the P-operation. Since resources of various kinds ask for different management policies, it is very unlikely that a single strategy embedded within a P operation will suffice for all applications. An additional problem is that the V operation must select a process in the waiting list. If critical sections can take a very long time, there may be many processes waiting in a P operation. In this case the V operation must carefully analyze which process should be awakened. In other cases, if the critical section is very short, the probability that a process has to wait in a P operation, is very small. In that case the V operation can apply a simple selection policy.

It is impossible to find a scheduling policy which can be put in the V operation and satisfy all applications of P and V. Therefore, we investigate how selection of waiting processes can be explicitly programmed where needed instead of being hidden in the V operation. This section shows how that can be done by using private semaphores.

Let a group of processes $P_1, \ldots, P_n$ share the resources $R_1, \ldots, R_m$, where $n > 1$ and $m > 0$. Each process has a request flag RF[i], an allocation indicator Al[i], and a private semaphore psem[i]. Private means that the semaphore will be exclusively used to signal process P_i. This means that other processes will use this semaphore as an argument in a V operation, but no other process than P_i will ever perform a P operation on this semaphore. Private semaphores eliminate the selection problem in the V operation, because P_i is the only process that can wait on private semaphore psem[i].

The processes use the procedures *request* and *release* for acquiring and returning resources. The procedures take the place of a P operation at the beginning of using a resource and a V operation at the end. Request is followed by a potential delay which goes into effect if no resource can be allocated. This delay is programmed as a wait operation on the private semaphore. The resources are inspected in a critical section using semaphore inspsem.

The first version of the programs is

```
initialize {inspsem = 1,avail = m,RF = Al = 0, all resources R free and
  all psem[i] = 0}
procedure considerallocationto(x) =
  if allocationto(x) is deadlock free then
    Al[x] ← select(free resource); avail ← avail−1
    R[AL[x]] ← in use
    RF[x] ← 0; signal(psem[x])
  fi
request[i]:
  when inspsem do RF[i] ← 1
    if avail > 0 then considerallocationto(i) fi od
  wait(psem[i])
  ⟨use allocated resource⟩
release[i]: R[AL[i]] ← free; Al[i] ← 0
            when inspsem do avail ← avail+1
              if RF = 0 then local j = selectfrom(RF)
                 considerallocationto(j) fi
            od
```

In the initialization of the programs above, all the private semaphores are initialized to zero. These semaphores cannot be passed right away. The initialization to +1 of the critical section semaphore for the inspection of the allocation state means that this semaphore can be passed without delay the first time. This initialization is typical for a critical section semaphore. If the value of the semaphore is restricted to the range [0:1], the semaphore is called a boolean semaphore. The stack example of the preceding section shows that it is sometimes convenient to let a semaphore start at a value larger than 1. Such semaphores are called counting semaphores.

The programs given here work much better than if the use of the resources were programmed as one critical section. First, the selection is not hidden in the V operation. Second, the programs can take care of deadlocks which the P and V cannot take care of (that would be too much overhead).

Third, and most importantly, the two critical sections in the programs are small and short. There is no potential delay in this code. The chance that a process has to wait is very small, but the chance that two processes are waiting is negligible. Thus, no elaborate scheduling is needed in the V operation.

There must be a potential delay somewhere in the programs, because if there are no resources free, a process must wait until a resource is returned. The delay is not in the critical sections, but outside. The delay is programmed as a wait operation on the private semaphore psem[i]. The procedure considerallocationto is able to find which processes are waiting by an inspection of array RF. The way in which the next process is selected can be programmed as part of procedure considerallocationto. Moreover, if the wait operation is implemented as a P operation, we have the advantage that process P_i is put to sleep if a delay is necessary, so that its processor can be allocated to another process.

4.2.2 Another way of managing the resources $R_1, \ldots, R_m$ is to program a monitor process which supervises the allocation of resources. Private event names are also very useful in this case.

The monitor program is very simple if there is no potential deadlock. In that case, the processes $P_1, \ldots, P_n$ signal a request to monitor AR through the event name *monitor*. A process P_i sends a request by setting request flag RF[i] to one. When AR grants the request, it will set the flag to zero, transmit the index of the allocated resource in AI[i] and signal P_i to go ahead. When P_i finishes, it resets AI[i] so as to release the resource and it signals the return to AR.

```
version 2
initialize {RF, AI = 0; monitor = 0; avail = m and all resources R free}
Pi: ———
     RF[i] ← 1; signal(monitor); wait(psem[i])
     ⟨use resource indicated in AI[i]⟩
     R[AI[i]] ← free; AI[i] ← 0; signal(avail)
     ———
AR: repeat local k
        wait(monitor); k ← selectfrom RF; RF[k] ← 0
        wait(avail); AI[k] ← index of free R; R[AI[k]] ← inuse
        signal(psem[k])
    until machine halt
```

However, if the monitor must watch out for deadlocks, it may not be possible to allocate a resource although some resources are free. The monitor must now also be activated when a resource is returned, because the allocation state may change such that a resource can be allocated, which was not possible without the returned resource. Monitor AR must now be activated at every potential state change of the resource pool. Thus, instead of the command signal(free), a process P_i must notify the monitor of a release by signal(monitor). It now becomes necessary to specify the reason for calling upon monitor AR. For this purpose process P indicates a return in the flag RF[i] by the value −1.

```
version 3
initialize {RF, AI = 0; monitor = 0; avail = m; and all R free}
P_i: ———
     RF[i] ← 1; signal(monitor); wait(psem[i])
     ⟨use resource indicated in AI[i]⟩
     RF[i] ← −1; signal(monitor); wait(psem[i])
     ———
AR: repeat own avail; local k*
        wait(monitor)
          if some k in [1:m] sat : RF[k] = −1 then
          R[AI[k]] ← free; AI[k] ← 0; avail ← avail+1; RF[k] ← 0;
            signal(psem[k])
          else
            k ← selectkforwhich(RF[k] = 1)
            if avail > 0 and allocationto(k) is deadlock free then
              AI[k] ← index of free R; R[AI[k]] ← in use; avail ← avail−1
              RF[k] ← 0; signal(psem[k])
          fi fi
     until machine halt
```

The modification in P_i is not substantial. However, when it returns a resource P_i must now wait for an acknowledgment of AR that it noticed the return. Abstracting from the meaning of the values of RF[i], the statements wait(psem[i]) can be viewed as "wait until RF[i] has been cleared."

A centralized management as presented here is a valid alternative to the distributed control presented earlier, because considerallocationto(x) can be executed by only one process at a time anyway.

PROBLEMS

1. Suppose each of the processes $P_1, \ldots, P_n$, sharing three line printers, has a relative priority which is recorded in the i-th element of array PRTY[1 . . . n]. The value of the priority indicator is immaterial if there is

*The declarator *own* means that a variable so declared exists outside the environment in which declared, but is only accessible within that environment. It gives the environment its private piece of global storage space.

an LP free when one is requested. But if several processes are waiting for an LP when one is released, this one is allocated to the process with highest priority. Program this LP allocation strategy.

2. Processes $P_1, \ldots, P_n$ may request data blocks of four different sizes: s, 2s, 3s and 4s. If a block of size $<$ 4s is not available when requested, a block one size larger is split, if available, in order to satisfy the request and the remainder is added to the free blocks of its size. Two policies are proposed: proposed:

   a. One central monitor manages the free blocks; all request and returns are addressed to this central supervisor.
   b. Four monitors each manage blocks of a particular size; requests and returns are sent to the appropriate manager.

Program both policies and compare them with respect to complexity of program, length and efficiency. The question of merging adjacent blocks can be left out of the discussion. It is assumed that from time to time a cleaning process sweeps through all the free blocks and coalesces adjacent blocks.

3. Traffic at the intersection of two two-way streets is regulated by a policeman who devised the following strategy for himself. He watches each of the four directions in succession and he uses as criterion to switch to the next direction: "20 cars have passed coming from the direction I am watching or there are no longer cars coming from that direction." This implies that, when he watches South, for instance, at most 20 cars from that direction are allowed to pass, no East or West bound cars can pass, but an indeterminate number of cars coming from North can pass while he watches South. Program the behavior of the policeman and the car drivers.

4. In section 3.5 we discussed the example of three classes of processes sharing six MTs. Reconstruct a necessary and sufficient condition to avoid deadlocks. Program the three process models and program a monitor that manages the MTs applying a deadlock avoidance algorithm. Make sure that permanent blocking is not possible in your programs. Check whether or not one of the following policies suffices to prevent permanent blocking of the processes: once a request can not be granted to a process P_i,

   a. no other request will be granted until P_i can be satisfied.
   b. no processes will be allowed to join or reenter the group $P_1, \ldots, P_i$ until all pending requests have been satisfied.

5. Storage is divided among a large number of computations $c_1, c_2, \ldots, c_n$ $(n > 7)$. Each computation occupies some fixed part of storage. Between each two computations some space is left that can be claimed by either one of the two (the two computations at the extremes have only one neighbor).

Suppose the pattern of behavior of a computation is that it sometimes needs both areas on either side of its fixed storage part, but at other times gives them up again. Program the behavior of the computations with regard to storage management with and without a monitor and make sure that the programs are deadlock free.

In problems 6 and 7 we discuss once more the idea of programming a monitor to manage resources $R_1, \ldots, R_m$.

6. At a first glance it seems much nicer to express the reason why a process P_i calls upon monitor AR in the event name itself instead of in an additional flag RF. This is essentially the way the second version works. RF is still needed to indicate who is calling AR for a request, but it seems that the use of RF when a resource is returned as in the third version is superfluous. Modified in this way, the monitor program is

```
initialize {RF, R, AL = 0; monitor = 0; all psem = 0; free = m}
AR:  repeat
        begin local k; wait(request); k ← selectfrom RF
           wait(free)
           if allocationto(k) is deadlockfree then
              AI[k] ← index of free R
              RF[k] ← 0; signal(psem[k])
           fi
        end
     until machine halt
```

a. Find and explain what is wrong with this program.
b. Suppose that there is no potential deadlock; show that this version can be simplified still further and show that it works correctly.

7. Looking at the programs of the third version, it seems that it is not necessary for process P_i to wait after returning a resource R, because it does not need a resource to continue. It seems that the last statement wait(psem[i]) in P_i and the first signal(psem[i]) in AR can be eliminated. Find and explain the reason why this is not true.

Alternatively, the second wait statement in P_i could be moved to the very beginning, preceding the statement RF[i] ← 1, before another resource is requested. Show that this modification works out correctly if the initialization is changed accordingly and explain what improvement is achieved by it. Another suggestion worth considering is to replace monitor AR by two monitors, one for handling requests and one for handling releases. This leads to a version in which P_i is as simple as the second version. Write programs for the two monitors and specify the initialization.

4.3 QUESTIONS AND ANSWERS

4.3.1 P and V are primitive operations, of the same nature as LOCK and UNLOCK. The advantage of using the former instead of the latter is that a process waiting in a P operation goes to sleep, whereas a process looping in a LOCK operation is wasting the time of a processor which it may share with the very process that will wake it up. P and V are adequate brackets for a small critical section which has no potential delay in it. These small critical sections combined with private semaphores are sufficient to implement any desirable scheduling algorithm.

On the other hand, a proper choice of semaphores and wait and signal commands can be used to implement a desirable ordering of execution (called *fixed scheduling*). Some examples of such arrangements are discussed in this section.

A relationship which frequently exists between groups of processes is the one of question and answer. A process of a group *Q* has a question and it expects to receive a reply from one of the processes in a group *R*. The program (version 1)

Q_i: —prepare question; signal(question); wait(reply)—
R_j: —wait(question); prepare answer; signal(reply)—

assures that as many replies are sent back as questions asked. The arrangement is rather chaotic because many processes of group *Q* can ask questions and all the answers are given, but there is no way to sort out which reply belongs to which question.

This ambiguity can be removed if a question carries a tag indicating which Q process asked it. Instead of finishing with wait(reply), a process can then wait on the reply to its particular question by wait(psem[i]), where psem[i] is the private semaphore of process Q_i asking the question. The program is basically the same (version 2):

Q_i: —prepare question[i]; signal(question); wait(psem[i])—
R: —wait(question); select question[j]; prepare answer; signal(psem[j])—

This form of question and answer is found in the timesharing system of section 2.5. The group *R* consists of the character transmission processes. All user processes belong to group *Q*.

The ambiguity in the relation of question and answer can be avoided if all questions are inhibited until a reply to the current one has been received. The result of such a strategy is that question and answer strictly alternate in time. Since only one reply is in preparation at a time, there is no point in having more than one process R in group *R*. The program (version 3, one R only)

Q: —prepare question; wait(permission); signal(question); wait(reply)—
R: *repeat* wait(question); prepare answer; signal(reply); signal(permission)
until R halt

is still not adequate because if there is a lazy process Q, two Q processes may pass wait(reply) in the wrong order and pick up each other's answers. This problem can be solved if either a Q process explicitly notifies R that it received an answer, or if the Q processes treat ordering of asking questions as an internal affair.

The program with an acknowledgment of receipt is nicely symmetric (version 4, one R only):

Q: —prepare question
wait(permission)
signal(question); wait(reply)
signal(receipt)—

R: *repeat* signal(permission)
wait(question); prepare answer;
signal(reply)
wait(receipt)
until R halt

These programs correspond to the monitor version of the resource allocation discussed in the preceding section. The permission semaphore adds the rule that the monitor processes the requests serially.

Ordering the questions in time can be treated internally in group Q if asking a question and waiting for reply are considered as a critical section for processes in Q (version 5, one R only):

Q: —prepare questions; {signal(question); wait(reply)}
R: *repeat* wait(question); prepare answer; signal(reply)
until R halt

If this program structure is applied to the batch system of section 2.2, the request vector RF can be replaced by a single element, because now only one process can ask DC for a data transfer to or from the drum.

The structure of version 5 is somewhat simpler than that of version 4, but both have the drawback that the programs get rather complicated if scheduling Q processes is necessary. Version 5 has the nice property that process R is not affected by such a modification because the scheduling can be arranged by a critical section and a private event name local to group *Q*. The second version is probably the best solution.

Another variation of version 1, in which group *R* has more than one process again, is worth considering because of its symmetry (version 6):

Q: wait(reply); prepare question; signal(question)
R: wait(question); prepare answer; signal(reply)

In this form it has the same drawback as the first version. Moreover, a Q process is unable to wait for a reply to its own question, because the function of the statement wait(reply) at the beginning in a Q program (instead of at the end) is merely to obtain permission for asking a question. However, if group *Q* consists of only one process that repeatedly asks questions, this structure would certainly be a nice one to implement (version 7, one Q only):

Q: *repeat* wait(reply); prepare question; signal(question);—
until Q halt
R: —wait(question); prepare answer; signal(reply)—

The structure of version 6 is more relevant when information flows only in a single direction. The information sent by a Q process must then be considered as a message instead of as a question and there is no need to wait for reply. The reason a Q process starts with a wait this time is to gain permission for sending a message (version 8):

Q: prepare message; wait(permission); send message; signal(message);—
R: wait(message); accept message; signal(permission); process message

If permission is initialized to a number $n > 1$, up to n Q processes can send messages in overlapping time intervals. Such an arrangement is the basis for communication among processes and is discussed in more detail in chapter 5.

4.3.2 It sometimes happens that processes execute critical sections of a class s, but one of them, a process R, has a privileged status in that R should always be selected first if it wants to execute a critical section of class s. Such a situation occurs if a monitor R manages a set of resources for a group of processes *Q*.

This kind of fixed priority rule is easily implemented in a program. The timing should be arranged in such a manner that, when a Q process finishes and R is waiting, the latter will be selected over any of the Q processes. Representing a critical section by a bracket pair, a solution is given by

R: {A} and Q: [{A}]

R has to wait if there is a process in the critical section s, represented by the bracket pair { }. This must be a process Q, because there is only a single process R. This Q process is then at the same time in the critical section represented by the square bracket. Thus, all other Q processes (if any) are held up at [and none can be waiting at {. As soon as Q leaves critical section { }, it will wake up a process waiting to enter this critical section. But the only process waiting at that moment is R! Thus, R is indeed selected at the earliest possible moment.

One can easily think of generalizations of this situation; process R can be replaced by a group *R* comprising more than one process having the privileged status, or a third class *T* could be added with even lower priority than Q. The problem presented is particularly relevant, because it is the basis for a solution to all such problems. The generalizations can be programmed by a monitor process which has higher priority than the processes it serves. The process R and the group *Q* have such a priority relationship.

PROBLEMS

1. Reconsider the eight versions of the question and answer relation between processes for the cases that either group *Q* or group *R* or both are reduced to one process. Investigate what sort of simplifications can be made in those cases and see which versions reduce to the same structure. If the reductions do not lead to the same structure, characterize the differences.

2. The drum controlling process, DC, in the batch system of section 2.2 answers questions for various processes in the system. Analyze the structure of DC and classify it as one of the versions discussed in this section. Consider an implementation of DC in the form of the other versions presented in this section and discuss which one is the most suitable in the given circumstances.

3. It was noticed that versions 4 and 5 did not cater to scheduling Q processes. Rewrite these versions so that they implement the scheduling algorithms as discussed in the preceding section either by a monitor or by proper sections in the programs themselves. Investigate the simplifications in the programs that result from reducing either group *Q*, or group *R*, or both to one process.

4. Consider two different strategies for managing a set of n identical magnetic tape units ($n > 1$). The first design is one in which all units are controlled by one single process MTC. MTs are so slow compared to the CPU that MT interrupts are rare and can be handled easily by one process. The second strategy ignores this observation and attaches (for conjectured convenience) a controlling process to each MT. Processes using an MT are assumed to have reserved it beforehand as was discussed in earlier sections, but that point is irrelevant here. Processes can perform certain standard operations on tapes such as READBLOCK, WRITEBLOCK, SKIP, REWIND, STOP, etc. Each of those must be viewed as a question that needs an answer. Compare the two strategies, and design the program of the processes using the tape commands and of the processes controlling the MTs.

5. Suppose *R* is a group of processes with a monopoly position which a group *Q* lacks with respect to execution of some action A. The rules are:

1. If a R ϵ *R* is performing A, no Q ϵ *Q* nor another R may execute A.
2. Any process may start A if none is executing it yet.
3. (monopoly rule) No process of group *Q* is allowed to start action A as long as there are processes in group *R* either executing A or waiting for permission to do so.

An implementation in the spirit of version 4 is inadequate because only one of the groups can start action A if rule (1) is satisfied, but this violates rule (2).

Programming execution of A as a critical section is sufficient to implement rules (1) and (2), but is probably not adequate for rule (3).

The basis for a solution to implementing such a monopoly rule is to require that each process in the underprivileged group *Q* ask permission to start action A individually, whereas an R-type process asks permission for the group as a whole. The effect of the latter is achieved if the first R process asks permission to execute the action A. Once acquired, this permission is not given up until the last R-process has completed action A. We use the notation ( )* to indicate a critical section entered by a group instead of an individual process. This means that the first process of that group enters the critical section in the normal way and the last process exits the critical section in the normal way. However, all processes of that group between the first and the last may execute the code of the critical section without executing the P at the beginning and the V at the end. In this manner, the critical section is reserved for a group as long as there are processes of that group interested in executing the code of the critical section.

Using the star notation, the problem described above is solved by

R: ({A})* Q: [(acquire permission)]{A}*.

a. Show that, if a process R and a process Q are both waiting for permission, process R will gain permission before Q.
b. Solve the problem for the three remaining variations that action A is either not a critical section for group R, or not for group Q or not for both. (The Readers and Writers problem [CACM 14 10, October 1971] is a special case of this one.)
c. Design an implementation for the group execution of a critical section (the star notation).

4.4 IMPLEMENTATION OF SOFTWARE SIGNALS

4.4.1 The specifications of P and V operations describe precisely what is needed to implement a small critical section. They also fit the definition of wait and signal. A process which is suspended when it executes a P operation is put on a waiting list. Each semaphore has its own waiting list. We use (for convenience) circular lists in all cases. (The last element of a circular list points back to the first element instead of indicating that it is the last.)

The argument of a P operation must indicate whether or not it can be passed. A suitable data structure for the argument is a record composed of two fields:

a. A value field which shows how many processes still can pass. The range of the indicator usually is [0:1], but we have seen that a range [0:n|n > 1] is sometimes useful.
b. A pointer to the list of waiting processes. This pointer gives us access to the waiting list. If there are no processes waiting, its value is *nil*, indicating that the list is empty; otherwise, it points to the last element in the list allowing fast access to both front and rear of the list (see figure 4.4a).

Each element i of a circular list has a pointer "succ[i]" which indicates the element next to element i in the list. For the list of figure 4.4a we find succ[a] = b, succ[y] = z, succ[z] = a and succ[ptr[sem]] = a because the value of ptr is z. We define as a special case succ[*nil*] = *nil* to account for the case of an empty list when the value of ptr = *nil*. A circular list has the special characteristic that, if i points to a genuine list element, succ[i] will not be *nil*.

Two standard operations on lists are: *insert* and *remove*. The function of insert is to add an object to a list at an indicated place and the function of remove is to take away an indicated element from the list. These functions have a special meaning when applied to a *queue*. A queue is a data structure from which only the first element can be removed and to which a new element can be appended only at the rear. Applied to a queue, the functions remove and insert are always interpreted in this restrictive sense.

4.4.2 Returning to the subject of waiting lists, we observe that it must be possible to select a process to be removed from a list. That is to say, it must be possible to decide for any pair in the list which one of the two should be removed first. Thus, between every pair of elements there exists a priority

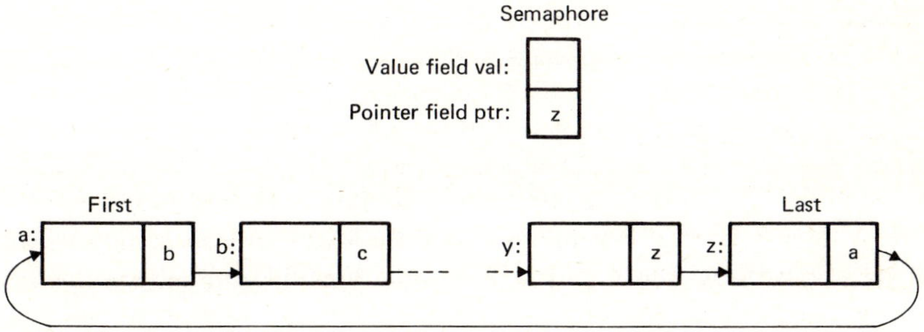

Figure 4.4a A semaphore and its waiting list

relation "$<$" which is transitive ($a < b$ and $b < c$ implies $a < c$) and irreflexive ($a \nless a$). Such a total ordering defines a linear ordering analogous to the ordering less than for integer numbers. A linear ordering of the waiting processes based on their arrival time is called an *arrival time queue*.

It is convenient to order a waiting list by the selection priority if the latter does not change while a process is present in the list. The order is maintained by searching for the right place when a process is inserted into the list. A process is selected by removing the first element of the list. However, if the selection priority may change while a process resides in a waiting list, an order based on selection priority is probably not suitable, because the advantage of having a simple selection procedure is not likely to match the disadvantage of intermediate reorderings. In that case, the insert procedure can be simplified by merely placing a newly arriving process at the end of the list. Selecting a process then requires a more elaborate procedure. It requires a search for the process with maximal priority. In this case the list structure merely serves the purpose of enumerating the waiting processes.

A very efficient strategy results if the selection priority is fixed on the basis of arrival time. This strategy combines the advantage of a simple procedure for both inserting a process and selecting one for removal. When a process arrives, it has lowest priority of all. Thus, it must be appended at the end. The top element automatically has the highest priority, and is chosen when a process is removed from the list. Thus, neither insert nor select and remove requires a search through the list. The structure of the waiting list in this case is a simple arrival time queue.

In the preceding sections it was argued that P and V must be used only for small critical sections. All scheduling with respect to priorities existing outside the waiting list and issues such deadlocks cannot be handled by P and V. Therefore, the best implementation of a semaphore waiting list is an arrival time queue. In practice it may be convenient to design special versions of P and V which have waiting lists not ordered by arrival time, but by some form of external priority; we exclusively use arrival time queues for P and V. Lists not associated with semaphores are not subject to such a restriction.

When a process is not on one of the waiting lists, it is able to run. However, the number of processes that will actually run in parallel is restricted to the number of available processors. Thus, the non-waiting processes can be split into two groups, the running processes and the processes ready to run, but not actually running. Ready to run processes are placed in the ready list to facilitate enumeration of the ready to run processes. Although, in the colloquial sense of the word, processes in the ready list are also waiting (waiting for a processor), we will use the term *waiting* in a technical sense and apply it only to processes that were put on a waiting list by calling a P operation. For processes in the ready list we use strictly the term *ready to run* or *ready*. If there is a chance for confusion, we will use the term *blocked* as an equivalent for *waiting*. When a process is selected from a waiting list, it is promoted to the ready list. It depends on its priority relative to the other processes in the list (and probably also on the ones running) whether or not it is immediately further promoted to the running state. Unlike in semaphore queues, the relative priority of processes in the ready list changes dynamically as a function of the amount of used processor time (see sections 2.4 and 2.5). It is therefore not efficient to order the ready list by linear priority. Which structure fits best depends on the chosen processor scheduling algorithm. This topic is discussed in more detail in chapter 6.

Let us assume that every process P_i is identified in the operating system by a process control block. Its base address is PCB[i]. It contains the vital information about P_i (when P_i must give up the CPU it is using). The processor state is saved in the PCB so that its value can be restored when a processor is allocated.

Since a process frequently resides in a list, but in only one at a time, it is useful to reserve in each PCB[i] a field for succ[i], the pointer to the next element in a list. Furthermore, we incorporate in a PCB for clarity a state field which reveals whether a process is running, ready or waiting. Figure 4.4b gives an idea of the structures involved.

In section 3.4 we reasoned that P and V must themselves be implemented as critical sections. If P and V on a particular semaphore can be executed by different processors, it is necessary to use LOCK and UNLOCK on a fixed lock bit as entry and exit of P and V. Furthermore, we will see in the next section that our interrupt on a processor should be considered as V operation executed by a peripheral device. Therefore, we do not allow an in-

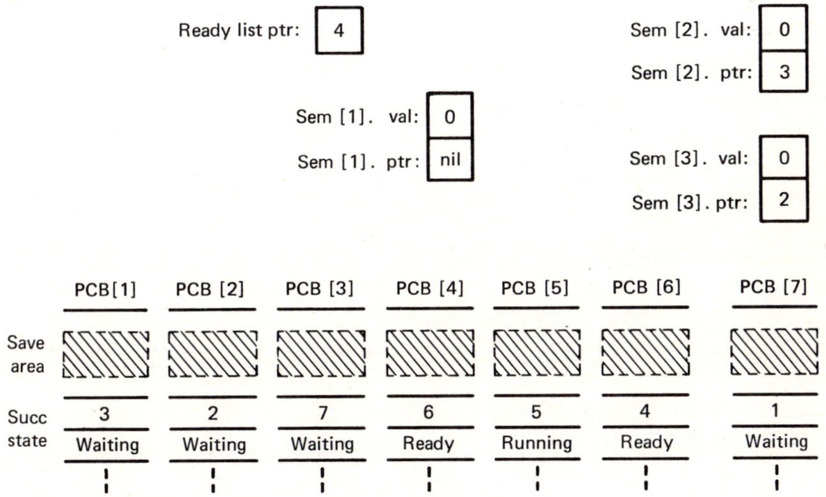

Figure 4.4b PCBs in the ready and waiting lists

terrupt to occur while a processor is executing a P or V operation. This can be done, as we will see in the next section, by masking off all interrupts, or executing P and V at the highest interrupt level.

On the other hand, the execution of a P or V offers an excellent opportunity to gather some information about a process. It would be penny-wise but pound-foolish to neglect such a chance for the sake of saving some overhead in execution time. It is very useful to know how much time a process spent on a CPU. This information is helpful for accounting and CPU allocation strategies. It can easily be collected in a P operation when a process is blocked and the processor is allocated to another process. Another example: when a process enters a critical section, it essentially acquires a system resource. It makes sense to temporarily assign a higher priority to such a process in order to speed it up and get the semaphore released as soon as possible. Details of such additional information are not relevant here; they will just be referred to in this section by the collective noun *control information*.

4.4.3 Let *current* indicate the index of the process currently running on a processor and let this process call P(sem) or V(sem). The programs for P(sem) and V(sem) are, in view of the preceding discussion:

```
P(sem) =
begin
   disable interrupt; LOCK(PV lockbit)
   if val[sem] > 0 then val[sem]−1
   else save processor state (current)
      close control information (current)
      STATE[current] ← "waiting"
      insert(current into semqueue[sem])
      current ← select from ready list
      STATE[current] ← "running"
      open control information (current)
      restore processor state (current)
   fi
   UNLOCK(PV lockbit); enable interrupts
end
V(sem) =
begin
   disable interrupts; LOCK(PV lockbit)
   if ptr[sem] = nil then val[sem]+1
   else local k; remove(k from semqueue[sem])
      insert(k into readylist)
      STATE[k] ← "ready to run"
   fi
   UNLOCK(PV lockbit); enable interrupts
end
```

The operation "insert" places a new element at the rear and the operation "remove" takes away the first element of a queue. Applied to a queue the programs for insert and remove are:

```
insert (g,x)  =  if g = nil then succ[x] ← (g ← x)
                 else succ[x] ← succ[g]; g ← (succ[g] ← x) fi
remove (g,y) = begin y ← succ[g]
                 if g = y then g ← nil else succ[g] ← succ[y]; succ[y] ← y fi
                 end
```

Note that remove function assumes that the list is not empty. This is true in the V operation because the call of remove is preceded by an explicit test for an empty queue. It is true in the P operation, because the ready list will contain a NULL process that can always run (see section 3.4). The given version of the V operation does not promote the process which is removed from the waiting list to the running state. This wasn't done, because, unlike in the P operation, the caller can always continue to use the processor. Further promotion can be considered if there is a way to compare the relative priority of the awakened process and the one currently running. It may be worthwhile to consider such a strategy in an implementation of the signal operation. A program for the modified V operation is:

```
V(sem) =
begin
  disable interrupts; LOCK(PV lockbit)
  if ptr[sem] = nil then val[sem]+1
  else local k; remove(k from semqueue[sem])
    if priority(k) > priority(current) then
      save processor state(current)
      close control information(current)
      STATE[current] ← "ready to run"
      insert(current into readylist)
      current ← k
      STATE[current] ← "running"
      open control information(current)
      restore processor state(current)
    else
      insert(k into readylist)
      STATE[k] ← "ready to run"
  fi fi
  UNLOCK(PV lockbit); enable interrupts
end
```

PROBLEMS

1. Let elements of a circular list L consist of two fields: (a) a priority value and (b) a successor pointer. Assume that the list is arranged in decreasing

priority order. Suppose the priority value of an element is variable: When it changes, the element must be replaced such that the proper ordering is maintained. Write a program for replacing an element. Once this program has been written, verify the remark made earlier in this section that the advantage of a quick selection if the priority order is maintained does not match the disadvantage of rearrangement through replacements. Investigate whether or not it would pay to use doubly linked circular lists.

2. Consider once more the three list ordering strategies:
   a. ordering as an arrival time queue
   b. ordering according to a fixed external priority
   c. ordering according to a changing external priority(*external* means not based on arrival time, but determined by unknown sources).

It has been stated several times that P and V must be used preferably in those circumstances where the probability that many processes are waiting is very low. It could therefore well be that the amount of work associated with each of the three strategies is not much different after all if the semaphore queues are very short. Evaluate this statement for the cases that the average queue length is respectively 1, 2 or 5.

3. Assuming that the *else* part of P and V are rarely executed compared to the *then* part, it may be worthwhile to consider optimizations which would speed up the *then* parts. Two proposals are: (a) restrict the semaphores to Boolean variables; (b) (the other extreme) allow also negative values of the semaphore and let a P operation always decrement and a V operation always increment. Investigate how the P, V programs must be modified for either (a) or (b). Sketch an assembly code version of P and V, disregarding the *else* parts. See if either (a) or (b) would mean a saving in assembly code or execution time of the *then* parts.

4. Yet another idea based on the assumption of short waiting lists is to replace the V operation by the operation FREE. The operation FREE will also check the waiting list, but instead of selecting one process, it removes *all* processes from the waiting list and resets their program counters such that each of them will redo its P operation. Write a program for the operation FREE and discuss the conditions under which it is an acceptable alternative to a V operation.

5. Suppose we want to extend the family of wait and signal operations with two others: STOP and START. A process P_i can call STOP(j) in order to stop process P_j and it can call START(k) to start a stopped process P_k. The states running, waiting and ready are for this purpose extended with a state *stopped*. Associated with the state stopped is a list of stopped processes.

Write programs for the operations STOP and START and investigate whether or not the P, V programs must be modified. When such an extension was considered, it was observed that it would be a bad policy to STOP a process when it is executing a critical section. Thus, we do the following. In the case mentioned, STOP will not have the immediate effect of stopping the process, but, instead, set a flag to indicate that a STOP was requested for this process. The STOP is brought into effect when the process has left all its critical sections.

Modify your programs for STOP and START and the P, V programs. What are the implications of allowing nested critical sections?

4.5 IMPLEMENTATION OF HARDWARE SIGNALS

4.5.1 The available hardware prescribes the way a central processor and device processors such as channels and control units can cooperate. It does not leave much flexibility in programming such a cooperation. In chapter 1 we saw that a CPU initiates work on peripheral devices by sending commands and the device in question indicates when it has completed the work. Ideally, the control program of a device is

```
device_k: (hard wired)
          repeat  wait(BUSY_k)
                  interpret command
                  record command completion
                  signal(READY_k)
          until   device halt
```

while the program of the controlling process running on a CPU will contain this particular piece of code:

```
controller (programmed):
—prepare command; signal(BUSY_k); wait(READY_k)—
```

We can easily verify that these programs provide the necessary cooperation between a device and its controlling process. The semaphores $BUSY_k$ and $READY_k$ are both initialized at 0. Suppose a fixed field, called the command buffer, is reserved in storage or in the device processor to hold a command. Initially, the device idles and waits for the BUSY signal. The controlling process places a command in the buffer before it sends the BUSY signal to the device and won't send another command until it receives a READY signal. Because by that time the device has already completed the current command, the device and controlling process cooperate satisfactorily. It is, however, not realistic to expect that a hardware implementation of wait and signal is wired into a device. We must investigate whether or not the given hardware can be extended with programs that have the desired effect.

The eventnames $BUSY_k$ and $READY_k$ are in reality not more than a pair of bits which can be set by the device or under program control. The (hard-wired) structure of a device control program is:

```
device_k: (hard wired)
          repeat
             repeat look at flag BUSY_k until BUSY_k = 1
             BUSY_k ← 0
             interpret command
             record command completion
             READY_k ← 1
          until device_k halt
```

The first statement expresses the fact that a device processor continually inspects the BUSY flag when it idles to see if another command has arrived. When it finds one, it resets the BUSY flag to zero and after completing the command, the READY flag is merely switched ON.

Given this hardware structure we see that programming signal($BUSY_k$) in the controlling process is very simple: all that is needed is the statement $BUSY_k \leftarrow 1$. Setting the ready flag normally has the side effect of causing an interrupt. This results in the execution of one of the instructions of a table in a fixed storage area. This is a general characteristic of all interrupt systems. There exists a wide variety of implementations of which we will discuss only the major characteristics.

We investigate first how signal($READY_k$) and wait($READY_k$) can be programmed for a simplified form of device interrupt system. After having done that, we will discuss how similar implementations can be designed for more realistic interrupt systems.

The program counter PC of a CPU is extended with a bit vector MASK which has one bit for every bit in the READY vector. When $device_k$ has completed a command, it will set $READY_k$ to 1 as indicated in the device program. All bits can be set to either 0 or 1 under program control. An interrupt occurs at the very moment that for any k the state ($MASK_k$, $Ready_k$) equals (1,1) when the CPU starts another fetch-execute cycle. An interrupt can have either one of two possible causes:

a. The device assigns a one to $READY_k$ while ($MASK_k$,$READY_k$) = (1,0)
b. $MASK_k$ is set to one under program control while ($MASK_k$,$READY_k$) = (0,1). In the latter case we say that an interrupt is *pending*.

When an interrupt occurs, the CPU executes an interrupt instruction instead of the next instruction of the program it is working on. This instruction is a subroutine call. It has the effect of saving the current value of the program counter and jumping to the address given by the interrupt instruction. Since the MASK vector is adjoined to PC, the value it has when

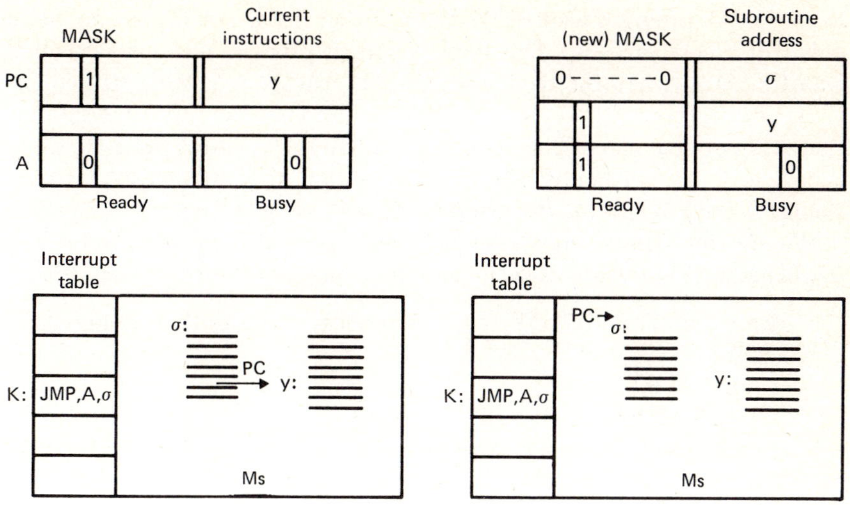

Figure 4.5a State before and after interrupt by device_k

the interrupt occurs is saved with the address of the current instruction of the interrupted program. The value of MASK in the new PC is set to all zeros. This has the effect of masking off all interrupts and thus, of disable interrupts (see figure 4.5a).

An interrupt subroutine call disables all other interrupts. The interrupt subroutine is essentially that part of a V operation that wakes up a process. A comparison of the program below and the second version of the V operation presented in section 4.4 shows the strong similarity between the two routines.

interrupt subroutine_k =

begin
  $\text{MASK}_k \leftarrow 0$; $\text{READY}_k \leftarrow 0$ $ changes are made in the saved state
  save processor state (current)
  close control information (current)
  $\text{STATE}_{\text{current}} \leftarrow$ "ready to run"
  return (ready list,current)
  current ← k $ k is the index of the device control process
  $\text{STATE}_{\text{current}} \leftarrow$ "running"
  open control information (current)
  restore processor state (current)
end

Since this interrupt routine version of the V operation always wakes up a process, this process must be waiting. Bit MASK_k is used to guarantee that this is so. We program wait($READY_k$) such that it sets $MASK_k$ to one if and only if it blocks $process_k$. This implies that, if $process_k$ has not yet called wait($READY_k$) when the device sets $READY_k$ to one, $MASK_k$ still equals zero, so an interrupt, and consequently execution of the interrupt subroutine, will not take place. The operation wait($READY_k$) must put P_k to sleep if $device_k$ is not yet ready. The implementation of wait($READY_k$) is very similar to the P operation discussed in the preceding section.

We use for convenience the terms *hardware P,V operations* for the implementation of wait($READY_k$) and the matching interrupt subroutine.

```
hardware P on READY_k =        $ process_k is currently running
begin
   disable interrupt
   if READY_k = 1 then READY_k ← 0
   else  save processor state(k)
         close control information(k)
         STATE_k ← "waiting"
         MASK_k ← 1
         current ← select from ready list
         STATE_current ← "running"
         open control information (current)
         restore processor state (current)
   fi
   enable interrupts
end
```

The presentation here is only a model. In practice there are minor differences of implementation such as where exactly PC is saved when an interrupt occurs, how the arrays READY, BUSY, MASK and the interrupt table are named and implemented, where these are located, how interrupts are disabled or enabled, etc.

4.5.2 Three issues are not properly reflected in the presentation up to this point: (a) priority levels of interrupt, (b) access to devices via channels and control units, and (c) the structure of commands, in particular blocking and chaining. The latter topic is a matter of how communication between processes and devices is organized and is therefore discussed in section 5.3.

The interrupts discussed up to this point all arise from input/output operations. However, an interrupt can also be used for purposes other than cooperation of processes and devices. Two such pruposes of major importance are for calling system functions and for dealing with certain error conditions.

The objective of designing an operating system is to create a virtual machine which provides the proper environment for running programs and accessing semi-permanently stored data. The hardware is defined by the instructions one can write. Providing a virtual machine means creating a modified set of rules for writing instructions. Instructions of the virtual machine that do not exist in the hardware must appear as elementary instructions, although in reality they are implemented as instruction sequences for the underlying machine. Examples of such virtual instructions or system functions are P and V and the procedure COPY (see section 2.5). Execution of such a virtual instruction may involve facilities or data to which the calling environment has no direct access at all (disable interrupt or waiting queues). It is customary to speak of a privileged mode in which a virtual instruction is executed. Many machines have hardware facilities for marking instructions or data as privileged and the interrupt mechanism can be used to switch from unprivileged mode to privileged mode (a well known example is an SVC call on the IBM/360).

Certain error conditions that may arise in a program are detected by hardware facilities. Standard examples are arithmetic overflow and division by zero. If the occurrence of such an error condition results in an interrupt, it is as if at that point a subroutine is called. The activated interrupt routine can sort out the nature of the error and transfer control to an appropriate error handling routine. Hardware failures can be treated in a similar way.

4.5.3 The interrupt table is not arranged by device in most machines, but by class of interrupt. The connection between classes and table entries is either fixed in hardware (five priority classes in the IBM/360) or can be set by program control (PDP-10, PDP-11). The index of an entry in the interrupt table is then considered the priority level of the interrupts associated with that level. This has the following effect: when an interrupt has occurred, all interrupts of the same or lower levels are automatically inhibited, but those on higher levels can still occur. The ability to set the priority level of an interrupt under program control has the advantage that other interrupts can be inhibited selectively instead of by a uniform disable operation.

The interrupt table has in reality not many entries, usually one for each class instead of one for each separate interrupt as in the presented model. This has the drawback that, when an interrupt occurs at a certain level, the true cause must still be found. This can be found out by inspecting the vectors READY and MASK. The hardware of many machines includes clever instructions which make the search for the cause of an interrupt very cheap. An example of such an instruction is the one that computes the index of the leftmost one in a bit vector stored in a machine word.

Commands and data are transmitted to and from devices through channels and control units. It is sufficient for our purposes to pretend that a control unit is the device it controls, since the manner in which a control unit manipulates a device has little bearing on how an operating system should work.

A channel is a specialized processor that has a cycle time comparable to

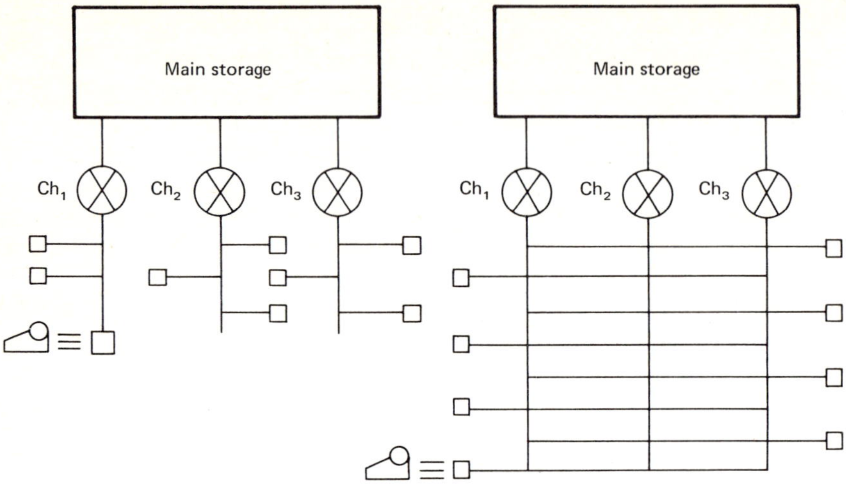

Figure 4.5b Fixed and variable data paths

that of a central processor. It is specialized in the sense that its instruction set is particularly tailored to the devices it serves. Channels serve a practical purpose: without a channel the data flow from a device to main storage (or the other way around) would have to be controlled either by the CPU, as in first generation machines, or by the control units of the devices. Control by the CPU (referred to as *cycle stealing*) makes it hard to exploit any of the parallel capabilities of a machine configuration. On the other hand, hardware is getting cheaper and cheaper. A device processor can be built nowadays for a few hundred dollars, so channels are not so urgently needed as they used to be when we could not afford to let a device processor idle.

Connections between devices and channels are either fixed (IBM/360) or variable in the sense that a data path can be established between any one device and any one channel, but a device is connected to one channel at a time (Burroughs 6500, see figure 4.5b).

The wiring between channels and devices in the variable scheme acts as a switch operated under control of connection requests. There are two variations on this theme: either a request for access to a device is sent to a particular channel which will accept the request when it can and establish a data path; or, a request for access is broadcast to all channels and one which is able to do so will accept it and establish a path.

A channel services only one device at a time. This implies that a process which controls a device must set up a path through a channel every time it wants to activate its device. Thus a control process and a channel must cooperate as described in these programs:

```
control process: —                      channel:
      wait(channel free)                repeat  wait(channel request)
      send device address[k]                    establish connection device[k]
      signal(channel request)                   signal(channel ready)
      wait(channel ready)                  CH:  control path to device[k]
  CD: send command                              signal(channel free)
      signal(BUSY[k])                   until   channel halt
      wait(READY[k])
      —
```

A channel maintains a data-flow path in a conversational mode or in burst mode. In conversational mode one data item is sent across for every channel request, whereas in burst mode a data path is maintained for a flow of a great number of items sent in sequence. The conversational mode is typically applied to the slower sort of devices such as card readers, teletypes or line printers. Watching a channel serving some slow devices, we observe a sequence of items passing through directed to different devices. The data flow between these devices and main storage is interleaved by the channel which provides a multiplexing function. A channel working in burst mode also has such a multiplexing function on a larger time scale; in terms of the time scale at which data is transferred, such a channel is temporarily reserved for a particular device. Burst mode typically applies to faster devices such as drums, disks or magnetic tapes. Variations on the manner in which commands are handled in burst mode are discussed in section 5.3.

PROBLEMS

1. Suppose a machine has a very simple timer interrupt system: after every so many instructions have been executed the regular sequence of instructions is interrupted and, instead of the next one in sequence, an instruction is executed from a fixed place which contains a call to the interrupt subroutine. The machine has a disable interrupt flag, DIF, which can be set under program control. If DIF has the value zero when the interrupt would have occurred, it is kept pending until DIF is set to one.

Investigate whether or not the programming of P and V for device communication as proposed in this section has to be modified. What order of magnitude should the length of the instruction sequence between two timer interrupts be?

2. Suppose a multiprocessor machine has three not entirely identical processors A, B and C. Processes $P_1, \ldots, P_3$ run on these processors, but they cannot run on all processors. Their ability to run on a processor is expressed by P_1(A,B), P_2(A,B), P_3(B) and P_4(A,C). Each process has a fixed priority $p_1 < p_2 < p_3 < p_4$. The objective is to have the processes of highest priority running at any one time (to the extent that this is possible).

Consider a situation in which three processes are running and the fourth one is selected from a waiting list. The awakened process must not only be compared with the one that it wakes up, but must also be compared with the processes running on the other processors. Investigate how the second version of the V operation in section 4.4 should be modified to implement the priority rules described here.

3. It is not possible to store the current value of the program counter PC in a fixed register if the machine has a multi-level interrupt system, because an interrupt of higher level could overwrite a saved value. Design a technique for saving PC, for setting up a new MASK vector and check in detail what happens if an interrupt of higher level occurs while the interrupt subroutine for a lower level is being executed. Would it be possible to allow a higher level interrupt to occur when a P-operation is being executed?

4. Suppose the MASK vector does not match the READY vector, but instead, there is only one MASK bit for every interrupt level. Show that this hardware is insufficient to implement hardware P and V as described in this section. Discuss what additional data is needed, how it must be used and where it must be updated.

5. Suppose a multiplexing channel has a cycle time of 1 microsecond. Suppose one 20-line/second line printer and two 15 card/second card readers are attached to it. If the channel has to control every character between device and channel, every word between channel and main storage and every command between channel and control process, figure out how heavy a load these devices are for the channel assuming that all are working at full speed.

READING LIST

A classical synchronization problem is discussed in [1]. Several beautiful examples are presented in [2]; most famous are the "dining philosophers" and the "sleeping barber." An example of microprogrammed system functions is [3].

1. Courtois, P. J., F. Heymans, and D. L. Parnas, "Concurrent Control with 'Readers' and 'Writers,' " *Comm. ACM* 14, 10 (October 1971).

2. Dijkstra, E. W., "Cooperating Sequential Processes," in *Programming Languages*, Academic Press, 1968.

3. Liskov, B. H., "The Design of the Venus Operating System," *Comm. ACM* 15, 3 (March 1972).

5. Communicating Processes

5.1 COMMUNICATION TECHNIQUES

5.1.1 This chapter discusses the various ways processes send information to one another. We saw in chapters 1 and 2 that an operating system comprises a variety of processes such as a drum controller, a teletype manager, or a user process. Though any one of them performs its function autonomously, its activity is usually driven by requests from outside. A clear example is the drum controller (see section 2.2). Its task consists of activating the drum device and controlling the data traffic between the main store and the drum. The manner in which it performs this task is an internal matter, but its activity is usually instigated by a data transfer request from another process. Such a request is just one instance of interprocess communication.

The term *communication* denotes the activity of data transmission between processes. In some cases, as for instance in case of the drum controller and the drum device, data is indeed physically moved from one site to another. In other cases, if communicating processes share the same physical storage, data is not actually moved, but the right to access the data is transferred from one process to another.

A data transmission is controlled by an exchange of question and answer between the communicating processes. We will use the term *message* for such questions and answers, since it is a more general term than *command* or *instruction*. The term *command* has the flavor of a master process sending an imperative question to his servant and the term *instruction* is frequently used to mean machine instruction. The term *message* does not have such connotations. Moreover, this term can be used for both question and reply.

In its most general form, a message consists of four parts: an identification of the process which sends it (the source or the sender), an identification

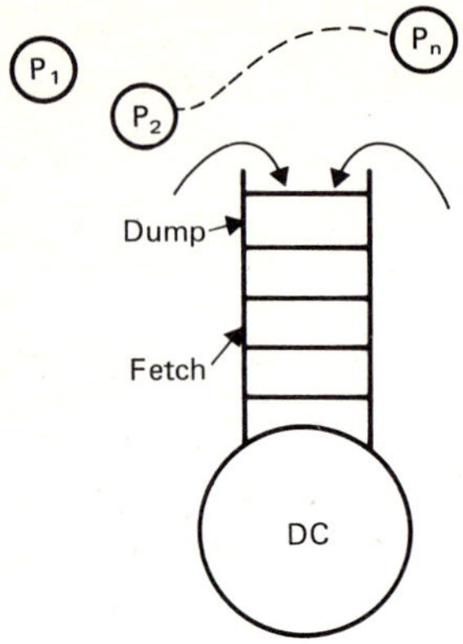

Figure 5.1a Single message queue attached to destination

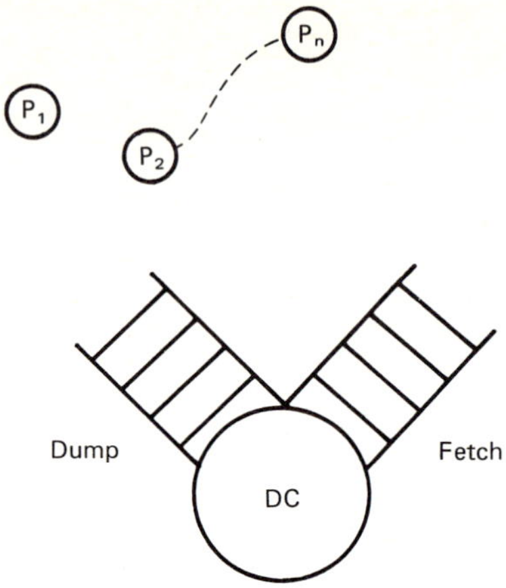

Figure 5.1b Two message queues sorted by instruction

of the process to which it is being sent (the destination or the receiver), a description of the data involved (the data description), and a description of what must be done (the instruction). However, in particular instances any of these four parts may be absent if the necessary information can be derived from other sources. This point is demonstrated below by a variety of communication protocols for a drum controller, DC.

We can attach to DC a message queue; i.e., a space for a message array in which other processes can deposit a message. An indication of the receiver is superfluous with such an arrangement because the destination is known to be process DC (see figure 5.1a).

Alternatively we can give process DC two message queues, one for the messages asking for data from the secondary store, the other one for sending data to the secondary store. In this case the instruction part of messages is no longer needed (see figure 5.1b). Alternatively, every process may have a queue (or two separate queues, one for each direction) for data transmission requests. Process DC scans the queues in some order. In this case no indication of source or destination is needed.

Finally, suppose the main store is divided into blocks of fixed and equal size, called *page frames*. The status of the page frames is described in the frame table containing one entry for each frame. A page frame descriptor indicates whose information momentarily resides in its corresponding frame. Using the frame table, DC can decode a message containing the instruction "swap out process P_i", without requiring any further data description (see figure 5.1c) to identify the pages in use by process P_i.

When DC determines that a data transmission process P_i has been com-

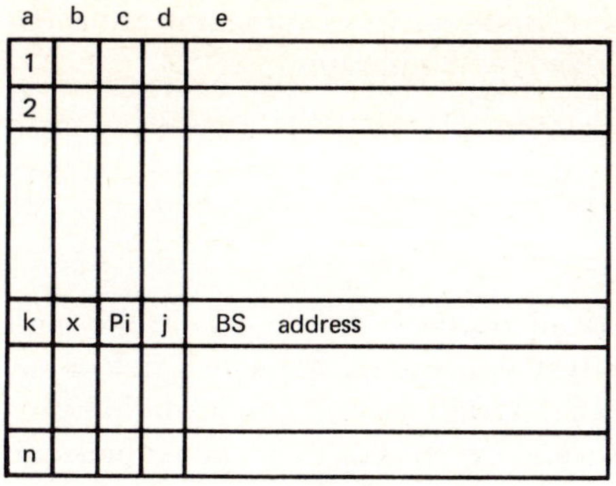

a: Frame number
b: STATUS (e.g, free, copy etc)
c: Process which uses this frame
d: Index of process' page table entry
e: Corresponding page on backing store

Figure 5.1c Sketch of a frame table

pleted, it sends a message in answer to P_i's transmission request. If process P_i sends only one request to DC at a time, no confusion can arise about the completed transmission, and a data description and an instruction are not needed in the notification message. If, in addition to this, process P_i sends only one message at a time, it will not be necessary to mention the source of the notification message, because P_i can derive this information from the last message it sent. In such a case the notification message reduces to signalling through a private semaphore; chapters 3 and 4 contain several examples of such rudimentary notification messages.

The command which a device controller sends to its device can be viewed as a message in which sender and receiver do not have to be indicated. The device answers with the simplest form of message, saying "DONE" (see section 4.5) (or "READY").

Even a sequence of machine instructions can be viewed as a series of messages sent by a programmer to a central processor. The data and instruction part are clearly present, but source and destination are not identified in the message (and don't have to be). A notification message is not explicitly created in this case, but is implicitly present because the machine continues to the next instruction. On the other hand, an explicit notification that the whole sequence of instructions has been completed may be sent to the user.

5.1.2 The substance of chapters 3 and 4 makes it easy to implement process communication. Chapter 3 shows how critical sections can be used to prevent two processes from sending messages to the same process simultaneously. Chapter 4 shows how question and answer can be ordered in time by placing synchronization commands in the programs.

We discuss three basic methods of implementing communication between processes. They are characterized by the phrases

1. master-servant system
2. dialogue system
3. mailing system

A typical example of a master-servant system is a device controller and its device. The servant is at all times available, except when he is sick or has a day off! The master schedules the work for the servant and it would be his own mistake if he confused the servant by sending him more than one command at a time. The servant regards it as his duty to notify his master when he completes a task so that he can accept another command. The major characteristics of a master-servant communication system are:

a. the master does not have to ask permission for using his servant
b. the servant's activity is entirely controlled by the master
c. the connection between source and destination is fixed

A dialogue system is similar to a facility whose services can be requested by telephone. Prospective users of the facility compete for service, and the number of customers that can be simultaneously handled depends on the structure of the service facility. However, once a connection between user and facility has been established, the user can ask a series of questions which will be answered until he is done, assuming that he does not place an unreasonable demand on the service facility. A typical example of a dialogue system is the set of user processes competing for the use of magnetic tape units. Before a process is able to manipulate one of its tapes it must request the use of an MT. In this respect it competes with others. The MT monitor decides on matters of allocation. However, once the connection between a process and an MT has been established, the user has temporary monopoly of using the device. The major characteristics of a dialogue system are:

a. a user must acquire permission for using the service facility
b. the activity of the facility is triggered by the user's requests, but controlled by the facility itself
c. the connection between user and service facility is established temporarily

In a mailing system messages are sent whether or not they can be processed right away. Messages are not sent directly from source to destination. Instead, senders and receivers communicate via a shared data area, for which the terms *mailbox* or *communication buffer* are used. Senders deposit their messages in the mailbox and receivers take them out in due time.

A mailing system is the most general communication system. It allows, among other things, for the situation in which the number of messages sent varies in time. We say that the senders operate in *burst mode*. The purpose of having a mailbox is then to bridge the gap between the changing rate at which messages are sent and the rate at which these can be received. Messages which cannot be processed right away remain in the mailbox.

Another advantage of a mailbox system is that a sender does not have to wait until its message is processed. It can continue doing other things, including sending another message to the same mailbox. This arrangement is particularly convenient when a sender does not care about an acknowledgment or notification of completion. An example of such a situation is a user process producing output for a line printer. Suppose the line printer controller, LPC, receives print requests from other processes via a mailbox. A user process can immediately dispose of its printer output while depositing descriptive messages in LPC's mailbox. The sender may continue without waiting until the line printer has actually printed its output.

5.1.3 The drum controller of section 2.2 communicates with other processes via a mailbox. The mailbox is the request vector RQ. This example illustrates another reason why, in certain situations, a mailing system might be preferred to a dialogue system. In the latter kind of system, a sender must acquire permission for asking all its questions in advance. However, if a process wants to ask only a single question, asking the question implies asking permission for doing so. This makes a separate request for permission superfluous! In this particular case there is no need to establish a connection between source and destination before a message can be sent. At the very moment such a connection is established it can immediately be broken again, because the next message will probably come from another source. A mailing system is more appropriate in such a situation than a dialogue system. A mailing system is characterized by

a. the size of the mailbox permitting, a sender does not need permission to send a message
b. the senders have no control over the receivers
c. there is no particular time interval during which a sender and a receiver are directly connected
d. the mailbox provides a buffering facility for the time that messages are sent faster than they are processed

Two basic functions are needed for accessing a mailbox: deposit(m) and remove(m), where m is a message. It is obvious that a receiver must not try to remove a message before the whole message is in the mailbox. Thus, the operations remove and deposit must be synchronized. We introduce for this purpose the semaphore "mesnum," and design deposit and remove as follows:

```
deposit(m) =                        remove(m) =
  begin local x                       begin local x
    select empty frame(x)               wait(mesnum)
    mailbox_x ← m                       select full frame(x)
    mark(x, "full")                     m ← mailbox_x
    signal(mesnum)                      mark(x, "empty")
  end                                 end
```

(It is assumed that marking a frame empty or full is done in one storage access, behaving as a critical section.)

If eventname mesnum is initialized to zero, then these programs guarantee that the number of deposits is at all times greater than or equal to the number of removes. In other words, the receiver is not able to get ahead of the sender (of course it should not).

On the other hand, it is not likely that we can afford to let the sender get arbitrarily far ahead of the receiver, because then we would need a mailbox of infinite size. Assuming that a mailbox has a finite capacity for storing messages, we must adjust the procedure of deposit and receive so that the mailbox cannot overflow. Another way of phrasing this additional requirement is: the sending should not get arbitrarily far ahead of the receiver in consuming empty frames.

Note the duality between handling messages and handling frames. In case of messages, the receiver must wait until the sender has produced at least one message; in case of frames, the sender must wait until the receiver has created at least one empty frame. Thus, the limited size problem can also be solved by synchronization: the sender must ask for an empty frame and wait if there is none; when it has cleared a frame, the receiver must notify the sender if the latter is waiting for a frame. For this purpose we introduce a semaphore "framnum" in which the number of empty frames will be recorded. The initial value of framnum is equal to the total number of frames in the mailbox. The modified programs for the operations deposit(m) and remove(m) are:

```
deposit(m) =                        remove(m) =
  begin local x                       begin local x
    wait(framnum)                       wait(mesnum)
    selectemptyframe(x)                 selectfullframe(x)
    mailbox_x ← m                       m ← mailbox_x
    mark(x, "full")                     mark(x, "empty")
    signal(mesnum)                      signal(framnum)
  end                                 end
```

These versions of deposit and remove ensure that the receiver cannot get ahead of the sender (if the initial value of mesnum = 0), and also, that the sender cannot get ahead of the receiver by more than the number of frames in the mailbox.

The programs for deposit and remove can easily be extended to handle communication between more than one sender and more than one receiver. The current versions are adequate for the case of one sender and one receiver, because the sender has filled a frame x before the receiver processes it, and the sender does not write in frame x again unless the receiver has cleared it.

If there are many senders, we must make sure that no two of them select the same empty frame and overwrite each other's messages. This cannot happen if "select empty frame (x)" includes within one critical section both selection of an empty frame and its removal from the set of empty frames. The result of such a strategy is that a frame x temporarily can be in an intermediate state between being empty and full. After having been selected, frame x is not empty anymore, but it is not marked full until the message has been delivered. The strategy can be implemented by using two arrays, EMPTY and FULL, which reflect the state of all the frames. The elements of array EMPTY are intially all *true* and those of FULL *false*. The combination $EMPTY_x = FULL_x =$ *true* is the only one out of four possibilities which can never occur.

Adding the critical sections we come to the final version:

```
deposit(m) =                          remove(m) =
  begin local x                         begin local x
    wait(framnum)                         wait(mesnum)
    when s do                             when r do
      selectempty(x);                       selectfull(x);
        EMPTY_x ← false                     FULL_x ← false
    od                                    od
    mailbox_x ← m                         m ← mailbox_x
    FULL_x ← true                         EMPTY_x ← true
    signal(mesnum)                        signal(framnum)
  end                                   end
```

The arrays EMPTY and FULL can be efficiently implemented if both arrays are coded as bit vectors. Test operations on bits are very efficient in most machines.

PROBLEMS

1. Suppose a computer configuration has n disk units (n > 1) which are used as backing store devices. Process DC_i controls the data transmission to and from the i-th disk unit. Two communication policies are considered:

a. Each process P_j and DC_i has a message queue. Page frames are identified by a number pair (d,k), where d is the number of a disk unit and k the index of the frame on disk d. The main store is named disk $d = 0$. Each process P_j controls the moving of its own pages. If a process needs a free frame on one of the disks or in the main store, it can request one by calling a system function which remains unspecified here. A process P_j needs the assistance of a DC_i for an actual data transfer.

b. A process P_j possesses two queues, one for listing data transmission requests, one for receiving answers. A process has no control over the absolute location of its pages. Instead, its address space is defined in a page table whose entries carry a tag indicating whether or not the corresponding page is directly accessible. A process can ask to make a particular page accessible (or inaccessible) by placing a message in its request queue. An additional process, called the page manager, scans the request queues, interprets the space requests and sends off the transfer requests to the disk controllers. The page manager has one message queue for receiving the answers from the disk controllers and translates these answers into transfer completion notifications which it sends to the processes P_j.

Devise for both strategies the layout of those messages which describe requests and those which describe answers to requests. Discuss which information is known by default.

2. The batch system discussed in section 2.2 contains various communicating processes. For each communication describe the layout of the messages and characterize the communication as master-slave, dialogue system, or mailing system. Do the same for the communication with the teletype controller and swapper in the timesharing system discussed in section 2.5.

3. A system has n line printers, $n > 1$. The line printers can be used in a dialogue communication or in a mailing system. If the first arrangement is chosen, a process first requests a line printer and, after getting one, sends lines to be printed one by one to the allocated line printer. When all lines have been printed, the process releases the line printer. If a mailbox system is implemented, a process prepares its output as a sequence of lines before it sends anything to the line printers. When all the output is ready it sends a message to the central mailbox for all printers in which it requests the printing of its output. Design both systems. Specify the system functions that must be available in each of the systems and discuss the layout of the messages. Try to compare the two systems by discussing some of their merits and drawbacks.

4. We consider some properties of the mailbox communication for which the procedures deposit and remove are used.

a. Prove that in the one sender-one receiver case, a frame x cannot be accessed simultaneously by sender and receiver if we use the second version of the procedures.
b. Suppose we replace the two arrays EMPTY and FULL by one array STATE whose entries have one of the values empty, full, or in use. "In use" is the result of selection and holds until the mark-instruction. Investigate whether this implementation is acceptable in the many senders-many receivers case.
c. Prove that at all times the number of empty frames is less than or equal to the counter of eventname framnum. Prove from this property that the action of selecting an empty frame in deposit is always successful.

5. A fixed area of the main store is reserved for messages (the message pool). A link field is added to each message which points to the next message of its queue. The last message points back to the first, that is, a queue is implemented as a circular list. The empty frames are all linked together in one list and all messages are supposed to require the same amount of space. Each queue is identified by a header whose content points to the last message if the queue is not empty. All headers are listed in a unique queue table, implemented as an array. The number of messages in a queue is restricted. The procedures remove and deposit have two parameters, m and q, where m represents a message and q the index of a header in the queue table. Reprogram deposit and remove for this case. Write programs for deposit and remove which fit the specifications above.

5.2 THE DESIGN OF A MESSAGE SWITCHING FACILITY

5.2.1 An operating system modifies the bare hardware into a machine which supports the concurrent execution of user programs. It does so by hiding part of the hardware from the user and substituting in its place commands which are more convenient to use and which enforce the rules for sharing the system facilities. An example of hiding and substitution is the procedure COPY which defines the interface between terminals and user programs in section 2.5. The user programs do not have to be concerned about serving keyboard and teleprinter interrupts and character transmission. All the user program has to do is call the procedure with the proper parameters. An example of enforcing the rules is the code of P and V. If a program is blocked in a P operation, the operating system allocates the free-coming CPU to another program. Another example is the application of resource allocation rules and the avoidance of deadlock states.

A natural method for designing an operating system is the incremental machine design. Following this method several aspects of the original machine are modified one by one until the desired operating system has been achieved. In the preceding chapters we primarily paid attention to two of these aspects, the hardware interrupts and the control of the peripheral devices. The hardware interrupts have been replaced by P and V which at the same time change the machine to a multiprogramming machine. The device control processes remove the need for user programs to operate the I/O devices.

The adjective *incremental* refers to the fact that a newly designed extension builds on what already exists. For example, the device control processes of chapter 4 use P and V for synchronization purposes; interrupts have completely disappeared from their programs. A system built following the incremental design method consists of a number of layers which define a functional hierarchy. A program written for layer L_i (the i-th extension) uses commands which are defined at the lower levels. This implies that the proper functioning of such a program depends on the proper functioning of the lower layer programs. This functional dependency determines the program hierarchy.

In this section we illustrate the incremental design method by designing a process communication facility. In doing so, we actually go one step backwards in the hierarchy, because this extension builds only on the multiprogramming layer and not on device control. The communication facility makes it possible for processes to send messages to one another. This feature is also useful for user programs which send requests to I/O control processes. Therefore, the multiprogramming extension comes first in the program hierarchy, followed by this new communication facility, while the control of the peripheral devices can be rewritten to use both facilities.

5.2.2 The communication facility will replace P and V by a set of procedures which allow the user processes to communicate. Processes are classified as sending or receiving processes (a process may belong to both categories). A sender process has a sender queue and a receiver process has a receiver queue. When a message is sent from a process P_i to a process P_j, it is placed in receiver queue RQ_j. When P_j sends an answer to P_i, a message is placed in sender queue SQ_i (see figure 5.2a).

All messages are stored in a storage area to which the processes have access only through the procedures defined by the communication facility. The procedures relevant to our discussion are:

```
buycredit(n)
send(m,j)          receive(m)
waitanswer(m)      sendanswer(m,i)
```

Procedure buycredit determines how many messages a particular process may have in the message pool. This procedure assures that a process is not able to monopolize the message storage area.

After preparing a message, process P_i calls send(m,j) to transmit message

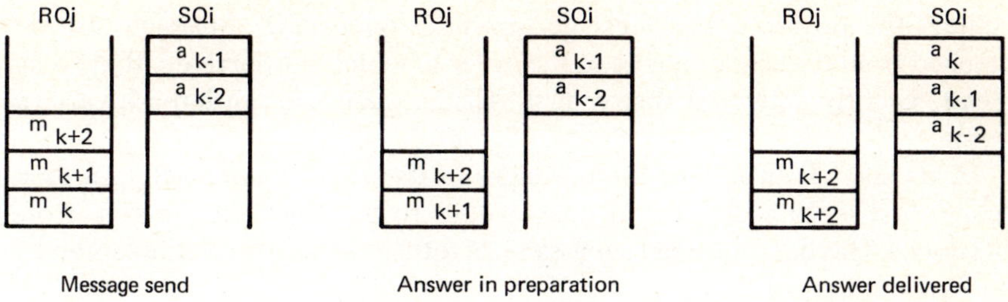

Figure 5.2a Questions and answers of processes P_i and P_j

m to receiver queue RQ_j. The procedure appends the index i of the sender to the message so that the receiver can send an answer to sender queue SQ_i. When the sender places a message in RQ_j, the sender's credit is decremented by one.

A process P_i cannot have more unanswered messages than its credit allows. When its credit limit is reached, the sender must call waitanswer (m,i) before it can send another message. (Procedure waitanswer can, of course, be called before the credit limit is reached.) Waitanswer returns the answer to the least recently issued message, but causes a delay if none of the messages of process P_i have been processed by the receivers (that is, if SQ_i is empty). When a message arrives, waitanswer takes it out of the sender queue and increments the sender's credit by one.

The programs of send(m,j) and waitanswer(m) are:

```
send(m,j) =
  if CREDIT_i = 0 then reportlackofcredit
  else
    CREDIT_i ← CREDIT_i − 1
    when rq_j do insert(m into RQ_j) od
    V(question_j)
  fi
    where i is the index of the calling sender process;
      semaphore rq_j prevents an access conflict to receiver queue RQ_j;
      semaphore question_j counts the number of questions in receiver
        queue RQ_j
waitanswer(m) =
  P(answer_i)
  when sq_i do remove(m from SQ_i) od
  CREDIT_i ← CREDIT_i + 1
```

where semaphore $answer_i$ counts the number of messages in sender queue SQ_i and semaphore sq_i gives processes exclusive access to sender queue SQ_i.

The fact that a caller of waitanswer was able to pass $P(answer_i)$ guarantees the presence of a message in sender queue SQ_i. Messages are detached from the sender queue in the order in which they arrived, that is, the least recently delivered answer first. All the queues are ordered by arrival time.

A receiver P_j processes the messages in its receiver queue RQ_j in first-come first-serve order. P_j calls receive(m) to get the next message from its queue. Having processed a message, P_j returns an answer to the sender by calling sendanswer(m,i).

The programs of receive(m) and sendanswer(m,i) are

```
receive(m) =
    P(question_j)
    when rq_j do remove(m from RQ_j) od
    return(m)
```

where j is the index of the receiver process.

```
sendanswer(m,i) =
    when sq_i do insert(m into SQ_i) od
    V(answer_i)
```

5.2.3 The production of messages is limited by the credit policy allowing the senders to have only a certain number of unanswered questions. This credit policy makes it possible to set aside a finite storage area in which all messages can be stored. However, the policy does not guarantee that messages will actually be removed from the pool in due time. As it stands, the communication facility is not able to cope with the malfunctioning of a receiver or a sender. If a receiver does not work properly and does not process a particular message owing to internal errors, that message takes up space forever and its sender will never receive an answer. As a result, the sender's maximal credit is effectively decreased by one.

The system must protect itself against malfunctioning processes. For that purpose we design a special receiver Rt and a special sender St which belong to the communication system. Receiver Rt and sender St are activated at regular time intervals through an external timer, like the one discussed in chapter 2. Messages will be tagged with their time of arrival in a queue. The function of Rt and St is to clear the queues of all messages which remain in a queue longer than a certain time interval. The length of this interval is determined by the communication facility.

This new strategy puts a critical time constraint on senders and receivers. Both questions and answers must be received within the given time interval or else they will be deleted from their queue. The special receiver Rt can at least send an answer to the unlucky sender whose question was not properly received, telling the sender that its question was not answered in time. The special sender St, however, can do nothing else other than delete an overdue answer, assuming that the sender is at fault. The critical time interval selected must be large enough so that processes, under all normal circumstances, will react to the messages being sent and answered.

The special receiver Rt cannot wait on semaphore $question_j$. Since it is trying to delete overdue questions, it should not wait if a particular queue is empty. On the other hand, when procedure receive successfully passed $P(answer_i)$, Rt should not get a chance to remove a message just before procedure receive gets to it. This potential access conflict can be resolved by a critical section programmed in Rt and in procedure receive, using semaphore "$cleanrq_j$". It is likewise necessary to prevent an access conflict between special sender St and procedure waitanswer. Another semaphore, "$cleansq_i$", serves that purpose. The modification of the procedures receive and waitanswer consists of embedding the procedure body respectively in the critical sections

when $cleanrq_j$ *do . . . od*

and

when $cleansq_i$ *do . . . od*

The program of Rt is

```
special receiver Rt =
  local j = index of first Receiver Queue; set timelimit
  repeat
    when cleanrq_j do
    when rq_j do
      repeat local ptr = ref leastrecentmessageinRQ_j
        $ a link field of a list element of a ref variable
        $ a ref variable is a pointer to a data object
      until arrival time(ptr) > timelimit do
      mark(message(ptr), "no answer")
      P(question_j)
      send(ptr to senderof(message(ptr)))
    od od od
      j ← index of next Receiver Queue
  until all Receiver Queues have been inspected
```

The program of ST can easily be derived from this program.

The communication facility is an implementation of a mailing system discussed in the preceding section. The communication of processes which use this facility does not need to be programmed in line using P and V. Building such a layer has the great advantage that it can be tested and debugged independently of the layers below and the higher ones to come. If the communication is coded in line using P and V, one has to verify in each place that it has been correctly programmed. Moreover, the self-contained facility makes it much easier to guarantee that the user programs cannot violate the rules or have an adverse effect on each other's results.

PROBLEMS

1. It seems as if a sender can get more than its initial credit if it calls procedure waitanswer a sufficient number of times, because this procedure increments CREDIT unconditionally. Show that a sender trying this will get itself in trouble. Would it be necessary to modify procedures waitanswer and send to test for either underflow or overflow of CREDIT compared to the initially bargained amount? Argue that such a modification is of less importance to the proper functioning of the communication facility than the extension of the clean-up processes St and Rt. Why is it not necessary to introduce a credit policy for the receiver processes?

2. Suppose all the sender processes get the same amount of initial credit. Procedure buycredit then becomes superfluous. The messages are now stored in an array whose rows correspond to the sender processes and whose number of columns equals the credit. It is assumed that the messages and the number of senders are small enough so that the space for the message array can be reserved permanently. It is assumed, furthermore, that the average number of messages in a row is so small that the receivers can afford to scan the messages and rows one by one when looking for a next message. Program the four communication procedures and the clean-up processes given these specifications.

3. It seems on first sight unnecessary to introduce the additional critical sections

$$\textit{when}\ \text{cleanrq}_j\ \textit{do} \ldots \textit{od}$$

and

$$\textit{when}\ \text{cleansq}_i\ \textit{do} \ldots \textit{od},$$

because the critical sections using semaphores rq_j and sq_i already ensure exclusive access to, respectively, receiver queue RQ_j and sender queue SQ_j.

a. Give an example of what goes wrong if the critical sections are not added.
b. Why is it not necessary to embed the procedures send and sendanswer in those critical sections?

4. It is possible for the processes using the communication facility to run into a deadlock; (for example, process P_1 sends a question q_1 to process P_2 while P_2 sends a question q_2 to P_1 and both decide to wait first for an answer before sending an answer to the other process). Consider two proposals to avoid such deadlocks by the additional rules:

a. If a process P_i has a right to send a question to a process P_j, then P_j never has the right to send a question to P_i.
b. The set of processes is partitioned in a number of fixed classes. These classes form a hierarchy in the sense that a process in $class_i$ has the right to send a question to a process in $class_j$ if and only if $i < j$.

Rule (a) defines a hierarchical relation between every pair of processes, rule (b) defines a class hierarchy. Investigate which rule provides a sufficient condition for preventing communication deadlocks.

5. The way in which machine MS is specified in this section makes it possible for a sender to find the answers to its questions in an order different from that in which the questions were sent. If this leads to ambiguities, the problem can be solved as long as all the sender processes do not use more than a credit of one. Suppose, however, that we reject such a trivial solution and nevertheless require that answers be received in the order in which messages were sent. The senders can buy a credit of more than one and they may use all of their credit. Modify the four procedures and the clean-up processes so the strict question-answer ordering rule is obeyed.

5.3 DEVICE COMMUNICATION

5.3.1 Communication between a central processor and the peripheral devices requires special attention because the implementation of service facilities must follow the rules prescribed by the hardware. Device communication is discussed with respect to a classification of hardware features. This classification is based on the capability of a peripheral device control unit or channel to process:

a. A single command
b. A batch or block of commands
c. A queue of linked commands

The simplest form of device control unit sends a notification to a central processor when it completes a command and then waits until it receives another command from the central processor. The notification consists of no more than setting a READY flag as an indication that the device can accept the next command. After setting the READY flag, the device (the peripheral device control unit or channel) waits for the next command by continually inspecting the BUSY flag. It starts interpreting the command buffer as soon as it finds the BUSY flag set.

In section 4.5 the behavior of the device was described by

device: *repeat*
    repeat inspect $BUSY_k$ *until* $BUSY_k = 1$
        $BUSY_k \leftarrow 0$
        interpret command
        record the outcome
        $READY_k \leftarrow 1$
    until device halts

The central processor does not transmit the data; all it does is send a command and set the BUSY flag. The BUSY flag is set by the command $BUSY_k \leftarrow 1$. As soon as the device detects a one in $BUSY_k$, it resets $BUSY_k$ to zero and interprets whatever it finds in its command buffer as the current command.

After finishing the current command, the state information of $device_k$ reflects what happened during command execution. The occurrence of a parity error while a command is executed is reported in the state of $device_k$ and is detectable after completion of the command. The status of a channel or device in many machines contains a set of reserved fields for error reports which are typical for that device. (Sometimes an error causes a particular kind of interrupt which identifies the nature of the error.) The normal outcome of executing a command is usually characterized by the absence of any error report.

Not reflected in the representation of $device_k$ is the possible side effect that setting the READY flag can have. In section 3.5 we discussed the function of the $MASK_k$ and found that an interrupt occurs at the moment that the condition $(READY_k, MASK_k) = (1,1)$ becomes true (provided that no interrupts at higher levels are pending or in operation). This condition becomes true either if $MASK_k$ is set to one while an interrupt coming from $device_k$ is pending: $(READY_k, MASK_k) = (1,0)$, or if the state is $(READY_k, MASK_k) = (0,1)$ and the device assigns a one to $READY_k$ after finishing a command. We discussed in section 3.5 how the effect of an interrupt can be interpreted as the operation signal($READY_k$).

5.3.2 When an interrupt occurs, two things must be done: first, the process on whose behalf the command was executed must be notified of the completion, including an error report, and second, another command must be sent to the device. This second step involves a slight timing problem. Mechanical devices such as card readers or line printers have the awkward property of coming to a complete stop if a next command is not presented within a short period of time after finishing a command. If this critical time constraint is not met, the device must be started again at the next command, causing it to operate at a reduced speed.

The critical time constraint is even more serious for a device such as a disk or a drum. Information on such a device is usually divided into blocks with several blocks on one track (see figure 5.3a). The critical time constraint is determined by the rotation speed of the device and the length of a small gap that is left unused between two consecutive blocks. The control system must give the next command within a time interval equal to the time it takes a reading head to pass a gap. If a command is not given within this time limit, the device is too late for the next sector. If the control system is consistently too late, the page transfer slows down by a factor of two or more.

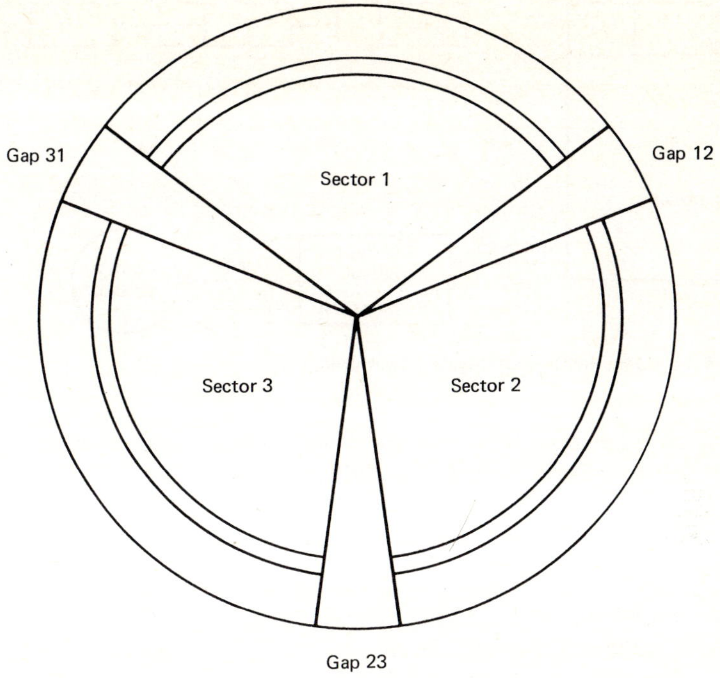

Figure 5.3a Three blocks in three sectors on a disk track

Because of this critical time constraint, the device control process must first place the next command (if any) in the device command buffer before it sends a completion notification for the command just completed. If the command queue is empty, the control process should not wait for the first command to arrive in the queue, because this would cause an unpredictable delay in sending the completion notification. However, this implies that if a command is placed in an empty queue, the device must be restarted. In order to minimize restarting, the control process should not delete the current command from the queue until it has received the READY signal from the device. Following this reasoning, we come to the organization of device communication described below (see figure 5.3b).

A process sends a command (m,i) to command queue CQ_k, where m is the command proper and i the source identification. If the queue is empty, it also places m in the device command buffer. The process is then free to do other things (preparing another command, for instance). When it cannot continue unless the device has processed the command, it waits for the completion notification by calling waitanswer(e), where e is the formal name for the error report it receives in return.

The device control process waits until awakened by the interrupt routine. After copying the error report from the device command buffer, it sends the

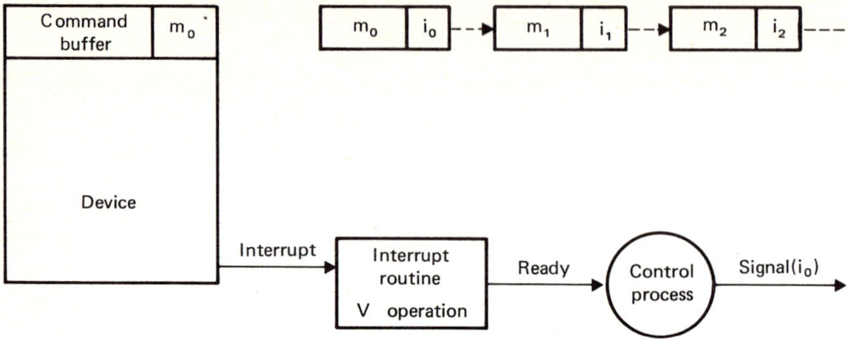

Figure 5.3b Organization of device communication

next command (if any) and deletes the completed command from the queue. Finally, it forwards the completion notification.

5.3.3 The programs for sending a command and for the device control process are:

```
procedure command((m,i),CQ_k) =
  when CQ_k accessible do
    insert((m,i) into CQ_k)
    increment(queue length)
    if queuelength_k = 1 then
      command buffer_k ← firstcommand(CQ_k)
      signal(BUSY_k)
    fi
  od

Device Control Process: local errorreport, m, j
  repeat wait(READY_k)
        errorreport ← devicestatus_k
        when CQ_k accessible do
          if queuelength_k > 1 then
            commandbuffer_k ← secondcommand(CQ_k)
            signal(BUSY_k)
          fi
          remove((m,j) from CQ_k)
          decrement(queue length)
        od
        sendanswer(errorreport,j)
  until DCP halt
```

Deleting a command from the command queue *after* the device has processed is crucial after all. It guarantees that when a process sends a command and finds the queue empty, the device is not still busy processing the last command; otherwise it would overwrite this command with its own.

In the batch system of section 2.2 the order of sending the next command and the completion notification of the preceding command is the wrong way around. In that particular case we can afford to send the completion notification first, because this action is a simple instruction which resets an element of a fixed vector to zero. This action is quite unlike sendanswer in that it contains no potential delay. Thus, in that particular example the critical time constraint can still be met.

5.3.4 Interestingly enough, we don't need a device control process at all if we add the requirement that a sender must immediately wait for an answer. All we need is a little change in the interrupt routine and most of the control program can be added to the program of procedure command.

We reserve a field destination in the work space of the interrupt routine and change its program so that it performs the operation signal($psem_i$) instead of signal($READY_k$), where $psem_i$ is the private semaphore of the sender process P_i. The procedure command not only sends a command to the queue, but also waits until the device is done, places the next command (if any), and deletes the first command from the queue. The program of procedure command is (implementing the wait immediately rule):

```
procedure command((m,i),CQk) =
  when CQk accessible do
    insert((m,i) into CQk)
    increment(queue length)
    if queuelengthk = 1 then
      commandbufferk ← firstcommand(CQk)
      destinationk ← firstprocess(CQk)
      signal(BUSYk)
    fi
  od
  wait(psemi); errorreportk ← device statusk
  when CQk accessible do
    if queuelength > 1 then
      commandbufferk ← secondcommand(CQk)
      destinationk ← secondprocess(CQk)
      signal(BUSYk)
    fi
    delete(firstcommand from CQk); decrement(queue length)
  od
end
```

In many cases, however, the extra requirement of immediately waiting is not very practical. Consider as an example the management of accessible and inaccessible pages. Accessible pages reside in primary store and, as the name expresses, information on such a page can be referenced directly. Inaccessible pages reside in secondary storage. Information residing on an inaccessible page cannot directly be referenced. An attempt to do so results in a page fault. Suppose that one of the available operations on pages is SWAP(p_k,p_j) where p_j and p_k are two pages owned by the process that calls procedure SWAP. The procedure has no effect if both pages are accessible or both are inaccessible. However, if they are not of the same kind, the result of SWAP is that the accessible page is now inaccessible and the page that was inaccessible is now accessible. The process which used SWAP for pages in different states traded one page for the other. Procedure SWAP must send two commands, one to swap out the accessible page and one to get the inaccessible page into the main store. If there is a device controller, the process could first send both commands and then wait for the two completion notifications; without the device controller, the process cannnot send the second command until it received an answer to the first. This may imply an extra restart of the device and a waste of CPU time, because the device and the process are forced to operate serially.

5.3.5 The information unit which a device can handle in one command is much smaller than the unit which suits the logic of the processes. Two examples:

1. Transfer of a coherent piece of information, for instance a page, must be split in single word transfers to be handled by a disk, whereas the device controller should send notifications in terms of whole pages.
2. A line printer builds up a line image as a sequence of storage words, whereas the logical unit is a printed line.

The discrepancy between the two units leads to numerous unnecessary signals unless the command handling is modified. This problem has been recognized by hardware designers and has been solved by some additional features of hardware devices. The first modification is in the processing of a certain type of commands. A chunk of information dumped on or fetched from a relatively fast device such as a magnetic tape unit or a disk or a drum occupies an area of consecutive storage cells. Instead of sending a command for each separate word of such an area, the device accepts a command which indicates a starting address and a count. The address and the count determine the area. The device treats the command as a program loop, decrementing the count by one for each word transferred and it terminates the command execution when the count reaches zero. It is not necessary to send a command to the device for each word. The device control process is not signalled until the whole area of consecutive storage cells has been transferred.

Another technique, called *blocking* of commands, allows the control system to form its own dispatch units. It requires quite a bit more sophistication of the device in the following sense: instead of a single command, the device accepts a batch of commands arranged in a linked list. When the device is finished with a command it automatically advances to the next command in the batch (if any) without the help of the device control process. The device finds the next command of a batch through a link field which is attached to every command. The device gives the READY signal when it has processed the whole batch of commands.

The technique of blocking commands can be useful for slow serial devices such as a card reader or a line printer. Since a card image is composed of a set of columns and a page is composed of a set of lines, a list of commands can be assembled to create dispatch units that correspond to the notion of reading a card or printing a page.

When the technique of blocking commands is applied, the control process is responsible for sending a new batch to the device. The last technique to be discussed here, *chaining of commands*, obviates this need. The device advances to the next command through the link field of the current command just as in the case of blocking commands. However, in contrast with the blocking technique, the device does not have to observe batch boundaries and can start itself again when a command arrives in an empty command queue. How this is done is explained below.

Up to this point, setting BUSY $\leftarrow$ 1 indicates that there is one command available to the device, and setting READY $\leftarrow$ 1 indicates the the device has processed one command. Command chaining lifts the restriction of counting only up to one. The device control unit is extended with a BUSY count, Bc, and a READY count, Rc. They count respectively the number of commands available to the device and the number of commands processed by the device. Before fetching the next command, the device attempts to decrement Bc by one, but will proceed and do so only if the value of Bc is positive. After completing a command, the device increments Rc by one. In addition to incrementing Rc, the device sets the READY flag if and only if it changes the value Rc = 0 into Rc = 1. The procedure command increments Bc_k by one when it inserts a command in the device queue and the device control process decreases Rc_k by one when it deletes a command from the queue.

The program of a device which can handle a command chain is

```
device_k: repeat
              while Bc_k = 0 do "nothing" od
              decrement(Bc_k)
              commandfield_k ← linkfield(commandfield_k)
              commandbuffer_k ← command(commandfield_k)
              ⟨interpret command⟩
              copy(devicestatus_k into command(commandfield_k))
              if Rc_k = 0 then READY_k ← 1 fi
              increment Rc_k
          until device halt
```

The next command is loaded by copying it into the command buffer; the command is not delinked from the command queue.

The programs of procedure command and the device control process are now entirely released from sending a command to the device.

```
procedure command((m,i),device queue_k) =
   when devicequeue_k access do
      insert((m,i) into DQ_k)
      increment(Bc_k)
   od
Device Control Process: local m, j
   repeat
      if Rc_k > 0 then READY_k ← 0
      else wait(READY_k) fi
      when device queue_k access do
         remove((m,j) from DQ_k)
         sendanswer(m to j)
         decrement(Rc_k)
      od
   until DCP halt
```

If the control process finds $Rc = 0$, it must wait until the device finishes another command. In that case, the device wakes up the control process when it sets the READY flag; because $MASK_k$ is set in wait($READY_k$), an interrupt is caused when both get set. The interrupt routine, when activated, performs signal ($READY_k$). Note that the order in which both the device and its control process operate on the READY flag and counter Rc is essential.

It is assumed that the increment and decrement operations applied to Bc_k and Rc_k are single store access instructions which act as critical sections. If interleaving were possible, the operations could leave wrong values in the variables Bc_k and Rc_k.

PROBLEMS

1. Suppose a line printer, LP, can handle command blocking. LP has a line buffer of 120 characters, partitioned in 30 sections of four character positions each. An LP command has two parameters, the index of a section and the address of a storage cell. LP transfers the contents of this cell to the section of the buffer indicated by the first parameter. LP prints out the line buffer as soon as a "newline" or a "newpage" character is placed in the line buffer, or if a character is placed in the 120th position of the line buffer.

The design goal is to allow a process to send the output of a whole program to LP in one message. This message will consist of a single data item, the address of the first line. A line image consists of a header followed by a number of cells that contain the successive characters of the line. The header contains the number of cells of the line and a pointer to the cell where the next line begins (if any). It is assumed that printing is reliable enough so that the processes which produce the output do not need notification when the printing is done. The only thing to be done when the device has finished a block of commands is to release the space occupied by those commands.

Printer control is divided between two parallel processes, the LP controller and the decoder. The latter receives the output messages of the processes, translates such a message into a series of command blocks, one for each line, and passes these blocks on to LP. Write a program for the decoder process.

2. A disk D has 2080 storage words per track and a transfer rate of 40,000 words per second. The system works with a block size of 512 words, so four blocks fit on one track. The work to be done in between two block transfers consists of the interrupt routine, which saves the CPU state of the current process and signals the controller, and reloading the CPU state of the controller. Assuming that the disk controller is already waiting to give the next command, estimate for a one-microsecond cycle time machine whether or not the gaps between pages on disk D are large enough to meet the critical time constraint. Would blocking or chaining of commands improve the situation?

3. Programming control processes which operate on data that they share with hardware devices is always difficult because the only form of critical section available is the exclusive access to a storage cell. The programs of a command chaining $device_k$ and its control process contain conditional operations on $READY_k$ using the counter Rc. Verify that the operations on these variables are correct in the sense that the controller cannot be waiting while there are completed commands, or process a command that has not yet been finished by the device.

4. In section 2.2 we discussed the idea of a see-saw buffer: while one half of the buffer is filled by an input device, the other half is being transferred elsewhere. If command chaining or blocking of commands can be applied, the link fields of the two halves could be set to point to each other permanently.

   a. Investigate whether or not the counters Bc and Rc provide sufficient control in the case of command chaining to prevent the device and its controller from getting too far ahead of each other.
   b. In case of blocking commands, the device control process must record and maintain the state of the see-saw buffer. Write the controller program for this case.

5. Suppose that the pages of information which are shared among several processes are all recorded in a single table, SPT. An entry in SPT contains state information, a counter and a pointer to the location of the shared page. The state information tells whether the shared page is accessible, in which case the pointer is the address of a cell in primary store, or inaccessible, in which case the pointer is the address of a cell in secondary store. The state information can also reflect whether or not the shared page is in transition from one level of store to the other. The counter indicates the number of processes that share the use of a page when it is accessible.

Processes can ask for access to a shared page by calling procedure "request(x)" where x is the index in SPT of the desired page. When a process loses interest in a page it calls procedure "release(x)" where x is again the index in SPT of the shared page in question. Program the procedures request and release assuming command chaining and assuming that a process needs a completion notification in all cases.

5.4 COMMUNICATION WITH THE OPERATOR CONSOLE

5.4.1 One terminal of a general purpose computing facility has the special function of allowing a human operator to assist the running programs. Messages may be sent to the operator console where the operator can read them and take appropriate action. A request for mounting a particular magnetic tape on an indicated tape unit is a typical example of such a message. After having processed a message, the operator sends an answer telling the sender that the request has been satisfied. In this section we discuss some of the operating system facilities which serve the communication with the operator console.

A terminal is a combination of two independent devices, a keyboard and a printer (or scope). In section 2.5 we discussed how these two devices can be controlled by two processes, KCP and PCP, one for keyboard control and one for printer control.

A user program calls COPY(in,x) for transferring the contents of its input buffer into a storage area pointed at by x. If the user process wants to write output, it places a line image in the output buffer by calling COPY(out,y), where y points to the storage area where the line image is. Copying the input buffer must not coincide with typing, and filling the output buffer must not coincide with printing. The version of the control programs based on interrupts is found in section 2.5. Converting that version to one using wait and signal is left as an exercise to the reader (see problem 1).

5.4.2 We consider several possible ways of organizing the communication between a set of user processes and the human operator. One simple policy requires that the operator give a final answer to one question before accepting the next question. A more advanced policy allows the operator to tell a process to hold on for a moment while other questions are answered.

We use the term *conversation* for the set of actions which begin when a process sends a message to the human operator and end when the sender receives the final answer. The format of all possible conversations between a process and the operator is strictly defined by the operating system. All the possible questions a process can ask are listed in a table. Each question has a predefined set of answers. A question sent by a process consists of the index of an entry in the question table and the necessary parameters that go with this particular question. For example, a process may assemble the question (14, NH02.5,2) where the question list contains

14. remove ⟨tape number⟩ from tape unit ⟨number⟩.

It is a nuisance if the operator has to look up the text of the question which goes with a certain number (though many operators have shown a remarkable memory for such associations). Therefore the list of possible questions is not only kept on paper, but also in the machine. When a process sends a message such as the one above, the operating system decodes and prints it in textual form on the operator console:

14. remove NH02:5 from tape unit 2.

Readability of computer logs is well worth the cost of generating and printing the text of such messages.

If the simple console communication policy is adopted, only one conversation may take place at a time. A question Q_i must be followed by answer A_i before any process is permitted to ask question Q_{i+1}. The interface between the user processes and the operator console consists of the two procedures WRITE outbuf and READ inbuf. The buffer "outbuf" is used for sending a question to the operator and the buffer "inbuf" for getting the answer. It is assumed throughout this discussion that a message is no longer than a printer line so that it fits in both outbuf and inbuf, and can be written or read in one call of WRITE or READ.

The programs for READ and WRITE are very simple.

procedure READ(x) =
begin wait(inbuf full); copy(inbuf into x); signal(inbuf empty) *end*
procedure WRITE(y) =
begin wait(outbuf empty); copy(outbuf from y); signal(outbuf full) *end*

The programs assure that two processes can neither simultaneously write into outbuf nor simultaneously read from inbuf. This implies that a question Q_i cannot be overwritten by question Q_{i+1} before Q_i has been printed and that the operator cannot overwrite answer A_i before inbuf has been read out. However, if the processes use the procedures WRITE and READ without further restrictions, there is nothing that prevents message

Q_{i+1} from being typed before answer A_i has been given. Even if the operator did not give any answer at all, the flow of questions could not be stopped. This problem was earlier discussed in section 4.3.

There are two ways of implementing the policy of strictly sequential conversations. The first implementation assumes that a user is willing to wait for an answer immediately after asking a question. In that case the whole conversation can be cast in a critical section of this form:

```
procedure ask operator(x) =
begin local m = decode(x)
  when conversation permitted do WRITE(m); READ(m) od
    x ← recode(m)
end
```

where the operation "decode" translates the numeric format of a message as generated by a process into the textual format that can be read by the operator, and operation "recode" translates the answer. The critical section guarantees that question Q_{i+1} cannot be asked until answer A_i has been received.

Compared to the speed of computations, and even compared to I/O operations, the preparation of an answer by the operator is a very long process (for example, removing a tape and placing it in a particular place on a shelf). Thus, while the operator prepares an answer, a process may use its time to do something else instead of waiting. In that case the critical section solution is inadequate, because it relies on the fact that each process waits for an answer immediately after asking a question.

5.4.3 Another implementation of the strictly sequential conversations is achieved by introducing a conversation control process, CCP, which has the monopoly of interaction with the operator console. Instead of calling WRITE and READ, the processes send a message to process CCP, which sends it on to the operator, waits for an answer, and dispatches this answer to the sender (see figure 5.4a).

This policy can be implemented on a machine with message sending facilities as discussed in section 5.2. A process calls send(m,CCP) which has the effect of placing a message in CCP's message queue. The process can determine at its convenience when it needs to call waitanswer (see section 5.2).

The program for process CCP is very straightforward:

```
Conversation Control Process:
  local k,m,x
  repeat receive(m)
    k ← m.processindex; x ← decode(m)
    WRITE(x); READ(x)
    m ← recode(x); sendanswer(m,k)
  until CCP halt
```

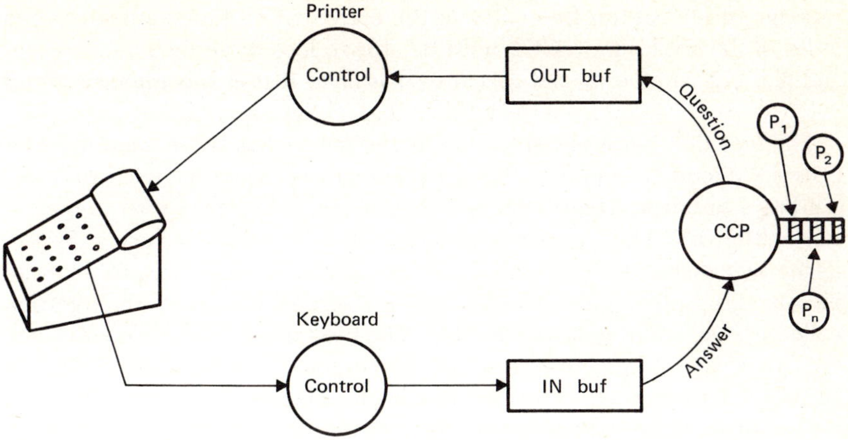

Figure 5.4a Communication with the operator console teletype

The sequential conversation policy is not adequate if the operator has the option of postponing a final answer for one reason or another. It is very convenient for the operator to have this option; for instance, the operator may not be able to immediately satisfy a request because of other demands on the operator's time. Moreover, it gives the operator a chance to prepare answers for several questions at the same time or, to a certain extent, reverse the order of answering questions. This is useful if, for example, a request to remove a tape follows a request for mounting one on the same unit.

The more advanced policy permits the operator to break off a conversation and send a final answer at a later moment. Also, several conversations may proceed simultaneously up to a fixed upperbound N. To break off a conversation, the operator sends a message asking the sender to wait. This changes the behavior of a sender from a single waitanswer call essentially to *repeat* waitanswer *until* final answer. The calls on waitanswer may in reality be separated by other actions the process performs in the meantime.

Since answers are not necessarily generated in the same order in which the questions arrive, the conversation control process must know, when it receives an answer, to which question it corresponds. It is therefore necessary for CCP to pass a conversation identification to the operator which can be used to forward the answer to the right place. The index of the sender could be used for this purpose, but would imply that a process cannot have more than one conversation open at a time. Such a restriction is not necessary if CCP numbers the conversations. On the other hand, CCP must map this number into a process index when it forwards the answer.

Since we wish to restrict the number of conversations to a maximum, N, CCP can maintain an array of N elements, one for each conversation. The conversation number is used as the array index. When CCP receives a new message, it allocates a free entry in the conversation table and stores the index of the sender in it. CCP must be able to look at an incoming answer and find out whether or not this answer is final. It uses this information to delete a conversation from the table so that a new conversation can start.

The fact that questions and answers are not in strictly sequential order causes a dilemma similar to the one encountered when we tried to order sending a command completion notification and sending the next command (see section 5.3). The question is: should CCP wait until a message arrives in its message queue or READ inbuf and forward an answer? The problem can be solved by splitting the control into two parallel processes: the question collector, Qc, and the dispatcher, Dp. The former receives the messages in the queue and enters conversations in the conversation table, the latter READs and forwards the answers, and deletes a conversation when it finds a final answer. Since both processes operate on the conversation table, care must be taken that no conflict arises when the two processes try to access the table simultaneously.

5.4.4 The processes Qc and Dp are described in the programs below. The conversation table is represented by array CT.

```
Question Collector Qc: local k,m,x
repeat wait(number of conversations)
  receive(m)
  when access to CT permitted do
    k ← index of free CT entry; CT_k ← m.processindex
  od
  x ← decode(m); WRITE((x,k))
until Qc halt
Dispatcher Dp: local i,k,m,x
repeat READ((x,k)); m ← recode(x)
  when access to CT permitted do
    i ← CT_k
    if x is a final answer then CT_k ← free; signal(number of conversation) fi
  od
  sendanswer(m,i)
until Dp halt
```

The eventname "number of conversations" is initialized to the upper-bound N.

Once the decision has been made to keep a record of the current conversations, there is an opportunity of implementing additional rules which improve the reliability and usefulness of the operator console communication. As an example we discuss a method for decreasing the possibility that the operator can forget to answer a message.

We compensate for the operator's forgetfulness with the following addi-

N = 4

CT before answer to P_9				
Sender index	12	9	12	7
Retardation count	0	1	4	1

CT after answer to P_9				
Sender index	12	9	12	7
Retardation count	1	0	5	2

↑ Conversation 3

Figure 5.4b Operator forgetting conversation P_{12}

tional rule: let r be a given number greater than or equal to N; every set of r consecutive answers must contain at least one answer for every existing conversation. That is to say, if the operator does not address a particular conversation in a series of r answers, it is assumed that this conversation has been forgotten. In such a case the corrective action to be taken is to remind the operator of the existence of the conversation in question.

To implement this rule, each element of CT is extended with a counter in which the control processes record the order in which the operator responded to the existing question. When Dp forwards an answer as part of conversation k, it resets the counter of conversation k to zero and adds one to all the others (see figure 5.4b). While adding one to the other counters, Dp checks them for overflow which occurs if their value exceeds the constant r.

Process Dp reminds the operator of a particular conversation by printing a DON'T FORGET message on the console printer. It passes as parameter the number of the conversation, which is also known to the operator. The dispatcher now operates on the conversation table in the following manner:

when access to CT permitted *do*
  for i *in* [1:n] *do*
    if $i \neq k$ *then* $CTcount_i \leftarrow CTcount_i + 1$
      if $CTcount_i > r$ *then* WRITE("DON'T FORGET",i)
    fi fi
  od
  $CTcount_k \leftarrow 0$; $i \leftarrow CT_k$
  if x is a final answer *then* $CT_k \leftarrow 0$; signal(number of conversations) *fi*
od

This program is not an exact implementation of the additional rule because it does not force the operator to send an answer to a neglected conversation after receiving the DON'T FORGET message. On the other hand, if the operator does not address the forgotten conversation right away, the DON'T FORGET message will recur.

There are, of course, many variations possible with respect to implementation or additional features of console communication. This section showed the major distinction between sequential and nonsequential console communication and gave an example of how such a system can be improved through implementation of additional rules. Some alternative implementations and features are discussed in the problems that follow.

PROBLEMS

1. The keyboard and printer hardware of a terminal are described by

keyboard hardware:
  repeat
    wait(TBUSY); put typed character in keyboard transmission buffer
      signal(READY)
  until terminal off

  printer hardware:
  repeat wait(PBUSY); print character in printer transmission buffer
    signal(DONE)
  until terminal off

The transmission buffers can hold only one character at a time.

The processes KCP and PCP (respectively for keyboard control and printer control) have been described using interrupts in section 2.5. The interface with user programs is defined in this section by the procedures WRITE and READ. There are two proposals for implementing the echo feature:

a. We use the echo buffer in addition to inbuf and outbuf (see section 2.5).
b. KCP immediately places an input character in the printer transmission buffer to get it printed.

Process KCP competes with process PCP for access to the printer transmission buffer. Write the programs for KCP and PCP using wait and signal instead of interrupts for both proposals and compare their effects.

2. Consider the following variation on the strictly sequential conversation rule. The operator sends not only answers, but can also send a note to a process. A note originates at the console and has a process as destination. The operator does not need an answer. We assume that a note is distinguishable from the questions or answers of an ordinary conversation. Since a note does not cause ambiguity with regard to the current conversation, it can be allowed to occur either in the middle of a conversation or in between two conversations. However, operator notes should have a high priority. That is to say, the console communication control system should

not wait for the next conversation to start while ignoring a note placed by the operator in inbuf. Design the modified sequential conversation system.

3. If the processes that communicate with the operator can be users sitting at a terminal, a greater flexibility of the message text can be allowed. The content of a message can be a string in which a user can place an arbitrary question for the operator. However, a user may make a mistake or change his mind about what he just asked. It would therefore be nice if the user could retract his statement if so desired. Suppose a user can send a message that says RETRACT. The effect of sending such a message is that the operator acknowledges the control system that the RETRACT message has been noticed so that the control system can terminate the conversation. A RETRACT message coming from a process which has no current conversations going is discarded and does not reach the operator at all. Complete the design specification of this additional facility and write the programs of the question collector and the dispatcher.

4. Assume that 80% of all conversations are terminated by one answer and 98% by not more than two answers. We investigate whether this knowledge can be used to reduce the overhead of the overdue message detection, particularly the updating of all the entries in the conversation table every time that an answer is forwarded by the dispatcher. The proposal is to move most of the work from Dp to Qc and simplify it as follows. The process Qc uses a pointer, ptr, which cycles through the conversation table. When a new conversation is started, ptr is advanced from where it was left last time until it points to a free entry. If the pointer passes a non-free entry, it does not skip this element, but it increments the count by one. If the count reaches the value 3, then it is assumed that the operator has neglected this conversation and the DON'T FORGET message is sent. When Dp forwards an answer, it resets the count to zero.

Discuss the merits of this implementation compared to the implementation presented earlier in this section. Write the modified versions of the programs for Qc and Dp using this design.

5. Consider a stricter interpretation of the overdue message rule: as soon as the dispatcher detects that the operator did not pay attention to some conversation in the last r answers, the operator is inhibited from sending another answer, the processes cannot start a new conversation, and Dp informs the operator about the trouble. Normal conversations should not resume until the operator sent a message to the troubled conversation(s).

Revise the programs of Qc and Dp in this sense. (The objective of this exercise is partly to show the superiority of the DON'T FORGET strategy which excels in simplicity and provides an entirely acceptable approximation of the stricter rule.)

5.5 VIRTUAL DEVICES

5.5.1 An important design tool is that of *abstraction*, that is, considering what different objects have in common, while ignoring the differences. The designer may, for instance, abstract from the physical properties of a computer. The notion *inaccessible page* is an abstraction from the physical devices which constitute the backing store. In the context where this notion is used, it does not matter whether the secondary storage device is a drum or a disk or any number of those devices. All that is relevant is the set of operations which make it possible for a page to be converted from inaccessible into accessible and vice versa.

It is very common for abstractions to be built upon abstractions. For instance, this is the case if an operating system is composed as a set of layers (see section 5.2). The P, V extension abstracts from hardware interrupts and from the actual number of CPUs. The communication system abstracts from the layout and space allocation of messages, etc. Another example of abstraction is an automatic paging system. Page-transfer operations make backing store look like a set of message queues in which data transmission requests can be placed. Most of this abstraction is based on a process communication system. We discuss in this section some other cases in which a useful abstraction is based on communication.

5.5.2 Suppose we design a system with a set of processes which can compile, load, and execute user programs. We set as our design objective that the processes must continue executing user programs as long as programs are supplied through one of the input media, but independently of the actual number of input devices. A user control process is not tied to a particular input device. This has the advantage that, if a device fails, the system can still work. In addition, the system does not have to be changed if new devices are added. The processes are also designed to be independent of the speed of the input devices so that an input device can be replaced by a faster one without having to modify the system.

To each process we allocate a receiver queue in which its input will be placed. The receiver queue acts as *the* input device for the process to which it is attached. The queue is called a *virtual input device* or *virtual reader*. The virtual reader consists of a string of messages. A message points to a place in the store in which input data is stored. Figure 5.5a shows a snapshot of the three processes with their virtual readers accepting jobs from three central mailboxes.

Process P_i in figure 5.5a is processing the second input page of job c. Process P_j has just filled its virtual reader with job a. Process P_k is going to select another job. If it selects a job from the mailbox with the short jobs, it will receive job d.

In this example user jobs are divided into three groups: short jobs, medium-size jobs, and long jobs. Such an arrangement makes it possible for jobs to be selected not just by arrival time, but also by characteristics of the job itself (here its size). The purpose of having the three groups is that now a higher priority can be attached to short jobs to shorten their turnaround time (the time which elapses between submitting a job and the time the results are produced).

The major advantage of virtual input devices is that their use does not require a computational process to get involved in assembling input pages from various types of real input devices. The virtual input devices provide the proper abstraction from equipment peculiarities which are irrelevant to the task of the computational processes. The gain is not only flexibility in number and nature of real input devices, but also clarity of system structure.

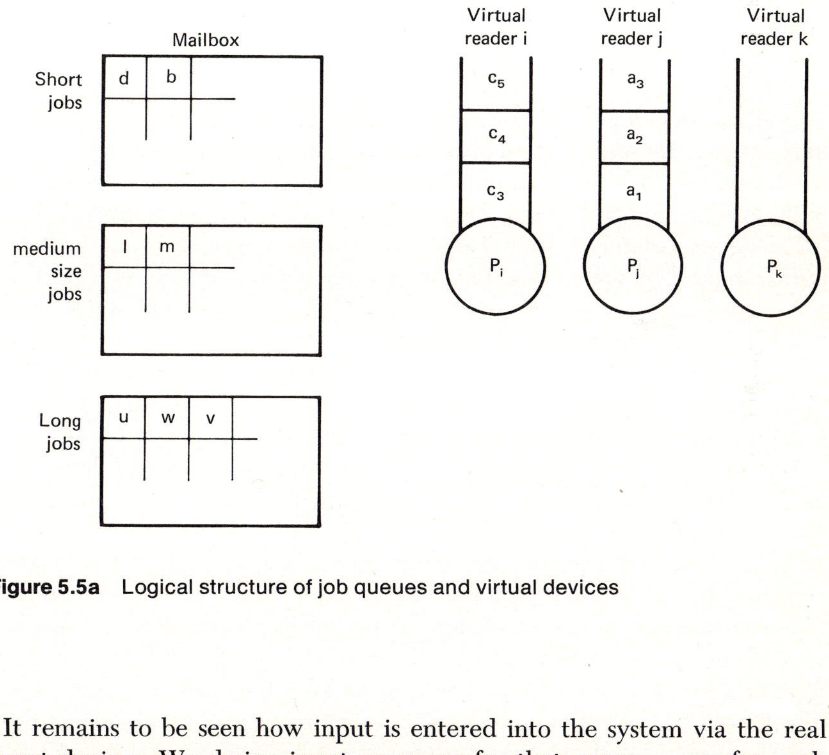

Figure 5.5a Logical structure of job queues and virtual devices

5.5.3 It remains to be seen how input is entered into the system via the real input devices. We design input processes for that purpose, one for each input device. The task of such an input process is to receive input from the device and place it in storage frames of the central mailboxes. The structure of an input process is presented in the program below.

Input Process:
repeat local k ← newqueue; number of frames ← 0
wait(number of input frames)
repeat local f = newframe; i ← 0
repeat command (m(f,i), input device); advance(i)
until eof *or* i ≥ framesize
send(f,k); increment number of frames
until eof
if number of frames small *then* send(k, short job queue)
else if number of frames large *then* send(k, long job queue)
until Input Process halt

An input process builds a new message queue describing the new job. The input process needs a free entry in the queue table for building a new queue. The process counts the number of frames so that at the end it can determine to which mailbox the job must be sent. The operation wait(number of input frames) prevents the system from getting saturated with input pages that cannot be processed. The computational processes must signal the number of input frames when an input page is received from a virtual input device. Once this wait has been passed, the creation of a new input page is allowed. The target address of an input portion is determined by the pair (f,i) where f is a pointer to a frame and i the relative address within that frame. The procedure command has been discussed in section 5.3 on device communication. Depending on the particular input device, it is incremented by the number of storage cells needed for one input portion. For example, a card can be stored in 20 cells, assuming four characters in a cell and 80 columns on a card. If the card is not full (which is normally the case), the amount of cells needed may be substantially less. When a frame is full, it must be appended to the job. When end-of-file is reached, all of the input has arrived, so the job can be placed in the appropriate job queue.

Output devices can be treated in much the same way as input devices. If each of the computational processes is equipped with a virtual input device and a virtual output device, the process looks like a virtual machine able to compile, load and execute user programs in a given input and output format. The translation of input and output from, and into, external representations is hidden from this virtual machine, including the devices performing the necessary transformations. The design of virtual output devices lends itself to a demonstration of the point raised earlier about scheduling. The selection of the job output that should be processed next can be designed with much more sophistication than is possible with ordinary arrival time scheduling.

5.5.4 Suppose the user processes $P_1, \ldots, P_n$ each have a virtual line printer which contains a string of messages pointing to output pages. We assume that an end-of-file indicates the end of a job. The output of the next job does not continue on the same page, but starts on a new page. The output of a job is removed from a virtual printer by an output process (analogous to an input process) which sends the commands to the real output device. Output jobs are classified into two categories, selected, and unselected, depending on whether or not an output process is working on this job. There are two space restrictions on virtual printers; each individual virtual printer may contain not more than one unselected job, and all the virtual printers together may not take up more frames than a given upperbound MOF.

A user process P_i is not allowed to create a new output page unless the two restrictions are met. Once a new frame has been acquired, output can be produced. When an output page has been created, it is placed in the virtual printer. While output pages are added to a job, their number is counted. This information is used later on to determine the status of a virtual printer. When an output job is completed, the output processes are notified through a signal of the eventname "number of output jobs."

An output process does not start until it finds that the number of output jobs is positive. When it starts, it selects a new output job in a way that is discussed in detail later on in this section. Once a virtual printer has been selected, the associated user process is permitted to start another output job while the pages of the current job are being printed one by one. When all the information on an output page has been printed, the number of output frames increases by one.

Before turning our attention to the scheduling issue, we present the programs for output processing as described above.

```
User process Pi produces output:
  wait(number of unselected jobsi)
  repeat local f; local number of frames = 0
    wait(number of output frames), f ← new frame
    fill next output page(f)
    send(f, virtual printeri); increment number of frames
  until eof
  when access to state information permitted do
    STATEi ←initial priority (number of frames)
              $ this action is discussed below
  od
  signal(number of output jobs)
Output Process:
  repeat local j
    wait(number of output jobs)
    when access to state information permitted do
      j ← select index of next output job
          $ this action is discussed below
    od
```

signal(number of unselected jobs_j)
repeat local m,d = 0
  receive(m, virtual printer_j)
  repeat command((m,d), Line Printer); d ← d+1
  until eof *or* d = frame size
  release(m); signal(number of output frames)
until eof
until Output Process halt

The critical sections in these two programs operate on the state of the collection of all virtual printers. The state is described in a STATE vector which has one element for every virtual printer. We decide to distinguish between four different states:

Value of STATE_i	Meaning
0	no selectable job
1	highest priority job
2	medium priority job
3	lowest priority job

When process P_i produces output, STATE_i is set to high, medium or low priority depending on whether P_i produced a small, a medium large or large output job.

The STATE vector is used in procedure "select index of next output job" for job scheduling. The objective of our scheduling strategy is to give high priority to the small output jobs. If there is a great demand for output stemming from small jobs, there is the chance that it will take a long time before the output of a large job is printed. Such a situation arises if the virtual printers 3 and 4 are filled with a high priority job by the time that the virtual printers 1 and 5 have been emptied and vice versa (see figure 5.5b).

State vector	Index	Value
	0	2
	1	1
Pointer ptr →	2	3
	3	0
	4	0
	5	1

Figure 5.5b State vector indicating output priority

This can be avoided by the following policy. The selection procedure maintains an own variable, ptr, which points to one of the entries in the STATE vector which has one entry for each virtual pointer. When the select procedure is called, ptr cycles through the indices of the STATE vector until it points to an element of highest priority. However, instead of skipping an element of medium or low priority, the STATE element is decreased by one when ptr passes it. The effect is that the pointer passes an element of lowest priority twice, and an element of medium priority once, before this element becomes eligible as a high priority job. It is still possible for a high priority job to be selected before a low or medium priority job although the latter arrived earlier. (The ranges of the three priority classes can of course be extended to an interval greater than one.)

The program of the selection procedure is simply:

```
procedure select index of next output job =
  own ptr ← 0        $ no initialization when the procedure is called
  begin repeat ptr ← (ptr+1) mod(STATE vector length)
               if STATE(ptr) > 1 then STATE(ptr)−1 fi
         until STATE(ptr) = 1
               STATE(ptr) ← 0
               return(ptr)
  end
```

If the most output jobs are in the same priority class, the scheduling algorithm reduces to round robin. This may or may not be a desirable property. If the computation time and the time it takes to produce the output are indeed close to the average for jobs with equal priority, then a round robin scheduling algorithm is acceptable. Otherwise, we may consider a refinement of the priority classes based on other factors, such as computation or production time. We do not discuss this in more detail here. Related scheduling issues are investigated in chapters 6, 7 and 8. The point of the discussion here has been to show that virtual output devices give us more flexibility in scheduling output jobs than do a central mailbox or a single receiver queue attached to an output control process. A deviation from arrival time scheduling makes it impossible in the latter cases to use the simple operations send and receive for linking and delinking messages onto and from queues. Much more elaborate search procedures would be needed in addition to procedures for inserting and deleting messages from anywhere in a queue. Moreover, realize that all these operations have to be programmed as critical sections to avoid access conflicts. Expanding such operations is therefore not very attractive.

On the other hand, the scheduling is not the most important aspect of virtual devices. As stated earlier, the usefulness is primarily in clarity of system structure, abstraction from device pecularities in the context of a computation, graceful degradation of service when I/O equipment fails, and flexibility in the nature of hardware devices. These properties apply to input and output alike.

PROBLEMS

1. A device control process dispatches transmission completion notifications to all the processes which can send a command to the attached device (see section 5.3). However, if virtual input devices are used, the input process of a device would be the only process ever to receive such notifications.

Investigate how the device control process and the input process of an input device can be merged into one process and write a program for it.

2. In the batch system described in this section it is entirely up to the operator to determine which programs will be read into the machine next. Suppose the decision is moved to the user processes. It is then no longer necessary for input to be read in units of whole user programs and data. A user process may assemble a program from several identifiable modules and ask for those separately. Another modification we consider is for a user process to be allowed to have more than one virtual input device. The design permits a process to find an input process in a pool of such processes to which it identifies a virtual input device. The process then sends a message to the operator console in which it identifies the input it desires to receive and the input process it was able to reserve. Complement the proposed design where necessary and write a new program for the input process and the relevant part of a user process.

3. The restriction that a virtual printer may contain only one unselected job is used in the design of the STATE vector, because with this restriction there is only one priority to remember for each virtual printer. Suppose this restriction were replaced by another requiring that the total number of unselected jobs in all the virtual printers together not exceed a given upperbound. Revise the maintenance of the STATE information and the programs that deal with the virtual printers.

4. The situation may occur in which there are no output frames left consumed although not a single job has been completed in any of the virtual printers. In that particular case an output job should be selected although the STATE vector contains all zeros. We wish to make sure that there will be enough space available to complete this selected job; if there is not, the system runs into a deadlock. Therefore, a small number of output frames (two) is reserved for this situation. These frames may not be used for

production of a job while still unselected, but they will be used in case an incomplete job is selected in the rare situation described above.

Show that this strategy is sufficient to avoid a deadlock. Modify the programs to handle this situation. Is it necessary to design an analogous strategy for virtual readers?

5. The system proposed in problem 2 has the advantage of making the central mailboxes superfluous. On the other hand, if processes are allowed to have more than one virtual input device, a deadlock may arise in certain situations, because there is only a fixed number of real devices. Characterize such deadlock states and their causes. Invent rules that the operator can enforce to prevent such states.

READING LIST

A good example of message switching is [1]. An attempt to introduce better constructs than P and V is [2]. The usefulness of a process hierarchy is discussed in [3]. The use and abuse of the term *hierarchy* is discussed in [4].

1. Brinch Hansen, P., "The Nucleus of a Multiprogramming System," *Comm. ACM* 13, 4 (April 1970).

2. Brinch Hansen, P., "Structured Multiprogramming," *Comm. ACM* 15, 7 (July 1972).

3. Dijkstra, E. W., "Hierarchical Ordering of Sequential Processes," in *Operating System Techniques* (Hoare and Perrott, eds.), Academic Press, 1972.

4. Parnas, D. L., "On the Buzzword Hierarchical Structure," Proceedings of the IFIPS congress, Stockholm, 1974.

6. Scheduling Policies

6.1 SOME ELEMENTARY SCHEDULING DISCIPLINES

6.1.1 The preceding chapters contained several examples of serial devices (devices and resources which can be used by only one user at a time, such as the backup store, I/O devices, and critical sections). If several users wish to use a serial device, it must be determined in which order it will be allocated to them. An algorithm which determines such an order is called a scheduling algorithm. The set of rules on which such an algorithm is based is called the scheduling policy, scheduling strategy, or scheduling discipline.

It is customary to use the term *job* for the task which a user wants to be performed by a serial device. The jobs are generated by the *source*. In this context the serial device or resource is called the *service facility* or *server*. The *schedule* is an ordered list of job descriptions for which a limited amount of storage space is set aside. Scheduling takes place when the source adds a new job to the schedule, and when the server selects the next job. Some examples follow below.

a. The server is a backup store device; the source consists of the processes which request data transmissions. A job description is a message which indicates two storage areas, one in the main store and one on the backup store, the size of these areas, and an identification of the process requesting the transmission. The schedule is determined by the request queues. Scheduling takes place mainly at the time when a message is sent.

b. The server is a set of critical sections sharing semaphore s; the source consists of the processes trying to enter one of these critical sections. The job description is merely the identity of a process waiting to enter the critical section. The schedule is the waiting list of semaphore s. Scheduling takes place when a process enters the waiting queue.

c. The server is a set of line printers; the source consists of the processes producing printer output. If we follow the design of section 5.5, the job descriptions are the output job descriptors which are placed in the output queues of the processes. Scheduling takes place when a process adds an output job to its output queue, and when the service facility selects the next output queue from which it takes an output job.

d. The server is a central processor which is multiplexed among a set of processes. A job consists of the sequence of instructions between two consecutive waiting periods of a process. The schedule is the ready list which contains a status description of every ready-to-run process. Scheduling takes place when a process enters the ready list, but may also take place when the next process is selected to run. Various strategies for this case are discussed later in this chapter.

6.1.2 The messages in a sender or receiver queue are most naturally ordered by arrival time. The messages are removed from the queue in the same order, by the "first in first out" or "first come first serve" (FIFO or FCFS) scheduling discipline. This discipline is applied in all cases in which there is no reason to give preference to one job over the other. A FIFO discipline is very attractive because the operations of inserting or removing a job are very simple. The same is true for a "last in first out" (LIFO) discipline for which a stack is used. Insert is a push operation and remove a pop operation. We applied such a policy to the management of free blocks of storage space in the beginning of chapter 3. However, a LIFO scheduling discipline is generally not desirable (imagine what would happen if data transmission requests were treated LIFO!). It is acceptable in the particular case of allocating free blocks of storage, because one free block is as good as any other.

The probably that the source adds a new job to the schedule in a unit of time is generally assumed to be a Poisson distribution. This is justified if the jobs behave similarly to a waiting queue at a window in a bank or the telephone calls coming through a telephone exchange. The typical property of a Poisson distribution is that the time of arrival is totally independent of the current state and earlier arrivals. We assume that is also true for jobs arriving at the servers discussed below.

We assume that the number of jobs serviced per time unit is also a Poisson process, just as serving people in a bank or on the telephone. The probability that a bank employee helps a certain number of clients per time unit or that a telephone call lasts a certain time is, again, entirely independent of the current state or the recent history. We choose the Poisson distribution because we assume that the time the server needs to carry out a particular job is independent of when the job arrives and also independent of the service time needed by preceding jobs.

6.1.3 Let α be the "arrival rate," that is, the observed rate at which jobs are added to the schedule per time unit. Let β be the "service rate," that is, the observed rate at which jobs are processed per time unit. A Poisson distribution states that the probability that x jobs arrive in a time unit is

$$\Pr(x) = e^{-\alpha} * \frac{\alpha^x}{x!}$$

The factor $e^{-\alpha}$ assures that $\sum_{x=0}^{\infty} \Pr(x) = 1$, because $\sum_{x=0}^{\infty} \alpha^x/x! = e^{\alpha}$ The expectation value (or arithmetic mean) of the number of jobs arriving per time unit is

$$E(x) = \sum_{x=0}^{\infty} x \neq \Pr(x) = e^{-\alpha} \sum_{x=1}^{\infty} \alpha^x/(x-1)! = e^{-\alpha} \sum_{y=0}^{\infty} \alpha^y/y! = \alpha,$$

where y is substituted for x−1. Thus, the expectation value is equal to the observed arrival rate. The probability that exactly x jobs are serviced in a time unit is

$$\Pr(x) = e^{-\beta} * \beta^x/x!$$

with expectation value $E(x) = \beta$.

The probability that x jobs arrive in a time interval t can be found by observing that we may expect αt jobs in that interval. Thus, this probability is found by substituting αt for α:

$$\Pr(x(t)) = e^{-\alpha t} * (\alpha t)^x/x!$$

The probability of no arrivals at all in an interval t is

$$\Pr(x(t) = 0) = e^{-\alpha t}$$

Hence, the probability of at least one arrival in that interval t is

$$\Pr(x(t) > 0) = 1 - e^{-\alpha t} = \alpha \int_0^t e^{-\alpha u} du \text{ (see figure 6.1a)}$$

This probability is a function of time and can be seen as a cumulative probability distribution of which the adjoint density function is

$$d(t) = \alpha * e^{-\alpha t}$$

with expectation $E(t) = \int_0^{\infty} t d(t) dt = \alpha \int_0^{\infty} t * e^{-\alpha t} dt$

Applying partial integration we find

$$E(t) = -t * e^{-\alpha t} \Big|_0^{\infty} + \int_0^{\infty} e^{-\alpha t} dt = 0 - e^{-\alpha t}/\alpha \Big|_0^{\infty} = 1/\alpha$$

This says that the expected time interval between two successive arrivals (the interarrival time) is equal to $1/\alpha$. This corresponds to the expected

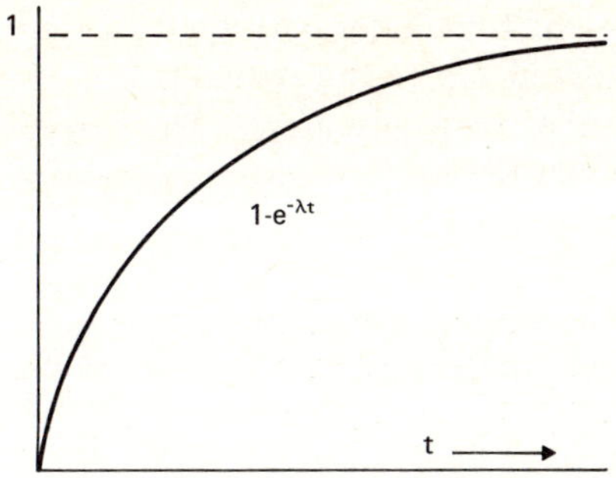

Figure 6.1a Probability of at least one arrival

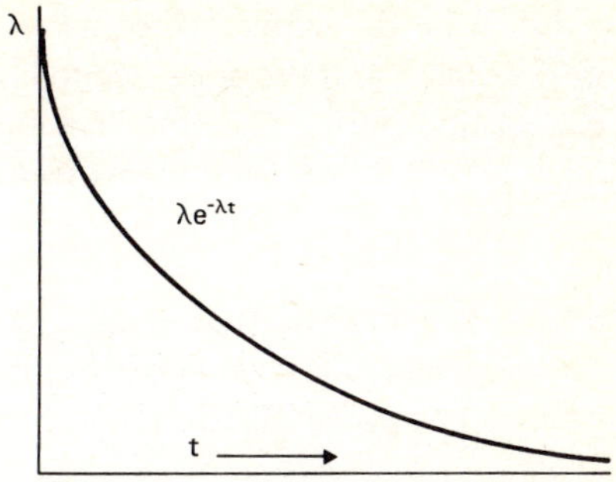

Figure 6.1b Inter-arrival density function

arrival rate α. The probability distribution function for the arrival time is negative exponential (see figures 6.1a and 6.1b).

The probability that no job leaves the system in a given interval t is $\Pr(x(t)=0) = e^{-\beta t}$, so the probability that at least one job leaves the system in the interval t is

$$\Pr(\text{at least one departure}) = 1 - e^{-\beta t} = \beta * \int_0^\infty e^{-\beta u} du$$

The expectation value for a departure can be derived from the probability density function $\beta * e^{-\beta t}$ in a similar manner as for interarrival times.

$$E(t) = \beta \int_0^\infty t * e^{-\beta t} = 1/\beta$$

This says that the expected time interval between serving two jobs (the average service time) is $1/\beta$.

6.1.4 The total time a job j spends in the system depends not only on its service time, but also on the time it takes to serve all the jobs in the job queue when j arrives. This total time, for which we use the term *response time*, is seen by the source as being the time it takes to complete a job. In order to get some feeling for the ratio of response time to service time, we must estimate the number of jobs that we may expect to be in the system when a job arrives.

It is intuitively obvious that the expected length of the job queue depends on the parameters α and β. In particular, if α increases while β is fixed, we expect that the average queue length will grow. Furthermore, things will entirely get out of hand if α exceeds β, because this means that jobs arrive at a higher rate than they can be served. On the other hand, if α is much smaller than β, there is a fair chance that an arriving job finds the queue empty.

Let T be the expected response time, which includes both waiting time in the queue and the time needed to be served. Given the arrival rate α, we expect that during this time T a number of αT new jobs arrive. Thus, when a job leaves the system, we expect a number of

$$n = \alpha T$$

jobs to be in the system. This equation, describing a relation between the arrival rate and the expected number of jobs in the system and the response time, is known as "Little's result."

6.1.5 We are particularly interested in those system states in which the arrival rate α and the service rate β do not noticeably change. After an initialization period the system arrives at an equilibrium referred to as the steady state. This state is characterized by the fact that the probability of finding exactly "i" jobs in the system is constant in time:

$$p_i(t) = P(\text{number of jobs in the system} = i)$$

is constant, thus its time derivative

$$p'_i(t) = 0$$

One can prove that the system indeed reaches a steady state if the arrival time and the service time are negative exponentially distributed.

The values of $p_i(t)$ are needed to compute the expected value of the number of jobs in the system so that an estimate of T can be computed using Little's result. We proceed as follows: let Δt be a small time interval.

$$Pr(+1) = Pr(\text{one arrival in } \Delta t) = \alpha\Delta t * e^{-\alpha t} = \alpha\Delta t + O(\Delta t^2)$$

where $O(\Delta t^2)$ indicates that the sum of the remaining terms contains a factor Δt^2. Similarly,

$$Pr(-1) = Pr(\text{one departure in } \Delta t) = \beta\Delta t * e^{-\beta\Delta t} = \beta\Delta t + O(\Delta t^2)$$

for $i > 0$. If there are no jobs in the system, no job can depart, so

$$Pr(-1) = 0 \qquad \text{for } i = 0.$$

The probabilities of more than one arrival or departure in Δt are all of the order $O(\Delta t^2)$ or higher. The probability that neither arrival nor departure takes place is

$$Pr(\text{no change in } \Delta t) = 1 - (\alpha + \beta)\Delta t + O(\Delta t^2) \qquad \text{for } i > 0$$

and

$$Pr(\text{no change in } \Delta t) = 1 - \alpha\Delta t + O(\Delta t^2) \qquad \text{for } i = 0$$

Ignoring terms of the order $O(\Delta t^2)$ and higher, we have

$$p_i(t+\Delta t) = Pr(0)*p_i(t)+Pr(-1)*p_{i+1}(t)+Pr(+1)*p_{i-1}(t) \qquad \text{for } i > 0$$

and

$$p_0(t+\Delta t) = Pr(0)*p_0(t)+Pr(-1)*p_1(t)$$

After substituting Pr(0), Pr(+1) and Pr(−1), dividing by Δt and taking the limit, we find

$$p'_i(t) = -(\alpha+\beta)p_i(t)+\beta p_{i+1}(t)+\alpha p_{i-1}(t) \qquad \text{for } i > 0$$

and

$$p'_0(t) = -\alpha p_0(t)+\beta p_1(t) \qquad \text{for } i = 0$$

Since equilibrium is characterized by $p'(t) = 0$, the probabilities for finding a certain number of jobs in the system are related by the equations:

$$(\alpha+\beta)p_i(t) = \beta p_{i+1}(t)+\alpha p_{i-1}(t) \qquad \text{for } i > 0$$

and

$$p_1(t) = \alpha/\beta p_0(t)$$

Successive substitution leads to $p_i(t) = \rho^i * p_0(t)$ where $\rho = \alpha/\beta$. Since $\sum_{i=0}^{\infty} p_i(t) = 1$, we find $p_0(t)*\sum_{i=0}^{\infty} \rho^i = 1$.

This limit sum exists only if $\alpha < \beta$ and in that case

$$\sum_{i=0}^{\infty} \rho^i = 1/(1-\rho), \text{ so } p_0(t) = 1-\rho$$

Our intuitive reasoning that α must be less than β appears to be justified. Moreover, the latter equation says that the probability of finding the system empty in the steady state is $1-\rho$, so the probability of finding the system not empty is $\rho = \alpha/\beta$.

The expected value for the number $n = E(i)$ of jobs in the system is:

$$n = E(i) = \sum_{i=0}^{\infty} i*p_i(t) = p_0 \sum_{i=1}^{\infty} i*\rho^i = (1-\rho)*\rho/(1-\rho)^2 = \rho/(1-\rho)$$

Using Little's result, we find

$$T = 1/\alpha*\rho/(1-\rho) = 1/(\beta-\alpha)$$

A comparison of the expected time T that a job spends in the system and the expected service time $1/\beta$ shows how much a job is slowed down because of the competition:

$$\beta T = 1/(1-\rho)$$

All the equations above clearly show that the behavior of the service system is predominantly determined by the value of ρ. If ρ is close to one,

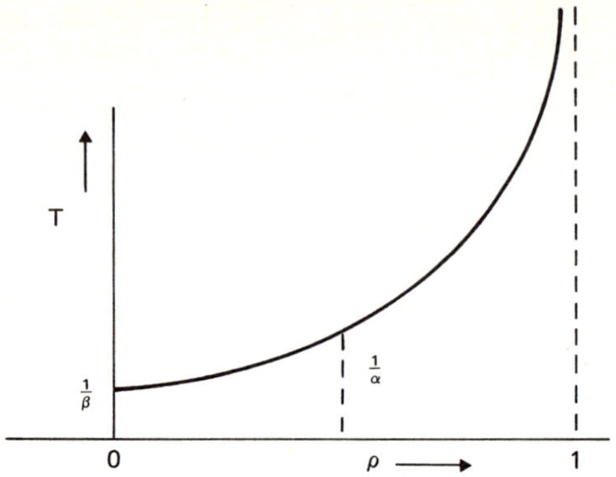

Figure 6.1c The expected response time as function of ρ

the probability of finding the queue not empty is high, and we have a serious slowdown problem if ρ gets too close to one. If ρ is less than 1/2, the chance of finding the queue empty is greater than the chance of finding jobs waiting and jobs are slowed down by a factor less than two (see figure 6.1c).

6.1.6 Suppose that the system serves two kinds of jobs, short jobs and long jobs, and that both have a Poisson distributed arrival rate and service rate with parameters (α_1,β_1) and (α_2,β_2). One can prove that the composition of two Poisson processes again yields a Poisson process (see problem 1). The arrival rate of the composition is $\alpha = \alpha_1+\alpha_2$. The average service time is:

$$\begin{aligned} 1/\beta &= \alpha_1/(\alpha_1+\alpha_2)*1/\beta_1+\alpha_2/(\alpha_1+\alpha_2)*1/\beta_2 \\ &= 1/(\alpha_1+\alpha_2)*(\alpha_1/\beta_1+\alpha_2/\beta_2) \end{aligned}$$

Thus,

$$\alpha/\beta = \alpha_1/\beta_1+\alpha_2/\beta_2 \text{ or } \rho = \rho_1+\rho_2$$

Suppose short and long mean that the service time $1/\beta_1$ is much smaller than the service time $1/\beta_2$. We found that for a FIFO scheduling discipline the expected response time is

$$T = \frac{1}{\alpha} * \frac{\rho}{1-\rho}$$

where $\alpha = \alpha_1+\alpha_2$ and $\rho = \rho_1+\rho_2$.

This implies that the expected time spent in the system is the same for all jobs. This places the short jobs in a very unfavorable position, because the short jobs are not expected to get through the system any faster than the long jobs.

The round robin (RR) scheduling discipline remedies the indiscriminating behavior of the FIFO strategy. RR scheduling has been very popular since the design of the first multiaccess systems, and still is, because of its simplicity and fairness. We will see that, if an RR policy is applied, the expected time a job spends in the system is related to its service time, meaning that short jobs will get through much faster than long jobs.

The basic idea of an RR scheduling discipline is that the server is allocated to a job only for a time quantum of fixed length. When a job runs out of its time slice (quantum), it cycles back to the rear of the job queue to wait for another time slice. An RR discipline can be applied only to a preemptive resource such as a CPU, not to a nonpreemptive resource such as a line printer. (A nonpreemptive resource cannot be deallocated until its user is willing to give it up; a preemptive resource can be deallocated by an operating system monitor and reallocated at a later time.)

The arrival rate of an RR discipline is much higher than of a FIFO discipline, because jobs which did not finish are fed back to the job queue. An estimate of the arrival time is found by the following reasoning. If the time quantum is q and the service time $1/\beta$, then the job is exepcted to need k time slices where $k*q = 1/\beta$. If a particular job needs exactly k time slices, it arrives k times in the job queue instead of just once.

Let $k_1*q = 1/\beta_1$ for the short jobs and $k_2*q = 1/\beta_2$ for the long jobs. The arrival rate of new jobs is (as before) $\alpha = \alpha_1+\alpha_2$. The service time is also the same, because

$$1/\beta = \alpha_1/\alpha*k_1q+\alpha_2/\alpha*k_2q = 1/\alpha*(\alpha_1/\beta_1+\alpha_2/\beta_2)$$

Thus, we find again $\rho = \rho_1+\rho_2$.

This means that the average response time is the same for the FIFO and the RR scheduling discipline. However, the mean number of jobs in the system when a job arrives is given by

$$n = \rho/(1-\rho)$$

while every job in the queue is serviced for a period of time equal to the quantum q. Hence, a particular job which passes k times through the queue has an expected response time of

$$T(k) = k*[q*\rho/(1-\rho)+q] = k*q/(1-\rho)$$

That is to say, the expected response time of a particular job is proportional to its service time. Applied to the system serving the short and long jobs, it means that both can get through in a time proportional to the amount that each one individually needs independently of the other. In such a system the small jobs won't suffer as much from the presence of long jobs as in the FIFO system.

A FIFO service system has an advantage over an RR system in one respect which has been left out of the discussion here. Allocation of the server to another job involves updating the status information of the departing job and the job to be served next. The time required for this switching from one job to another may not be negligible compared to the service time. Applying an RR policy, the overhead is proportional to the number of time slices a job needs, whereas in a FIFO system the price of such overhead is paid only once. This observation leads to two conclusions: first, if there are no large differences in job needs, a FIFO scheduling strategy is preferable; an RR scheme is justified only if some jobs are seriously slowed down because of others. Second, the quantum q should be chosen as large as possible so as to avoid unnecessary job switches. In the example of the short and long jobs, a proper choice would be to fix q so that most of the small jobs can get through in one time slice.

PROBLEMS

1. The probability that an event x occurs under the condition y is denoted by $Pr(x|y)$. This probability is equal to the product $Pr(x)*Pr(y)$ provided that x and y are independent. The arrival rates of the short and long jobs in the mixed system are indeed independent. Thus, if x represents the arrival rate of a system purely consisting of short jobs, y the arrival rate of a system purely consisting of long jobs and s of the composition of the two systems, we find

$$\begin{aligned} Pr(s) &= Pr(x=s|y=0)+Pr(x=s-1|y=1)+ \ldots + Pr(x=0|y=s) \\ &= Pr(x=s)*Pr(y=0)+Pr(x=s-1)*Pr(y=1)+ \ldots + Pr(x=0)*Pr(y=s) \end{aligned}$$

Prove that the arrival distribution of the mixed system is a Poisson distribution if both pure systems are Poisson-distributed and prove that the arrival rate of the mixed system is equal to the sum of the arrival rates of the pure systems.

2. A system S processes jobs which require a service time close to a given figure. Once in a while, however, a much smaller type of job needs service, but this happens very rarely. It is therefore decided not to apply an RR discipline, because it would cause unnecessary job switching overhead. Instead, the following scheme is proposed: any new standard job is appended at the end of the queue as usual; if such an exceptional job arrives, it is inserted into the queue at the rear of all the small jobs already present, but preceding all standard jobs in the queue. The server always takes the first job from the queue.

Design the job queue as a linked list and write the programs for inserting an exceptional job. Would an array implementation be suitable?

3. $C_1, \ldots, C_5$ are five classes of jobs all ariving at the same rate in a job queue, but the relation between their service rates is $\rho_1 = 2*\rho_{i+1}$ for $i = 1,$

2, 3, 4. Given that arrival and service are Poisson-distributed, express the expected length of the job queue and the expected time spent in the system in the system parameters and also the probability of finding the queue empty.

4. It seems advisable to implement an RR scheme for the system of problem 3 with quantum size q equal to $1/\beta$. Express the expected value of the response time T_i of a job which belongs to class C_i in the parameters α and β. Is this value proportional to the service time of a job in class C_i?

5. It was observed that execution of a user request interpreted in an interactive system took on the average 100 milliseconds. Assuming that request arrival and execution are Poisson-distributed, estimate how many users the system can support guaranteeing an average response time of one or two seconds.

6.2 LINEAR PRIORITY SCHEDULING

6.2.1 An RR scheduling discipline can be applied only to the allocation of preemptive devices. In contrast to a nonpreemptive device, a preemptive device can be taken away at any moment and reallocated at some later time without affecting its user. A CPU and the main store are typical examples of preemptive resources. A line printer is an example of a nonpreemptive device. Because output jobs must not be mixed, an RR policy cannot be applied. In this section we discuss a range of scheduling disciplines for preemptive devices. The FCFS discipline is the lower bound of the range and the pure RR discipline is the upper bound.

We found in the preceding section that the short jobs severely suffer from the long jobs if an FCFS discipline is applied. An RR discipline works in favor of the short jobs, because the expected response time is then proportional to the required service time. An RR discipline slows down all jobs by the same factor. On the other hand, we may argue that the RR policy is somewhat unfair towards the long jobs by accepting every new job and giving it an equal share of service. The system ought to recognize some obligation towards the jobs to which the system has already committed itself. Following this reasoning, a newly arriving job should not immediately receive its share if the service facility is in use by other jobs. In this section we discuss a scheduling discipline in which the admittance condition depends on the arrival time of the new job and the number of jobs currently sharing the service facility. A new job is placed at the end of the job queue as is done in both RR and FCFS disciplines. However, the difference from an RR strategy is that a job which received a service quantum is not fed back to the end of the queue, but to a place somewhere in the middle of the queue (see figure 6.2a).

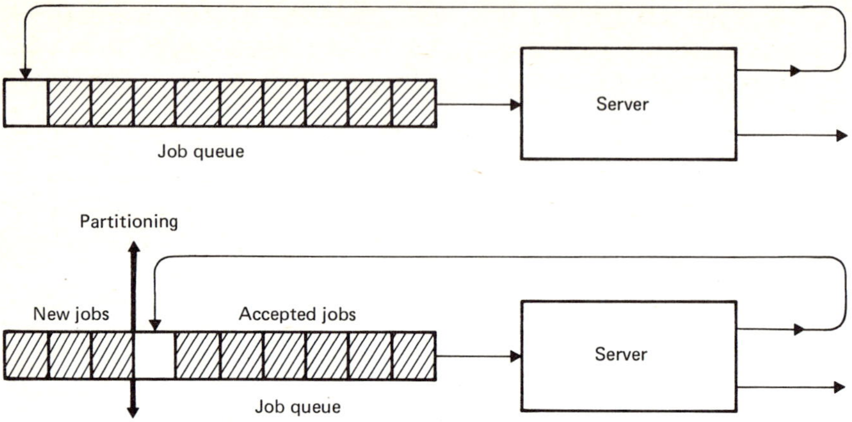

Figure 6.2a RR and other feedback scheduling

Jobs competing for the service facility are divided into new and accepted jobs. The accepted jobs are scheduled RR, and a job which has just received a service quantum is fed back to the position in the queue following the last accepted job. A new job does not receive any service at all. However, when a certain condition is met, the new job which is first in line will be accepted and appended to the accepted part of the job queue. A new job is accepted by moving the partition between accepted and new jobs one step to the left.

The condition for accepting a job is determined by the priorities of the jobs in the queue. When a new job arrives, it starts off with a priority equal to zero. The priorities are a linear function of time. The rate at which the priority of a new job changes in a time interval Δt is given by

$$\Delta p = a * \Delta t \qquad (a \neq 0)$$

The priority of an accepted job changes by

$$\Delta p = b * \Delta t$$

If a new job arrived at t_0, the priority it accumulated up to the current time t is

$$p(t) = a(t - t_0)$$

If the job started at t_0 and has been accepted at t_1 its priority at the current time is

$$p(t) = a(t_1 - t_0) + b(t - t_1)$$

The acceptance rule says that a new job is accepted as soon as its priority has reached the same priority as an accepted job, or when the accepted set is empty. Assuming that we start with a single accepted job, the rule implies that all the accepted jobs have the same priority (see figure 6.2b). The proof is left to the reader (see problem 1).

6.2.2 The priority as defined above has a serious drawback with respect to an implementation because the priority changes for both new and accepted jobs. This implies that all the priorities must be updated after every time slice! The overhead incurred by updating all the priorities is unacceptable for the sake of efficiency. We demand that our system satisfy the following implementation principle: the status information of a job is updated when a job is placed in a queue but not while a job is waiting in a queue. This means that the feedback system is not allowed to update any of the new jobs and, out of the accepted job set, only the one which is fed back to the queue at the end of a time slice.

The implementation principle can be satisfied by applying a linear transformation to the priority measure (that is, by replacing p by $v = x*p+y$, $x \neq 0$). A linear priority order is invariant for linear transformations because $p(i_1) \leq p(i_2) \leq \ldots \leq p(i_n)$ is transformed into $v(i_1) \leq v(i_2) \leq \ldots \leq v(i_n)$ if $x > 0$ and into $v(i_1) \geq v(i_2) \geq \ldots \geq v(i_n)$ if $x < 0$. In the latter case the order is reversed.

It is not hard to satisfy the implementation principle for the accepted jobs. Since the accepted jobs all have the same priority, the priority of the accepted jobs can be recorded in a variable ap and updated at the end of a time slice q by adding $b*q$ to ap. Variable ap is set to zero when the set of accepted jobs gets empty and it is set to the priority of the first accepted job when it arrives. It is not necessary to record the priority of the individual jobs in the accepted set.

The priority of a new job depends on its arrival time. It is therefore

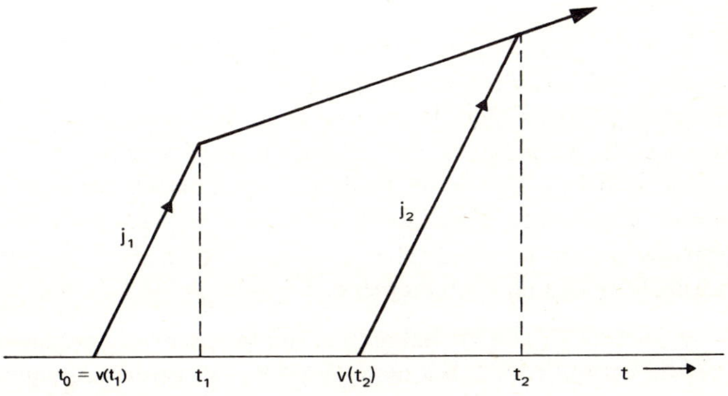

Figure 6.2b Priority of new and accepted jobs

necessary to record the priority of each new job separately. The implementation principle is satisfied for the new jobs by applying this linear transformation to p: $v = -p/a + t$ so that $v(t) = t_0$ for a new job and $v(t) = t_0 + (1 - b/a)(t - t_1)$ for an accepted job where t_0 is the arrival time and t_1 the time of acceptance.

The function v(t) is constant for a new job, so updating is not necessary. The function v(t) is the virtual arrival time. The virtual arrival time is the parallel projection of the current value of p(t) on the time axis, parallel to the slope α (see figure 6.2b). The name expresses that this is the point on the time axis where the job would have started if it had gained its current priority by waiting alone.

The coefficient of the linear transformation $x = -1/a$ is negative if we choose $a > 0$. The highest priority then corresponds to the smallest value of v. Thus, the leftmost virtual arrival time on the time axis is the virtual arrival time of the accepted jobs. This is the only point that travels along the time axis, because the virtual arrival times of the new jobs are constant. The set of accepted jobs is never empty if the set of new jobs is not empty, because the leftmost job is immediately accepted if the last accepted job leaves. If the virtual arrival time of the accepted jobs, av, meets the virtual arrival time of a new job, the latter is absorbed by the former and the job is accepted. The speed at which av travels along the time axis depends on the parameter $r = (1 - b/a)$. We investigate some of the possibilities for $a > 0$.

1. $r \leq 0$ for $b/a \geq 1$. The virtual arrival time of the accepted jobs is a decreasing function of t for $r < 0$ and it does not move if $r = 0$. This means that av never meets the virtual arrival time of a new job. Thus, a new job is not accepted until the currently accepted jobs leave. Assuming that two jobs cannot arrive at exactly the same time, there is only one accepted job at a time. Thus, the policy is a pure FCFS discipline (see figure 6.2c). Varying the value of r has no impact for negative r.

2. $0 < r < 1$ for $0 < b/a < 1$. The virtual arrival time of the accepted jobs increases, so av travels to the right. Since $r < 1$, av moves slower along the time axis than the current time. When a new job arrives, it takes a while before av catches up with it, but it eventually will, even if no accepted jobs leave (see figure 6.2d). Kleinrock called this policy "selfish round robin," because it seems as if the accepted jobs try to keep the server for themselves, but do not entirely succeed. The waiting time of a new job increases if $r \rightarrow 0$.

3. $r = 1$ for $b = 0$. The virtual arrival time increases as fast as time, so av is the current time t. If a new job arrives, its priority is equal to the priority of the accepted jobs, so it is immediately accepted. Thus, the policy is now a pure RR without delaying new jobs.

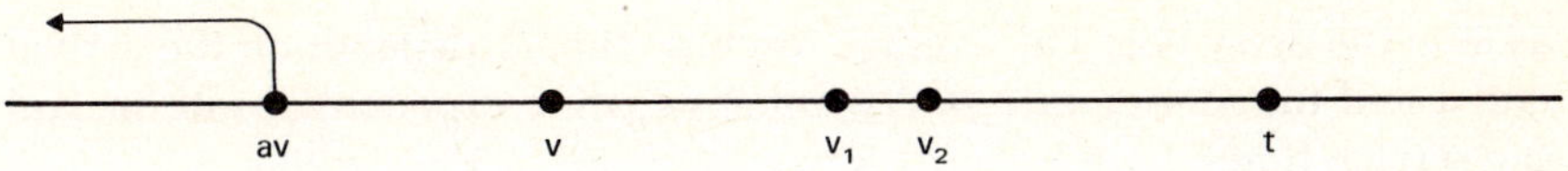

Figure 6.2c FCFS scheduling for $r \leq 0$

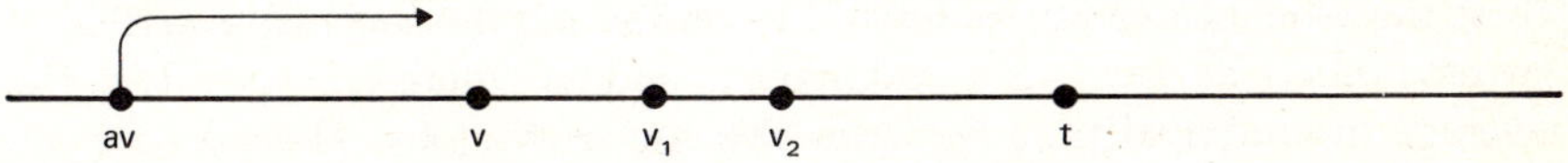

Figure 6.2d SRR scheduling for $0 < r < 1$

6.2.3 A job is fed back to the rear of the queue for $r = 1$ (as in RR) and it is fed back to the head of the queue (which corresponds to FCFS) for $r = 0$. The SRR disciplines in between these two extremes favor the accepted jobs over the newly arriving jobs. How close the SRR policy comes to FCFS or pure RR depends on the parameter value.

We found in section 6.1 that when applying an FCFS discipline, the response time is the same for all jobs and, when applying an RR discipline, the response time is proportional to the required service time. Since the SRR disciplines are flanked by the FCFS and RR disciplines, we expect the response time of short jobs to come out less favorable in an SRR discipline than in the RR policy, but much better than in FCFS. We expect that the response time of short jobs will improve if $r \rightarrow 1$. An analysis of the response time of an SRR discipline follows below.

Applying an SRR discipline, new jobs must first spend some time in a delay box, as it were, before being admitted to the service facility (see figure 6.2e). A new job remains in the delay box so long as its arrival time is greater than the virtual arrival time of the jobs being served.

The time spent in the delay box depends on the speed at which av (the virtual arrival time of the accepted jobs) catches up with the arrival time of

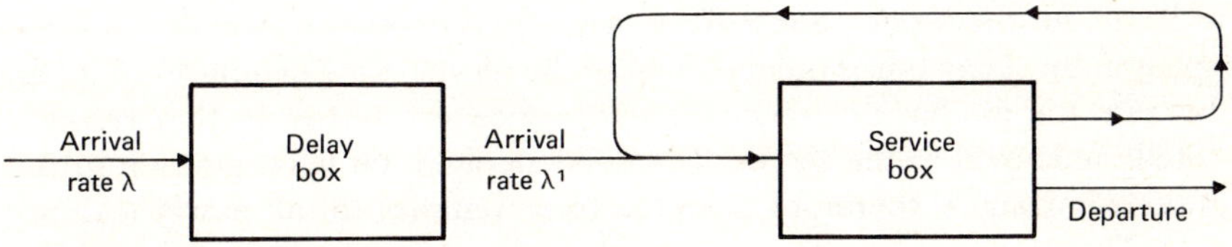

Figure 6.2e New jobs passing the delay box

a job in the delay box. The average response time T depends on the arrival rate α and the service rate β. Assuming negative exponential interarrival and service times,

$$T_{SR} = 1/\beta * 1/(1-\rho) = 1/(\beta-\alpha)$$

where $\rho = \alpha/\beta$ (see section 6.1). The arrival rate at the service box, α', depends on the arrival rate α and the parameter r. The relation between these three quantities can be found by considering the successive arrival of two hypothetical new jobs at moments t_1 and t_2, where $t_2 - t_1 = 1/\alpha$, the average interarrrival time between two successive jobs. The jobs are admitted to the service box when av is equal to their virtual arrival time (which is identical to their arrival time). That is, the jobs are admitted to the service box at moments t'_1 and t'_2 such that

$$v_s(t'_1) = t_1 \text{ and } v_s(t'_2) = t_2$$

Applying to the definition of virtual arrival time,

$$1/\alpha = t_2 - t_1 = v_s(t'_2) - v_s(t'_1) = r(t'_2 - t'_1) = r * 1/\alpha'$$

because $1/\alpha'$ is the expected interval between two arrivals at the service box. The effect of the delay box appears to be a slowdown of the arrivals at the service box to the rate

$$\alpha' = r * \alpha$$

The response time of the feedback system as a whole can be split in two terms, one for the time spent in the delay box and one for the response time of the service box.

$$T_{SR} = T_d + T_S$$

The response time of the service box is (see section 6.1):

$$T_S = 1/(\beta - \alpha')$$

Thus, the average time spent in the delay box is

$$\begin{aligned} T_d &= T_{SR} - T_S \\ &= 1/(\beta-\alpha) - 1/(\beta-\alpha') = (\alpha-\alpha')/\{(\beta-\alpha)(\beta-\alpha')\} \end{aligned}$$

We found in section 6.1.6 that the response time of a particular job is proportional to its service time if a round robin discipline is applied. This is still true for the service box if RR scheduling is chosen. However, the time spent in the delay box is independent of the service time of a particular job, because the job has not received any service yet and is, in that respect, totally unknown to the server. The delay depends on what goes on in the service box and is therefore expected to be uniform for all newly arriving jobs. That is to say, T_d is the expected delay for every job. The response time of a particular job is the sum of two terms: the first depends on the system as a whole and is the same for all jobs; the second term is proportional to the number k of time quanta q needed by this job (see section 6.1.6).

$$T_{SR}(k) = T_d + T_S(k) = (\alpha - \alpha')/(\beta - \alpha)(\beta - \alpha') + kq/(1 - \rho')$$

where $\rho' = \alpha'/\beta$. Thus,

$$\begin{aligned} T_{SR}(k) &= 1/(\beta - \alpha) - 1/(\beta - \alpha') + kq * \beta/(\beta - \alpha') \\ &= 1/(\beta - \alpha) - (1 - kq\beta)/(\beta - \alpha') \end{aligned}$$

The last expression for the response time T(k) of a job which needs k time slices conveys some interesting properties of the selfish round robin discipline compared to the response time in an FCFS or RR scheduling system. The response times for these disciplines are, respectively, $T_{FC}(k) = 1/(\beta - \alpha)$ for a pure FCFS discipline, and $T_{RR}(k) = kq * \beta/(\beta - \alpha)$ for a pure RR discipline.

The second term of T_{SR} vanishes if $kq = 1/\beta$, which is the case for the job whose service time equals the average service time. The response time of this job is apparently the same for all three disciplines. Short jobs are characterized by $kq < 1/\beta$; long jobs need more than average service time, so, for those jobs, $kq > 1/\beta$. Comparing the response times for the various disciplines, we find $T_{RR} < T_{SR} < T_{FC}$ for short jobs, and $T_{FC} < T_{SR} < T_{RR}$ for long jobs. The selfish round robin discipline apparently does not favor the short jobs as strongly as does an RR discipline, but it also does not discriminate so strongly against long jobs as does an RR discipline. The opposite is true comparing this feedback discipline with an FCFS policy. Finally, if $\alpha' \rightarrow \alpha$ (that is, if $r \rightarrow 1$) the SRR discipline changes into the RR discipline. If $r \rightarrow 0$, and consequently $\alpha' \rightarrow 0$, the feedback discipline gets further away from the RR discipline and behaves more like the FCFS discipline.

PROBLEMS

1. We assume that it is not possible for two jobs to arrive exactly at the same moment. The acceptance rule precludes the possibility that a new job (not accepted) has a higher priority than any accepted job. Prove that the accepted jobs have the same priority at all times. Is it possible for the priority of the accepted jobs to decrease sometimes even if we choose $b > 0$?

2. If the parameter $r = (1 - b/a)$ is chosen in the interval [0:1], the virtual arrival time of the accepted jobs (av) increases, although not as fast as time. If we choose $r > 1$, av travels faster than time. Characterize the policy determined by $a > 0$, $r > 1$.

3. The smallest virtual arrival time corresponds to the highest priority if $a > 0$, because the coefficient $x = -1/a$ of the linear transformation $v = -p/a + t$ is negative. If we choose $a < 0$, then the coefficient is positive. In that case the highest priority corresponds to the greatest value of v. Investigate the case $a < 0$ and characterize the disciplines which are found for various values of $r = (1 - b/a)$.

4. A service facility SF consists of a delay box and a service box (see fig. 6.2e). The delay box is in reality a queue in which jobs await admission to the job queue of the jobs which receive service in an RR schedule. We apply an SRR discipline. Every job carries an indication telling when it arrived in the admission queue. Time can be read by calling READTIME which returns as value the current time.

Write a program for the procedure ASKADMISSION which is called when a job enters the admission queue and write the program for the action of the service box at the end of a time slice. This action updates the virtual arrival time of the service box and applies the admission rule.

5. The service time t of a job which needs k time slices is $t = k*q$, where q is the quantum size. If q approaches zero while k increases such that $t = k*q$ remains true, the response time of a job whose service time is t becomes a continuous function of t. The response times for an RR, an FCFS and an SRR discipline are

$$T_{RR}(t) = t*\beta/(\beta-\alpha)$$

$$T_{SR}(t) = 1/(\beta-\alpha) - 1 - t*\ \beta/(\beta-\alpha')$$

$$T_{FC}(t) = 1/(\beta-\alpha)$$

where $\alpha' = r*\alpha$. Plot $T_{RR}(t)$, $T_{FC}(t)$ and $T_{SR}(t)$ for various values of r against t for $(\alpha,\beta) = (50,100)$ and also for $(\alpha,\beta) = (80,100)$.

6. A service facility SF has two job queues, one for high priority jobs and one for low priority jobs. A job is charged for the services at a rate of f* its service time, where f is proportional to the ratio of service time over response time. The jobs in the high priority queue are serviced round robin, the jobs in the low priority queue are serviced FCFS. However, the low priority queue is serviced if and only if the high priority queue is empty. If at the end of a time slice allotted to a low priority job the high priority queue is not empty, the low priority job is returned to the low priority queue and the RR scheduling of the high priority jobs is resumed. Write a program for the selection of a next job at the end of a time slice, and a program for the service charges.

6.3 LONG RANGE CPU SCHEDULING

6.3.1 The scheduling decisions taken on behalf of a job between its arrival and departure from a service facility are considered as short term decisions. The mechanism which brings such decisions into effect is local to the service facility and the nature of such decisions is a characteristic of that service facility. In the scheduling policies discussed in the preceding section all jobs are treated alike upon arrival. Their history regarding previous passes through the service facility are not taken into account. The arrival of a job is considered its birth and a job ceases to exist when it leaves the service facility.

In this section we discuss some long range scheduling policies in which the history of previous passes through a service facility are taken into account. The variables which describe the history of a job belong to the service facility. These variables are not deleted when a job leaves the service facility, but are not accessible during the absence of the job and their values are frozen during that time. However, when the job returns, the history variables, with their final value of the previous pass, become accessible again.

CPU scheduling is the typical example of a situation in which long range scheduling is useful. A process has no use for a CPU while it is waiting for the completion of an I/O command. Therefore, it leaves the service facility when it is blocked and returns when it is ready to run. A long range scheduling policy rates the priority of a job by the service received during previous passes as well as by the recent history since the last arrival.

6.3.2 If a long range scheduling policy is applied, a job is inserted into the job queue by the priority it accumulated in previous passes through the service facility. As always, we are concerned about providing service in accordance with the demand of a job. Small jobs should not suffer too much from the presence of long jobs.

Instead of applying a single scheduling discipline to all jobs, we consider long range policies which use different disciplines depending on the service history of a job. The scheduling policy has several stages, each stage subject to an individual scheduling discipline. A job enters stage s_i when its accumulated service time exceeds a given threshold t_i. This threshold t_i is a fixed attribute of stage s_i. It is less than threshold t_{i+1} for $i = 1, 2, \ldots$. When a job enters the service facility for the first time, it enters stage s_1; therefore, we choose threshold t_1 equal to zero.

We discuss a long range scheduling strategy which distinguishes between three stages. The thresholds t_2 and t_3 are chosen such that a short job finishes before it reaches the second stage. The jobs of medium service time length depart before reaching the third stage and only jobs which require very long service times enter the third stage.

The service facility places a job in one of three queues corresponding to the stage of the job. The server schedules the job as follows. If the first queue (corresponding to stage 1) is not empty, the next job is taken from that queue. Otherwise, a job is taken from the second queue if that queue is not empty. A job is taken from the third queue only if the first and second queue both are empty. This selection policy favors the short jobs over the longer jobs.

Since the subdivision in three stages is influenced by long range effects, we may still assume that the interarrival and service times of short jobs show a negative exponential distribution. In other words, it can still be assumed that there is considerable randomness in the arrival and service times requested by short jobs. Therefore, a suitable scheduling discipline for the first stage is round robin. This discipline guarantees a response time proportional to the service time requested by a short job (see section 6.1.6).

A job which reaches the second or third stage contributes to the average service time of the first stage only while being in the first stage. The service time in further stages has no impact on the first stage. It follows that short jobs which depart before reaching the second stage are serviced faster than when the RR scheduling discipline is uniformly applied to all jobs, irrespective of stage.

The RR discipline is not a suitable policy for the third stage. This stage is reached by the very long jobs. The FCFS discipline is the best scheduling policy for long jobs. It has the advantage of minimal job switching overhead. In addition, the system limits the number of large jobs that execute in parallel. Long jobs are likely to have a high demand for system resources. It is bad policy if the main store is shared by too many long jobs at a time. The FCFS discipline forces the long jobs to execute serially.

The obvious choice for the middle stage is a feedback policy between FCFS and RR. The SRR discipline with $0 < r < 1$ fits nicely in between those two. The parameter r can be used to tune the system. *Tuning* means that the parameter r is set to a value for which the system shows the best performance. This value is found by measuring the performance for various values of r, assuming that the demands on the system made by the user community remain the same during the measurements. Furthermore, the scheduling can easily be refined if stage s_2 is subdivided into several stages. Each substage is attached to a different value of the parameter r and this value of r is used when the feedback scheduling algorithm is applied to a job in such a substage. If at the same time the threshold t_3 is moved upwards, we see that the partitioning into three units can easily be generalized to an arbitrary n-partitioning corresponding to a sequence of ascending values of the parameter r.

6.3.3 The service facility of a three stage system uses four job queues: three for the jobs in the three stages, and one which implements the delay box of the

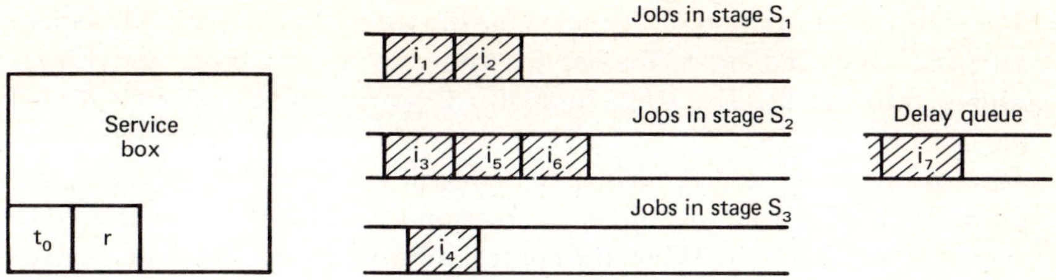

Figure 6.3a A three stage scheduling system

SRR discipline. Jobs in the delay queue are tagged with their virtual arrival time so that this quantity can be checked against the virtual arrival time av of the service box (see section 6.2 and fig. 6.2e). The virtual arrival time of a job in stage s_2 is the moment of arrival in the delay queue (see figure 6.3a). The test whether or not jobs should be transferred from the delay queue to queue q_2 (the queue adjoined to stage s_2) is carried out when another job is selected for service.

Applied to CPU scheduling, the four queues together form the ready list. Transitions from the list to the running state or vice-versa occur in three situations:

a. in a P operation, if a process is blocked
b. in a V operation, if the awakened process has a higher priority than the process currently running
c. at the end of a time slice

The actions of P and V relevant to the discussion here are:

1. close control information (current)
2. current ← select from ready list
3. open control information (current)

Time slice end is handled by a CPU control program which is activated when a time slice expires. The control information of a process is closed when it is forced to give up a CPU. It is reopened when a CPU is reallocated to it. If the three stage scheduling policy is applied, a process is selected from the ready list in the way described in section 6.3.2: the next process is taken from the front of the first non-empty queue in the order q_1, q_2, delay queue, q_3. A process returns to the front position of the queue that corresponds to its stage s_i if it is awakened in a V or if it called V and the process awakened has a higher priority than the calling process (see section 4.4.5). If a process runs out of a time slice, a process in stage s_1 or s_2 is not returned to the front, but fed back to the end of the queue of its stage.

6.3.4 The control information of a process for the three stage scheduling policy contains a stage indicator, the service time, its arrival time, and its remaining time credit. The stage indicator is set when the time slice of a process runs out depending on how its accumulated service time compares to the thresholds t_2 and t_3. When the control information is opened, the time of day is read from the universal clock and this value is remembered in the arrival time variable. When the control information is closed, the arrival time is subtracted from the current time of day and the result is added to the service time variable. This variable reflects the accumulated service time.

The arrival time of a process is set when a process enters the delay queue. This happens if a process must leave stage s_1 when it runs out of a time slice and its accumulated service time is equal to threshold t_2. When the control information is opened, the value of the remaining time credit is copied into the TIMER device. The TIMER starts decrementing the time credit and, if the credit runs out, causes an interrupt which results in running the CPU control program. This program allocates the CPU to the highest priority process. When the control information of a process is closed, the current value of the TIMER is copied into the variable which holds the remaining time credit. If a process blocks itself in the middle of a time slice, it can continue when it is awakened from the point where it left. The virtual arrival time of the accepted jobs in queue q_2 (av) is incremented by r* the elapsed time if the job is in stage s_2. (r is the coefficient of the SRR policy applied to stage 2, see section 6.2.) In addition, the stage indicator is updated and its arrival time is set. This value is its virtual arrival time when it is placed in the delay queue.

Control information is opened and closed as follows:

```
open control information(k) =
begin
   arrival time_k ← time of day
   TIMER ← time credit_k
end

close control information(k) =
begin local elapsed time ← time of day − arrival time_k
   service time_k ← service time_k + elapsed time
   time credit_k ← TIMER
   if stage_k = s_2 then av ← av + r*elapsed time fi
      $ av is the virtual arrival time of the accepted jobs
      $ r is the parameter of the SRR discipline (see section 6.2)
   stage_k ← if service time_k < threshold t_2 then 1
         else if service time_k < threshold t_3 then 2 else 3 fi fi
   arrival time_k ← time of day
end
```

The next process to run is taken from the first non-empty queue in the ready list in the order q_1, q_2, delay queue, q_3. If all queues are empty, the NULL process is selected.

```
select from ready list =
begin local k
while delay queue not empty and new job acceptable do
   k ← remove(delay queue); insert(k into q2); av ← arrival time_k
od
      $ a new job is acceptable if its arrival time ≤ av
   select ← if some k in [1:3] sat queue_k not empty then
         remove (queue_k) else NULL job fi
end
```

Selection from the ready list takes place only if it has already been decided that the currently running process must give up the CPU. Therefore the selection procedure must always be successful in finding a process to run. (This issue has also been raised in section 4.4.). The virtual arrival time of the accepted jobs in stage s_2 may have been increased before another job is selected from the ready list. Therefore, the delay queue is inspected and all acceptable jobs are transferred to queue q_2. The condition for accepting a job is described in section 6.2.

6.3.5 The CPU control program is activated when a process runs out of a time slice. It has a dual function:

a. the currently running process must be appended to the queue of its stage
b. the CPU must be allocated to the highest priority process.

The control program can make a shortcut if the current process does not change its stage and its corresponding queue is empty. The fact that a process of stage s_i is running implies that the queues corresponding to the higher priority stages are empty. Thus, if the queue of stage s_i is also empty, the currently running process has the highest priority. The CPU is not deallocated in this case; instead, the TIMER is reset to the quantum size so that the current process can run during the next time slice.

The NULL process, and the processes in stage s_3 which are treated on an FCFS basis, can have an infinite time slice, because the V operation which returns a process in stage s_1 or s_2 attaches higher priority to the awakened process and allocates the CPU to it. Thus, since only processes in stage s_1 or s_2 (being served in an RR schedule) can run out of their time credit, the CPU control program is activated only if a process in stage s_1 or s_2 is currently running.

The acceptance rule assures that the delay queue is empty if q_2 is empty. This implies that a job, coming from s_1, should immediately be placed in q_2

and not in the delay queue. If av is set to the time of day, the arrival time of the job, coming from s_1, is equal to av, so it will be placed in q_2 when the next job is selected. If a job leaves s_2 and q_2 gets empty, av is also set to the time of day so that new jobs can be accepted from the delay queue. The CPU control program handles the switching from one process to another in a manner similar to P and V (see section 4.4.5). Since they operate on shared data, these programs must not be executed concurrently. The CPU control program is therefore embedded in the same LOCK and UNLOCK pair as P and V. The control program runs at the highest priority level so that interrupts are inhibited while it is running.

A program for CPU control is

```
begin LOCK(PV lockbit)
   local k; close control information(current)      $ stage(current) is updated
if q2 empty and service time(current) = threshold t2 or t3
   then av ← time of day fi
   $ q2 can now accept new jobs from the delay queue
time credit(current) ← quantum size
   $ the current process starts at the end of the queue with a new time slice
if all k in [1:stage(current)] sat queuek empty then
   timer ← quantum size; open control information(current)
else save processor state(current)
   STATE(current) ← "ready"
   if service time(current = threshold t2 then
      insert(current into delay queue)
   else insert(current into queue(stage(current))) fi
   current ← select from ready list
   STATE(current) ← "running"
   open control information(current)
   restore processor state(current)
fi
   UNLOCK(PV lockbit)
end
```

There is no need to save and restore a processor state if the currently running process is allowed to continue. In that case the TIMER is simply reset to the quantum size q so that this process can continue during the next time slice.

6.3.6 The scheduling priority of a process is composed of two components: the stage indicator and the relative position in the job queue. These two components reflect, respectively, the total service in the past, and the relative amount of service during the recent pass through the service facility. No priority distinction has yet been made based on the nature of the job itself.

Some processes should always have higher priority with respect to CPU allocation than some of their competitors. This is typically the case for device control processes which have to meet critical time constraints in order to keep the peripheral devices working at their maximal speeds. Such processes should have priority over all user processes, independent of recent or long-range history.

There is a fixed number of this kind of processes that must have higher priority than all the others. If the relative priority of these processes is fixed, the ready list can be extended with a queue q_0, containing the set of high priority processes arranged in order of relative priority. If there are not too many of these high priority processes, the high priority queue can be implemented as a vector, where the index corresponds to the relative priority. The stage indicator of a high priority process is permanently equal to zero. Its accumulated service time has no impact on its priority. Instead of an arrival time indication, the control information of a high priority process contains the index of its position in q_0 so that the process can easily be inserted in the right place in q_0. The time credit of a high priority process is infinite.

PROBLEMS

1. The extended version of the V operation in section 4.4.5 preempts the CPU from the current process if it wakes up a process of higher priority. This priority test was represented in the form:

$$\text{priority(k)} > \text{priority(current)}$$

where k is the index of the process being awakened.

Suppose the ready list is organized as presented in this section; it consists of the high priority vector q_0, the queues q_1, q_2, and q_3 corresponding to the three stages, the delay queue and the NULL job. The notion of priority is defined by the rules:

a. A process in stage s_i has higher priority than a process in stages s_j if $i < j$.
b. The lower the index in vector q_0, the higher the priority.
c. The awakened process has higher priority than the process which wakes it up if they are in the same stage s_i where $i > 0$.

Write a program for the priority test of the V operation applying these rules.

2. There are two arguments in favor of incorporating the priority test in the V operation: (1) in the case of a hardware V operation (see section 4.5), the awakened process is a device control process; (2) if the NULL job is running, it should be stopped as soon as any other job is inserted in the ready list.

On the other hand, there is no need to test the priority in the V operation if we do not have a NULL job. The only place where the priority is ever inspected is in the selection program. Therefore, the program "select from ready list" can be designed in such a way that it cycles until a job enters the ready list or a device performs a V operation on the CPU. Modify the selection procedure according to this design. Make sure that the program is interruptable while it cycles.

It has been proposed to design the software V operation the simple way, that is, without priority test, and to design the hardware V operation such that the CPU is always allocated to the process being awakened. This also implies that no priority test is needed in the hardware V operation. Discuss the pros and cons of this proposal, in particular with respect to the possibility of several hardware V operations in rapid succession.

3. The SRR scheduling makes the management of the ready list somewhat complicated. A much simpler strategy is the one applied in the CTSS time sharing system mentioned earlier in problem 4 of section 2.2. The basic idea of that strategy is that the same scheduling discipline is applied to every stage (we opt for RR), but the time slice allotted to a process in stage s_i is q^{2i-1}, where q is the quantum size for stage s_1. The transition from one stage to another depends on the accumulated service time and the given thresholds, while the selection is subject to the same precedence rule: a process in stage s_i is chosen if and only if q_i is not empty and $q_1, \ldots, q_{i-1}$ are empty.

Write the programs for the maintenance of the control information, return into the ready list, selection from the ready list, and the control of a CPU for this strategy.

4. Consider the following alternative to organizing stage s_2 into the two separate queues, q_1 and the delay queue. Instead of the two queues, we have a single queue so that selection is simplified to taking the front element. However, insertion depends on the virtual arrival time av of the service box and the arrival time of a process in stage s_2. If its arrival time is greater than av, the process is inserted at the end of the group of processes already in the queue for which this is the case; otherwise, the process is inserted at the end of the section containing the accepted processes. Write a program for inserting into the ready list for this design.

5. A process which is in the middle of a critical section is tying up a system resource. Therefore, such a process should be forced to complete this critical section as fast as possible. Such a process has temporarily an exceptional priority.

Assuming that P and V are used for entrance and exit of a critical section, and are distinguishable from synchronization signals, a process can carry an indication whether or not it is in a critical section. The CPU control program which is activated when a time slice runs out will not return a process which is in a critical section to the ready list, but allocate the next time slice to it.

Investigate the necessary modifications in the P and V and the CPU control program.

6.4 VIRTUAL PROCESSOR SCHEDULING

6.4.1 In the preceding section we designed the scheduling strategy such that it distinguished between various sorts of jobs and applied different scheduling disciplines to different types of jobs. In this section we discuss yet another approach to CPU scheduling: that of several subsystems, each of which has its own virtual processor. For a subsystem to be able to run, a real central processor must take the place of the virtual processor. Thus, the various subsystems share the use of the available real processors and allocation of these real processors to the subsystems requires a scheduling strategy.

Subsystems can be formed in many useful ways. For example, a general purpose system is conveniently split in three subsystems, one for the real time jobs, one for the batch stream of user programs and one for the time sharing activities of the system. Instead of one subsystem handling the batch stream, we may prefer having several subsystems, corresponding to a size classification of user programs. The short programs are handled in one subsystem, the medium-size programs in another, and the long programs in a third subsystem.

Every subsystem can have its individual processor allocation scheme. A time-sharing subsystem allocates CPU time probably on a RR basis, whereas a batch system for long user jobs serves its jobs in all likelihood on an FCFS basis. In order to avoid confusion between scheduling of subsystems and scheduling within subsystems, we assume here that all subsystems treat their jobs in a simple FCFS order. Also for simplicity, we consider a single CPU system.

We discuss in this section two methods of scheduling virtual processors. The first method allocates CPU time to the subsystems taking the history into account. The objective of this method is to ascertain that every subsystem receives its fair share of CPU time, an amount of CPU time depending on the accumulated service time. The other method is known as deadline scheduling. This guarantees each subsystem a certain amount tf CPU time within a given period of time. The CPU allocation system considers the end of a period as a deadline for allocating that amount of CPU time.

6.4.2 The fair share policy not only takes into account the accumulated service time of a virtual processor, but also how long ago that service was received.

Let $C_i(t)$ be the characteristic function of subsystem i; its value is one while subsystem i has the CPU in use and zero otherwise. We restrict ourselves to a single CPU system so that $\sum_{i=1}^{n} C_i(t) = 1$.

The utilization function $B_i(t)$ is defined as a function of the service time such that the service time contributes less according to its distance in the past (see figure 6.4a). An expression satisfying this specification is:

$$B_i(t) = c_i * \int_{-\infty}^{t} C_i(u) * e^{c_i(u-t)}$$

If all constants c are chosen equal to a single constant c, then

$$\sum_{i=1}^{n} B_i(t) = c * \int_{-\infty}^{t} \sum_{i=1}^{n} C_i(u) * e^{c(u-t)} du = c * e^{-ct} * \int_{-\infty}^{t} e^{cu} du = 1$$

It can be shown that $\sum_{i=1}^{n} B_i(t)$ is also equal to one if not all constants c_i are equal.

Unfortunately, the chosen utilization measure $B_i(t)$ does not satisfy the implementation requirement which says that the value of the measure must not change while no service is received (see section 6.2.2). The change is caused by the factor $e^{-c_i t}$, because

$$\Delta B_i = B_i(t+\Delta t) - B_i(t)$$

$$= c_i * e^{-c_i(t+\Delta t)} * \int_{-\infty}^{t+\Delta t} C_i(u) e^{c_i u} du - c * e^{-c_i t} * \int_{-\infty}^{t} C_i(u) e^{c_i u} du$$

If virtual processor i receives no service in time interval t to $t+\Delta t$, then $C_i(u)$ is zero. Thus, the integrands are equal. However, the two terms are not equal, because the coefficients of the integrals are not equal. The increment of $B_i(t)$ while the system is waiting is given by

$$\Delta B_i = \{e^{-c_i \Delta t} - 1\} * c_i e^{c_i t} \int_{-\infty}^{t} C_i(u) * e^{c_i u} du$$

The value of this expression is not zero, unless system_i has not yet received

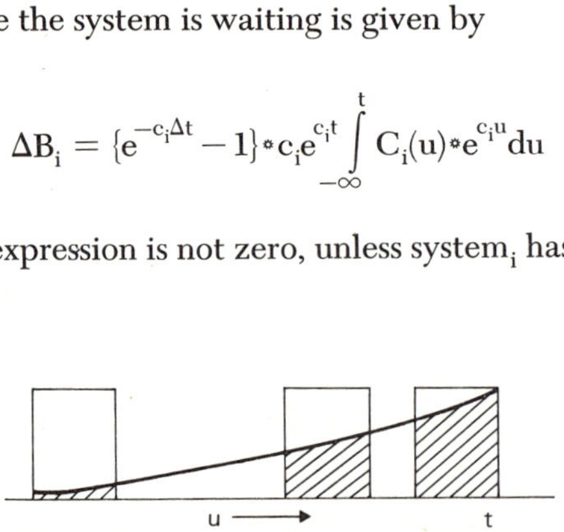

Figure 6.4a CPU utilization of subsystem i

any service at all. Since the problem is caused by the factor $e^{-c_i t}$, we define

$$S_i(t) = e^{c_i t} = c_i * \int_{-\infty}^{t} e^{c_i u} du$$

and

$$b_i(t) = B_i(t) * S_i(t) = c_i * \int_{-\infty}^{t} C_i(u) * e^{c_i u} du$$

Function $b_i(t)$ satisfies the implementation principle (see section 6.2), because

$$\Delta b_i = c_i * \int_{-\infty}^{t+\Delta t} C_i(u) * e^{c_i u} du - c_i * \int_{-\infty}^{t} C_i(u) * e^{c_i u} du$$

is equal to zero if $system_i$ is not serviced in time interval $[t:t+\Delta t]$. The increment during a service interval is

$$\Delta b_i = c_i * \int_{t}^{t+\Delta t} C_i(u) * e^{c_i u} du = e^{c_i t} * (e^{c_i \Delta t} - 1) = S_i(t) * (e^{c_i \Delta t} - 1)$$

because $C_i(t)$ is equal to one during that time interval. The function $S_i(t)$ increases by the same amount in that time interval:

$$\Delta S_i = e^{c_i(t+\Delta t)} - e^{c_i t} = S_i(t) * (e^{c_i \Delta t} - 1)$$

Ignoring terms of the order $O(\Delta t^2)$ and higher, we have

$$\Delta S_i = S_i(t) * c_i * \Delta t$$

6.4.3 In order that each subsystem gets it fair share, the highest priority is assigned to the virtual processor with the smallest B_i. The priority of a waiting virtual processor increases in time, because

$$\Delta B_i = \{e^{c_i \Delta t} - 1\} * B_i(t)$$

is negative. If we write $B_i(t+\Delta t) - B_i(t)$ for ΔB_i, we find

$$B_i(t+\Delta t)/B_i(t) = e^{c_i \Delta t} - 1 = -c_i * \Delta t + O(\Delta t^2)$$

This equation expresses the decay of $B_i(t)$ during an inactive period. It can be viewed as a measure of the speed at which the priority of virtual processor i grows.

The constant c_i is a parameter which can be used to tune the speed ratios of gaining priority. If all constants c_i are equal to a single constant c, all

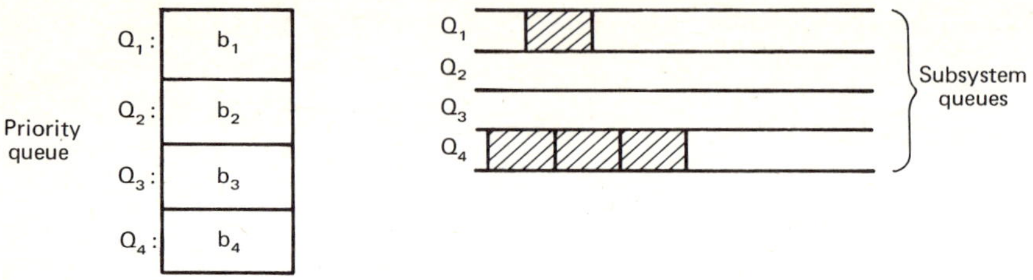

Figure 6.4b Readylist composed of priority and subsystem queues

virtual processors gain priority at the same speed. This implies that, if all subsystems have jobs to run, the CPU is allocated on a RR basis. If one of the subsystems requests less service than others, its priority increases relative to the others. Thus, if the low request system comes with a request for service, it has the highest priority, so it will be serviced immediately.

This discipline is an example of an autoregressive scheduling mechanism. It regulates itself automatically in that it balances the CPU allocation based on information it records about past behavior. If applied to an ordinary general purpose system, a single constant c is sufficient. The real time subsystem is the most crucial one, because if not serviced within a critical time limit, it fails. Assuming that the real time system does not need a large fraction of the CPU time, it will have gained a high priority by the time that it requests service if it operates at regular time intervals. In the subsequent discussions we assume that a single coefficient c suffices.

6.4.4 The ready list consists of the job queues belonging to the subsystems, and a priority queue which determines the current priority order of the virtual processors (see figure 6.4b). The priority queue lists the values of the functions $b_i(t)$. The correspondence of index and subsystem is fixed.

The control information consists of the parameter c, the function $S(t) = e^{ct}$, and three variables for each virtual processor indicating, respectively, the accumulated service time, the remaining time credit, and the value of $b_i(t)$. The value of $B_i(t)$ can be derived from $b_i(t)$ and $S(t)$. However, only the relative position in the queue is important. This can be directly derived from $b_i(t)$, because

$$b_i(t) < b_j(t) \text{ implies } B_i(t) < B_j(t) \qquad \text{for all pairs } i,j$$

The control information is updated when a job releases the CPU. $\Delta S = S*c*\Delta t$ is evaluated and added to $S(t)$ and b_i, where i is the index of the process releasing the CPU. A job carries an indication as to which subsystem it belongs so that the correct control information set can be accessed.

The next job is selected from the highest priority subsystem whose job queue is not empty. The highest priority subsystem is found by a search through the priority list for the smallest value of b(t). Instead of fixing the order of the subsystems in the priority list, the priority list can be arranged in ascending order of b(t). The selection is in that case somewhat simpler: the first subsystem whose job queue is not empty must be selected. However, the priority list must then be kept partially ordered, implying that every time the control information of a job is closed and $b_i(t)$ is updated, $subsystem_i$ must be removed and reinserted in the correct place according to its new value of $b_i(t)$. If the priority list remains in a fixed order (see figure 6.4b), then reinserting when $b_i(t)$ changes is not necessary. The priority list must now be searched if a next job is selected. If the list is not very long, then searching is not expensive. The priority list is not longer than the number of subsystems, which probably is a small number anyway. The issue of searching and sorting the priority list is discussed in more detail in section 6.5.

6.4.5 The virtual processor scheduling must be implemented as part of the actions:

1. close control information(current)
2. select(current from ready list)
3. open control information(current)
4. CPU control program at time slice end

The open and close programs are essentially the same as described in section 6.3.4, except for the additional maintenance of S(t) and $b_i(t)$. (Be aware that we assumed for simplicity that every subsystem serves its jobs FCFS.) The next job is the first job in the queue of the highest priority subsystem with non-empty job queue measured by $b_i(t)$. When a V operation returns a process to the ready list, this process is placed at the head of the job queue of its subsystem.

The CPU control program is entirely different from the program in the preceding section. It more closely resembles P and V. The programs implementing the fair share scheduling of virtual processors are listed below.

open control information(k) =
begin
TIMER ← time credit($subsys_k$)
end

close control information(k) =
begin local elapsed time = time credit($subsys_k$) − TIMER
  time credit($subsys_k$) ← TIMER
  service $time_k$ ← service $time_k$ + elapsed time
  $\Delta S \leftarrow S * c *$ elapsed time; $C \leftarrow C + \Delta S$; b($subsys_k$) ← b($subsys_k$) + ΔS
end

```
select from ready list =
begin
   UNLOCK(PV lock bit); while ready list empty do od; LOCK(PV lock bit)
   local j,k = 1; local min ← ∞
   for j in [1:priorlistlength] do
      if queue_j not empty and min > priorlist_j then min ← priorlist_j; k ← j fi
   od
   select ← remove(queue_k)
end

CPU control program =
begin LOCK(PV lockbit)
   save processor state(current)
   close control information(current)
   STATE(current) ← "ready"
   time credit(subsys(current)) ← quantime size
   insert(current into ready list)
   current ← select from ready list
   STATE(current) ← "running"
   open control information(current)
   restore processor state(current)
   UNLOCK(PV lockbit)
end
```

6.4.6 We discuss next another method of scheduling virtual processors, deadline scheduling. A deadline schedule guarantees that a virtual processor, while it is ready, receives a certain amount of service within a given period of time. For example, for a general purpose system one may decide to allocate 60% of the CPU time to the time sharing subsystem, 35% to the batch system and 5% to the real time system. These figures determine which fraction of CPU time should be allocated to each subsystem. However, it is not sufficient to guarantee that the service a particular virtual processor receives will, on the average, amount to a given fraction of CPU time. The 60% share reserved for the time sharing system can then be allocated in one chunk of 36 minutes of every hour to time sharing, with the result that time sharing users are locked out for a whole period of 24 minutes! Therefore, in addition to the figures which specify the fraction of CPU time that each subsystem should receive, we specify the duty cycle within which this fraction must be allocated. For example, we may fix the duty cycle of the time sharing system at one second. This means that the time sharing subsystem must receive 60% of every successive period of one second. The duty cycle of the batch system can be chosen much larger, for instance, five or ten minutes. For the real time system a duty cycle in the order of 10 milliseconds might be appropriate.

The deadline scheduling strategy works as follows. Let CPU time be allocated in quanta of size q. Think of the time a virtual processor is ready to run as a succession of time intervals in length equal to the cycle time c_i which is chosen as a multiple of the quantum size q. If the fraction of CPU time which virtual processor i should receive is fixed at f_i, the scheduler guarantees that virtual processor i receives at least $q_i = f_i * c_i$ quanta of service in every successive cycle of ready time. The term *ready* is used here in the sense of *not blocked*; in this sense a virtual processor is ready if any of its jobs is running or in the ready list.

Every subsystem has its own pair (c_i, f_i) that specifies its deadlines and fraction of CPU time. The worst case for the CPU scheduler occurs if all subsystems are ready and claim their fraction of service. The scheduler of a single CPU system can satisfy a given collection of virtual processors in the worst case only if $\sum_{i=1}^{n} f_i \leq 1$. However, in practice it may be possible to allow a situation in which this sum exceeds one. The demand is less than the possible maximum during the time one of the subsystems is blocked. While a subsystem is absent, the scheduler is able to anticipate its future demands and allocate to an unblocked virtual processor more quanta than necessary before the next deadline. The scheduler serves such a virtual processor ahead of schedule. This leaves some spare time in the future which could be used for additional service if $\sum_{i=1}^{n} f_i > 1$. On the other hand, the scheduler is not able to handle the worst case if this sum exceeds one, so this situation should be allowed only if it does not matter that some deadlines are occasionally not met.

The possibility of an idling subsystem is entirely disregarded from here onwards. That is, we assume from now on that a subsystem never idles, and that it contains at least one job that can run. If necessary, every subsystem can be thought of as having its own NULL job.

6.4.7 The ready list consists of the job queues of the subsystems, and a priority queue split in two sections, u list and s list (see figure 6.4c). The u list contains the virtual processors for which service is urgent. These virtual processors must yet receive some quanta before their next deadline is reached. The s list contains the satisfied virtual processors, which have already received the necessary quanta up to their next deadline. A virtual processor moves from the s list to the u list when it enters its next cycle (when its deadline is reached) and from the u list to the s list when it has received the necessary quanta of its current period. Both lists are arranged in order of ascending deadline. This implies that a virtual processor must be inserted by its deadline value when it moves from one section to the other. The highest priority is assigned to the head of the u list. This is the virtual processor which has not yet received all its quanta and whose deadline is closest of all.

If $\sum_{i=1}^{n} f_i$ is strictly less than one, the u list is sometimes entirely empty.

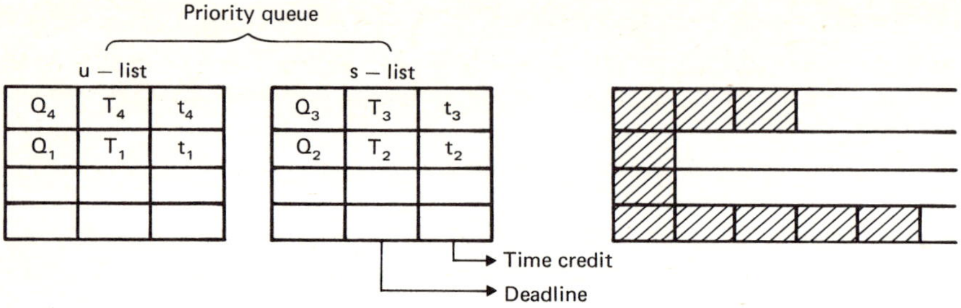

Figure 6.4c Readylist for a deadline scheduling system

This becomes clear if we check how much CPU time must be allocated in a period L, where L is the least common multiple of all the cycle times c_i. The fraction of CPU time which must be allocated to virtual processor i in period L equals $f_i * L$. The total CPU time allocated if all the deadlines are met is $L * \sum_{i=1}^{n} f_i$, which is less than L if $\sum_{i=1}^{n} f_i < 1$. Thus, if fewer quanta are allocated than strictly necessary to meet the deadlines, there comes a time when, although all quanta have been allocated, not one deadline has yet been reached. Such a situation describes exactly the case that the u list is empty, while all virtual processors reside in the s list. There is no reason to let such a situation exist for long. If the u list gets empty, the scheduler can transfer the head of the s list to the u list and process ahead of its deadline schedule.

The control information of a virtual processor consists of two constants, representing its duty cycle and its share, and two variables, representing its next deadline and its remaining time credit. The constant $share_i$ is equal to $q_i *$quantum size, where q_i is the number of quanta which must be allocated in one period. The motivation for introducing the constant $share_i$ is that it is more conveniently used in the implementation than either the number q_i or the fraction f_i. Any one of these three constants will do, because any one of them can be expressed in the other two, the duty cycle and the quantum size.

The remaining time credit is operated upon in the usual way. It is copied into the u TIMER when the control information is opened. The deadline is incremented by the duty cycle when a virtual processor is transferred from the s list to the u list. The deadline is used for three purposes:

a. to insert a virtual processor into the u list
b. to insert a virtual processor into the s list
c. to time out its presence in the s list

When a virtual processor arrives at the head of the s list, the s TIMER is set to the difference of its deadline and the current moment in time. The s

TIMER starts decrementing this time interval and causes an interrupt when the deadline of the first virtual processor is reached. The interrupt activates a second CPU control program which transfers the first virtual processor in the s list to the u list.

6.4.8 In order not to confuse the scheduling of virtual processors with the scheduling of jobs within one subsystem, we assume again that every subsystem treats its jobs on an FCFS basis. The actions in which the deadline scheduling is implemented are:

1. open and close control information
2. select from ready list
3. CPU control activated when u TIMER interrupts
4. CPU control activated when s TIMER interrupts

The corresponding programs are listed below.

```
open control information(k) =
begin arrival time_k ← time of day
  u TIMER ← time credit(subsys_k)
end

close control information(k) =
begin local elapsed time ← time of day − arrival time_k
  service time_k ← service time_k − elapsed time
  time credit(subsys_k) ← time credit(subsys_k) − elapsed time
end

select from ready list =
begin local k
  if u list empty then k ← firstof(s list)
    deadline_k ← deadline_k + duty cycle_k;
    insert(remove(k from s list) into u list)
    s TIMER ← if s list empty then ∞
                else deadline(firstof(s list)) − time of day fi
  fi
  select ← firstof(queue(firstof(u list)))
end

CPU control activated when u TIMER interrupts =
  $ this program activates the first element on the u list
begin LOCK(PV lockbit)
  save processor state(current)
  STATE(current) ← "ready"
  close control information(current)
```

```
if time credit(subsys(current)) = 0 then
   time credit(subsys(current)) ← share(subsys(current))
   insert(remove(u list) into s list)
   if current = firstof(s list) then
      s TIMER ← deadline(subsys(current)) − time of day fi
fi

   return(current to readylist)      $ "return" places a job at the head of a list
   current ← select from ready list

   STATE(current) ← "running"
   open control information(current)
   restore processor state(current)
   UNLOCK(PV lockbit)
end

CPU control activated when s TIMER interrupts =
   $ this program transfers the firstof the s list to the u list
begin LOCK(PV lockbit)
   local k = firstof(s list)
   deadline_k ← deadline_k + duty cycle_k; insert(k into (u list))
   s TIMER ← if s list empty then ∞
                  else deadline(firstof(s list)) − time of day fi
   if k = firstof(u list) then u TIMER ← 0 fi
   UNLOCK(PV lockbit)
end
```

If the inserted element happens to be the first in the u list, it should immediately receive service. Setting the u TIMER to zero has the effect that u TIMER interrupts and activates the first element of the u list.

PROBLEMS

1. One of the subsystems served by a fair share CPU scheduling system is a time sharing system which serves its jobs round robin with a quantum size equal to the one used by the fair share scheduler. The system needs only one TIMER device by virtue of the equal quantum sizes.

Investigate whether or not the procedures for updating the control information need to be modified. Write a modified version of the CPU control program which also takes care of the RR scheduling within the time sharing subsystem.

2. The use of N (N > 1) different coefficients c_i in a fair share scheduling

system has the disadvantage that the scheduler must maintain N different functions $S_i(t) = e^{c_i t}$. All these functions must be updated when the control information of a virtual processor is closed. The coefficients always occur in connection with time. Consider therefore the following alternative.

A single coefficient c will be used. Instead of real time, t counts the number of quanta allocated. The functions S(t) and $b_i(t)$ are used in the same way as before, but now as functions of the number of allocated quanta. The quantum size, however, will not be equal for all subsystems; each has its own quantum size.

Write the program for closing the control information for this strategy. Analyze whether the ratio of the quantum size for a batch subsystem and time sharing subsystem should be smaller than one or greater than one.

3. A foreground-background scheduler attempts to optimize the utilization of CPU time. The idea is that the CPU is first allocated to foreground jobs (usually time sharing jobs). The background jobs (usually belonging to a batch stream) serve as fillers; as soon as no foreground job can run, one of the background jobs is activated, but is stopped immediately if one of the foreground jobs becomes ready to run again.

Investigate whether or not the coefficients of a fair share system or the constants duty cycle and fraction of CPU time can be chosen such that the design approximates a foreground-background system. Do the same for a pure FCFS and a pure RR system.

4. One version of the V operation compares the priority of the process calling the V operation with that of the one being awakened. Program this priority test for the fair share scheduling system and also for the deadline scheduling system.

5. The two timers of the u list and s list can be implemented sharing one physical TIMER device. The scheduler maintains for that purpose two additional variables: utimer and stimer. These two variables must be programmed to act just like the corresponding hardware devices. That is, the variable stimer must time out the presence of the first job in the s list and the variable utimer must gradually decrement the time credit of a virtual processor and cause an interrupt when the credit runs out. It can do the latter, of course, only with the aid of the single physical TIMER device. Therefore, the TIMER is always set to the minimum of utimer and stimer so as to cause all the necessary interrupts.

Rewrite the maintenance programs for the control information of the deadline scheduling system, and the selection from the ready list and also both CPU control programs using these two software timers and the single TIMER device.

6.5 IMPLEMENTATION ISSUES AND MULTIPROCESSOR SCHEDULING

6.5.1 Round robin and first-come first-serve scheduling cause the least overhead in maintaining a job queue. Selection of the next job is the simple action of removing the first element from the queue and a job is inserted into the queue by simply appending it to the rear of the queue.

Scheduling policies which account for service time received in the past require a more elaborate job queue maintenance. The priority of a job changes in time and so does its priority position relative to the other jobs. RR is a simple policy, because, if a job runs out of a time slice, its priority drops to the lowest of all, and it is placed at the end of the queue. Similarly, FCFS is simple, because a newly arriving job has the lowest priority, while the relative priority of the jobs does not change at all.

There are basically two maintenance strategies for a time-dependent priority scheduling policy:

a. The queue is partially ordered by decreasing priority
b. Every element in the unordered queue carries a priority indicator

Method (a) has the advantage that selecting a next job is simple, but has the disadvantage that a job must be inserted into the queue in a position which corresponds to its priority; method (b) is just the opposite. We discuss in this section the impact of these two methods on scheduling virtual processors and their application to a system with several central processors. If a system is divided into subsystems by different types of jobs, one may assume that a simple scheduling policy suffices per subsystem: RR, FCFS or SRR. Time-dependent priority scheduling is more appropriately applied to the virtual processors for these systems.

6.5.2 Let the information relevant to scheduling virtual processors be kept in a priority list which is arranged following either method. The priority list is consulted or updated, when a process

1. is blocked
2. is awakened
3. runs out of time credit

The next job that has absolute highest priority is selected in a P operation or in the CPU control program which is activated when a time slice ends. When a process is awakened in a V operation, it is possible to switch to the highest priority process. On the other hand, there is no need to do so, because the running process has not run out of time credit.

The decision as to what should be done in a V operation depends on a choice between two possible units on which the notion of relative priority can be based: time, or service quanta. If time is chosen as the basic unit, the highest priority process should run at all times. Selecting the highest priority process in a V operation is consistent with that idea. If a service quantum is chosen as the unit, the relative priority should not change until the end of a time slice. The priority measure is updated in a P or V in order to affect the change in priority between disjoint time slice segments, but this change is not reflected until time slice end. Taking this point of view, there is no need for a general selection of the highest priority process in a V, because the priority has not changed in the meantime. That is, the currently running process or the one awakened has the highest priority.

Time fits better as basic unit of method (b), whereas quanta are the more natural units for method (a). If quanta are used as unit for method (b), we need an additional piece of control information: priority change. This variable is to be used when control information is opened or closed, but it is not added to the priority variable until a time slice end is processed. We assume here that such a refinement is not necessary. A comparison of the two methods is presented in figure 6.5a.

	Block	Wakeup	Time Slice End
a. REORDER	no	no	yes
SELECT	take first	no	take first
b. SELECT	search	omit search for efficiency	search

Figure 6.5a Maintenance of an ordered and an unordered schedule

6.5.3 It is not necessary to sort the whole priority queue when it must be reordered at the end of a time slice. The fact that a particular virtual processor was running has had no effect on the priority of the other virtual processors. Another virtual processor may have been running in the meantime and its priority may therefore have changed. Such changes will have been accounted for if it reached its time slice end. Thus, only the virtual processor that ran out of time credit must be replaced in the priority list.

The most obvious way of maintaining an ordered priority queue is by keeping a linked list or an array in which the elements are ordered by descending priority. Removing the highest priority element is simply done by taking the first element from the list or array. However, inserting requires a search for the correct place where the new element fits so that the order is maintained. This search is proportional to the length of the queue. Thus, if the average length of the queue is n, the time it takes to insert m elements is proportional to n*m. If this linear ordering method is used, a list structure is more appropriate than an array. The latter has the drawback that all the elements following a newly inserted element must be shifted one place in the array.

There are several methods for ordering a priority queue which perform much better than the straight linear ordering. A beautiful method is based on the "heap sort" algorithm invented by J. W. J. Williams. The priority queue is maintained as a partially ordered set which can be represented as a binary tree. The order is determined by the rule that a node (if it is not a leaf) must have a higher priority value than both its offspring. An example is given in figure 6.5a in which the priorities of ten elements are partially ordered in a binary tree.

The binary tree can easily be represented by a linear array. The nodes are numbered starting at one from left to right and from top to bottom. The indices of the elements along the leftmost path through the tree, starting at the top, are, respectively, 1, 2, 4, 8, ... Williams gave the name *heap* to the array representation of the partially ordered set of priority values. An array A[1:n] is a heap if

$$A[j//2] \geq A[j] \qquad \text{for } j \in [2:N]$$

where the symbol // represents integer division. Note that the parent of the j-th node in the tree of figure 6.5a has the index j//2. Thus, the heap characteristic of an array corresponds to the priority ordering rule of the tree.

The heap ordering of the priority queue has two important advantages over the linear ordering. First, the heap can be implemented as an array. This makes the link fields entirely superfluous. Secondly, we will see shortly

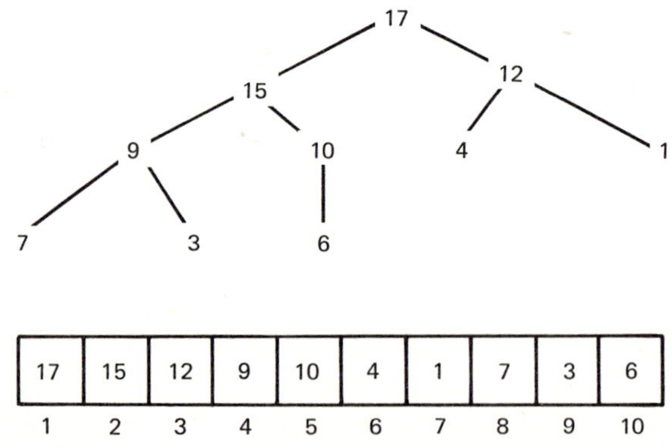

Figure 6.5a A partially ordered priority queue

that inserting and removing an element require one comparison per tree level instead of one comparison per element of the linear priority list for inserting. Therefore, the remove and insert algorithms take $O(m*\log_2 n)$ time for m operations on a heap of average size n. Removing the highest priority element from a linear priority queue is a trivial operation, but inserting an element is an $O(m*n)$ operation. Thus, the priority heap performs better than the linear priority list, particularly for large n. The linear priority order should be used if n is small (say $n < 5$).

A new element is inserted into the heap by creating a new array element and assigning to it the given priority value. This addition may disturb the heap rule, because the new element A[last] may be greater than the element A[last//2]. If so, the two are interchanged. The new value now resides in A[j] where j = last//2. It is possible for the new value to also be greater than its new parent A[j//2]. If so, the two values are again interchanged. This process is continued until the inserted value has found a parent with a larger priority value or until it has reached the root of the tree (the first element in the array). Figure 6.5b shows how the value 16 is "sifted up" through the heap of figure 6.5a in three steps. The new position of the inserted value is shown by the little circle.

Let array A[O:N] be reserved for a heap of priority values. The upperbound N is chosen large enough to allow for fluctuations in the number of elements in the queue. The unused elements of the array have the value zero. The element A_0 is added to facilitate the test for the end of the array. Its value is permanently equal to zero. We assume that a priority value is a positive integer. The index of the last significant array element is recorded in the variable "last". The initial value of last is zero. A program for inserting a new value into heap A is

```
procedure insert(x into A) =
begin local i, k; i ← (last ← last+1)
   repeat k ← i; i ← i//2 until i = 0 or Aᵢ ≥ x do Aₖ ← Aᵢ od
   Aₖ ← x
end
```

The program differs a little from the description of the algorithm in that the new value is not placed into the heap until the proper array element is

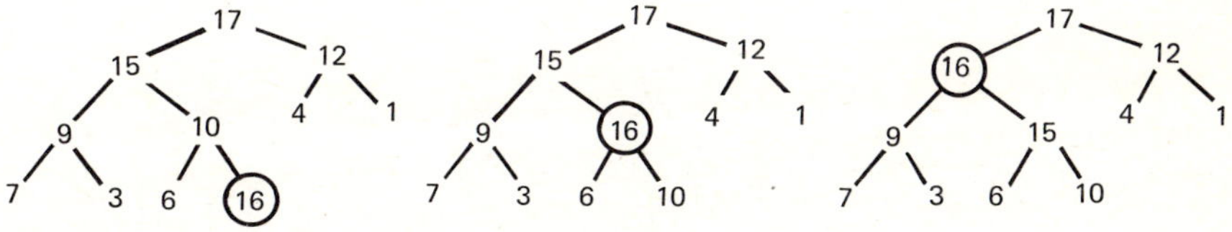

Figure 6.5b The successive stages of inserting into a heap

found where it belongs. The element A_0 has been added to make sure that the repetition test does not fail for $i = 0$.

The largest priority value is always in the root of the tree (the first element of the array), because the root of a (sub-)tree is larger than or equal to all its nodes. Therefore, finding the highest priority value is no problem. However, the heap must be reconstructed after the root has been removed. This is done by sifting down instead of sifting up. The priority value stored in A_{last} is moved to the root A_1. It is possible that this value is smaller than one of the priority values in the offspring A_2 and A_3. If so, the largest of these two is interchanged with the value in A_1. In its new position, the value may again be smaller than that of one of its offsprings. We keep interchanging the sifted value with that of one of its offsprings until we reach a leaf or the offspring has a smaller value than the one sifted down. The remove procedure returns as value the priority value which was in the root when the execution started.

```
procedure remove(A) =
begin local v = A₁; local i,k = 1; local save = A_last; last ← last−1
  repeat i ← k; k ← 2*i
    if k < last then if A_k < A_k+1 then k ← k+1 fi fi
      $ k is now the index of the largest offspring (if any)
  until save > A[if k > last then 0 else k fi] do A_i ← A_k od
  A_i ← save; return v
end
```

The value "save" is not returned to the array until the proper place has been found where it belongs. The repetition test compares the saved value with its largest potential offspring if there is one, or with A_0 otherwise. In the latter case the test is always true, because save > 0 and $A_0 = 0$. The procedure of sifting down when the root is removed is shown in figure 6.5c.

The heap arrangement is one of the best methods for keeping a set of priority values partially ordered. It has the advantage of low storage requirements, the absence of link fields and their updating and, last but not least, good performance of inserting and removing elements. Balanced

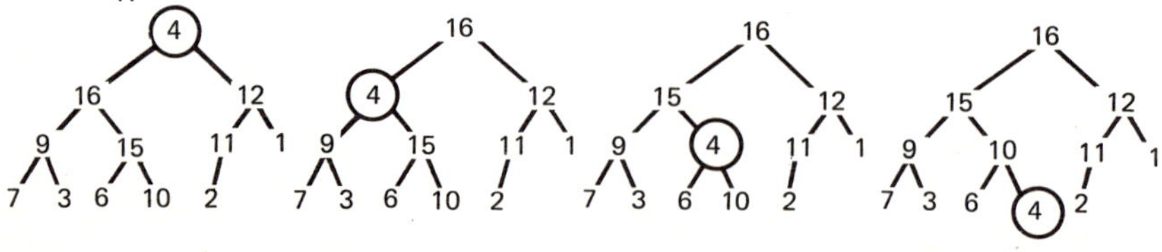

Figure 6.5c The successive stages of removing from a heap

trees and other methods for ordering a set of priority values, performing nearly as well as the heap method, are discussed in the literature.

6.5.4 A slight advantage of method (b) is that because an element can easily be excluded from selection for a variety of reasons, all eligible and ineligible items can be kept in one list. Only if there is a chance that the search for the highest priority eligible element slows down too much because of a great number of ineligible items, then organization in separate lists is recommended. On the other hand, such an organization is rather simple if the lists are unordered. An element entering the list can always be appended or placed at the head of the list.

An interesting intermediate form is the batch schedule. Suppose the job queue is at some time completely ordered by priority. The jobs will be served in that order as by an RR scheduler. However, when all jobs have received a quantum, the queue is reordered in accordance with the priorities which may have changed in the meantime.

This method has the advantage that the operations remove and insert are as simple as for an FCFS or RR discipline, but the effect of a time-dependent priority can still be brought to bear. However, the question is whether the queue can easily be reordered after a batch has been served.

We discuss briefly two methods for sorting the priority queue. The first is the heap sort, mentioned earlier. When the sorting starts, the queue is first transformed into a heap (such that $A[j//2] \geq A[j]$ for $j \in [2{:}N]$). Next, the elements are pulled off the heap one by one. The heap property is restored every time an element is taken from the root in the same manner as in the procedure remove described earlier in this section. This is an efficient sorting method which operates in $O(n \log n)$ time, where n is the number of elements in the heap.

Another efficient and elegant method is "quick sort," invented by C. A. R. Hoare. We keep two pointers, "left" and "right," initially pointing, respectively, to the first and to the last element of the array. The elements A[left] and A[right] are compared while decreasing right by one until A[left] < A[right] or left and right meet. If a left element is found less than a right element, the two elements are interchanged and now the left pointer starts moving to the right until, again, A[left] < A[right] or left = right. By the time left = right, the element A[left] is in its proper place, because

$$A[i] \geq A[\text{left}] \geq A[j] \qquad \text{for } 1 \leq i < \text{left} < j \leq N$$

The procedure can now separately be applied to the section to the left of A[left] and the section to the right of A[left], because it is certain that no two elements in different sections have to be interchanged.

The quick sort method turns out to work more efficiently than one might expect from the worst case. The procedure takes $O(n^2)$ time in the worst case, because the procedure may have to be repeated n times while each step requires linear time. However, one can show that for a randomly ordered queue the expected execution time is $O(n \log_2 n)$. This has been confirmed by experiments. Unfortunately, the method works rather badly if the queue is already almost sorted by priority. One can check this by applying the method to a queue in which only one adjacent pair of elements is out of place. Thus, if the time-dependent priority does not change much during the period of processing the whole queue, quick sort may not perform satisfactorily.

6.5.5 If every virtual processor carries its own time credit the scheduler can easily be extended to a multiprocessor system. A virtual processor is completely independent of the particular CPU on which it runs and it can therefore run on different CPUs at different times.

The scheduling systems discussed in this and the preceding section are designed for central processors with a general machine instruction set capable of executing user programs. In places where the number of central processors was assumed to be one, the extension to several central processors is obvious. The schedulers presented are nowhere critically dependent on the number of central processors. Thus, if a given multiprocessor system has a set of identical central processors which can serve any one of the subsystems, then the fair share or deadline scheduling system can also be used for such a multiprocessor system.

A system with identical central processors is at one extreme end of the spectrum of possibilities. At the other end we find a multiprocessor system in which every CPU has a special function and no subsystem is served by more than one CPU. Such a system can be treated as a composition of single CPU systems. A configuration of particular interest in between these extremes is one in which every subsystem can be served by a subset of CPUs, while the intersection of these subsets may be non-empty. For example, we could have a dual processor system in which one CPU serves all the real time processes while the other supports the time sharing subsystem, but both allocate CPU time on a secondary priority basis to the batch subsystem. Or, a particular group of users may have a privileged status. One CPU is reserved for their work, while another CPU serves every subsystem equally. Such multiprocessor systems have the general characteristic that certain subsystems are precluded from running on certain processors. This inequity is assumed in our further discussions.

The designer of a scheduler for a multiprocessor system is also faced with the choice between maintaining a partially ordered priority list or selecting jobs from an unordered list by searching. In the remainder of this section we briefly discuss some design and implementation issues for both methods with respect to a multiprocessor system.

6.5.6 Suppose that the virtual processors are not ordered by priority, but that every virtual processor carries control information from which its priority can be derived. Every time a next job is selected, the list of virtual processors is scanned for the eligible processor of highest priority whose job queue is not empty. Whether a processor is eligible depends on information such as "satisfied until next deadline" and also on the indication on which CPUs this virtual processor can run. It is not possible to split the list of virtual processors in two disjoint parts, one for the eligible processors and one for the others, because a given virtual processor may be eligible for one CPU and not for another. An alternative would be to list the eligible virtual processors for every CPU separately. However, such an arrangement implies that a virtual processor is listed as many times as there are CPUs on which it can run. The problem of inserting and removing a virtual processor from several lists probably defeats the purpose of cutting down on the search. Moreover, the separate lists cannot be simultaneoulsy consulted and modified by independent CPUs, because the information is not independent.

If we have one priority list which is totally or partially ordered (for instance by increasing deadline), a search cannot be entirely avoided, because the highest priority virtual processor may not be able to run on the CPU which is selecting a job. The search takes less time than for an unordered listing of the virtual processors, because it can be terminated as soon as the first runnable virtual processor is found. Although the list of virtual processors cannot be split along the lines of eligible and ineligible, a partitioning is possible in which one sublist contains all the virtual processors which cannot or should not run at all. The search process benefits from such partitioning in any case, whether or not the list of virtual processes is ordered.

The presence of several CPUs causes the following problem with regard to inserting an awakened process into the readylist. It can easily be established which of the awakened process or the running process has the highest priority. However, both may have higher priority than one of the processes being served by one of the other CPUs! If the scheduler aims at running the highest priority processes, it must reallocate all the central processors when a process is awakened. If the relative priority of the processes currently running on the CPUs is recorded, one can try to run the awakened process on the lowest priority CPU possible. The fact that every process cannot run on any CPU complicates the procedure even further. The most general implementation seems so unattractive that we should look for a reasonable alternative.

Unfortunately, the problem cannot entirely be ignored. In certain cases a comparison of the running process and the awakened process is not sufficient. For example, one real time process may wake up another real time process, while another CPU is executing a background job. In such a case the background job should indeed be forced to give up its CPU.

The example shows a possible alternative solution. Let a precedence relation be defined for the CPUs which corresponds to the relative priority of the virtual processor it is serving. That is, CPUs serving jobs of one subsystem have equal precedence. When a process is awakened, the priority of its virtual processor is compared to the priority of the virtual processor served by the lowest precedence CPU. If the CPU carries lower priority, the awakened process replaces the process running on that CPU. If not, the priority of the awakened process is compared to that of the process which caused the wake up and the higher priority process gets the CPU. In any case, the loser returns to the readylist.

Such a policy is feasible if it is not too hard to find the CPUs in the lowest precedence class. If the relative priority of the virtual processors changes in time (as in the fair share and the deadline scheduling systems), then the precedence order of the CPUs also changes in time. It is then necessary to search for the lowest priority virtual processor which is running on a CPU on which the awakened process also can run. This CPU is a usable one of lowest precedence. Similar difficulties do not arise in a single CPU system, because no search is necessary when a process is awakened using several processors.

PROBLEMS

1. If the list of virtual processors which share a single CPU is not ordered, the next job is selected by searching. Suppose that a deadline scheduling policy is applied and that the number of virtual processors is small enough to keep two bit vectors in machine words which represent, respectively, "not yet satisfied until next deadline," and "corresponding job queue is not empty." Among the machine instructions that operate on bit vectors of machine word length are logical operations such as AND, OR and COMPLEMENT, and in particular TEST A,B and ROT A,B, where A is a machine register and B a register or a storage operand. The test instruction finds the index of the first one in the binary representation of A scanning from left to right and places this value in B. The rotate instruction rotates the bits in A over a number of bit positions as given by B (to the left if $B > 0$, to the right otherwise). Assume furthermore that array DEADLINE is accessible in primary storage.

Choose the necessary instructions of a hypothetical machine in addition to the given instructions, and program a machine instruction sequence which implements the search of the next virtual processor as described in section 6.5.4.

2. The fair share scheduler of a single CPU system maintains two separate lists, one for all eligible virtual processors and one for the others. A virtual processor is not eligible while its job queue is empty. The eligible list is kept in order of highest priority first.

Write the programs for entering and exiting from both sublists and describe when these programs must be executed. Investigate also whether a similar implementation can easily be designed for a deadline scheduling system.

3. A dual processor system serves three kinds of jobs: class A contains jobs which can run only on CPU_1, class B jobs can run on both CPU_1 and CPU_2, and class C jobs can run only on CPU_2. All jobs in one subsystem belong to the same class. The virtual processors are listed in three separate heaps corresponding to the three classes; each heap is partially ordered in descending priority. When a next job is selected, the priorities of the first element in the two heaps are compared and the higher priority virtual processor is selected.

Write the selection program and write a program for reordering at the end of a time slice for the case of fair share scheduling.

4. A multiprocessor system has four CPUs and four subsystems A, B, C and D. The control information of a subsystem consists of the value of b(t) computed by the fair share scheduler, an indication "job queue non-empty", a list of CPUs it can run on, and the CPUs which are currently running jobs of the subsystem. The list of CPUs on which the subsystems can run is fixed and is given by A(2,3,4), B(1,3,4), C(1,2,4) and D(1,2,3).

At any moment the processors must be allocated to the processes with the highest priority. This implies that it may be necessary to reallocate a processor if a process is awakened. Ready to run processes to which no processor is allocated are placed in the readylist. Write a program which puts an awakened process in the right place and updates the necessary control information.

5. The deadline scheduler of a multiprocessor system maintains three heaps: one for the satisfied virtual processors, one for the virtual processors whose job queues are empty and one for the eligible virtual processors. When a next job is selected, the process with closest deadline which can run on the selecting CPU must be chosen.

Discuss the transition of a virtual processor from one of the three heaps to one of the other heaps. Indicate the causes of such a transition and describe the necessary updating of control information at that time. Compare this design with the one in which all virtual processors are listed in a single list or heap. Does the additional overhead of maintaining the three heaps outweigh the disadvantages of the longer search through a single list or heap?

READING LIST

Heapsort and Quicksort algorithms are described in [1] and [6]. There is an extensive literature on scheduling and modeling of systems. Only a few papers are listed here [2, 4]. Some, involving storage allocation, are listed at the end of chapter 8. References to most of the relevant literature are found in [3, 5]. [3] describes analytic models for a variety of operating system problems. [6] is a well-written standard textbook on queueing theory. [7] discusses the practical aspects and goals of performance evaluation.

1. Aho, A. V., J. E. Hopcroft, and J. D. Ullman, *The Design and Analysis of Computer Algorithms*, Addison-Wesley, 1974, 87–92.
2. Belady, L. A., and C. J. Kuehner, "Dynamic Space Sharing in Computer Systems," *Comm. ACM* 12, 5 (May 1969).
3. Coffman, E. G., Jr., and P. J. Denning, *Operating System Theory*, Prentice Hall, 1973.
4. Kleinrock, L., "A Continuum of Scheduling Policies," *Proceedings of the AFIPS SJCC* 36 (1970).
5. Kleinrock, L., *Queueing Systems*, vol. I: *Theory*, John Wiley, 1975.
6. Knuth, D., *The Art of Computer Programming*, vol. 3: *Sorting and Searching*, Addison-Wesley, 1973, 145–150.
7. Lynch, W. C., "Operating System Performance," *Comm. ACM* 15, 7 (July 1972).

7. Storage Management

7.1 MULTI-LEVEL STORE

7.1.1 In this chapter we discuss some widely applied methods of managing a two-level store consisting of primary and secondary storage. The general objective of this management is to put that part of the information which is not immediately needed in secondary storage. The reason for having the active information spread over two levels of store is a matter of economy. A fast access storage device is used as primary store, because the instruction execution time of a central processor is critically dependent on the cycle time of the store from which a CPU fetches the instructions and the operands. However, it is not economical to store information which is not immediately needed in a fast store if there are much cheaper devices which can hold that information. We encountered an application of this rule in section 2.2. The batch of programs ready to run is stored as a job queue on a drum. There is no point in placing these programs in the fast primary store, because programs are executed by that system one at a time. The access speed of a primary storage device is even more important than its size, but, for secondary storage, size is more important than access speed.

We introduce here some useful terminology:

a. The term *name* is used to denote the symbolic representation of a data object or executable procedure in the way this is done in a program written in a programming language.
b. The term *location* is used for a physical storage cell in which an instruction or data item is stored.
c. The term *address* (sometimes called *virtual address*) refers to a unique label that distinguishes a location from other locations.

It will hardly be necessary to draw the reader's attention to the extreme usefulness of names as a symbolic representation of programs and data. The use of symbolic names not only increases the readability of programs, but also allows the user to abstract from storage allocation issues which generally are irrelevant to the logic of the program in which the names are used. The use of addresses can be elucidated by an example taken from the domain of compiler design. Suppose code is to be compiled for a recursive procedure FIB(n) which computes the n-th Fibonacci number of a given non-negative integer n.

procedure FIB(n) =
FIB ← *if* n = 0 *or* n = 1 *then* 1 *else* FIB(n − 1) + FIB(n − 2) *fi*

It is impossible to reserve one fixed location for the parameter n, because, owing to the recursion, several instances of the parameter may exist at one time when the n-th Fibonacci number is being computed. Therefore, the compiler translates the name n into an address of the form W[d], where W represents the starting point of the work space which will be allocated when FIB is activated and d is the offset from the base of this workspace. W[d] is an example of a (virtual) address.

Names used in a program must eventually be translated into references to locations which contain the instruction or data item corresponding to the given name. A central processor cannot access the instruction or data item until such a translation has taken place. The translation is accomplished in two steps.

$$\text{name} \xrightarrow{T_1} \text{address} \xrightarrow{T_2} \text{location}$$

The set of addresses into which the names of a given program can be translated is known as the *virtual store* or *virtual memory* of this program. The notion of virtual store is an abstraction from physical storage, because the addresses determine only the positions of information items related to one another disregarding the exact physical locations.

The mapping T_1 is largely an issue of language system design. Mapping T_2, however, belongs to the domain of an operating system. The language system considers the virtual store as *the* store of the target machine on which compiled programs are supposed to run. An implementation of mapping T_2 transforms the given hardware into a machine which has the properties of the virtual store. Mapping T_2 accomplishes a machine transformation as discussed in section 5.2.

The design of the virtual store and the implementation of mapping T_2 are the two degrees of freedom left to the design of an operating system. The domain of mapping T_2 is the virtual store, while its range is the two-level store consisting of primary and secondary storage (the main store Ms and a backup store Bs). System designers have taken advantage of this situation and used mapping T_2 for implementing a suitable management of the two-level store. The language system programmer has the illusion that every program works in its own virtual space, while the operating system interprets the virtual addresses in such a way that the information resides at the proper storage level.

7.1.2 The data flow between the two storage levels can be placed under explicit control of the program in which the information is used, under control of the operating system, or under joint control of both. Each of these three approaches has its pros and cons, which we will discuss in due course. In this section we discuss an example of the first kind, dynamic overlay.

Suppose a machine has a primary store Ms of 2^{12} words and a secondary store Bs of 2^{16} words. When an instruction is loaded into the instruction register, the 12 least significant bits are interpreted as a location in Ms. A location in Bs can be accessed only through a device command. The operating system provides two transfer operations:

$$\text{save}(l_1, l_2, n) \qquad \text{and} \qquad \text{fetch}(l_1, l_2, n)$$

where l_1 is a location in Ms and l_2 a location in Bs. The save operation copies the locations $l_1, \ldots, l_1+n-1$ into the location $l_2, \ldots, l_2+n-1$; the fetch operation does exactly the opposite. Both operations result in an error message in the abnormal case that

$$l_1+n > 2^{12} \text{ or } l_2+n > 2^{16}$$

We choose the identity transformation for mapping T_2. However, an address is interpreted as a location in Bs only if it is used as second parameter in one of the operations save or fetch; in all other instructions an address is interpreted as a location in Ms.

Suppose that the programs for this machine are written in a programming language in which names obey scope rules as in PL/1 or a language of the ALGOL family. A program written in such a language may have a block structure as shown in figure 7.1a. The scope rule allows a block to reference local names defined in this segment and names defined in the ancestor blocks (for example, block K has access to the names defined in K, F, B and A, but not to names defined in L and E, or C and D and their offsprings).

The dynamic overlay technique is applied in the following way. The compiled code and the data for all the blocks is placed in the secondary store Bs. The execution of the program is started by loading block A into the primary store Ms and setting the program counter to its first instruction. Because block A does not have access to any name defined in the inner blocks, none of the inner blocks are needed while block A executes. The blocks are compiled as subroutines. When control is passed to an inner block, the code and data area for this block are loaded into Ms and the program counter is set to the first instruction of the inner block. When a block is finished executing, its code and data are moved back to the secondary store. The nesting rule for blocks assures that all the inner blocks have finished by the time a parent block finishes.

The total Ms space needed for the execution of a block structured program is far less than the sum of the space requirements of all the blocks. Figure 7.1a shows that the maximum space requirement in the example is determined by the combination: A B E, A B F K, A B F L, E C G, A D H, A D I and A D J, because only one of these combinations will ever be in Ms.

If the programmer carefully designs the block structure of his program, it may be able to run in an area of Ms considerably smaller than the size of the entire program. On the other hand, the larger the number of blocks, the more overhead is added to the execution of the program because of the searches through Bs for the block to be loaded. A programmer must look for the golden mean between two extremes: (1) a program which has only a few inner blocks runs the risk of not fitting in Ms; (2) a program which is meticulously split in blocks may run very slowly and leave Ms space idle! A programmer who is not familiar with the behavior of a system which uses overlays may have serious difficulties in finding the proper balance. On the other hand, the overlay technique may work out very well for a program which is frequently executed in an area of known size. The code of a compiler is an example of such a program.

Implementation of dynamic overlay is worth considering for the simple batch system discussed in section 2.2. However, dynamic overlay is an inadequate method of allocating space in the main store of a general multiprogramming system. In such a system the two levels of storage are shared by several partly executed programs of which a variable subset can run. This causes the availability of space at the primary level to vary in a manner which can be predicted by neither the programmer nor a compiler.

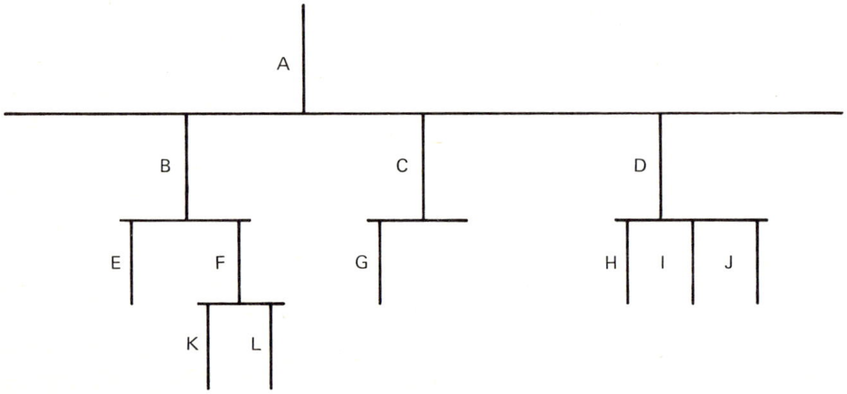

Figure 7.1a Block structure of a program

Conditions outside the control of an individual program determine whether or not the effort of dynamic overlay pays off. In the next sections we discuss the techniques of paging and segmentation. If one of these techniques is applied, space in the two storage levels is allocated with proper regard for the entire collection of running programs and their states. Therefore, these techniques are much more amenable to multiprogramming than dynamic overlay.

PROBLEMS

1. Look up some data about information transmission speeds of various devices and information storage density on some information carriers. Suppose a language system is 60,000 lines long written in a programming language. Its compiled code consists of 12,000 machine instructions for the compiler part, 4000 machine instructions for the runtime support section and 2000 machine instructions for its library. Compare the space needed to store all this information on cards, magnetic tape, disk or drum (all of your choice). Estimate the average time it will take to load the compiler or a library routine from these long range storage media.

2. A program has the following structure:

A: *begin* ⟨320⟩ B: *begin* ⟨240⟩ C: *begin* ⟨180⟩ *end* ⟨200⟩ *end*
D: *begin* ⟨450⟩ *end*
⟨600⟩
end

The numbers between angle brackets represent the number of instructions which the compiler generates for that section. Let Ms be a store of 4096 words and suppose the compiler applies the dynamic overlay technique. Determine the Ms location of the blocks A through D at runtime.

3. Compiler C applies dynamic overlay. A conditional statement of the form: "*if* BE *then* stat 1 *else* stat 2 *fi*" is coded by jump instructions, one following the evaluation of the Boolean expression BE which has as target statement stat 2, and one at the end of stat 1 which transfers control to whatever follows after the delimiter *fi*. A problem similar to that of an inner block arises when the compiler has found the places where the jump instructions must be inserted. Since the exact runtime location in Ms of this block is not yet known, these jumps must be fixed when the position in Ms is known. This position is determined at the end of the block.

Design a method for coding a conditional statement (or a repetition statement) for a compiler which applies the described overlay technique, and extend the program which handles block end to fix up the necessary references to runtime locations.

4. An overlay technique can also be applied to variables and arrays declared at the head of a block. Assume that these array declarations may have variable bounds (of which the values are not known at compile time). Design a stack discipline for the management of variables and arrays such that data items in parallel blocks use the same space at the primary level Ms.

5. Suppose the Ms workspace of a library routine MUL(A,B,C) is restricted to 64 cells including space for its local variables, but not for its parameters. The routine multiplies two matrices given as first and second parameter and places the result in C. The number of rows (columns) of an array can be found by calling the library routine rowlength (columnlength) with a matrix as parameter. Design routine MUL such that it can multiply n by n matrices under the given constraint where $64 \leq n < 128$.

7.2 SWAPPING AND RELOCATION

7.2.1 In a multiprogrammed machine the execution of several programs may be under way. Some are ready to run, while others are waiting for the completion of a data transmission. The waiting times are generally very long. Data transmission through slow devices such as a card reader or teletype takes on the order of 0.1 to 1 second. Data on fast devices such as a drum or disk is usually transmitted in large quantities because of the seek time. Such a transfer of data takes some 10 to 100 milliseconds. It would be a waste of valuable storage space if the program and data of a waiting process were kept in the main store. Ideally, the primary store should contain only processes that are ready to run.

This objective can be achieved in various ways. We discuss in this section the swapping method. The principle of the method is that program and data of a process that is going to wait are swapped out of the main store Ms and are saved on the backup store Bs. When the waiting period is finished and the process is again ready to run, it is placed in the swap list. When it has reached the head of the swap list, it is swapped into Ms as soon as there is enough space.

First we design the system procedures for swapping programs and data out of Ms. Next we discuss the system process which controls the backup store Bs and allocates Ms space to the programs that can run. Finally, we look at the special case of a multiprogrammed timesharing system. This is an extension of the timesharing system described in section 2.5 which did not have multiprogramming.

7.2.2 First a matter of design strategy. We don't want to follow the awkward practice of window allocation which is common in banks and post offices. There a customer must make up his mind and choose a window when he enters, and is supposed to stick to that window no matter how long he may have to wait. People entering later may be served long before him. The right way to go about it is to assign a customer to a window when it is his turn to receive service rather than at the moment he enters. Analogously, a process in a multiprogramming system must not be tied to a particular area in Ms; a process whose turn it is to run should be loaded into the first sufficiently large area available. This, however, implies that a process which was swapped out may be loaded into an area of Ms other than the one in which it was previously running. Thus, references to data items or places in a program should not be expressed in terms of physical locations of Ms, but in terms of positions relative to the beginning of the area in Ms allocated to the process. Such references correspond to addresses in a virtual store. If the references in a program are expressed as virtual addresses, the program is called (for obvious reasons) a relocatable program.

The translation from virtual addresses to physical locations can easily be performed at execution time. The exact location is derived by adding the contents of a base register or relocation register to a virtual address. The value of this register is the starting location of the area in Ms in which the relocatable program and its data are loaded. Thus, the address translation rule applied at runtime is:

$$\text{location} = \text{base} + \text{virtual address}$$

A program runs in a contiguous block of Ms space whose lower bound is determined by the relocation register. Since there are several programs in Ms at the same time, we need to be certain that a program does not access locations beyond the upperbound of its allocated space. The hardware of many machines is designed to perform a simple address check. In addition to the starting location, either the size or the ceiling of the allocated area in Ms is kept in a register. When a virtual address is translated into a location, the hardware checks whether or not the result is within the allocated area. (Using the size instead of the ceiling has the advantage that the check can be performed in parallel with the relocation addition). If the check fails, the attempted operation results in an address fault. This simple check assures that a program cannot access information outside its own area, and protects a program and its data against mistakes or malicious actions of other programs. Of course, it should not be possible for a program to violate the protection by assigning an arbitrary value to the register containing the base, the size or the ceiling.

In this section we assume that the areas in Ms in which a program and its data are placed are all of the same size. In the problems at the end of this section we consider a simple variation of this assumption. A contiguous block of Ms space in use by a process P_i is moved out of Ms and saved on Bs by the procedure SWAPOUT(i). A contiguous block is moved from Bs to Ms by calling SWAPIN(i), where i is the process index.

7.2.3 The function SWAPOUT(i) saves the information on the secondary store device Bs (for example, a drum). This is achieved by placing a message in the device queue (see section 5.3). If the queue is empty, the command is also placed in the device command buffer; otherwise, it is merely appended to the device queue. The command consists of the base and ceiling of the Ms area, the base of the area in Ms where the contents should be saved, and an indication that this is a save command. A complete message consists of this command and the identity of the sender. Thus, a program for swapping out an area from the primary store is:

```
SWAPOUT(i) =
begin local m
   m.base ← base_i; m.ceiling ← base_i + size_i
   m.direction ← "out"
   m.destination ← base of free area on back up store
   backupstorebase_i ← m.destination
   command((m,i), device queue)
end
```

We assume that Bs is so large that a free area can always be found.

The swapping system maintains a swap-in queue which contains the processes ready to return to Bs. If a process is placed in an empty swap-in queue and there is room in Ms, the process is immediately swapped in; otherwise, it is appended to the swap queue.

Similar to SWAPOUT, the function SWAPIN prepares and sends a message to the device queue of the secondary store device, but it sends a load command instead of a save command. A program for swapping in is:

```
SWAPIN(i) =
begin local m
   m.base ← base_i; m.ceiling ← base _i + size_i
   m.direction ← "in"
   m.source ← backingstore base_i
   command ((m,i), device queue)
end
```

SWAPIN and SWAPOUT both insert a message into the device queue of Bs without waiting until the transfer is completed. This has several consequences. In the first place, the area in the primary store occupied by a process which is swapped out cannot be used as free space in SWAPOUT until the information has been saved. Secondly, it is possible for a process to not yet be completely swapped out when an answer arrives and SWAP-IN decides to swap this process in again. This causes no real problem, because the load command is placed further on in the device queue than the save command. Thus, by the time the load command is executed, the save command has been processed. Finally, the completion of a transfer in either direction must be noticed by the control process of the backup store device. The function of this process is discussed next.

Let BSC be the process which controls the backup store device. Process BSC is awakened when the device has completed a transfer. Its primary task is to delete the current command and send the next command to the device. If a save command has been completed, the status of the primary store is updated, because the area in the primary store occupied by the saved process is really free. The free space is allocated to the first process in the swap-in queue, or, if the queue is empty, it is recorded as free. The free space is entirely controlled by process BSC. Its program is a variation on the general program for device control processes presented in section 5.3. In order to avoid unnecessary complexity and to improve readability, error reporting and the repeated use of the index which indicates the device are omitted from the program below. If an error occurs, the source is still available, so BSC can try the same command once again. If still unsuccessful, the failure should be reported to the human operator.

```
Backup Store Control process: local m,j,k
repeat wait(READY)
   when device queue accessible do
      if queuelength > 1 then
         commandbuffer ← second command (device queue)
         signal(BUSY)
      fi
      (m,j) ← remove(device queue); queuelength ← queuelength − 1
      if m.direction = "in" then V(psem_j)
      else if swapqueue empty then recordfreespace(base_j)
           else k ← remove(swapqueue); base_k ← base_j; SWAPIN(k)
         fi fi
   od
until BSC halt
```

A little reorganization can save a considerable amount of swap time. If programs are written or compiled as reentrant code, the space in Bs occupied by the program part is not released when program and data are loaded into Ms so that it is not necessary to copy the program part when the process is saved. Only the data part must be saved when the process is swapped out. Some swapping time can also be saved when a process is brought into Ms by sharing the code of library programs and systems. Sharing the code of a program such as a compiler does not only save swapping time but also valuable space at both storage levels, because only one copy of a relatively large program is stored in each storage device instead of one copy for each user.

7.2.4 The swapping technique fits very well in a multiprogrammed timesharing system. Such a timesharing system can have the same management of terminals as the system described in section 2.5, but the user processes are controlled differently. The primary store is not allocated to just one user process at a time, but shared by a number of users. The objective of the storage management is to have only ready to run processes in Ms. In a timesharing system the waiting times are caused by copying input and output from the input buffer and output buffer.

The interface between a user's terminal and a user process was described in sections 2.5 and 5.4. As far as a user process is concerned, the fixed input buffer "inbuf" acts as a virtual input device from which lines of input can be obtained by calling READ. The fixed output buffer "outbuf" acts as the virtual output device into which output lines can be written by calling WRITE. The buffer outbuf can also be viewed as a receiver queue reserved for a particular user process; the function of WRITE is then to send a message to this queue. This receiver queue can hold only one message at a time. Therefore, though the primary function of WRITE is to send a message, it waits for an answer to the preceding message so as to assure that the next message cannot be sent until the answer has been received.

We add to outbuf a state indicator which can have one of three values: empty, nonempty or requested. "Requested" indicates that a user process found that it could not yet write the next output line, because outbuf was not yet empty.

procedure WRITE(y) =
begin
  when outbuf_i accessible *do*
    if STATE_i = empty *then* $\text{V}(\text{psem}_i)$
    else $\text{STATE}_i \leftarrow$ requested; SWAPOUT(i)*fi* *od*; $\text{P}(\text{psem}_i)$
  $\text{outbuf}_i \leftarrow$ y; $\text{STATE}_i \leftarrow$ nonempty
  raisereadyflag_i; $\text{signal}(\text{READY}_{out})$
end

Index i identifies the process which calls WRITE.

The printer control process (see section 5.4) must place the user process on the swap list if the latter has been removed from Ms and is ready to run again. It can detect this situation by inspecting the status of outbuf described in the variable STATE. The statement signal(outbuf empty) in the program of section 5.4 is replaced by a piece of program that corresponds to the swapping version of sendanswer.

Printer Control Process:
repeat $\text{wait}(\text{READY}_{out})$
  i $\leftarrow$ index of raisedreadyflag; dropreadyflag_i
  if outbuf_i underflow *then*

when $outbuf_i$ accessible *do*
if $STATE_i$ = requested *then*
  if room in primary store *then*
  $base_i$ ← free area in $Ms(size_i)$; SWAPIN(i)
  else insert(i into swapqueue) *fi*
else $STATE_i$ ← empty *fi*
od
else transfer character from $outbuf_i$ to $printer_i$; signal($BUSY_{i,out}$) *fi*
until PCP halt

The program for PCP has been designed such that a single process controls the printing on all user teletypes. This process is activated through a single semaphore $READY_{out}$ and the particular terminal or user process requesting assistance makes itself known by raising its flag. This design makes sure that the control process essentially starts with the statement

$$\text{wait}(READY_{i,out}\ \textit{or}\ READY_{2,out}\ \textit{or}\ \ldots\ \textit{or}\ READY_{n,out})$$

where n is the number of user terminals.

Procedure READ corresponds to the action of receiving a message if we view inbuf as the receiver queue of a user process. Therefore, the swapping of receivers can be programmed similar to the swapping of senders and the procedure READ and the keyboard control process can be modified accordingly. The programming of this process and related procedures is left as an exercise to the reader.

PROBLEMS

1. The swapping technique has been implemented in the procedures waitanswer and sendanswer. Consequently, swapping applies only to sending processes. An extension of the swapping technique to receiving processes requires modifications in the communication procedures send and receive. Write the programs for such modified versions of send and receive and check if it is necessary to change the procedures SWAPOUT and SWAPIN.

2. It is not realistic to assume that all user processes need the same amount of space in Ms. If areas of a uniform size are allocated, this size must match the largest permissible user process. This implies considerable waste of space, because the size is necessarily too large for most user processes. Therefore, consider a classification of user processes in three groups: small, medium, and large with three corresponding standard area sizes such that large area = 2*medium area and medium area = 2*small area. Redesign the swapping of sender processes using this classification of user processes. Investigate whether there should be one uniform swap queue or three separate queues, one for each standard size. An advantage of having sep-

arate queues seems to be that space which is too small for a large user process can be allocated to a small or perhaps medium-size process instead of remaining idle. On the other hand, we must make certain that the design does not lead to permanent blocking of the large user processes, which is possible if swappable processes are selected by size.

3. Suppose that every process has its own copy of the code of the communication procedures and this code is swapped just as the rest of the program and its data. However, the procedures SWAPOUT and SWAPIN are shared and belong to the operating system area which is never swapped out. Examine the procedures waitanswer and sendanswer and discuss what goes wrong if the communication is designed this way.

4. User processes working in a multiprogrammed timesharing environment should not only be swapped out while waiting for permission to output a line, but also while waiting for input. The procedure READ and the process for keyboard control must be modified for this purpose in a similar way to WRITE and printer control. Write modified versions of the programs for keyboard control and write a program for READ. The programs can be designed similar to those presented in this section for printer control and WRITE.

5. Suppose two bits of a machine instruction are used to indicate a base register. The coding 00 means no base register modification, and the codes 01, 10 and 11 mean the base registers which point, respectively, to the base of the shared programs, the program section, and the data section of a user process. When a user process is swapped out, only the data segment is saved, but the space of both program segment and data segment is released. When a process is loaded, its program segment and data segment are both loaded into the primary store. Assume that the processes use areas of equal size. Design the bookkeeping of free and used areas in both storage levels, and program the updating of the base registers. The CPU state of a process is saved in its control block when a process blocks itself; when it is selected to run, its CPU state is reloaded.

7.3 SEGMENTATION

7.3.1 If the variable data is separated from the reentrant program, a copy of the invariant program text can be kept on the backup store Bs so that only the variable data has to be saved. The basic idea of segmentation is that there is no need to load a program and its data in one contiguous area of the primary store Ms. Loading the program section and the data section in two separate—and possibly nonadjacent—areas has the obvious advantage of providing a more flexible storage allocation. Since space is continuously allocated and released, it is much harder to find one contiguous area for a large piece of information than two smaller contiguous areas for two separate pieces.

Once the usefulness of separating a program and its data has occurred to us, we notice that it may be useful to go further and divide the information into more than two pieces. Partitioning the information into several program segments and several data segments not only facilitates the layout of information in Ms but also improves the usage of Ms in other ways. Segmentation makes it unnecessary for all the information of a process to be loaded into Ms before the process can run. It is sufficient to load the program segment into which the program counter PC of a process is currently pointing together with the data segments it references. This means that the processes ready to run only have to be partially loaded into Ms. The average space requirement of a segmented process is much less than the size of its total information.

Obviously, there is some overhead involved in going from one segment to another. Therefore, the aim is to minimize the number of segment transitions. This goal can partly be achieved if instruction or data items within the same locus of control are placed in one segment. The natural locus of control for instructions is a program block or a procedure or subroutine. If an instruction in a subroutine is executed, it is more likely that another instruction (most likely the subsequent instruction) in that subroutine will be executed next rather than an instruction outside this routine. With regard to data, the natural unit is a data structure such as an array or a list. Again, if an element of a data structure is referenced, it is most likely that other elements of the same data structure will be referenced in subsequent instructions.

In this section we discuss the addressing of segmented space and the management of segments. The issue of finding or creating space in Ms to accommodate a segment is discussed in section 8.1.

7.3.2 The program and data of a process are partitioned into a set of segments which are randomly placed in Ms. A segment is described by a segment descriptor which, among other things, points to the base of the actual segment. The segment descriptors of a process are placed in the segment table. There is one segment table for each process. The base address of the segment table and its length are stored in the process control block.

A virtual address is defined as a pair (s,w) where s is an index into the segment table and w the position of the referenced item relative to the segment base. An address is transformed into a location by:

$$\text{location} = \text{base}(ST_s) + w$$

However, this address translation may fail in one of three different ways, two of which we consider as plain mistakes. A process control block is part of the operating system data and is therefore always accessible to the system. Although a segment table can be loaded before a process starts running and can be dumped when it stops running, we assume here that every segment table is locked in Ms with ST pointing to its base. Moving the segment table around may be a practical thing to do, but it has no impact on the segmentation logic. This simplification means that ST can be considered as a constant, and no address fault will ever arise from using ST in a translation.

The first mistake which may be detected during address translation is the use of an index s exceeding the upperbound of the segment table. This mistake is discovered in the test $s \leq$ STLENGTH at the beginning of the address translation and failure of the test brings the process into an error state which generates an error report. The second mistake which causes the translation to fail concerns the relative position given in w. If $w >$ length(ST_s), there is apparently an attempt to access information outside segment ST_s. Such a mistake also results in an error state and an error report.

The third case in which the address translation is not successful occurs if the referenced segment is not present in the primary store. Whether this situation must be considered a mistake depends on the implemented segmentation system. In this section we take the point of view that such an access fault is not a mistake and that it should be automatically corrected by the operating system. This viewpoint and the opposite one, which considers an access fault a mistake, are considered in more detail when discussing paging techniques (see section 7.4).

A segment descriptor consists of three attributes and three data fields (see figure 7.3a). The three attributes are runtime information, TYPE and STATE. The significance of the runtime information becomes evident later in this section. The TYPE attribute reveals what sort of segment is described. We distingiush between a program segment, a data segment, a descriptor segment and a shared segment. The STATE attribute determines whether a reference to the corresponding segment results in an access fault.

The field length determines the upperbound of the addressable items in the segment described. We assume that the length is determined once and for all when a segment is created. The two base fields point to the positions

Runtime info	TYPE	STATE	Length	Primary base	Secondary base

Figure 7.3a Layout of a segment descriptor

in the two storage levels. Either one of those may be void depending on the value of STATE. The STATE has one of three possible values. If the corresponding segment is present in Ms, the value of STATE is accessible. If the segment is in the secondary store, but not in the primary store, the value of STATE is inaccessible. A segment is still inaccessible when it is being loaded. If a segment is shared by several processes, it is possible for two or more processes to request the same segment. If these requests are handled in the same way, we end up with two copies of the shared segment in Ms. To prevent this, we check whether a segment has already been requested before sending a data transmission command to the backup store device. If it has, the segment is not loaded again, and the present copy of the shared segment is accessed directly when it has arrived. The detection of a multiple request for a shared segment is facilitated by marking the descriptor "arriving."

3.3 If a segment fault is not treated as a mistake, it can be used as an opportunity to swap segments. We shall see that it is no longer necessary to tie the swapping of segments to a particular operation such as READ and WRITE in a timesharing system. When a segment fault occurs, a system function SEGFAULT can be activated as if it was called by the process which caused the fault. The return address of this function call is the address of the instruction which caused the segment fault. The objective of procedure SEGFAULT is to get the referenced segment from the backup store and repeat the instruction which failed.

Procedure SEGFAULT must indicate to the backup store device an area in Ms where the segment can be placed. If there is not enough free space available, procedure SEGFAULT will make room by swapping out one or more segments. This means that a selection algorithm must determine which segments must be swapped out. A detailed discussion of several selection algorithms (commonly referred to as replacement algorithms) is found in the next chapter. At this point we simply mention that those segments are swapped out in which little recent interest has been shown. Such information can be derived from the first attribute in a segment descriptor, the runtime information. This reveals whether the segment in question has recently been referenced. The segmentation system does not need a swap list, because a program is not swapped out in its entirety.

Procedure SEGFAULT first checks whether the requested segment is arriving. If so, a request is placed in the dummy command queue. (A dummy command does not result in a data transmission. It is deleted when the requested segment arrives. The sender of the request is notified by that time that the segment is accessible.) If the segment is inaccessible, procedure SEGFAULT selects an area in Ms in which the segment can be placed. If it is necessary to clear an area, an area larger than needed may be obtained. SEGFAULT must then place the remaining space on record as being free. The process which caused the segment fault is still the currently running process. Thus, SEGFAULT finds the identity of the process which caused the segment fault in the variable current. The segment number s can be derived from the unsuccessful instruction through the return address. Finally, the process index is placed in a request queue so that the right process can be notified when the segment has arrived. A program for procedure SEGFAULT is:

SEGFAULT(s) = $ s is the segment descriptor in ST_i which caused the fault

begin local r
when Ms inspection *do*
  if STATE(s) = arriving *then* insert((current,s) into dummy queue)
  else base(s) ← free area in Ms(length(s))
    if more space became available than needed *then*
      record remaining free space *fi*
    while r = segment in selected area *do* STATE(r) ← inaccessible
      if TYPE(r) = datasegment *then* SAVE(r) *fi*
    od
    insert(current into request queue); LOAD(s)
  fi
od
    P($segf_{current}$)
end

The procedures SAVE and LOAD are just a slight modification of the SWAP procedures of the preceding section. The index of the segment descriptor is passed as a parameter. The segment descriptor gives access to the size of the segment and the base addresses of the destination in Ms and the source in Bs. The modifications of SWAPIN and SWAPOUT are left as an exercise to the reader. Procedure SEGFAULT concludes with a P operation on the private semaphore $segf_i$ (of which there is one for every process) reserved for handling segment faults. When this P operation is passed, the segment has arrived and SEGFAULT returns to the instruction which caused the fault. Note that the process in which the segment fault occurred also waits in P($segf_{current}$) if it sent a dummy command.

7.3.4 The swap procedures SAVE and LOAD end by sending a command to the device queue of Bs. SEGFAULT should not be allowed to finish until the commands are finished and can be deleted from the command queue. This can be done when the backup store device sends the READY signal for which the device control process is waiting. The function of this segment traffic control process (STC) is similar to that of the backup store control process in the swapping system discussed in the preceding section. It dispatches the notifications that the requested segments have arrived, it deletes the processed commands and it sends the next command to the backup store device. If the completed command loaded a segment into Ms, STC checks the dummy device queue to see for which dummy command the requested segment has arrived. If the segment has arrived, the dummy command is deleted and the sender of the dummy command is notified that the segment is accessible by performing V($segf_i$).

The completion of a save command requires no action from STC other than deletion of the command. Every save command originates in procedure SEGFAULT (by calling SAVE) and this procedure handles the cleared Ms space. The STATE of a saved segment has already been adjusted before the save command was given. A load command is also given by procedure SEGFAULT. When the segment has been loaded, STC must perform a V operation which releases the semaphore $segf_i$, where i is the index of the process in which the segment fault occurred. A program for segment traffic control is

```
STC: repeat wait(READY)
  when device queue accessible do
    local c = remove(device queue)
    if device queue not empty then
    copy(command(firstof(device queue)) into command buffer(Bs));
      signal(BUSY)
    fi
  od
when Ms inspection do
  local i = remove(requestqueue), s = requestedsegment(c)
  if STATE(s) = arriving then STATE(s) ← accessible; V(segf_i)
    for all q in dummy queue do
      if STATE(segment(q)) = accessible then
        V(segf[processindex(q)]); remove(dummy queue) fi
od fi od
until STC halt
```

7.3.5 The address translation of a segmentation system is much more complicated than that of a swapping system. If we save every intermediate result until it is not needed anymore, the address translation of a given address (s,w) into a location loc is

```
Address Translation in Segmentation System =
begin local seg,offset,TEMP
seg ← segment index
offset ← word offset
  if seg > Segment Table Length then report (Segment Table overflow)
  else TEMP ← ST_seg      $ get the segment descriptor
    if offset > length(TEMP) then report(Segment overflow)
    else
```

```
    if STATE(TEMP) = accessible then loc ← base(TEMP)+offset
    else SEGFAULT
  fi fi fi
end
```

This address translation causes a tremendous overhead, because it is invoked for every instruction fetch and every reference to a data operand in the store. Fortunately, the overhead can be reduced to reasonable proportions by some additional hardware. This is discussed below.

The majority of the tests are unnecessary. If a particular instruction has been fetched, it is very likely that either the subsequent instruction or an instruction in the same segment will be fetched next. The same is true for data items. Hence, we should exploit the fact that the tests worked out satisfactorily in the recent past and set a trap for any references outside the segments currently of interest. The hardware can assist nicely in the implementation of such a policy if a small associative memory is used.

An element of an associative memory consists of a tag field or key, a value field and possibly some other attributes. Instead of accessing by index, the statement

$$x \leftarrow AM[i]$$

means: store into x the value of the element in associative memory AM whose key is i. Access to an associative memory is extremely fast, not slower than access to an ordinary sequential store. When accessed, all elements simultaneously start testing their key against the given i and the element which has the corresponding key (if any) responds.

Suppose an associative memory AM of eight elements is available for implementing our segmentation system. We use AM essentially as a set of base registers. The keys correspond to segment descriptor indices and the values to their base and length (see figure 7.3b).

Address translation now proceeds as follows:

```
begin local seg,offset,TEMP
seg ← segment index
offset ← word offset
   TEMP ← base(AM[seg])
   if TEMP ≠ 0 then
      if offset > length(AM[seg]) then report(Segment overflow)
      else loc ← TEMP+offset fi
   else ADDRESSEXCEPTION fi
end
```

The overhead is minimal for the majority of references. In the most likely case, the address translation requires the same number of operations needed for address translation of relocatable code. That is, the address translation is the same for most references as in a relocating swapping

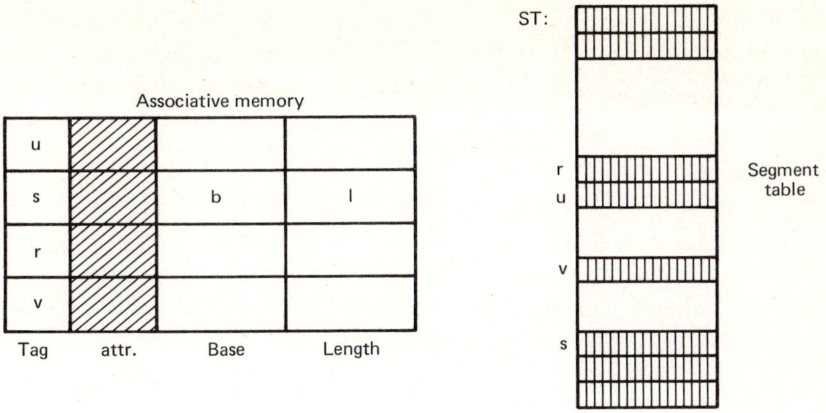

Figure 7.3b Sketch of an associative memory

system, while the three advantages that segmentation has over swapping are still preserved. Points in favor of segmentation are: (a) segments are much smaller than whole programs with their data, so storage does not have to be allocated in such large contiguous chunks; (b) only a small part of the information has to be present in Ms while a process runs; (c) the amount of information swapped in and out is much less, because only that which is needed is brought into Ms.

7.3.6 The address translation takes more time in the rare case that the referenced segment is not present in the associative memory. The segment may be accessible, though not present in the associative memory, or it is not accessible at all. In the first of these two cases, the segment descriptor is placed in AM, while the second case is handled by procedure SEGFAULT.

Suppose one of the attributes of an element in AM is the used bit which is set by the hardware when the particular element is used. After a new element has been brought into AM, we turn off all the used bits. When another segment descriptor must be loaded into AM, we search for an element whose used bit is still off. If one is found, this one is overwritten by the descriptor which must be brought in. If all used bits are on, we remove one in a round robin order or any order which seems appropriate. When an address exception occurs, the address translation continues in this way:

```
ADDRESSEXCEPTION:
      $ this program is a continuation of the preceding program
      $ the segment index is in seg
if STATE(ST[seg]) = accessible then
   TEMP ← select an element in AM
   overwrite element(TEMP) with (seg, base(ST[seg]), length(ST[seg]))
   clear all used bits and update runtime information
else SEGFAULT fi
```

The return address of ADDRESSEXCEPTION is the location of the instruction that caused the address exception. An instruction is tried twice if it references a nonaccessible segment.

PROBLEMS

1. The segment traffic control process needs the process index to find the proper segment table and needs the segment location to find the proper descriptor when a segment is swapped in. The latter is passed as a parameter into the swap procedures SAVE and LOAD.

Modify the swap programs given in the preceding section to fit the segmentation scheme of this section.

What difficulty arises if the segment location is not passed as a parameter to the swap procedures but, instead, if every process control block contains a variable sfault which is set to point to the segment for which a command is placed in the device queue (either for loading or for saving)?

2. The semaphore $segf_i$ is used for the synchronization of loading a segment and accessing it. Since the process which caused the segment fault is going to wait, it seems as if its private semaphore $psem_i$ could have been used. The semaphore $segf_i$ seems rather superfluous. Show that this reasoning is not correct and that the semaphores $segf_i$ are necessary.

3. Suppose that, if the offset w in a virtual address exceeds the length of a segment, this will be interpreted as a request for enlarging the segment by a factor 1.5 or by so much that the given offset falls in range. Since it is unlikely that the adjacent area is free either in Ms or in Bs, an area of the requested size must be reserved at the storage level in which the segment is currently *not* residing and a command should be sent to the drum device queue in order to move the already existing segment into the larger area. How could a segment be contracted?

Complete the design and reprogram the part of the address translation which reported a segment overflow.

4. The device queue receives two kinds of commands, save commands and load commands. The segment traffic control process passes save commands and load commands, but not dummy commands, onto the backup store device. It seems that the dummy commands could be placed in the device queue. This does not make much difference for the SEGFAULT procedure. However, STC must inspect a command before sending it to the device. If it is a dummy command, the segment has been loaded in the meantime, so the command can be deleted from the queue. Write a modified version of the STC program. Is it possible for STC to handle the command queue first-in first-out?

5. Processes must be able to create and delete segments. The system provides for this purpose two procedures: CREATE(t,s) and DELETE(seg). The latter gets a segment index as input and clears descriptor St[seg]. The former receives the type and size of the new segment as input and returns the index of the segment descriptor which it reserved in the segment table as value. (We assume that the segment table can always be extended.) Procedure CREATE places the given type in the TYPE field of the new segment descriptor, places the size in the length field, and initializes the STATE to the new value "empty". This value indicates a segment for which no space has yet been reserved in Ms, or in Bs. It also means that because CREATE does not reserve the space, the base field and backing store base field are void if STATE = empty.

Write programs for the procedures CREATE and DELETE. Modify the address translation procedure so that it can handle the case STATE = empty. If an empty segment is referenced, time has come to reserve the required space and change the value of STATE.

7.4 PAGING

7.4.1 The decision to restrict all segments of information to one uniform size turns out to have a significant impact on storage management. If all information is partitioned in pieces of equal size, we use the term *page* for such a piece of information. Where the term *segment* is used, it is always understood that two segments may be different in length. The differences between paging and segmentation and the pros and cons of both methods cannot be stated in a few words. A comparison is found in the next chapter. In this section we discuss the management of pages and the operating system functions which support a demand paging system.

7.4.2 The storage levels are partitioned into an array of frames, where a frame is a contiguous vector of storage cells starting at a location whose physical address is a multiple of the fixed frame size. The frame size is chosen equal to the page size so that a page fits in any one of the frames and a frame can host any one of the pages.

A virtual address in a paging system is a pair (p,w), where p is the index in the page table of the current process and w the offset from the base of this page. The page table consists of page descriptors similar to the segment descriptors in a segmentation system. The layout of a page descriptor is the same as that of a segment descriptor with the exception that the length field is missing, because, having the fixed size, recording the length is unnecessary. The address map of a virtual address (p,w) onto a location is given by

$$\text{location} = PT_p + w$$

where PT is the base of the current page table given in the process descriptor of the running process. We again assume, for simplicity, that page tables are locked in the primary store Ms so that PT can be treated as a constant.

Because of the fixed page size, a virtual address can very simply be represented in hardware. A field of fixed length, 18 bits wide for instance, is interpreted by the hardware as the combination of two fields, one for the page index p, 8 bits wide for instance, and one for the offset w, 10 bits wide (see figure 7.4a).

Virtual space appears to the programmer as one contiguous area (of 2^{18} cells in the example); the division into the two fields is immaterial to him.

The address translation is easily carried out by hardware and is very fast if an auxiliary associative memory is used like the one for the segmenting scheme in the preceding section. There is no need for an upperbound test, because the fixed size fields for page index p and offset w make table overflow and page overflow impossible. Moreover, the associative memory contains nothing more than the page index and the base. Using the associative memory AM, the address map for a given virtual address (p,w) works as follows:

> Address Translation for Paging System:
> pg ← page index
> offset ← word offset
> *if* pg *in* AM *then* loc ← AM[pg] + offset
> *else* ADDRESSEXCEPTION *fi*

Since p and w are found in fixed fields of an instruction, the hardware can very easily isolate the page index and the offset. The value of AM[pg] is a multiple of the page size and the offset is smaller than the page size. Therefore, the machine does not have to do a full scale addition. It simply places the value of AM[pg] in the high order bits of a register and the offset in the low order bits. Such an operation is as fast as moving a value from one CPU register to another. If the page descriptor is present in AM, the address mapping takes little more time than is needed to access a relocatable item via a base register. We may expect that a reference to a page not currently in use is rare compared to a reference to a page whose descriptor is in AM. This means that the majority of the address maps is entirely carried out in hardware at very little cost.

7.4.3 An address exception caused by an accessible page which is not in the associative memory is handled in the same way as in a segmentation system (see section 7.3.6). If a page is not accessible, control is transferred to procedure PAGEFAULT which makes the page accessible. This method is called *demand paging* and has basically the same structure as procedure SEGFAULT. However, the implementation is somewhat different for two reasons having to do with the STATE value "empty" and with the selection

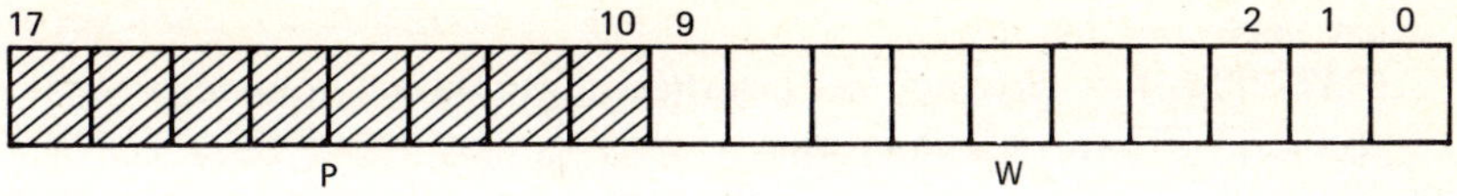

Figure 7.4a Decomposition of a page address

of a destination frame for loading or saving a page. The width of the process index field (8 bits in the example) determines the size of a page table (256 page descriptors in the example). Initially, and also after a page has been deleted, a page descriptor is in the STATE "empty", meaning that no information corresponds to this page descriptor. Referencing an empty page causes a page fault. At this time a frame in Ms must be selected and assigned to the empty page so that it becomes accessible.

When the system has reached its steady state, most of the frames in Ms will be in use. Therefore, there is a fair chance that all Ms frames will be in use when a pagefault occurs. If we follow the design of SEGFAULT, we would design procedure PAGEFAULT such that it selects a frame, generates a save command (if necessary) and generates a load command with the selected frame as destination. Likewise, the dump command would be prepared by selecting a frame in Bs and using this frame as destination. However, it is too early to choose a destination frame. A load command may have to queue up for a while before it can be serviced. During this time the situation in Ms may have changed. An inactive page may have been referenced again, or some pages may have been deleted with the result that some frames become free. Therefore, the selection of a destination had better be postponed until the load command is placed in the device command buffer. If Bs is a rotating device, the destination of a page had also better be selected when the save command is given. This gives us an opportunity to select the first free area on the drum or disk passing the reading heads. Had the decision been taken independently of the position of the rotating drum or disk, it would take, on the average, half a revolution before the starting address of the selected frame is found.

7.4.4 If the choice of a destination is postponed until the command in question is placed in the command buffer, a command cannot be prepared in its entirety when it is generated. This reduces the work in PAGEFAULT compared to SEGFAULT, but increases the work of the backing store control process which now must select a destination when it sends a command to the device. A program for handling page faults is:

```
PAGEFAULT(p) =        $ p = index of page causing the fault
begin
```

```
when Ms inspection do
   if STATE(p) = arriving then insert((i,p) into dummy queue)
   else if STATE(p) = empty then
begin local f = select free frame or old program page frame
   allocate frame(f) to page(p)
   if f = program page frame then remove page from frame(f) fi
         V(missing page(current))
   end
         else STATE(p) ← arriving        $ the STATE was "inaccessible"
         insert((i, p) into request queue)
      fi fi
   od
         P(missing page(current))
   end
```

The functions "remove page from frame" and "allocate frame to page" are explained in section 8.2. The dummy commands and the requests are placed in two separate queues so that the next device command can easily be accessed. The procedure which inserts into the request queue is discussed further on in this section.

It is not absolutely necessary to select an old program page when a frame must be cleared. A data page can be used as well. Selecting one among the program pages makes it possible for procedure PAGEFAULT to handle the reference to an empty page on its own, because in that case it is not necessary to swap out a page. As we will see shortly, the decision also helps to simplify the drum or disk control process.

When a program page is removed, there is a small chance that the associative memory AM contains a copy of the corresponding page descriptor. If that is so, this copy should be deleted from AM. The probability that AM contains a copy of a page which has been thrown out is very small, because presence in AM implies that the page descriptor was referenced more recently than others. It is therefore unlikely that pages accessible through AM are old and will be selected to make room for other pages in Ms.

The operating system should provide a simple CREATE procedure which takes a TYPE value as parameter and returns the index of an empty page if there is room in the page table. This gives the programmer who has access to CREATE a chance to create program pages, shared pages, and descriptor pages.

7.4.5 The control of page traffic could be organized in the same way as that of segment traffic. However, owing to the partitioning of both storage levels into equal size frames, a slightly more complicated organization leads to a better performance of the secondary storage device. We discuss two strategies for using a drum (or disk); in one case the device is divided into sectors and in another frames are layed out in a spiral on the drum (or disk). The first method, known as the paging drum, is discussed next; the spiral layout is discussed in the exercises at the end of this section.

If the page traffic control process PTC is designed analogously to the segment traffic control process STC, commands are processed in arrival time order. It then takes seven drum revolutions to process the command queue in the situation pictured in figure 7.4b. Since the read/write heads of the drum (or disk) have to pass a sector anyway, the commands had better be arranged in separate queues, one for every sector. The commands in the situation of figure 7.4b can then be processed in the order a1, a2, a3, b1, b2, b3, c1, c2, c3, d1, d2, d3, which requires only four drum revolutions.

The paging traffic control process PTC is activated (as usual) when the device has finished a command. It performs its task in four steps:

Step 1: Place a command in the device command buffer.
Step 2: Report completion of a load command and delete the request.
Step 3: Select a destination frame in Ms.
Step 4: Prepare command for the next sector and place it in the device queue.

Because there will always be a command added to the device queue in step 4, step 1 is never an empty action. The reason for always sending a command to the device is to make sure that the device wakes up PTC in time before the next sector comes up. The device is essentially used as a timer in the sense that it activates PTC every time the end of a sector is reached. The gap between two sectors should be large enough to carry out step 1, but the time interval does not have to include any of the other three steps. Step 1 is very straightforward; the command has already been pre-

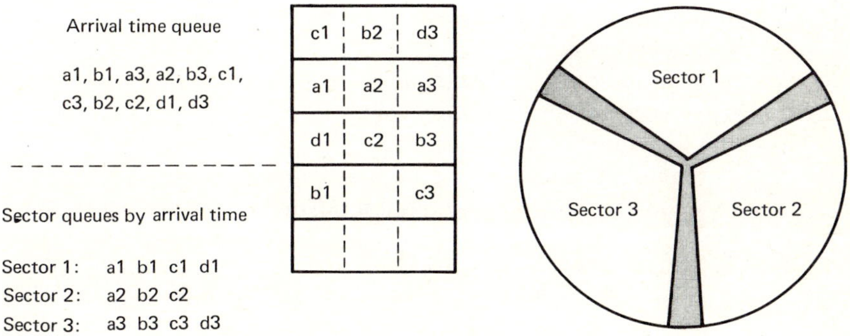

Figure 7.4b Device queue for paging drum

pared during the preceding activation of PTC in step 4. Moreover, PTC is the only process operating on the device queue, so step 1 does not contain a potential delay of any kind. Step 1 is implemented by the sequence of statements:

local c = remove(device queue)
copy(firstof(devide queue) into commandbuffer(Bs)); signal(BUSY)

7.4.6 The command that PTC places in the device queue is either a load command, a save command or a null command. A null command does not cause any information to be transferred, but causes the device to signal READY at the end of a sector just as it does when finishing one of the other commands. When STC finds in step 2 that a load command has just been completed, it must change the STATE of the page descriptor from "arriving" into "accessible" and signal the arrival to the process which is waiting for this page. This is also the right time to delete the corresponding request from the request queue. Recall that, when the request is generated in procedure PAGEFAULT, the destination is not yet selected. A request placed in the request queue consists of the pair (i,p) where i is a process index and p a page descriptor index. (A command is assembled from a request in step 4.) The request queue is arranged in separate sector queues as suggested in figure 7.4b. When the device reports that a fetch command in sector is finished, the first request of the corresponding sector queue can be deleted. The queue of dummy requests is then scanned for requests referring to the same page. If one is found, it is deleted and the arrival of the page is signalled to the process which generated the dummy request.

If a save command has been completed, the Ms frame involved is added to the list of free Ms frames. Recall that the completed command has been removed from the device queue in step 1, leaving only the command which is currently executed. A program for step 2 reads as follows:

Step 2 (reporting the completion of a command) =
local f = Ms frame of completed transfer(c)
if save command completed *then* add Ms frame(f) to list of free Mp frames
else if load command completed *then*
  when Ms inspection *do*
local i = process index(c), p = page index(c)
  STATE(p) ← accessible; V(missing page$_i$)
    for all q *in* dummy request queue *do*
    if p = requested page(q)
      then remove(q from dummy request queue);
V(missingpage$_i$)*fi*
    od
fi fi
advance current sector to next sector

Steps 3 and 4 prepare the command for the next sector. What goes on in step 3 depends on the choice of a page replacement policy and the application of the chosen selection algorithm. This topic is discussed in the next chapter. The selection of a frame does not result in changing a page descriptor. If there are free Ms frames, the selection algorithm picks one of those, otherwise it returns a pointer to a page descriptor of a program page. When step 4 is discussed, we will see that it is undesirable to select a frame used by a data page. We indicate this in a Boolean variable "restricted selection_k" where k is a sector number. A program for step 3 is:

```
Step 3 (select a potential destination frame) =
      $ the sector pointer has been advanced at the end of step 2
local f                         $ f will point to the destination
if restricted selection(current sector) then
   f ← select free frame or frame of old program page
   restricted selection(current sector) ← false
else f ← select free frame or frame of old page
   if current sector queue not empty and f is data page then
      restricted selection (current sector) ← true
fi fi
```

The program for step 3 is such that two successive selections with a nonempty sector queue will not both designate an Ms frame containing a data page.

Step 4 generates the command for the next sector and appends it to the device queue. It has a choice of generating a load command, a save command, or a null command. The choice depends on several factors: whether there is a load request, whether there is a copy of the destination designated in step 3 in Bs, and whether the sector in Bs has room for a new page. A decision diagram is given in figure 7.4c.

	sector queue is not empty	sector queue is empty
designated destination is free or has copy in Bs	(a) use designated destination and generate load command	(b) generate null command
designated destination is a data page and there is room in sector of Bs	(c) take designated destination and generate a save command for it	(d) take a designated destination and generate a save command for it
designated destination is a data page, but there is no room in sector of Bs	(e) generate null command	(f) generate null command

Figure 7.4c Decision diagram for generating a command

Cases (a) and (b) are self-evident. It is unfortunate that we must give priority in case (c) to generating a save command instead of processing the first load request in the sector queue, but there is no other choice, because the designated destination has not yet been cleared. A particular sector queue must not always end up in case (c), or this sector queue is permanently blocked. The occurrence of this situation is prevented by the restricted selection policy of step 3. This policy guarantees that, if case (c) or case (e) occurred once, it will not occur the next time that a command for this sector is generated.

Case (d) offers a nice opportunity to save a page so that a frame becomes free before the next sector is reached. Cases (e) and (f) are very unlikely. Bs should be large enough to hold all the information, and finding free frames should be no problem. If there is no room left in a particular sector, we cannot find a destination frame for a save command, so neither a load nor a save command can be generated for this sector at this time. We mentioned earlier that case (e) will not occur twice in a row because of the restricted selection in step 3. If all the sectors are completely filled, no page can be saved. We consider such a state of the system as a disaster and assume here that Bs is large enough so that this never happens. The problem is discussed in more detail in section 8.5.

A program for step 4 that matches the decision diagram is:

Step 4 (generate command for the coming sector) =
local m; *local*(i,p) $ the destination has been computed in step 3
if no space in current Bs sector *or*
  current sector queue empty *and*(f is free *or* f contains a program page)
then insert(null command into device queue)
else $ use the destination frame f and generate a save or load command
  if frame f = free *then* mark it "in transition"
  else remove page from frame(f) *fi*
  if removed page is data page *then*
    p ← descriptor(removed page); m.direction ← "out"
    secondary base(p) ← free Bsframe in current Sector
  else $ prepare a load command
    p ← first of(Sector Queue); m.direction ← "in"
  fi
insert(minto device device queue)
fi

Steps 3 and 4 are placed in one critical section

when Ms inspection *do* step 3; step 4 *od*

The critical section assures that another page fault cannot interfere with this part of the page controller. It is not necessary to place the code for sending a command to Bs in the same critical section.

PROBLEMS

1. The four steps of the page traffic control process for the paging drum have been designed such that a command is always ready when the drum can accept one. If sector queue q_k is empty and sector queue q_{k+1} is not, a save command should not take priority over the first load request in q_{k+1}, because a page can be saved in sector k before sector k + 1 is reached. Show that in these circumstances a load command will be generated for q_{k+1} assuming that every sector has some free Bs frames. Also, show that in between two save commands the Ms frame cleared by the first save command must have been used as destination of a load command.

2. Suppose an extended core storage (ECS) is used as backing store device. It does not need a device processor and does not have the problem of latency time (the time necessary to bring a rotating device in the right position for reading or writing). Therefore, an organization of the load queue as for the paging drum is not necessary; a queue is not necessary at all. The page traffic control process can also be deleted; the system procedure PAGEFAULT can do all the work. Also, there is no need for the STATE value "arriving." Procedure PAGEFAULT gets the requested page in Ms in three steps:

Step 1. Select a free frame or a frame of an old page in Ms.

Step 2. If the selected frame contains a data page, select a free frame in Bs and transfer the data page to that frame.

Step 3. If the requested page is inaccessible, move it to the cleared Ms frame.

Complete the design for this ECS paging system and make sure that parallel activation of procedure PAGEFAULT by concurrent processes does not give rise to conflicts.

3. The PTC process, which controls the paging drum, decides too early which command to process for the next sector. When the command is generated, there is still almost a whole sector to go; this may take several milliseconds, and the state of the pages may change in such a manner that the decision turns out premature. PTC ought to be awakened in time before the device has reached the end of a sector and then perform the steps in the order 3, 4, 1, 2. This way a destination is selected at the end of a sector instead of at the beginning. Therefore, a timer device is added to the paging system. Since the drum completes a sector at regular time intervals, the timer is set to the length of such an interval, such that it activates PTC early enough to complete steps 3 and 4 before the drum is ready.

Investigate the changes in procedure PAGEFAULT and control process PTC that are necessary to implement the timer/paging drum system. Show that the null commands are superfluous in this system.

In problems 4 and 5 we consider another layout of a drum (or a disk) which also has an impact on procedure PAGEFAULT and control process

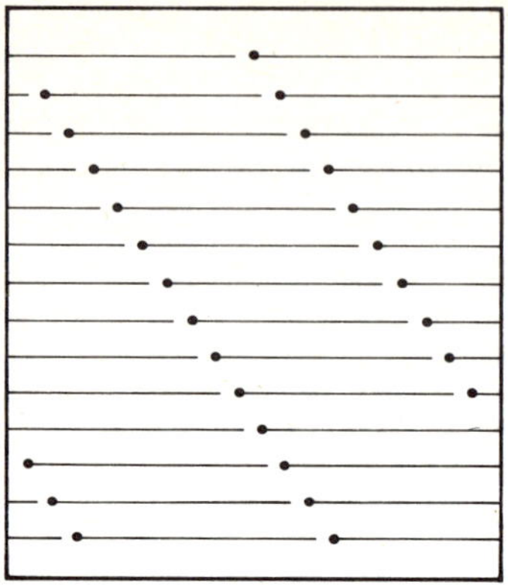

Figure 7.4d Frames laid out as spirals on a drum

PTC. The frames are laid out on Bs such that the starting addresses form a spiral on the drum (see figure 7.4d).

4. Whenever it is necessary to save a page, the first free Bs frame which will be encountered by the read/write heads of the drum is chosen as destination (we assume there is enough space on the drum). The save command gets priority over all load commands. There are three separate queues: one for load requests, one for save commands, and one for dummy requests. If a load command can be generated, one of the first four load requests in the queue is chosen. The request selected is the one whose source address on the drum is the closest to the current position of the read/write heads.

Design the page traffic control process for this paging system.

5. Procedure PAGEFAULT must be changed to handle the case of all queues being empty when a page fault occurs. The spiral drum cannot perform the timer function the way the paging drum does. Modify procedure PAGEFAULT to handle the first pagefault, but avoid a duplication of the work performed by process PTC.

7.5 SEGMENTATION AND PAGING COMBINED

7.5.1 Segmentation of programs and data has the advantage that only that part of the total information occupies space in the primary store which must be accessible in the near future. However, a segment may be so large that it becomes desirable to split it into smaller parts. It is easier to allocate space if a segment does not have to be loaded into one contiguous area. In addition, space allocation for variable size segments is more complicated than for fixed size pages. For these reasons it is worthwhile to consider the implementation of a segmentation scheme on top of a paging system.

It seems as if the optimal page size is one machine word, because the smaller the basic unit of contiguous space, the more flexible the space allocation is. However, there are also arguments in favor of large pages. Some disadvantages of a small page size are:

a. Every page needs a page descriptor; the smaller the pages the larger the number of descriptors.
b. A considerable amount of overhead is involved in starting a page transfer from one storage level to the other; the smaller the pages, the more serious this overhead is. Finding the optimal page size is one of the topics discussed in section 8.3. In this section the size of a page is chosen such that a small segment fits in one page, whereas a large segment needs several pages.

7.5.2 Virtual storage appears to the programmer as a segmented space in which an address is a pair (s,w) where s is a segment index and w the position of a word relative to the segment base. The system, however, interprets the offset w as a pair (p,w′), where p is a page index and w an offset within the designated page. Thus, from the system's point of view an address consists of three fields: s, p and w (see figure 7.5a).

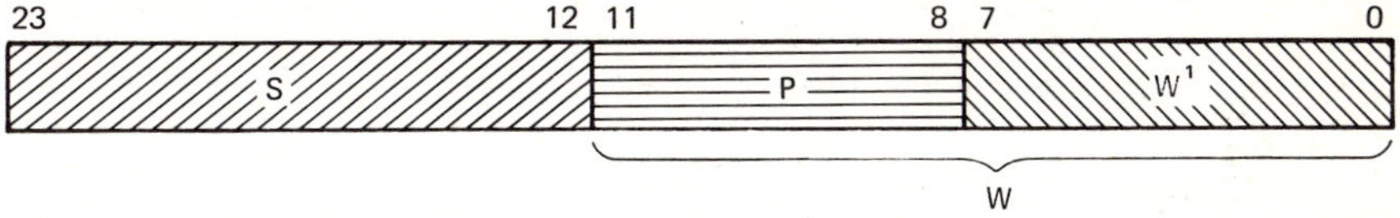

Figure 7.5a Decomposition of a virtual address

A segment descriptor points to a set of page descriptors and a page descriptor points to the frames (if any) in which the associated page resides (see figure 7.5b).

The meaning of the various fields is the same as in the preceding section. The first field in a page descriptor points to the segment descriptor which owns it. This pointer gives, among other things, access to the TYPE and runtime information of the segment to which this page belongs. The address translation of a virtual address (s,p,w′) into a location is given by:

$$loc \leftarrow PT[ST_S + p] + w'$$

where ST is the base of the segment table and PT the base of the page table.

When a word is present in the primary store Ms, it takes three steps to

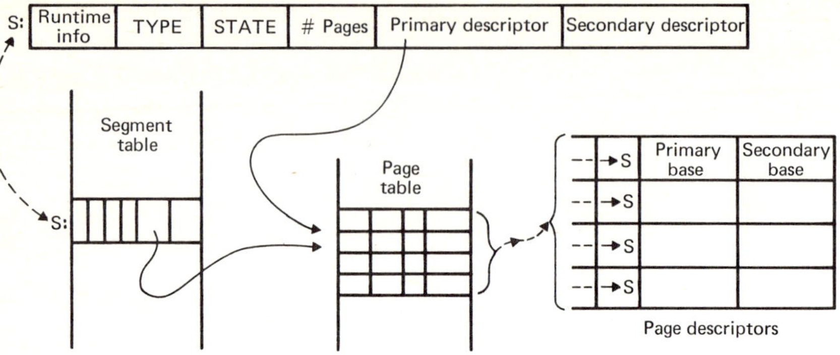

Figure 7.5b Layout of segment table and page table

access it: (a) get the index of the first page descriptor from segment descriptor ST_S; (b) add p to it and use the result to index into the page table; (c) extract the base from the computed page descriptor and add w′.

This elaborate address calculation can be bypassed for the majority of references in the same way as for a pure segmentation or pure paging system. Surprisingly enough, the address map can be as fast and simple as for the pure paging system. An associative memory AM uses as key the pair (s,p) and as value the base found in the corresponding page descriptor. The address map is then implemented as in a pure paging system:

Address Translation for Segmenting/Paging System:
pg ← descriptor address(ST_i) + p
offset ← w′
if pg in Am *then* loc AM[pg] + offset
else ADDRESSEXCEPTION *fi*

The base AM[pg] and the offset do not require a full scale addition. The machine concatenates the two values in adjacent but disjoint fields of a register. This operation is as fast as moving a value from one CPU register to another.

7.5.3 An address exception occurs if the key (s,p) is not found in AM. The possible reasons are:

a. Segment descriptor points to a page descriptor which points to an Ms frame. This is the case in which the page is in Ms, but its base is not in the associative memory AM.
b. p > # pages indicated in the segment descriptor. We treat this case as an error.
c. s > STLENGTH; a reference to a nonexisting segment. This is also an error.

d. Segment descriptor points to a page descriptor in STATE "empty."
e. Segment descriptor points to a page descriptor in STATE "arriving."
f. Segment descriptor points to a page descriptor in STATE "inaccessible."
g. Segment descriptor is in STATE "arriving."
h. Segment descriptor is in STATE "inaccessible."

While the STATE of the segment descriptor is "inaccessible" or "arriving," the STATE of the page descriptors of this segment is "inaccessible." This means that none of its pages can be accessible if the segment itself is not accessible. It is therefore not necessary to consider all combinations of segment and page STATE values.

In case (a) one of the AM elements is replaced by the referenced page in the same way as described in section 7.3. The key is the (s,p) part of the virtual address; the base is found through the segment descriptor and the page descriptor. Segments correspond to the natural procedure and data structure boundaries which are determined by a programmer. Since the segment structure is apparent to a programmer (or a compiler), the operating system ought to provide functions for creating and deleting segments. The parameter to CREATE is the TYPE of the new segment and an estimate of its size. The procedure derives from the estimated size how many page descriptors are needed, and sets up the segment and page descriptors. The segment descriptor is initialized to the STATE "inaccessible" and the page descriptors in the STATE "empty." The procedure DELETE needs a segment index as parameter. It erases all the page descriptors of this segment and the segment descriptor. If the descriptors are at the end of their table, the entries can be deleted and the variables STLENGTH and PTLENGTH can be adjusted; otherwise, procedure DELETE marks the descriptor as void.

Considering cases (b) and (c) as an error is compatible with this design. These cases ought to be treated as errors because reserving the space for all segment and page descriptors in advance leads to a waste of storage, and allocating the space and expanding sets of descriptors when case (b) or (c) occurs complicates the table management.

The cases (d) through (f) are handled by procedure PAGEFAULT (see section 7.4). The traffic between the two levels of storage is a matter of loading and saving pages. Therefore, any one of the page management systems described in the preceding section can be applied including the page traffic control process. The implementation of such a paging system has been described in sufficient detail in the preceding section.

7.5.4 How the two remaining cases (g) and (h) should be handled is a matter of taste. The two cases will not occur at all if both the segment table and the entire page table are locked in Ms during the time the process to which these segments and pages belong is present in Ms. In that case a segment descriptor always points to a set of accessible page descriptors in Ms, so the STATE of the former is permanently "accessible."

On the other hand, we may be somewhat concerned about the space required for storing the page descriptors. This may be a large number compared to the number of segment descriptors. The space occupied by page descriptors belonging to unused segments can easily be saved if a page descriptor set is treated as the "segment" to which a segment descriptor points. If the last page of a segment is swapped out, all the page descriptors are in the STATE "inaccessible." The set of page descriptors can now be swapped out too, and the segment descriptor is then marked "inaccessible." If the segment is referenced again, the set of page descriptors is fetched from Bs. While this is done, the segment descriptor is in the STATE "arriving." Once the set of page descriptors is back in the page table in Ms, the STATE of the segment descriptor is changed into "accessible." Finding space in Bs when a set of page descriptors is swapped out should be no problem. Room in Bs should be set aside for all the segment tables and page table of maximum length.

It is doubtful whether saving a set of page descriptors is worth the effort of moving such a small amount of information from one storage level to the other. Therefore, a less strict policy for saving page descriptors may be more suitable: when a process is brought into Ms, its segment table is loaded, but its page table is initially empty. Every time a segment is referenced for the first time, its STATE will be inaccessible, so its set of page descriptors is loaded and placed in the page table. If the last page of a segment is swapped out, the page descriptors are left where they are. Page descriptors are not swapped out until the whole process, including its segment table, is removed from Ms.

This policy implies that only the page descriptors which are really accessed are loaded into Ms. Another advantage of this policy is the simplicity of page table maintenance. It is not necessary to build the table in a contiguous block of storage. The descriptor sets can be placed in separate areas which do not have to be linked together, because a segment descriptor points explicitly to the base of its set. Since page descriptors are not removed from Ms until the whole process leaves, it is not necessary to reclaim any space allocated to those descriptor sets.

7.5.5 We mentioned earlier the importance of writing reentrant programs so that program pages can be overwritten. Another strong argument in favor of pure code has to do with shared programs. The use of shared programs (such as a compiler or a library function) in one process should be independent of its use in another process. This implies that the shared program may be used simultaneously by several concurrent processes. Obviously, the shared program must be written in pure code; for instance, if the first location of the code were used to store a return address, a second concurrent activation would overwrite the first return address.

Writing shared programs as reentrant code causes some problems regarding references to programs or data in the environment of the caller. We discuss two sorts of references: (a) the use of parameters and (b) references to global names.

Let us assume that parameters are passed either by value or by reference. It is customary to give a process some workspace delineated by two registers: WB, the workspace base which points to the first location of the workspace, and TOP which points to the first location beyond the workspace. Parameters are passed such that the code of the called program is invariant for all parameter instances and all environments in which the program can be called. This goal is achieved if parameters are passed through the caller's workspace. The calling environment saves the current value of WB, places the actual parameters in the workspace, resets WB to the location of the first parameter and calls the shared program. The shared program references its formal parameters as an offset from WB which is an addressing mode invariant for the environment in which the shared program is called.

In case of a value parameter the workspace location is used as an ordinary local variable location of the called program which happens to have an initial value. In case of a reference parameter, the shared program must access the given actual parameter through an indirect reference stored in the corresponding parameter location. The question is whether the parameter location is supposed to contain a physical location or a virtual address.

Passing a physical address as a reference parameter has the serious drawback that the segment in which the actual location resides cannot be relocated while the shared program is running. The impact of such a constraint on the paging system is prohibitive. Using a virtual address complies with the general addressing procedure for programs and data in the local environment. However, there is a slight difference: the address of an actual parameter must be interpreted relative to the environment of the caller which is defined by a segment table other than the local environment of the shared procedure. Therefore, either the parameter location must be extended by the ST base of the calling environment, or the exact location of the segment descriptor which gives access to the actual parameter must be substituted for the segment index. Thus, a virtual address for a reference actual parameter has the form (STbase,s,w) or (ST_s,w).

It is not possible to use a uniform ST base for all parameters. A procedure may call another procedure and pass some of its local names and some of the parameters passed to it as actual parameters. The ST base which the last called procedure must use for its parameters is not uniform for all of them. If a procedure passes a local name as actual parameter to another procedure, it must supply its own ST base as part of the virtual address of the parameter. If it passes one of its parameters as actual parameter to another procedure, it must copy the contents of its own parameter location into the corresponding parameter location of the called procedure. Hence, one could contrive examples in which every parameter needs another ST base.

7.5.6 Common data which is accessible in different environments (though different segment tables) is internal with respect to the environment in which it is created and external in all others. For an external name to be accessible, there must exist a global naming by means of which an access path can be established to the external object. Suppose there is such global naming and there are two mappings: one from external name to global name and one from global name to internal name. The first mapping is locally defined in the environment in which the common object is external, and the other mapping is locally defined in the environment in which the common object is internally defined. The question is how these mappings should be implemented and when they should be executed.

The simplest solution is to prohibit the use of global names entirely and to require that all external names be passed in via reference parameters. Such a solution may be realistic with regard to data, but is not feasible where procedures are concerned. Many procedures are provided as simple operations and should be callable without having been passed in as parameter (for example, functions provided by the operating system).

Another solution makes use of a LINKAGE EDITOR. When a program which uses external names is compiled, the references to an external name are linked together, and the head of the chain is recorded with the corresponding global name. Before the program is started, it is passed through a LINKAGE EDITOR together with all the segments which contain the internal definitions of the global names. The LINKAGE EDITOR performs the mapping of a global name to an internal name and chases down the chains of external references, substituting the internal name for the link information. This method has the drawback that recompilation of a segment which contains an internal definition makes it necessary to reinvoke the LINKAGE EDITOR. Such recompilation of independent segments can be avoided if the linking of segments takes place at loading time through a LINKING LOADER.

Access to external names can also be organized in an entirely dynamic manner similar to the implementation of reference parameters. The program which uses an external name must not be changed at runtime according to our reentrant code requirement. This implies also that references to external names must be invariant. These references are implemented in the program as indirect references through a workspace location determined at compile time. This workspace location is initialized with a trap and the global name. The invariant external name used in the program is this workspace location. When the external name is referenced for the first time, the trap catches the attempted access to the global name and invokes the mapping from global name to internal name which is substituted for the trap. In so doing the program uses an invariant external name, but the translation into an internal name takes place only once at the very first reference. All further accesses are as fast as to a reference parameter. Since external names may be internally defined in different environments, the virtual address substituted for the external name must be of the same structure as the reference parameter. This latter method implies that segments which are never referenced in a particular activation of a program produce no linkage resolution overhead.

PROBLEMS

1. Consider the following method of using the runtime information (RI) in a segment descriptor. An entry in the associative memory AM has a used bit (ub) and a dirty bit (db). When a new element is placed into AM all such bits in AM are cleared. The hardware sets the bits when it respectively accesses or writes into space which it reached through this AM element. When a segment descriptor is copied into AM, RI is set to "alive"; when it is thrown out of AM, the pair (ub,db) is copied into RI.

Investigate where in the address map the field RI must be updated. Suggest a use of the copied values of ub and db in RI and decide when RI should be cleared.

2. The secondary base descriptor of a segment descriptor points to the set of locations in Bs reserved for its page descriptors. Suppose it is decided to dump the set of page descriptors as soon as the last page of the set becomes inaccessible. The segment descriptor should also become inaccessible at that time. Write a program for saving page descriptor sets and investigate which modifications are necessary in procedure PAGEFAULT or the control process PTC.

3. The address field depicted in figure 7.5a is too long to fit in a small, or even medium-size, machine. Also, the additional address mapping hardware, especially the associative memory, may be too expensive. Suppose a machine has a set of double word registers (say four) where a double word pair carries exactly the same information as found in an element of the associative memory. A virtual address is defined as a pair (b,w′) where b is the number of one of the double word registers, and w′, as usual, is the offset from a page base. Address calculation consists of adding the second word of the pair indicated by b (which contains the page base) to w′.

Discuss a paging segmentation system built on such a machine. Design the machine instructions necessary to move from one segment to another.

4. The names of functions provided by the operating system can be seen as universal to every user. One fundamental requirement is that there should not be multiple copies of these functions at one storage level. Though

dynamic linking could be applied, it seems unnecessary to perform the mapping from global name to internal system name, because these two can easily be equated and be represented by a segment descriptor. It is therefore suggested that there be a universal segment table in which all segments containing system functions have a unique position. (Note that this design does not exclude independent recompilation of user or system procedures.)

Compare this approach with the method of LOADING program sets or dynamic linking of segments. Could this access method to system functions be added to the other systems?

5. Suppose we implement a paging segmentation system with dynamic linking of segments and access to external names. Trace the access path of a reference to a parameter in a procedure called within another procedure which passed an external name as actual parameter.

READING LIST

The MULTICS design has been described in many ways [1, 2]. It is particularly famous for the feature of linking segments dynamically. A nice overview of the various virtual memory strategies is [3].

1. Bensoussan, A., "The Multics Virtual Memory: Concepts and Design," *Comm. ACM* 15, 5 (May 1972).

2. Daley, R. C., and J. B. Dennis, "Virtual Memory, Processes, and Sharing in MULTICS," *Comm. ACM* 11, 5 (May 1968).

3. Denning, P. J., "Virtual Memory," *Computing Surveys* 2, 3 (September 1970).

8. Allocation Strategies

8.1 PLACEMENT OF SEGMENTS

8.1.1 The objective of storage management is to move information from one storage level to the other so that the primary store contains that part of the information which has the highest chance of being referenced in the near future. The various management systems—swapping, segmentation, paging, and paged segmentation—have this major objective in common. Which of these systems fits best for a given combination of machine and sort of jobs that are executed on it largely depends on the price in overhead one is willing to pay to achieve a satisfactory approximation of this objective. Therefore, a comparison of the characteristics of these systems is appropriate.

In the preceding chapter we discussed the implementation aspects of the two-level storage management. The implementation concerns primarily the mapping of virtual addresses onto locations and, as a consequence thereof, the treatment of access faults. Secondly, each management system needs a traffic control system which handles the flow of information between the two storage levels. In this chapter we analyze three matters of strategy concerning the following situations:

a. Before information can be brought into Ms, it must be decided where it is going to be placed.
b. If it is necessary to make some space free in Ms, it must be decided which page or segment should be swapped out.
c. It must be decided when information should be transferred from the secondary to the primary storage level.

The first issue is the question of placing information in Ms, the second is that of replacing accessible information. These matters have not been discussed in the preceding chapter in order to separate clearly implementation and strategy. The third issue concerns the choice between transferring information from the secondary to the primary storage level on demand or upon request. In the preceding chapter all information is fetched on demand, that is, a page or segment is automatically swapped in if it is inaccessible when it is referenced for the first time. Information is fetched on request if a process explicitly asks for segment or page by calling a system function especially provided for this purpose. A discussion of fetching on demand or request follows in section 8.3.

8.1.2 The fact that segments do not have a uniform size causes the problem of finding the right slot for placing a segment in Ms. (Such a placement problem does not exist for paging, because a page fits in any Ms frame.) When a segmentation system is in the steady state, we may assume that in the long run as much space can be cleared by deleting obsolete segments as is required for loading needed segments. However, a large segment may be replaced by a smaller one and the space of two adjacent small segments may be needed to load a larger one. As a result of moving segments in and out, a snapshot of Ms shows a partitioning in occupied and free blocks of various sizes (see figure 8.1a). This phenomenon is known as "checkerboarding" of Ms.

When space is requested for a segment of given size, a contiguous area of free space (a hole) must be found which is large enough to accommodate that segment. There is a chance that no hole will be large enough. We address this problem after discussing some methods for free space control.

Free space can be recorded in a link list which has a node for every hole. This well-known technique has the particular advantage that its cost in space overhead is minimal. The space for storing a node can be taken from the very hole described by that node, so there is never a problem of finding space for bookkeeping purposes when a new mode is created. In addition, the space is easily reclaimed when a node is deleted.

The task of the free space management system consists of:

a. Searching for a hole large enough for a segment of given size
b. Updating the link list of holes when space is allocated to a segment
c. Updating the link list of holes when the space of a segment is released

The way the link list is sorted has no significant impact on tasks (a) and

Figure 8.1a Checkerboarding of Ms due to segmentation

(b), but a proper ordering simplifies task (c) considerably. If the list is sorted by arrival time, a new hole is merely appended to the end of the list. In that case it is very hard to discover adjacent holes, because the nodes describing these holes are probably scattered through the list. However, at some time it will be necessary to merge adjacent holes to create holes of adequate size. At that time the whole list must be searched to find the neighbor of a given hole. This search can be in vain, because there is a fair chance that the space adjacent to a given hole will still be in use.

On the other hand, if the list is sorted by ascending (or descending) location number, then adjacent holes can easily be detected. There is a slight disadvantage in that in this case a new node, which is created when space is released, must be inserted into the list so that the ordering is maintained. On the other hand, it is now very easy to create holes as large as possible. When space is released and its neighbor holes have been found, a new node is created if the released space has no common boarder with its neighbors, but, if it has, the space is merely added to the already existing hole. In so doing, it won't be necessary to have a separate action for merging adjacent holes, because all possible merging took place when space was released.

8.1.3 A node in the link list describing the holes consists of two fields, one which points to its successor and one which represents the size of the corresponding hole. Let the list be a circular list and let a node be stored in the first two locations of a hole. It is convenient to fix the location of the first node so that the list can easily be accessed. Therefore, we reserve the first two words of the available storage pool M[0:N−1] for a fixed node which describes a hole of size zero. Initially, the list consists of two nodes pointing to each other. When the steady state has been reached, the list may contain many nodes in addition to the fixed NULL node (see figure 8.1b, c).

A method commonly used for searching for a hole larger than a given size is the first fit algorithm. The major characteristic of this algorithm is that the search is terminated as soon as a hole is found which is larger than the requested size. It has been shown that the performance of the algorithm

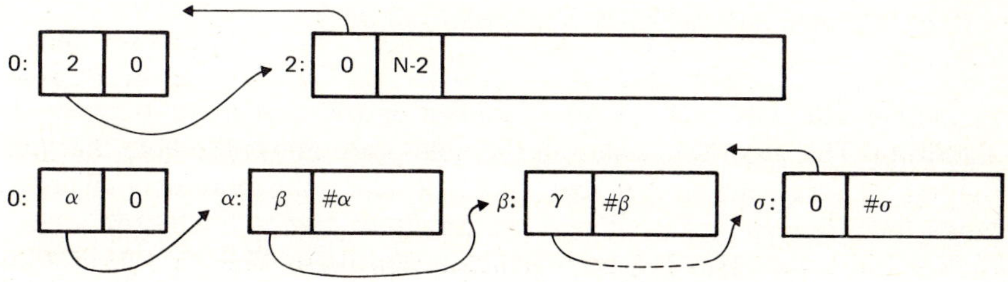

Figure 8.1b, c Initial state of the circular list of holes (above) and snapshot of the list of holes in the steady state (below)

vastly improves if the search is not always started at the NULL node. If the search is always started at the NULL node, the algorithm always selects a sufficiently large hole closest to the NULL node. As a result, the small holes left over after space allocation tend to accumulate at one end of the list. As a result, the larger holes at the other end are not scanned until all the small ones have been inspected. This has the effect of slowing down the search more than necessary. Instead of always starting at the NULL node, the search should be resumed at the point where the previous search terminated. Then, all holes are inspected with equal frequency and the small holes most recently left over are scanned last of all. Moreover, if the segments have a comparable lifetime in Ms, it is likely that the largest holes are just ahead of the search pointer, because the space in that neighborhood has probably been least recently allocated.

8.1.4 If the search algorithm selects a hole which matches the given size exactly, the selected hole must be entirely deleted from the list. A node can easily be deleted if the search algorithm results in a pointer to the predecessor of the selected node instead of the selected node itself. The actual space allocation is treated separately later on in this section. So is the question of what to do if not enough space is found.

A program for the first fit algorithm uses an *own* variable "trail", initialized to zero. A search leaves an indication of where it terminated in trail so that the next search can start from there. The list is sorted by ascending location. The first location of a hole is used as the link field pointing to the next node (if any) and the second location is used for recording the size of the hole.

First fit algorithm for given (size) =
own trail = 0
begin local space, dif; *local* x = trail
  space ← $M[M_x+1]$ $ space of the next hole
  if space < size *then*
    repeat x ← M_x; space ← $M[M_x+1]$ *until* x = trail *or* space ≥ size
  fi
  trail ← x; dif ← space − size
  if dif ≥ 0 *then* allocate space *else* report failure *fi*
end

Another alternative is a method known as the best fit or tightest fit algorithm. This algorithm scans all the holes and selects the hole that fits tightest for a segment of given size. That is, it selects the smallest of all holes larger than (or equal to) the given size. An alternative to the best-fit algorithm is the worst fit or largest remainder algorithm. This algorithm also scans all holes, but it selects the largest. Its objective is to avoid creating small holes which are left over when the best fit algorithm is applied. Obviously, the largest possible piece is left over if space is taken away from the largest hole. A comparative study of the algorithms has shown that the first fit algorithm is superior in performance, particularly if the search pointer cycles through the list instead of starting at the NULL node in every search. The programming of the alternative algorithms is left to the reader (see problem 1).

If space is taken from a hole β the node must be updated before the space is allocated. If the given size is equal to the size of hole β, the node must be entirely deleted. If the given size is smaller than hole β, the space is taken from the end of hole β so that the link fields don't have to be changed. Only the size of hole β must be updated in that case. The program for updating the link list when space is allocated forms the then part of the last statement in the first fit algorithm. The variable trail points at the predecessor of the selected hole (hole α in figure 8.1b, c) and variable dif equals space-size.

```
allocation from a selected hole  =
if dif = 0 then                   $ the location of the selected hole is in M[trail]
   M[trail] ← M[M[trail]]            $ copy the pointer to the successor
                                     $ into the link field of the predecessor
else M[M[trail]+1] ← dif fi          $ otherwise decrease size of selected hole
return M[trail]+dif as starting address of the allocated block.
```

It is assumed in this program that space is allocated in minimal quantities of at least three machine wordss. Otherwise the test dif $= 0$ must be replaced by dif ≤ 2 and the extra one or two words in which the node is stored must be allocated in addition to the requested size. Note that the NULL node is never selected, because its size equals zero. It is never deleted when space is allocated.

8.1.5 When space is released, a new node must be created. If the adjacent space is free, the released space should be coalesced with this free space. The four different situations are depicted in figure 8.1d. The fourth is a combination of cases two and three.

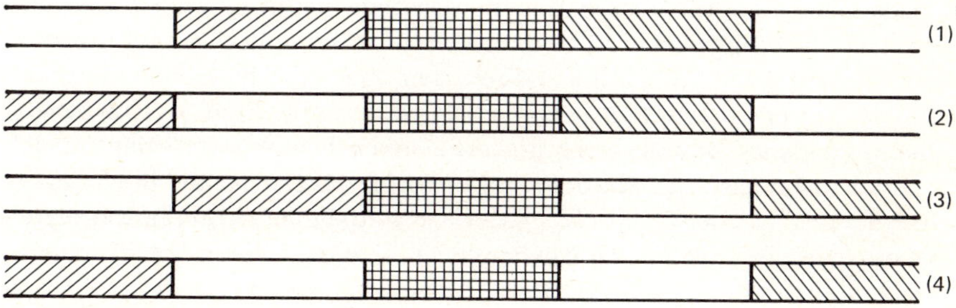

Figure 8.1d The new hole and its neighbors

A procedure which updates the free space when a segment is deleted must receive as parameters the first location and the size of the space to be released. The cases that must be handled by such a procedure can easily be derived from figure 8.1d. In the first case a new node must be created; in the second and fourth cases the space must be coalesced with its predecessor; in the third and fourth cases the space must be merged with the successor, but the descriptive node must be moved to the beginning of the new hole. A program for updating the link list of holes when space is released is:

```
release space(a, size) =
begin local x = 0
   while M_x < a and M_x ≠ 0 do x ← M_x od
   $ x now points to the rightmost hole to the left of the given address
   if x+M_{x+1} = address then     $ if hole x is adjacent to the released space
      M_{x+1} ← M_{x+1}+size       $ then add the space to that hole
   else                            $ otherwise, create new node
      M_a ← M_x; M_{a+1} ← size
      M_x ← a; x ← a               $ and let x point to it
   fi     $ x now points to the extended node or the new node
   if x+M_{x+1} = M_x then         $ if the right neighbor of x is a hole,
      M_{x+1} ← +M[M_x+1]          $ add its size to hole x and copy
      M_x ← M[M_x]                 $ its linkfield. This has the effect
   fi                              $ that the neighbor node is removed from
                                     the list
end
```

At the end of the first *if* statement, x points either to the enlarged node if the space is added to the left neighbor, or to the new node, if the predecessor is not adjacent to the released space. In either case x points to the hole that can possibly be merged with the righthand neighbor (cases three and four in figure 8.1d).

8.1.6 Most of the work that must be done when space is allocated or released is caused by the chosen data structure which represents the free space. When space is allocated, either a linkfield or a size field must be updated; when space is released, the overhead is more serious: before link and size fields can be updated, the list must be scanned to find the right place for inserting the released space. Allocating and releasing space can be reduced to much simpler actions if free and occupied space is represented as a bit string. Many machines provide very powerful and efficient instructions which operate on bit patterns. The advantage of using a bit string and the machine instructions that operate on bit patterns is in the elimination of the search when space is released. However, one has to pay the price of a more elaborate search for a hole of the right size when space is requested. Using the link list, the step from one hole to the next is very simple. If a bit representation is used, finding the next hole means finding a certain bit pattern. We discuss below the management of free storage by a bit string for a 64K word machine with a wordlength of 32 bits. We assume that space is allocated and released in multiples of 64 words.

The primary store is partitioned in 1024 blocks of 64 words each; all these blocks are represented in a bit vector of 1024 bits stored in 32 consecutive words. An element has the value one if the corresponding block of 64 words is free and zero otherwise. The first n blocks ($n \geq 32$) are permanently in use by the operating system, among other things for storing the bit vector. We assume that the machine has the common set of logical operations such as AND, OR, COMPLEMENT, SHIFT, and DOUBLESHIFT (to the left if the argument is positive, to the right if negative). Furthermore, the instruction set includes an instruction for testing the number of leading zeros or ones:

x ← TNLZ(w) places in x the number of leading zeros in w

x ← TNLO(w) places in x the number of leading ones in w

Assuming a two's complement machine, TNLZ(w) returns a zero if w is negative and TNLO returns a zero if w is zero or positive. The maximum result is 32; this result is returned by TNLZ if $w = 0$ and by TNLO if $w = -1$.

A window w of two consecutive registers is used for scanning the bit vector. We assume that segments have a maximum size of 32 blocks (of 64 words each). The window contains a copy of a substring of at least 33 consecutive bits copied from the bit vector (see figure 8.1e).

A pointer p indicates where the last scan left off. (This pointer corresponds to the *own* variable trail used in the first fit algorithm applied to the link list of holes.) Before a string is tested, the word to which p points and the next word are copied into the window (see step 1 in figure 8.1e). Subsequently, the bits in the window are shifted to the left until the bit corresponding to the one pointed at by p is in the leftmost position of the window. If the leading bits in the window are zeros, the pointer is moved to

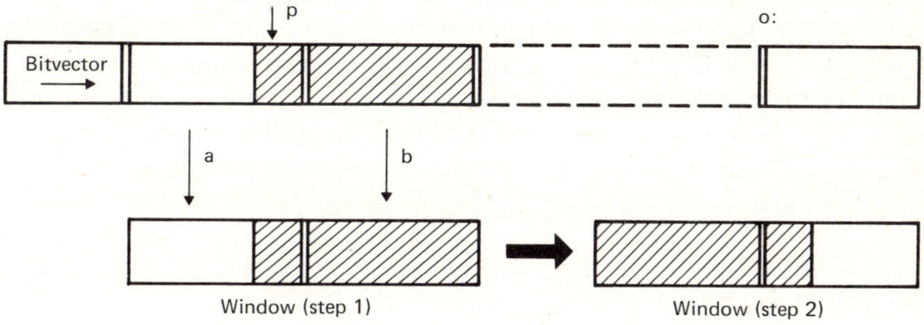

Figure 8.1e A bit string is placed and shifted in the window

the right until the first one is encountered. A string of ones corresponds to a free area, a pattern of zeros to an occupied area. In search of a hole large enough for a requested size, the number of leading ones is compared with the size. If it is insufficient, p is moved to the right just as in the case of leading zeros. If the amount is sufficient, an area of the requested size can be allocated. The algorithm terminates when a hole large enough for the requested size is found or when all holes have been inspected.

Applied to the 32 consecutive words of vector BV[0:31], a program for the first fit algorithm is

```
Bit string version of first fit algorithm for requested(size) =
own p = 1023
begin local x, window; local stop = p−1024
repeat
      window ← BV[p//32],BV[p//32−1]
                              $ // stands for integer division
   DOUBLESHIFT(window, 31−p%32)
                              $ % represents the remainder function
   x ← TNLZ(window); p ← p−x
   x ← TNLO(window); p ← p−x
   if p < 31 then p ← 1023; stop ← stop+1024 fi
until p ≤ stop or x ≥ size
if x ≥ size then allocate space else report failure fi
end
```

The integer division and the evaluation of the remainder can be implemented very cheaply as logical operations. Integer division by 32 is accomplished by a shift over five bit positions to the right. The expression 31−p%32 is computed in two instructions: load the complement of p followed by AND the result with 31. If the leading bits in the window are zero, the second test assigns zero to x. Thus, the relation $x \leq$ size is always false if the leading bits are zero.

Initially, stop has such a low value that p is able to reach the first word B[0]. We assumed that all the bits in B[0] are permanently zero, because the operating system uses the corresponding blocks of storage. Thus, as soon as p points to a bit in B[0], the pointer can be reset to the extreme left in order to continue the search for a pattern of contiguous ones. When p sweeps around to the left, stop is set to the original value of p so that the search can be terminated when p reaches the same point as where it started.

8.1.7 When space is allocated, p has already been moved to the right of the area from which space can be taken. The leftmost bit of this area is determined by p+x (figure 8.1f).

Space is allocated in three steps. First, the right wing of the window is filled with ones and the left wing with a pattern of q zeros in the least

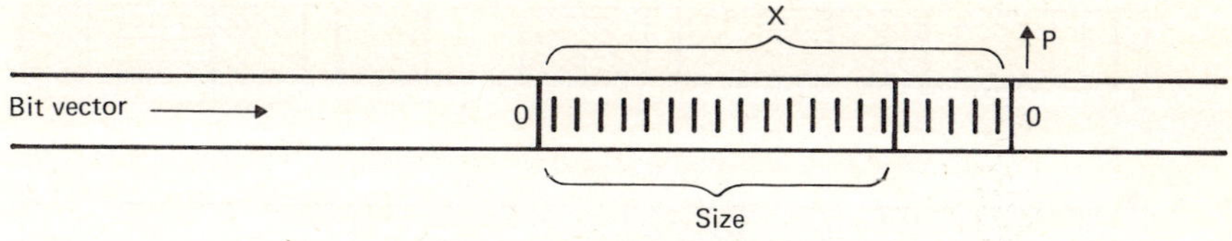

Figure 8.1f Space allocation after finding the space

significant bits where q = size. Secondly, p is set to point just left of the selected hole and the window is rotated over p%32-size bit position to bring the pattern of zeros in the window in line with the hole. Finally, the two words of BV in which the hole resides are masked off by the window through an AND instruction and p is moved beyond the allocated area. A program for space allocation is:

```
Allocate space from a selected hole =
leftwing ← −1; rightwing ← −1
SHIFT(leftwing, size)
p ← p+x+1                 $ p points just left of the selected hole
DOUBLEROTATE(window, p%32−size)
AND(BV[p%32], leftwing); AND(BV[p%32−1], rightwing)
p ← p−size; return as address of allocated area (64*p); p ← p−1
```

Releasing the space is as simple as allocating space since it is not necessary to search for the right place where the space must be inserted. Also, merging the space with a hole either to the left or to the right is not necessary. All that is needed is to set the bits corresponding to the released blocks to one. This is done in three steps just as in the case of allocating space.

```
Release space(address,size) =
begin local window(leftwing, rightwing)
  local q = address%64+size
      $ q points just to the left of the area in BV to be released
  leftwing ← 1; rightwing ← 0
  SHIFT(leftwing, size); leftwing ← leftwing−1
    $ leftwing contains now a pattern of ones in the least
    $ significant bits. The length of this pattern is equal to the given size
  DOUBLEROTATE(window, q%32−size)
  OR(BV[q%32], leftwing); OR(BV[q%32−1], rightwing)
end
```

8.1.8 When space is requested for new information, the operating system can take the opportunity to delete some obsolete information. The decision as

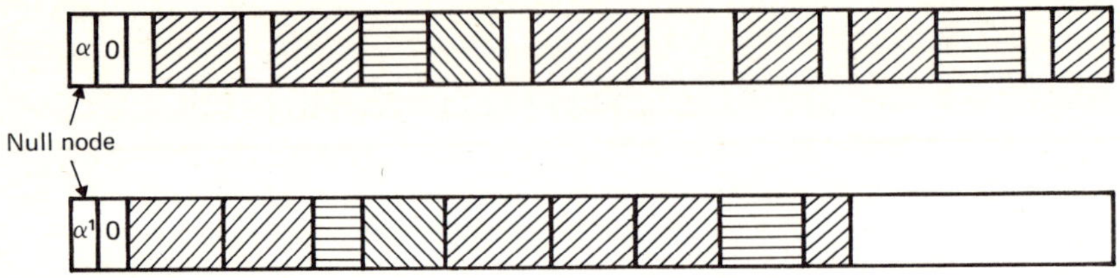

Figure 8.1g Storage layout before and after compacting

to which information can be removed from Ms is discussed in the next section. In a paging system it is sufficient to remove exactly one page for every page requested, but such a policy does not work in a segmentation system. Then it may be necessary to swap out more than one segment to clear the requested space. But even if this is done before the search algorithm is applied, the search may still be unsuccessful, because the available space may be scattered through the store in small pieces. What can be done about it is known as *compacting*. All the occupied areas are shifted towards one end of the storage pool so that all the small holes are replaced by one large hole at the other end (see figure 8.1g). The used storage can, of course, only be compacted if the segments are relocatable.

The position of segments that must be shifted by a compacting algorithm can be derived from the holes to the left and to the right. If x points to the left neighbor hole and z to the right neighbor hole, the occupied area in between starts at address $y = x + \text{size(hole x)}$. If a right neighbor hole exists, z is found in the linkfield of x, thus $z = M_x$. If the rightmost occupied area includes the rightmost location of the storage pool, this area has no hole as right neighbor. In that case z can be set to N, where N is the number of cells in the pool. An iterative compacting algorithm applied to the link list of holes has the following program:

Compacting algorithm for given link list of holes =
begin local k,x $= M_0$; *local* tot $= 0$; *local* y,z
while x $\neq 0$ *do*
  tot $\leftarrow$ tot$+M_{x+1}$; y $\leftarrow$ x$+M_{x+1}$ \$ M_{x+1} = size(hole x)
  z $\leftarrow M_x$; *if* z $= 0$ *then* z $\leftarrow$ N *fi*
  x $\leftarrow M_x$
  update segment description of segments between y and z
  while y $<$ z *do* $M_k \leftarrow M_y$; k $\leftarrow$ k$+1$; y $\leftarrow$ y$+1$ *od*
od
$M_k \leftarrow 0$; $M_{k+1} \leftarrow$ tot; $M_0 \leftarrow$ k; trail $\leftarrow 0$
end

It is necessary to move x to the next hole before the next area is shifted, because its linkfield is overwritten. The compacting algorithm must share the variable trail with the search algorithm, because the old value of trail loses its significance after compacting. The bookkeeping of segments presently in Ms is discussed in the next section. The record of these segments is used to update the segment descriptor when a segment is moved. Compacting is an expensive operation. Most of the time is spent in the inner *while* statement, moving the segments. Even if this statement is tightly coded using a push or auto increment instruction, its length in time will be in the order of ten microseconds on a microsecond machine. Using a block transfer instruction may reduce this time to one microsecond per word moved. Assuming that two-thirds of a 64K storage pool is occupied, it seems that compacting time will be on the order of 400 milliseconds or 40 milliseconds if a block transfer instruction is used. Thus, compacting should be applied as a last resort only if none of the remaining segments can be deleted.

PROBLEMS

1. The best fit algorithm applied to the link list recording the holes scans through the entire list and it selects the smallest hole larger than—or equal to—the given size. The algorithm of the largest remainder also scans the entire list and it selects the largest hole. Program these algorithms.

If you also program these algorithms for the bit vector recording of free space, you will observe how strongly the programs depend on the chosen data structure.

2. If the link list in which the holes are recorded is sorted by ascending hole address, a new node must be inserted in the right place when space is released. The search can easily be restricted to only part of the list at the cost of a few additional variables. Suppose that the available storage pool is divided in four sections of equal length. Three variables s1, s2, and s3 record the last hole address in, respectively, sections s1, s2, and s3. When space is released, a simple test reveals in which section it belongs. The search for the proper place of insertion can now be started at either the NULL node (if the space falls in the first section) or at the point indicated by sj (if the space falls in section j + 1). The variables s1, s2, and s3 may have to be updated when space is allocated or when a new node is inserted. Investigate how the first fit algorithm and the release program should be modified for this design. Space may be allocated from a hole which crosses the boundary of two sections.

3. The largest remainder algorithm takes the largest hole and allocates a block of the requested size from this hole. Let the holes be described by the

nodes of a heap (see section 6.5) which is arranged by descending hole size. The requested block must always be taken from the root. Write a program which allocates a part of the largest hole matching the requested size and inserts the remainder so that the heap remains ordered. Watch out for the case in which no space remains.

4. The execution time of the first fit algorithm operating on the bit string can be improved in several ways. Instead of executing both tests on leading zeros and leading ones every time, a simple test for a negative value in the window indicates which of the two tests is appropriate. Also, the test $p < 31$ is relevant only if a zero pattern is counted, because the first word in BV contains all zeros. Consider how the program should be modified to bring about these execution time improvements. Furthermore, observe that the test $p < 31$ is still carried out after resetting p to the extreme left. Modify the program so that this test is performed only while relevant.

5. Write the compacting algorithm as a recursive procedure (ignoring execution speed and updating of segment descriptors). Also write a compacting procedure for a space management system which uses the bit vector representation of free and occupied blocks.

8.2 REPLACEMENT ALGORITHMS

8.2.1 Before new information can be loaded into the primary store, we must find space in Ms. Free space in Ms is created either when information residing in Ms is deleted or by purposely swapping out information which is of no immediate interest any more. If information is deleted, the cleared space can simply be added to the pool of free space. If free space must be created by swapping, we need a criterion by which obsolete information can be distinguished from active information. In this section we discuss how the operating system finds obsolete information.

The right time to look for obsolete information is when Ms space is requested while the free space is insufficient. This is why an algorithm which selects the information to be swapped out is called a replacement algorithm. The name is somewhat misleading, because the algorithm does not actually replace the information. It merely designates the information which can be swapped out, but does not really activate the data transmission.

A replacement algorithm is applied by a demand paging system. Such a system allows the referencing of inaccessible pages. It interprets such a reference as a request to make the page accessible. The paging system discussed in section 7.4 is a demand paging system. The references to inaccessible pages are responded to by procedure PAGEFAULT. If handling page faults is left to the operating system, the operating system must find an obsolete page which can be exchanged for the requested page. The alternative to demand paging is a request paging system. In such a system a reference to an inaccessible page is an error. A request paging system provides explicit routines a user can invoke to load and save pages. In such a system it is more natural for a process to decide for itself which information can be swapped out. We will return to this subject in the next section. Most of what will be said about paging also applies to a segmentation system. Some minor differences are briefly discussed at the end of this section. In a paged segmentation system replacement is invariably applied to the paging subsystem. Because the paging aspects are entirely hidden from the user of virtual storage, a demand paging system is the most suitable. Thus, the discussion below applies as a whole to the paging subsystem of a paged segmentation system.

8.2.2 In order to find which page can be swapped out, the operating system must have access to the information which describes the pages present at the primary storage level. Only a small subset of all pages is in Ms at a given moment. Therefore, a search through all the page tables to find the page descriptors of pages in Ms is very inefficient. Instead, the operating system keeps a record describing the current use of the frames in Ms. The number of Ms frames is fixed, so a frame table (FT) of fixed length is sufficient. An entry in FT has the layout shown in figure 8.2a.

The number of frame descriptors, n, satisfies the relation n∗frame size = N, where N is the number of words in Ms. The base address of the frame corresponding to the i-th frame descriptor equals (i∗framesize). Therefore, the frame descriptor which corresponds to a page descriptor

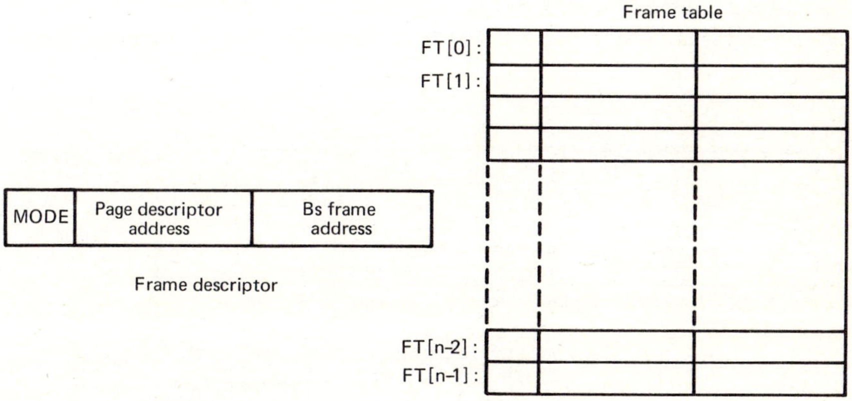

Figure 8.2a Frame table and frame descriptor layout

pointing to an accessible page can easily be derived from the primary base field in the page descriptor. The access path in the reverse direction, from frame descriptor to page descriptor, is explicitly established when a page is placed in a frame. At that time the address of the page descriptor is placed in the field of the appropriate frame descriptor.

The MODE field of a frame descriptor has one of four possible values: free, if no page resides in the corresponding frame; in use, if an accessible page resides in the frame; in transition, if the frame is involved in a load or a save operation; locked-in, if certain pages cannot be swapped out (for example, page tables and some parts of the operating system). If a frame is in use and contains a program page, there also exists a copy of this page in Bs. The address of the corresponding Bs frame is kept in the third field of a frame. At the moment that a page is transferred from Bs to Ms, we always enter its Bs frame address in the field of that name in the frame descriptor. This way some table space can be saved, because a page descriptor does not need a separate field for the secondary storage base. While a page is in Bs, the base field of its page descriptor can be used for recording its Bs base. When it is brought into Ms, its Bs base is transferred to the chosen Ms frame descriptor while its base field now contains the Ms base. This arrangement saves space, because there are far more page descriptors than Ms frame descriptors. The MODEs "in transition" and "locked-in Ms" are necessary to avoid the selection of such frames.

The runtime information of a frame is the same as that of the page residing in this frame. We assume that active page descriptors are kept in an associative memory AM (see sections 7.3 and 7.4). Thus information describing an active page and its frame is found in three places: in an AM entry, in the page descriptor, and in a frame descriptor (see figure 8.2b).

The reference bit (or used bit) and dirty bit (or written into bit, or changed bit) are set by the hardware, respectively, when the page is accessed and when a value is stored into it. We described in section 7.3.6 how the reference bit is used to find out which AM entries have not been accessed lately.

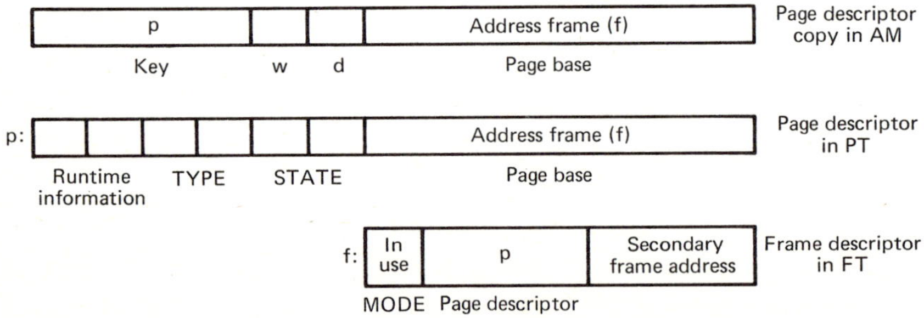

Figure 8.2b Information describing an active page

It is useful to have a copy of the dirty bit in the runtime information field of a page descriptor. When a page descriptor is removed from the associative memory AM, the value of the dirty bit in the AM entry is added to the dirty bit in the page descriptor using an OR instruction. This can save us some time in saving pages, because a frame pointing to a nonactive page descriptor in which the dirty bit is off contains a pure page. The fact that the dirty bit is not on means that no values have been stored into this page, and that the copy in Bs is still valid and, therefore, if such a page is removed from Ms, the page descriptor can simply be reset to its Bs base without saving the page. On the other hand, if the dirty bit is found on, the Bs frame indicated in the frame descriptor can be released, because the page in that frame is now useless. If a frame designated by a replacement algorithm is allocated to another page, the page currently residing in the frame must first be saved. These issues were discussed in section 7.4. Procedure PAGE-FAULT removes a page from a frame and allocates it to a new page when it handles access to an empty page. The page traffic control process allocates a frame when it finds a completed load command and it removes a page from the designated frame when it generates a save command. Given the data structures for an entry in the associative memory, AM, a page descriptor and a frame descriptor as depicted in figure 8.2b, programs for these two actions are:

```
remove page (z) from frame (f) =
begin
   STATE(z) ← inaccessible
   if copy of (z) in AM then
      copy runtime information into (z); clear (AM[z]) fi
   if dirty bit (z) off then pagebase (z) ← secondary frame (f)
   else clear (pagebase(z)); release Bs frame (secondary frame (f)) fi
   clear (runtime information (z))
   MODE(f) ← in transition; page descriptor (f) ← void
end

allocate frame (f) to page (z) =
begin secondary frame (f) ← pagebase(z); pagebase (z) ← f*framesize
   page descriptor (f) ← z; MODE(z) ← in use
   STATE(z) ← accessible
end
```

8.2.3 A replacement algorithm is applied only if no free frames are available. Its task is accomplished when it has found a frame that can be cleared. The decision whether or not the frame is actually used after the page presently residing in it has been saved (if necessary) falls outside the scope of the replacement algorithm. This matter has been discussed in detail in the second half of section 7.4 (step 3).

The overall objective of this two-level storage management is to have those pages available in Ms which have the highest probability of being referenced in the near future. Therefore, nearly all replacement algorithms have as their objective guessing which page in Ms currently has the lowest probability of being referenced. This page is then designated as the result of the replacement algorithm. The simplest algorithm selects a page at random. This algorithm is implemented by a designer who believes that it is not possible to make an intelligent guess as to which page is least likely to be referenced in the near future. Of course, implementation of this algorithm is trivial and the overhead it entails is minimal.

Two other straightforward replacement algorithms are: round robin and first-in-first-out. The RR algorithm uses an *own* variable lc which points to the frame *l*ast *c*leared. When the RR replacement algorithm is called, lc cycles through the frame table FT, starting from where it left off last time, until it finds a frame which is neither locked-in nor in transition. The algorithm selects the frame which has been longest in use, counting from where the pointer lc stopped last time. Implementation of this algorithm is very simple and no elaborate data structure is needed to support its execution. The choice of this RR algorithm is based on the expectation that the time intervals during which pages are referenced are reasonably close to an average time length. If this is true, the page with lowest reference probability is the one in the frame least recently selected. This is exactly the frame just ahead of the pointer lc, because the moment that lc pointed to that frame is the longest ago.

An FIFO replacement algorithm is based on the observation that the probability of referencing a page in the near future is likely to be a decreasing function of the time that this page resides in Ms. It seems therefore that the least harm is done if the oldest page is swapped out, that is, the page which was brought into Ms the longest ago. The FIFO replacement algorithm needs the support of a FIFO queue in which the pages in the frames are ordered by arrival time. The queue contains all the frames whose MODE = ‘in use’ and no others. The replacement algorithm is trivial: if a frame is requested, the first frame in the FIFO queue is designated; if a frame with a pure page in it is required, the queue is scanned from the beginning until such a frame is found.

Experiments and measurements have shown that the performance of the RR and the FIFO replacement algorithms is not good. Much better results are obtained with a variation on the RR scheme applied in many systems. It is known as the MULTICS algorithm, the second chance algorithm, or the clock algorithm. It is very attractive because of its simplicity and it performs surprisingly well. It is a good approximation of the least recently used algorithm which is discussed later on in this section. A description of the algorithm follows below.

If there are free frames, one of those is chosen by the replacement algorithm. Otherwise, one of the frames whose mode is in use is chosen. The algorithm uses an *own* variable lc (like the RR algorithm) which cycles through the frame table scanning the in use frames. The selection of the frame whose page will be removed depends on the runtime information, consisting of the used bit and the dirty bit. If the algorithm encounters an in use frame with (used bit, dirty bit) = (1,1) or (1,0) it turns off the used bit and proceeds to the next in use frame in the frame table. If it finds (used bit, dirty bit) = (0,1), it saves the indication that the page is dirty in another bit and changes the state to (0,0). It gives the dirty page a third chance. The pointer lc stops at an in use frame in the state (0,0). The page in this frame will be removed and saved in Bs if necessary.

The hardware changes the used bit and dirty bit when a page is referenced and changed. The result is that, for instance, the state of a frame which was changed from (1,0) to (0,0) by the algorithm may have been changed back to (1,0) by the hardware before the pointer reaches this frame the next time around. This has the effect of keeping the recently referenced pages in the main store. The algorithm also prefers a clean page over a dirty one. This saves valuable swap time, because there is already a true copy of a clean page in the secondary store Bs. Writing a program for the second chance algorithm is left to the reader (see problem 2).

8.2.4 The least recently used algorithm (LRU) recognizes the fact that some pages are used for longer periods of time than others. For example, a page containing part of a main program or the global data of a program usually has a longer lifetime than a procedure page or a page of temporary data. Therefore, the LRU algorithm is based on the assumption that the probability of referencing a particular page is proportional to the time interval between the last reference to a page and the present moment. The page which is selected by the LRU replacement algorithm is then the least recently referenced page.

An exact implementation of an LRU algorithm is not feasible because of its tremendous overhead on current hardware. It would be necessary to record the time of reference every time a page is referenced, because the operating system has no way of knowing which reference to a page is the last. The second chance algorithm is a good approximation of the LRU algorithm, because it holds on to the most recently referenced pages. Another approximation is the algorithm that uses the order in which pages leave the associative memory AM. When a page descriptor is removed from AM, its moment of last reference is later than that of the page descriptors which have already been removed from AM and is earlier than those which have not yet been removed.

This algorithm requires more work in loading and removing a page descriptor into and from AM. We need a last reference queue (LRQ) to which a page is appended when it is removed from AM. Unfortunately, we must reckon with the possibility that a page in LRQ is referenced. In that case the page descriptor must be removed from LRQ and copied into AM. A page is placed in LRQ when it is removed from AM and replaced by a copy of page descriptor q. This is done in the following way:

```
replace copy of (q) in AM by copy of (p) =
begin local TEMP ← address of AM[q]
   OR (dirtybit(ST_q), dirtybit(TEMP))
   append to LRQ(frame(q))
   if p in LRP old then
      delete from LRQ (frame(p)) fi
   update the page and frame description of p and q
   clear used bit and dirty bit in ST_p; TEMP ← p
end
```

The LRU replacement algorithm itself is very simple; it designates the first element of LRQ, or searches through LRQ from the beginning until it finds a frame with a pure page. Finally, procedure remove page from frame (f) must be adapted to remove the designated frame from LRQ.

The replacement of an element in the associative memory AM is rather elaborate. Moreover, the overhead is incurred at a time that we cannot afford it. The changes in AM must be as fast as possible to allow for frequent changes at a low cost. Therefore, the approximated LRU is inferior to the second chance algorithm.

8.2.5 Both the FIFO and LRU algorithms can be applied to a pure segmentation system if segments in Ms are linked together into a FIFO queue or an LRQ. The queues can be implemented the same way as for a paging system if every segment is assigned a number when it is brought into Ms. The frame table of a pure segmentation system is not fixed as in a paging system. It may be implemented as a list or as an array, but must be large enough to allow for fluctuations in the number of segments. If the second chance algorithm is applied, the frame descriptor for a new segment is inserted just preceding the pointer lc.

A replacement algorithm applied to a pure segmentation system may have to designate more than one segment if the first one found is not large enough for the requested size. It would make sense to keep around an *own* variable which reflects the total amount of free space. The replacement algorithm uses this variable to decide when to stop. It designates at least one segment and it terminates when the free space plus the space of the designated segments is larger than the requested size. However, except for these slight differences, the replacement algorithms work equally well for a pure segmentation system as for paging.

PROBLEMS

1. Write a transition diagram for the STATEs of a page descriptor and the

MODEs of a frame descriptor. Indicate in each diagram which actions cause the transitions, and list the states and modes which occur simultaneously. Extend the diagrams with the possible substates given by the runtime information and also indicate the actions which cause the changes. It seems as if the MODE field in a frame descriptor is superfluous if a second chance or LRU replacement discipline is adopted, because all the necessary information can be derived from the corresponding page descriptor or from the queue in which the frame descriptor resides. The TYPE field in a page descriptor also seems to be superfluous because of the runtime information collected and recorded in the descriptor copy in AM. Check all the places where MODE or TYPE are inspected or changed and see if both can be deleted.

2. The second chance algorithm distinguishes between dirty and referenced frames and frames which have not been referenced since the last inspection. Write a program for the second chance algorithm which selects an unreferenced frame whose dirty bit is turned off as described earlier in this section. Make sure that the program works correctly if there are no unreferenced or clean frames in the frame table.

3. The three replacement algorithms RR, FIFO and LRU are based on three different conjectures about the behavior of programs. Let a given program consist of a main program which fits on one page and a series of procedures which each fit on a page. The kernel of the main program is a loop in which it calls several of its procedures. The procedures very seldom call one of the other procedures. Main program and procedures frequently reference global data which also fits in one page. Suppose a number of programs with these characteristics run simultaneously. Which of the three replacement algorithms would give the best performance?

Since every one of the three algorithms guesses, it is possible to find a behavior of programs such that the chosen algorithm is the worst conceivable. Specify the characteristics of programs for every one of the three replacement algorithms which make the algorithm a very bad choice.

4. In a pure segmentation system to which an LRU algorithm is applied, because segments can be rather large it is conceivable for the LRQ to get empty and for there to be only a few replaceable segments in Ms. Convince yourself that an empty LRQ in a paging system must be considered as an error. Design the LRU algorithm for a pure segmentation system and write a program for it allowing for an empty LRQ.

5. There are three ways of sharing pages (or segments): 1) there is one shared page table accessible to all processes (in addition to their own page table); 2) each process has a copy of the page descriptor of a shared page in its own page table; 3) each process has a pointer to the unique descriptor of

a shared page in its page table. If the first method is adopted, all processes must use the same page index for a particular page. Access to a page is direct for the first and second method, but indirect through the pointer in the third method. Discuss how in each case the runtime information is maintained with or without an associative memory. Shared pages should not be chosen by the second chance algorithm if there are nonshared pages around unless no process shows interest in the shared page. Write a modified version of the second chance algorithm which accounts for shared pages. You may assume that a shared page is distinguishable from an unshared page. Would it be useful to have a counter with each shared page descriptor indicating how many processes share the page? When should the counter be updated? (This counter is called the reference count.)

8.3 THE USE OF LOCALITY

8.3.1 Simulation experiments and system measurements have shown strong evidence that processes do not access their pages at random, but at any one time tend to favor a subset of their pages. This phenomenon is commonly known as the principle of locality. It has been observed that the number of pages belonging to the locality is generally not very large (rarely more than 10 pages per process for a page size of 500–1000 words). It has also been observed that the locality changes slowly in the sense that the number of additions to—or removals from—the locality is very small compared to the number of references to pages in the locality. This gradual change of the locality causes what we may call the natural page flow of a process. Assuming that all the pages in a two-level store initially reside on backing store, a page must be transferred from Bs to Ms before it can be referenced for the first time.

The storage management would be optimal if the natural page flow were the only cause of page traffic between the two storage levels. However, another cause of page traffic is the phenomenon of the missing page. A page is said to be missing if it is not present at the primary memory level, although it belongs to the locality. A page can be missing for one of two possible reasons. The total space required by all the localities of the concurrent processes may be larger than the primary store Ms, or the space-management system may not precisely know which pages belong to the locality of a process at a given time.

In this section we analyze the efficiency degradation of processing a reference string if the localities can only partly be loaded into the primary store. It turns out that the performance is very sensitive to the phenomenon of the missing page. It is therefore important to determine the localities as accurately as possible.

8.3.2 If the primary storage is not large enough to hold all the localities of the active processes, some pages of the localities will be missing. These pages must be loaded into Ms before they can be referenced. The time (T) it takes to process a given reference string (s) depends on the length of the string (l), the average reference time to a page in Ms (r), the number of references to pages absent from Ms (a) and the transfer time (t) to fetch a page from the auxiliary store.

$$T(s) = l(s)*r + a(s)*t$$

The quantity a(s) is determined by the natural page flow (nat) and the number of missing pages (m). If the primary store is large enough to hold all the localities, a(s) is completely determined by the natural page flow. Therefore, the shortest time interval possible in which the given reference string s can be processed is

$$T_{min}(s) = l(s)*r + nat(s)*t$$

Define the relative efficiency of processing a reference string s as

$$\text{efficiency}(s) := T_{min}(s)/T(s)$$

The relative efficiency of processing a reference string s is equal to one if none of the pages are missing. The efficiency decreases if the number of missing pages increases.

The ratio $d = t/r$ is a measure of the speed discrepancy of fetching a page from the backing store and accessing a cell in the primary store. The ratio d depends on the chosen page size and the type of secondary storage device that is used. Given a page size of 512 words, a 70 word/millisecond drum with two to four pages per track and an average reference time $r = 3$ microseconds, the ratio d is in the range 4000–8000 (accounting for the latency of the drum). This figure is up to twice as high for a disk.

The ratio $f_{nat} = nat/l$ expresses the frequency of referencing a page for the first time in a given string. The principle of locality states that f_{nat} is very small. Observations of program behavior have shown that, for long reference strings 10^5 references or more and a page size of 512 to 1024 words, $f_{nat} = p(s)/\text{page size}$, where $0 \leq p(s) \ll 1$.

The ratio $f_{mis} = m/l$ represents the missing page frequency. The efficiency can be written as

$$\text{efficiency} = \{1+d*f_{nat}\}/\{1+d*f_{nat}+d*f_{mis}\} = 1/\{1+c*f_{mis}\}$$
$$\text{where} \quad c = d/\{1+d*f_{nat}\}$$

The coefficient c increases if the page size is increased. The ratio d is proportional to the page size if an Extended Core Store (ECS) is used as auxiliary store device. In that case the product $f_{nat}*d$ remains constant for various page sizes, so the coefficient c is also proportional to the chosen page size. (This is not exactly true for a drum or disk because of the latency time.)

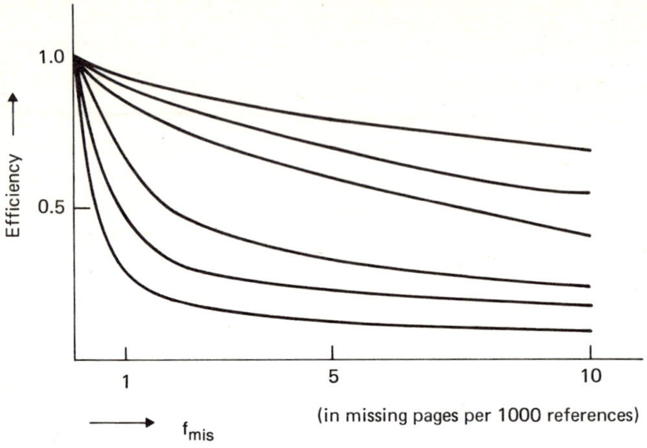

Figure 8.3a Reference efficiency as function of the missing page rate

The efficiency is plotted in figure 8.3a as a function of f_{mis} which is expressed in number of missing pages per thousand references. The value of the coefficient c is the parameter of the curves.

8.3.3 If Ms is not large enough to hold the pages of all the localities, a fraction q of all these pages must be placed in the secondary store. The expected value of $f_{mis}(s)$ for a given (long) string s depends on the number q and the probability distribution of referencing the pages in the localities. If the references to the pages in the localities are equally distributed, the expectation value $E(f_{mis}(s)) = q$. This is the worst possible case.

If, on the other hand, the reference probability for some pages is much smaller than for others, suitable page management can have a beneficial effect on the efficiency. We can expect that the value of $f_{mis}(s)$ is far less than q if the pages with lowest reference probability are kept in the secondary store. As a result, the efficiency will be greater than in the case that the pages are referenced at random. We investigate the effect of a more favorable reference distribution somewhat further for the case to which the least recently used replacement algorithm applies.

The LRU replacement algorithm, which was discussed in the preceding section, is based on the assumption that the most recently referenced pages have a higher reference probability than the least recently used pages. Let us assume that the reference distribution is geometric for an ordering of the pages from most recently used to least recently used (see figure 8.3b).

The page management system keeps the first y pages in Ms, and the remaining $(z-y)$ pages, which have the lowest reference probability, in Bs.

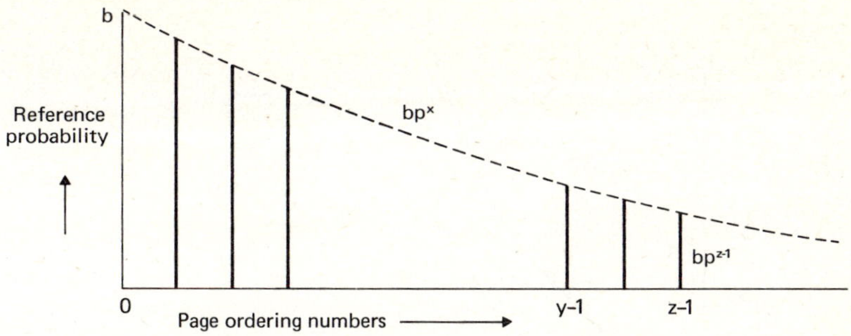

Figure 8.3b Reference distribution as function of the order of most recent reference

The fraction q of missing pages is equal to $(z-y)/z$. Assuming that the reference distribution is constant in time, the expected value of $f_{mis}(s)$ is

$$E(f_{mis}(s)) = \frac{\sum_{x=0}^{z-1} e^{-ax} - \sum_{x=0}^{y-1} e^{-ax}}{\sum_{x=0}^{z-1} e^{-ax}}$$

Evaluating and rewriting the righthand side results in:

$$E(f_{mis}(s)) = \frac{e^{-ay}-e^{-az}}{1-e^{-az}} = \frac{e^{qaz}-1}{e^{az}-1} = q * \frac{g(qaz)}{g(az)}$$

where $g(x) := \frac{e^x - 1}{x}$ (see figure 8.3c).

The improvement of the efficiency depends on the factor $g(qaz)/g(az)$. The function $g(x)$ has the property that for $0 \leq x_1 \leq x_2$

$$g(x_1) * g(x_2) \leq g(x_1 + x_2)$$

A proof is easily found if we substitute $x_1 = c-u$ and $x_2 = c+u$. The substitution implies that $x_1 + x_2 = 2c$ and $0 \leq u \leq c$.

$$g(c-u) * g(c+u) = \frac{(e^{c-u}-1) * (e^{c+u}-1)}{(c-u)(c+u)} = \frac{e^{2c}+1-(e^{c-u}+e^{c+u})}{(c-u)(c+u)}$$

$$= e^c \frac{(e^c+e^{-c})-(e^u+e^{-u})}{(c-u)(c+u)} = \frac{2e^c}{(c^2-u^2)}\left(\frac{1}{2!}(c^2-u^2)+\frac{1}{4!}(c^4-u^4)+\ldots\right)$$

$$= 2e^c\left(\frac{1}{2}+\frac{1}{4!}(c^2+u^2)+\frac{1}{6!}(c^4+c^2u^2+u^4)+\ldots\right)$$

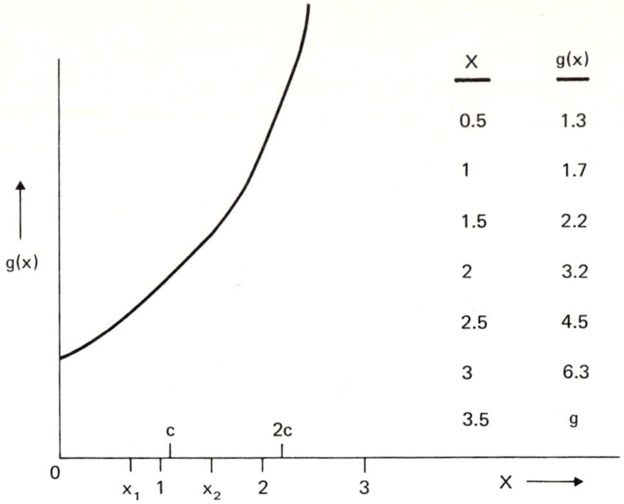

Figure 8.3c $g(x) = \frac{e^x-1}{x}, g(0) = 1$

The product $g(c-u)*g(c+u)$ is a monotonic increasing function of u. Thus, it reaches its maximum value on the given interval for $u = c$. This implies

$$g(c-u)*g(c+u) \leq g(0)*g(2c) = g(2c).$$

The proof that the function g(x) has the stated property is complete after resubstitution of x_1 and x_2.

The derived property can be used to give an estimate of the factor $g(aqz)/g(az)$. If x_1 is replaced by aqz and x_1+x_2 by az, then $x_2 = (1-q)az$, so $g(qaz)*g((1-q)az) \leq g(az)$. Thus,

$$E(f_{mis}(s)) = q*\frac{g(aqz)}{g(az)} \leq q*\frac{1}{g((1-q)az)} = q*\frac{(1-q)az}{e^{(1-q)az}-1}$$

The expected value of $f_{mis}(s)$ is smaller than q, because $g(x) \geq 1$ for all $x \geq 0$. If the reference probability is much smaller for the least recently used page than for the most recently used page, for instance a factor 5, then $e^{-az} = 0.2$ (see figure 8.3b), so $az = 1.61$. Assuming that the fraction of missing pages q is 12%, 8%, 4%, we find that the factor $1/g((1-q)*az)$ is respectively equal to

$$1/g(0.88*1.6) = 0.46,\ 1/g(0.92*1.6) = 0.44,\ 1/g(0.96*1.6) = 0.42$$

If the reference probability of the most recently used page is only 1.5 times that of the least recently used, the expected value of $f_{mis}(s)$ is approximately 0.8 q for $q = 10\%$. The efficiency increases rapidly with the size of the primary store, because a larger store means a smaller q and thus an increase of the argument $(1-q)az$. The steep increase of the efficiency is caused by the fact that $g(x)$ is an exponential function of x.

8.3.4 Unfortunately, it is not so easy to apply this theoretical result. The difficulty is that neither the operating system nor the programs which use the pages have precise knowledge about the reference probabilities of the pages. If the page management is entirely under control of the operating system, as in a demand paging system, all the system can do is make an intelligent guess. Such guessing was implemented for the first time by the designers of the operating system on the Ferranti-Atlas computer around 1960 in Manchester, England. This system assumes that the reference probability is correlated with the past frequency of referencing the pages. The most frequently referenced pages are assumed to have the highest reference probability. The system keeps the set of least frequently referenced pages on backing store, assuming that these pages have the smallest reference probability. Because the correlation of reference frequency and reference probability appears to be very strong, a page management system which counts the reference frequency for each page can do a good job at minimizing the number of page faults.

However, the overhead incurred by the least frequently used measure makes its application rather unpopular. A replacement algorithm based on this method must find the least frequently referenced page among the pages in the primary store. The cost of maintaining a list in which the pages are ordered by reference frequency is too high, because such a list must be updated too frequently when pages are referenced. Thus, the LFU replacement algorithm must compare the reference frequency of all the pages in the primary store in order to find the least frequently used page. In this respect the LFU algorithm compares unfavorably with other replacement algorithms, particularly the approximated LRU replacement algorithm. Moreover, the overhead of supporting the LFU algorithm is prohibitive without special hardware features. Every time a page is referenced, its frequency count must be incremented. This would not matter when a page cannot directly be referenced, but takes too much time in the normal case of a directly accessible page.

Another approach to controlling the number of page faults is the working set model invented by P. J. Denning. The working set of a process varies in time. The working set at time t consists of those pages which were referenced during the time interval $[t+1-T:t]$, where T is the working set parameter. One may expect that the working set size $s(T)$ is proportional to T for small values of T, but the locality principle says that $s(T)$ will level off for larger values of T and increase again for very large values of T.

The objective of the space management system applying the working set technique is to keep the whole working set of a running process in the primary store. However, there are two difficulties in applying the model. In the first place, there is too much overhead involved in recording the time of accessing a particular page (see the argument against implementing LFU earlier in this section). This problem can be solved by applying the LRU algorithm. Instead of a time interval T, we specify a fixed number K and interpret the working set as the last K referenced pages. However, we have seen that the LRU algorithm is not easily implemented either. We can use the second chance algorithm instead, but that leaves the other problem, the choice of T or K. If the value is chosen too small, the result will be that the working sets are only partly loaded, which results in a high page fault frequency. Denning called this phenomenon thrashing. If T or K is chosen too large, old pages in which a process is not interested anymore are kept too long in the main store. The result is that too few runnable processes share the main store.

The problem of choosing T or K can be solved in a very practical manner. The system measures the missing page frequency f_{mis} and uses T or K as a tuning parameter. If the frequency passes an acceptable upperbound (say one in 5000), the value of T or K is increased so that the page fault frequency decreases. If the page fault rate is too low, the main store is probably underutilized, and the value of T or K is decreased. This allows more runnable processes to share the main store at the cost of somewhat more page traffic.

As an alternative to demand paging, pages could conceivably be transferred on request. In a request paging system the programs which use the pages provide the information which pages belong to the localities and which pages can be discarded. For such a technique to work properly it will be necessary for the programs to also provide information about the size of their localities. Until this time not much data on the performance of request paging systems is available.

PROBLEMS

1. Given a machine with an average store reference time of 2 microseconds and a drum with a transfer speed of 80 words/millisecond and 1024 words per track, assume that the natural page flow frequency f_{nat} for a given string s is one-third times the reciprocal of the page size. Investigate the effect that changing the page size from 1024 words per page to 512, 256 and 128 words per page has on the relative efficiency of processing the given string s.

If we consider various alternative auxiliary storage devices, investigate whether it makes much difference if the relative efficiency of processing a given string is defined by $f_{nat}/(f_{nat}+f_{mis})$ instead of by the given definition.

2. The pages of a given set of localities can be partitioned in three classes. The first class consists of half the pages. These pages have the same refer-

ence probability. The second and third classes contain, respectively, two-thirds and one-third of the number of pages in the first class. The reference probability is the same for all pages in one class and is, respectively, two-thirds and one-third of the reference probability of the first class. The system keeps a number of pages with the lower reference probabilities in the auxiliary store. Use the given data to find an estimate for the expected value of the missing page frequency as a function of the missing page ratio q.

3. The objective of this problem is to compare the performance of the LRU and LFU algorithms in two special cases. First we need two procedures which generate a reference string to a given set of N pages. The first procedure is an implementation of the rule that the reference probability is a function which increases from the least recently referenced page to the most recently referenced page. The second procedure implements the rule that the reference probability is proportional to the frequency of past references. Both cases are initialized with a set of pages ordered by a fictitious set of last reference times and a fictitious past reference frequency. The first procedure of generating a reference sequence is applied to the first case and the second procedure to the second case. Measure in both cases the number of page faults if an LRU algorithm is applied and also if an LFU algorithm is applied. Carry out the simulation experiment for various values of the missing page ratio q, for instance 12%, 8%, 4% and 2%.

4. It is obvious that a direct implementation of an LFU algorithm causes too much overhead. However, consider the following approximation and compare its implementability with that of the approximated LRU technique. Assume the use of an associative memory AM in which copies of the directly accessible page descriptors are kept. Whenever a new descriptor must be placed in AM, the reference counts of all the descriptors in AM whose dirty bit has been set are incremented by one. After placing the new descriptor in AM, all the dirty bits are reset. Check all the places in the page management where the frequency counts must be updated and program an LFU replacement algorithm.

One could argue that the reference count is not accurate enough, because the time intervals between two updates of AM vary. An alternative to the reference frequency count would be a recording of the accumulated time that a descriptor resided in AM while its dirty bit was found on when tested. Check whether this modification causes more overhead in space or time and discuss whether it is worthwhile.

5. The working set parameter K (or T) and the missing page frequency can be measured in several ways. Compare two designs, one in which the parameter and the frequency are measured for the system as a whole and one in which they are measured for each process individually.

6. The working set parameter is used to tune the missing page rate and the use of the main store. If the frequency is too high, the parameter K (or T) is increased so that the processes are allowed to increase their working sets. However, when the parameter is increased, the main store is in use by the smaller working sets. Devise a strategy for making space available in the main store for the larger working sets. Also describe what must be done when the parameter is decreased.

8.4 EXTERNAL FRAGMENTATION

8.4.1 Paging is simpler than segmentation. The address map of a paged virtual store does not need an overflow test, whereas two overflow tests must be performed when an address of a segmented store is translated. A page table has a fixed length, but the length of a segment table is variable. Placing a segment in the primary store requires a search algorithm for a block of free space which is large enough to match the requested segment. Placing of a page is trivial; any frame is as good as any other. When a segment is deleted or removed from the primary store, reclaiming the space requires inserting in an ordered list and possibly merging with neighboring blocks of free space. A frame is reclaimed by appending it to a list of free frames of which the order is immaterial. In terms of space overhead, both methods pay a price in the form of a page table or segment table. The length of such a table depends on the chosen page size and the average segment size. We concluded earlier that it is easier to fit a large number of small segments in the primary store than a small number of large segments. A segment table could therefore be rather long. Moreover, a segment descriptor needs almost twice the space of a page descriptor because of the additional segment size field.

Using either method, some fraction of primary storage will be wasted. In a segmented store the waste occurs owing to the checkerboarding phenomenon. Segments have various sizes, and because of this, holes are created when a newly arriving segment does not precisely fit in the space left by removed segments. When placing and replacing segments has been going on for a while, the store looks like a checkerboard made up by blocks of used and unused space. This phenomenon is also known as external fragmentation.

It seems that a paging system is able to utilize all the available store. Indeed, it does not suffer from external fragmentation. However, storage is now wasted in another manner, known as internal fragmentation, owing to the fact that space is allocated in multiples of the chosen frame size. A segment (in the sense of a logically coherent piece of information) is divided into a set of pages of which the last contains less information than a frame is able to hold (unless different segments can share a page). So the waste of storage space is not as apparent as in a segmentation system, but it is nevertheless there. External fragmentation is discussed in this section and internal fragmentation in the next section.

8.4.2 The average amount of space taken up by the holes between the blocks of space allocated to segments is wasted. It is very difficult to find an estimate of the wasted fraction of storage because of the erratic behavior of the holes owing to the effect of splitting and merging holes. Knuth's fifty percent rule gives an estimate of the number of holes (h) as compared to the number of allocated blocks (n). The fifty percent rule states that on the average

$$h = p*n/2$$

where p is the probability that, when space for a segment is carved out of a hole, the remaining free space is large enough to be listed as a hole. The derivation of this rule is based on the reasonable assumption that, if the system is in its steady state, the probability that the number of holes increases when the allocation state is modified is equal to the probability that this number decreases.* If the segments vary widely in size, the probability p is very close to one. If $p = 1$, then $h = n/2$. The latter equation explains the name fifty percent rule. We can see by intuition that the rule is true if we observe that we may expect that on the average a segment has a hole on its right side half the time of its presence in the primary store and another segment the other half of the time. This implies that, on the average, half of the segments have a hole as a right side neighbor at any given time.

Although it is hard to give an estimate of the space wasted through external fragmentation, it is possible to relate the wasted fraction to the ratio of the average hole size and the average segment size. Let the ratio k be defined by the equation av(hole size) = k*av(segment size). Assuming that the variance in the segment size is large, so that we may set the probability $p = 1$, the fifty percent rule states that $h = n/2$. Let

$$\text{space(holes)} + \text{space(segments)} := M$$

Since space(segments) = n*av(segment size) and space(holes) = h*av(hole size) = n*k*av(segment size)/2, we find

$$M = (k/2+1)*n*\text{av(segment size)}$$

The fraction of space wasted is then

$$w = \frac{\text{space(holes)}}{M} = \frac{n*k*\text{av(segment size)}/2}{(k/2+1)*n*\text{av(segment size)}} = 1 - \frac{2}{k+2}$$

*The proof is found in D. E. Knuth, *The Art of Computer Programming*, vol. 1, sec. 2.5, pp. 445–446 (Addison-Wesley, 1969).

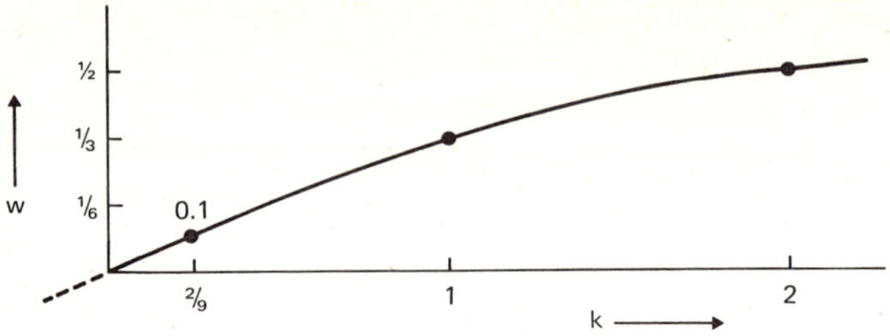

Figure 8.4a The fraction of wasted space as function of the relative hole size

This equation gives us an idea of the fraction of space wasted as function of the relative hole size (see figure 8.4a).

8.4.3 If paging is applied, it is sufficient for the replacement algorithm to designate exactly one page which must be cleared from its frame to provide space for a page arriving from secondary storage. In a segmentation system there is always a chance that a new segment does not fit in the space cleared by the segment designated in the replacement algorithm. The average hole size has an impact on the success of the replacement algorithm. In the extreme case of no holes, one may expect a fifty-fifty chance that a new segment fits in the hole created by a swapped out segment. If the average hole size increases, one may expect that fitting the new segment in the space created by a leaving segment and its neighboring hole gets easier. We can find a relationship between the fraction of wasted space and the probability that removing a segment creates enough space for a new segment to be loaded. If a slight increase of wasted space had a dramatic effect on the probability that swapping out just one segment is enough to bring in a new one, then such waste might be worth the trade-off in saving execution time of the replacement algorithm. We will see that this is so for small values of the relative size k ($k \leq 1$), but not for larger values. In other words, we will see that increasing the relative hole size k from one to two does not significantly improve the chance that removing one segment will create a hole large enough for bringing in another.

Let Pr(k) be the probability that a selected segment from backing store fits in the space created by the segment designated in the replacement algorithm and its neighboring hole. Let pr(x) be the probability distribution of the segment sizes and pr′(x) the probability distribution of hole sizes. The distribution functions are chosen such that

$$\int_0^\infty pr(x)dx = 1, \int_0^\infty pr'(x)dx = 1 \text{ and } \int_0^\infty xpr'(x)dx = k * \int_0^\infty xpr(x)dx$$

The latter equality states that the average hole size is k times the average segment size.

The probability that a given new segment of size x_1 fits in the space created by a designated segment of size x_2 and its neighboring hole of size x_3 is determined by the probability that $x_2+x_3 \geq x_1$. Assuming that the replacement algorithm does not select segments by size and assuming that there is no correlation between the size of a segment and the size of its neighboring hole, the probability that $x_2+x_3 \geq x_1$ is

$$Pr(x_2+x_3 \geq x_1) = 1-Pr(x_2+x_3 \leq x_1) = 1-\int_0^{x_1} pr(u) \int_0^{x_1-u} pr'(t)dtdu$$

The probability that an arbitrary new segment fits in the created space is then

$$Pr(\text{new segment fits}) = \int_0^{\infty} pr(x)Pr(x_2+x_3 \geq x_1)dx$$

$$= 1-\int_0^{\infty} pr(x) \int_0^{x} pr(u) \int_0^{x-u} pr'(t)dtdudx$$

Pr(new segment fits) is the function Pr(k), because the ratio between the mean values of pr'(x) and pr(x) is equal to k. We analyze Pr(k) for three different cases. The difference is determined by the choice of the distribution functions pr(x) and pr'(x). In the simplest case we assume that both are negative exponential distributions. This means that we assume that the number of segments and holes gradually decreases with their size. In the second case we again assume a negative exponential distribution for hole sizes, but the number of segments of a particular size is assumed to increase initially and decline for larger sizes. In the third case both distribution functions first increase and further on decrease for increasing sizes (see figure 8.4b). The distribution functions are given by

case 1: $pr(x) = e^{-x}$, $pr'(x) = ce^{-cx}$
case 2: $pr(x) = xe^{-x}$, $pr'(x) = ce^{-cx}$
case 3: $pr(x) = xe^{-x}$, $pr'(x) = c^2xe^{-cx}$

8.4.4 The size of a hole is expressed relative to the size of a segment. The relationship between c and k can be derived from the equality

$$\int_0^{\infty} xpr'(x)dx = k \cdot \int_0^{\infty} xpr(x)dx$$

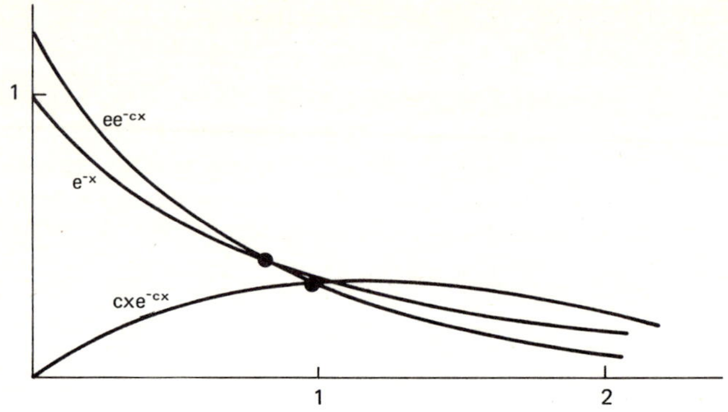

Figure 8.4b The distribution functions for segment and hole sizes

We find $c = 1/k$ in case 1, $c = 1/(2k)$ in case 2 and again $c = 1/k$ in case 3.

Observe that $1 = \int_0^\infty pr(x) \int_0^\infty pr(u) \int_0^\infty pr'(t)dtdudx$. Therefore,

$$Pr(k) = \int_0^\infty pr(x) \int_0^\infty pr(u) \int_0^x pr'(t)dtdudx - \int_0^\infty pr(x) \int_0^x pr(u) \int_0^{x-u} pr'(t)dtdudx$$

$$Pr(k) = \int_0^\infty pr(x) \int_0^x pr(u) \int_{x-u}^\infty pr'(t)dtdudx + \int_0^\infty pr(x) \int_x^\infty pr(u)dudx$$

The second term expressed the probability that the new segment fits in the space of the departing segment. It is therefore not surprising that this term has the value $\frac{1}{2}$ in all cases. Reversing the order of integration in an expression which has the same form as the second term has this effect on the integration boundaries:

$$\int_0^\infty f(x) \int_x^\infty g(u)dudx = \int_0^\infty g(u) \int_0^u f(x)dxdu$$

Since in the case at hand $f(x) = g(x) = pr(x)$ and

$$\int_0^\infty pr(x) \int_x^\infty pr(u)dudx + \int_0^\infty pr(x) \int_0^x pr(u)dudx = \int_0^\infty pr(x) \int_0^\infty pr(u)dudx = 1$$

it follows that the second term is equal to $\frac{1}{2}$.

We evaluate the first term for the second case where $pr(x) = x*e^{-x}$ and $pr'(x) = ce^{-cx}$. Replacing the integrand variable t by t/c gives

$$\int_0^x ue^{-u} \int_{c(x-u)}^{\infty} e^{-t}dtdu = e^{-cx} \int_0^x ue^{-(1-c)u}du$$

Substitution of $v = (1-c)u$ yields

$$\frac{e^{-cx}}{(1-c)^2} \int_0^{(1-c)x} ve^{-v}dv = \frac{e^{-cx}}{(1-c)^2} - \frac{e^{-x}}{(1-c)^2}((1-c)x+1),$$

so

$$\int_0^{\infty} pr(x) \int_0^x pr(u) \int_{x-u}^{\infty} pr'(t)dtdudx$$

$$= \frac{1}{(1-c)^2} \int_0^{\infty} xe^{-(1+c)x}dx - \frac{1}{(1-c)^2} \int_0^{\infty} x((1-c)x+1)e^{-2x}$$

$$= \frac{1}{(1-c)^2(1+c)^2} \int_0^{\infty} ye^{-y}dy - \frac{1}{8(1-c)^2} \int_0^{\infty} z((1-c)z+2)e^{-z}dz$$

where $(1+c)x$ is replaced by y in the first term and 2x by z in the second term. Evaluation of the integrals results in

$$\frac{1}{(1-c)^2(1+c)^2} - \frac{2(1-c)+2}{8(1-c)^2} = \frac{c^3-3c+2}{4(1-c)^2(1+c)^2} = \frac{c+2}{4(1+c)^2}$$

After substituting $1/(2k)$ for c and adding the second term we find

$$Pr(k) = \frac{1/2k+2}{4(1+1/2k)^2} + \frac{1}{2} = \frac{k+4k^2}{2(2k+1)^2} + \frac{1}{2} = 1 - \frac{3}{4(2k+1)} + \frac{1}{4(2k+1)^2}$$

Pr(k) can be evaluated in a similar fashion for the cases one and three. The result is

$$Pr_1(k) = 1 - \frac{1}{2(k+1)}$$

$$Pr_2(k) = \frac{3}{4(2k+1)} + \frac{1}{4(2k+1)^2} = 1 - \frac{3k+1}{2(2k+1)^2}$$

$$Pr_3(k) = 1 - \frac{1}{(k+1)^2} + \frac{1}{2(k+1)^3} = 1 - \frac{2k+1}{2(k+1)^3}$$

The minimum of Pr(k) is reached by k = 0 and is equal to 1/2 in all three cases. This corresponds to the fact that, if there are no holes, there is a fifty-fifty chance that a new segment fits. Pr(k) is a monotonic increasing function of k in all three cases (see figure 8.4c). This corresponds to the fact that the probability that a new segment fits increases if the holes are larger.

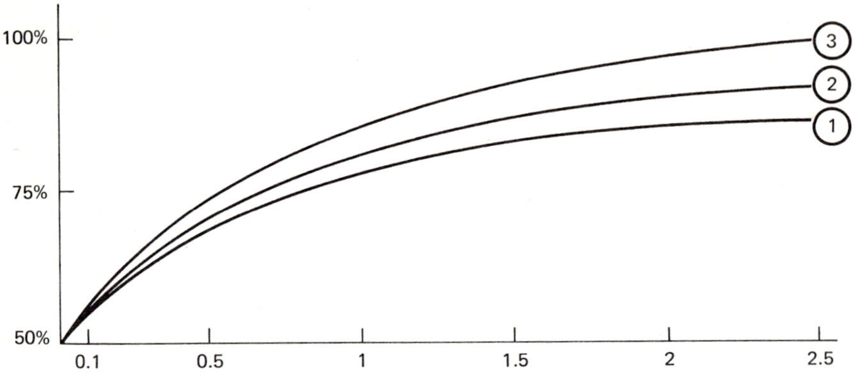

Figure 8.4c The probability that a new segment fits depending on the relative hole size

8.4.5 The three probability functions $Pr_1(k)$, $Pr_2(k)$ and $Pr_3(k)$ show a similar behavior. The probability that a new segment fits is significantly improved by increasing k from zero to one. Thereafter the probability increases at a much slower rate.

There is a clear trade-off between the overhead of exchanging segments in the two-level store and the fraction of space wasted in the primary store. If the relative hole size k is small, the fraction of wasted space is small, but there will be a fair chance that more than one segment must be removed to create a block of free space large enough to accommodate the arriving segment. If, on the other hand, the relative hole size is large, the overhead incurred by creating space for a new segment diminishes, but the fraction of wasted space is much larger. Comparing the wasted fraction w(k) and the probability that a new segment fits, Pr(k), in figure 8.4a and figure 8.4b, we see that Pr(k) is approximately 60% for w = 10%, 80% for w = 35% and 87% for w = 50%. Although it is hard to measure the tradeoff, it seems that the proper range for the relative hole size is between 0.5 and 1. The probability that a new segment will fit in the created space fraction of wasted space may be more than 20%.

PROBLEMS

1. Much of the overhead incurred when space is reclaimed or allocated is caused by updating the list of holes. In particular, if the set of holes is handled as described in section 6.3, searching through the list and merging holes are rather elaborate operations. The overhead may be considerably reduced at a slight cost of storing and updating some additional linking information. Let us reserve the first and last word of every block, whether it is a hole or allocated space, for bookkeeping purposes. All the blocks (and not just the holes) are listed in a double linked list ordered by ascending store address. The first reserved word of a block points forwards to its right neighbor, the last word points backwards to its left neighbor. In addition, every first and last word contains an indication whether the block is a hole or an allocated area. Program the allocation and return of space and see if a shorter execution time can be expected than when a single linked list, containing just the holes, is employed.

2. In subsection 8.4.4 the probability Pr(k) is computed for the case that $pr(x) = xe^{-x}$ and $pr'(x) = ce^{-cx}$, where pr(x) is the distribution of the number of segments of size x and pr′(x) the corresponding distribution for holes. Compute Pr(k) for the case that $pr(x) = e^{-x}$ and $pr'(x) = ce^{-cx}$ and for the case that $pr(x) = xe^{-x}$ and $pr'(x) = c^2xe^{-cx}$.

3. The computation of the probability Pr(new segment fits) is not entirely accurate. Space for a new segment is created by the segment designated by the replacement algorithm plus one neighboring hole. However, a segment may have a hole on both ends or it may have no hole at all as neighbor. Assuming that, on the average, half of the allocated blocks have a hole on the right end and half of them have a hole on the left end, the probability that a given segment will fit is equal to

$$\{Pr(x_2 \geq x_1) + 2 * Pr(x_2 + x_3 \geq x_1) + Pr(x_2 + x_3 + x_4 \geq x_1)\}/4$$

where x_1 is the stochastic variable representing the size of the arriving segment, x_2 that of the leaving segment, and x_3 and x_4 that of the neighbor holes. The probability that a new segment fits is

$$Pr(\text{new segment fits}) = \int_0^\infty pr(x)\{\tfrac{1}{4} * Pr(x_2 \geq x_1) + \tfrac{1}{2} * Pr(x_2 + x_3 \geq x_1) + \tfrac{1}{4} * Pr(x_2 + x_3 + x_4 \geq x_1)\}dx$$

Compute this probability for the case of a negative exponential distribution of the number of segments and holes of size x. The ratio between the average hole size and the average segment size is k.

4. The probability Pr(new segment fits) can be expressed directly in the wasted fraction of space, w. The function Pr(w) is obtained by eliminating k from the expressions for Pr(k) and w(k). Evaluate Pr(w) for the three combinations of probability distributions pr(x) and pr′(x). Plot the graphs of Pr(w) for $0 \leq w \leq 1$. Verify that in each case $Pr(w=0) = \frac{1}{2}$ and $Pr(w=1) = 1$.

5. The optimal range for the relative hole size k depends on the cost of execution overhead incurred when segments are exchanged and the cost of wasting some fraction of the primary store. Let us assume that the latter is proportional to the fraction of wasted space, cost(waste) $= c_1 w(k)$ and that cost(moving segments) $= c_2/Pr(k)$. The optimal value of k is found where the total cost reaches a minimum, that is, where $c_1\{w(k)+c/Pr(k)\}$ has a minimum for given c_1 and $c = c_2/c_1$. Compute the value of k for which the total cost reaches its minimum as a function of c. The factor c determines the relative cost of execution overhead versus waste of space. Check that the optimal value for k increases when c increases and explain what this relationship means.

8.5 INTERNAL FRAGMENTATION

8.5.1 A paging system does not suffer from external fragmentation, because an arriving page fits exactly in the space created when an old page leaves. However, storage space is wasted by internal fragmentation owing to the fact that space is allocated in multiples of the page size. This means that a segment of size s is stored in a number of n pages such that $(n-1)*\text{page size} < s \leq n*\text{page size}$, so an amount of $(n*\text{page size}-s)$ is wasted. The problem is primarily present in a system in which segmentation is built on top of paging. In a pure paging system a compiler or loader is able to pack the end of one code segment and the beginning of the next in one page. Our discussions concern a paged segmentation system. In this section we investigate how serious the internal fragmentation can be as compared to the external fragmentation of a segmentation system. Furthermore, we discuss the impact of the choice of the page size on the internal fragmentation.

8.5.2 For given page size p the size s of a segment can be written as

$$s = m*p+r$$

where r is a number such that $0 \leq r < p$. We assume for the time being that p is much smaller than the average segment size s.

Let x be a number in the range [0:p]. If pages and segments have a common unit of storage as building block (in all likelihood a storage word), then we expect that, for an arbitrary segment in a large group, the probability that $r = x$ is equal to $1/p$. That is to say, we assume that in a large set of segments all possible remainders are equally likely to occur. Since the waste incurred by storing a segment is equal to its remainder r, we expect that the absolute amount of wasted storage units in a large set of N segments is expressed as function of the page size by

$$w_N(p) = \{0+1+ \ldots +(p-1)\}*N*1/p = (p-1)*N/2$$

If s is the average segment size, the total space in which the N segments are stored is equal to

$$\text{total space}(N,p) = N*s+w_N(p) = N*(s+(p-1)/2)$$

The space needed for storing the average of the N segments is

$$\text{sas}(p) = s+(p-1)/2$$

The number of pages in which the N segments are partitioned is

$$\#\text{pages}(N,p) = N*\text{sas}(p)/p$$

The expression derived for sas(p) is not valid for values in the neighborhood of s and for values $p > s$. If p is exactly equal to s, and the number of segments of given size is distributed symmetrically around s, then segments in the smaller half fit in one page and segments in the larger half fit in two pages. In that case $\text{sas}(p=s) = (1/2+2/2)*s = 3s/2$. This value is still very close to the line $\text{sas}(p) = s+(p-1)/2$. However, for larger values of p the function behaves differently. If p is chosen so large that practically every segment fits in one page, then the space needed to store N segments is equal to $p*N$. Thus, for large values of p, the function sas(p) equals p (see figure 8.5a). The behavior of sas(p) is somewhat erratic in the neighborhood of $p = s$. It depends on the distribution function describing the number of segments of size x as function of x (see problem 2).

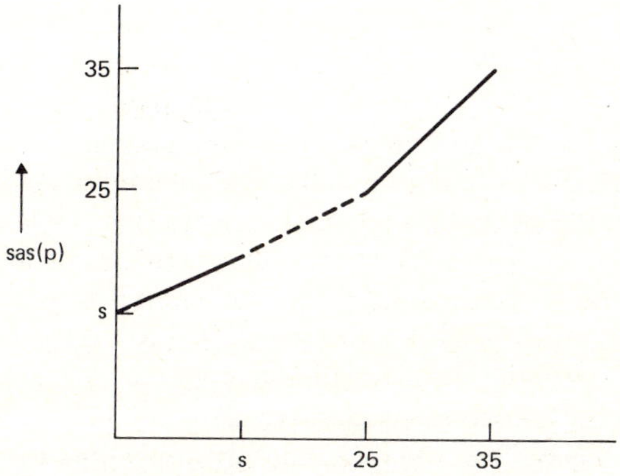

Figure 8.5a The space needed for the average segment as function of page size

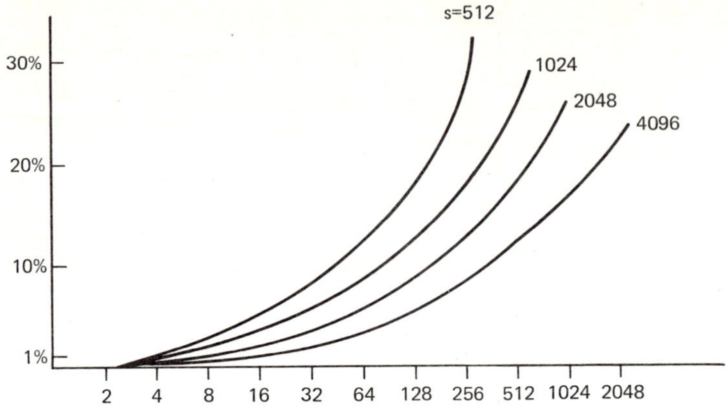

Figure 8.5b Internal fragmentation as function of page size

Let the internal fragmentation for a large set of N segments be defined as the ratio of the absolute waste $w_N(p)$ and the total space needed to store the N segments. If p is smaller than s, then

$$\text{intfragm}(p < s) = \frac{w_N(p)}{N * sas * (p)} = \frac{(p-1)/2}{s+(p-1)/2} = \frac{1}{2s/(p-1)+1}$$

If p is much larger than s, then $w_N(p) = N*(p-s)$ and $sas(p) = p$, so

$$\text{intfragm}(p \gg s) = (p-s)/p = 1-s/p$$

The internal fragmentation is plotted in figure 8.5b as a function of $\log_2 p$ for various values of the parameter s.

8.5.3 Looking at the graphs, it seems that the page size should be chosen as small as possible. As a matter of fact, if the page size is chosen equal to one storage unit, the internal fragmentation is exactly nil. However, there are other phenomena which tend to favor a larger page size. These are the swapping overhead and the storage needed for page and frame tables.

Every page is represented by an entry in a page table. Shared pages may even be represented by several page table entries. Likewise, the state of a frame in main storage is described by an entry in the frame table. The length of the frame table is equal to the number of frames in which Ms is partitioned. The number of page descriptors needed for a set of N segments is equal to the number of pages in which the N segments are split.

The page size must not be chosen too small or else the length of the tables is going to cost dearly. It would be absolutely impossible to adopt the basic storage unit as page size, because just the frame table would require at least as much space as the main store itself! Doubling the page size reduces the space needed for page tables and the frame table by a factor of two. In general the space that must be allocated to page tables and the frame table is proportional to the reciprocal of the chosen page size.

The overhead incurred by swapping a page is not proportional to the page size. There is a fixed average amount of time needed for getting a page transfer started, regardless of the page size. The magnitude of this fixed time overhead depends on the device. For a rotating secondary storage device the fixed time overhead is caused by the latency time. It takes on the average half a drum (or disk) revolution before a particular page is moved under the reading head, no matter how large or small the pages are. For a drum speed of 80 words/millisecond and 1024 words per track the latency time amounts to 6.4 milliseconds. This is a substantial time interval, because it is equal to the time it takes to swap a page of 512 words. The start-up time of a transfer from an ECS is typically 3 microseconds, which corresponds to the time it takes to move 30 words. However, the fixed time overhead of fetching pages from ECS finds its major source in software rather than in hardware. If a relatively slow device, such as a drum, is used as secondary store, a page is moved without CPU control and the transfer time is long enough to prepare the next transfer command and update the page descriptors while the page is moving. In case an ECS serves as backing store device, the preparation of a swap and updating the page descriptors cannot be performed in parallel. Therefore, the execution time of preparation and updating account for a fixed amount of time overhead which is independent of the page size. In order to avoid verbosity, we refer to this overhead also as latency time. Since shared data such as the frame table is involved, some synchronization will be necessary. Therefore, the average time overhead may be in the order of 100 microseconds.

The page size must apparently not be chosen too small but also not too large. We would like to find an optimal value for the page size which balances the two conflicting objectives of minimizing the internal fragmentation and of reducing the overhead of describing and moving the pages. An absolute measure for the optimal page size cannot be given. Therefore, we should set an upperbound for the internal fragmentation such that the swapping overhead is still acceptable. This is discussed next.

8.5.4 Define the space efficiency as a function of the chosen page size by

$$\text{space efficiency}(p) = \text{space needed}/\text{space used}$$

Without paging we need one storage unit per segment as segment descriptor and, on the average, s units for the information in a segment. Thus, the total space needed to represent N segments is equal to $N*(s+1)$. The space actually used consists of the pages in which the N segments are stored plus one page descriptor per page. This amounts to

$$\text{space used} = (p+1)*\#\ \text{pages} = (p+1)*N*\text{sas}(p)/p$$

Thus,

$$\text{space efficiency}(p) = N*(s+1)/\{(1+1/p)*N*\text{sas}(p)\}$$
$$= (s+1)/\{(1+1/p)*(s+(p-1)/2)\}$$

The space efficiency is a number in the range [0:1]. If $p \to \infty$, then the space efficiency goes to zero. It would assume the value one if no paging were applied.

The swapping efficiency is defined as

$$\text{swapping efficiency}(p) = \text{swap time needed}/\text{swap time used}$$

Let t be the number of storage units which could be transferred in a time interval equal to the latency time of the secondary storage device. Without paging, the time of loading a segment is proportional to its length incremented by t. So, the swap time needed to load N segments is equal to $N*(s+t)$. The swap time used is determined by the number of pages in which the N segments are stored and the swap time of one page. The latter is proportional to the page size p incremented by t*. Thus

$$\text{swaptime used} = (p+t)*\#\ \text{pages} = (p+t)*N*\text{sas}(p)/p$$

and

$$\text{swapping efficiency}(t,p) = N*(s+t)/\{(1+t/p)*N*\text{sas}(p)\}$$
$$= (s+t)/\{(1+t/p)*(s+(p-1)/2)\}$$

The swapping efficiency is also a number in the range [0:1]. If $p \to \infty$, then the swapping efficiency tends to zero. It would assume the value one if no paging were applied.

Observe that substitution of a one for the overhead t in the expression for the swapping efficiency yields the space efficiency. However, a realistic value for the swapping efficiency is found if t is set to a number on the order of 512. Both functions assume their maximum if the denominator has a minimum value. Let $F(p) := (1+t/p)*(s+(p-1)/2)$, the denominator of the swapping efficiency. The derivative of F(p) is

$$F'(p) = (p^2 - t(2s-1))/\{2p^2\}$$

F(p) reaches a minimum where F′(p) changes from negative to positive. This is so for $p = \sqrt{(t*(2s-1))}$. Since 2s is much greater than 1, we can approximate p by $\sqrt{(2ts)}$. The space efficiency reaches a maximum value for $p_0 = \sqrt{(2s)}$ (this is indeed a value in the range [1:s]). If $t = 512$ and $s > 1024$, then the swapping efficiency reaches a maximum value for $p_0 = 32*\sqrt{(s)}$. Unfortunately, the two maxima are in general rather far apart. This means that it is difficult to compromise between the space

*If several pages fit on a drum track and page requests are sorted by drum sector, the overhead per page can be much smaller than t. See problem 3.

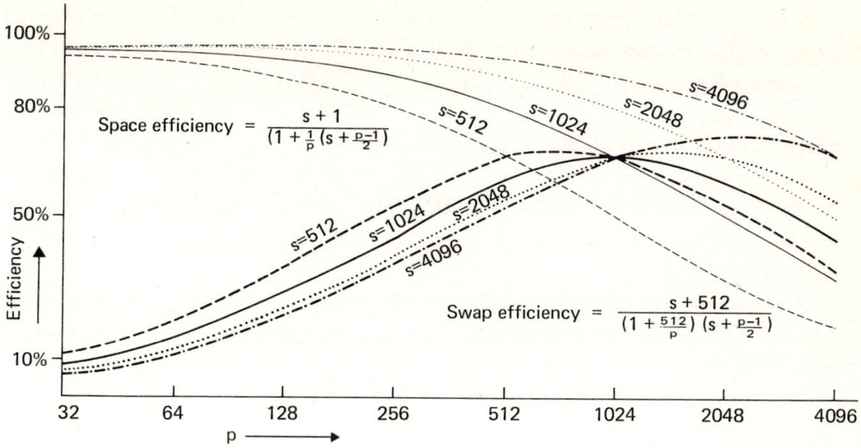

Figure 8.5c The space and swap efficiency as function of the page size

efficiency and the swapping efficiency. If p is chosen close to the point where one of the two reaches a maximum, then the other efficiency will be rather poor. This is shown in figure 8.5c in which both efficiencies are plotted for various values of the parameter s. The latency, measured in storage units, is fixed at $t = 512$.

Substitution of $p = s/k$ and $s = qt$ in the expressions for the internal fragmentation, the space efficiency and the swapping efficiency leads to the following close approximations:

$$\text{intfragm}(k) = 1/(2k+1)$$

$$\text{space efficiency}(k) = 2k/(2k+1) = 1-\text{intfragm}(k)$$

$$\text{swapping efficiency}(q,k) = \frac{2k}{2k+1} * \frac{q+1}{q+k} = \frac{q+1}{q+k} * \text{space efficiency}(k)$$

The table of figure 8.5d shows for some values of k and q how the efficiencies compare for an acceptable upper-limit on the internal fragmentation.

k	p	intfragm.	space eff.	swapping efficiency				
				q = 1	2	4	8	16
2	.50s	<20%	>80%	>53%	>60%	>67%	>72%	>76%
3	.33s	16	84	43	51	61	70	78
4	.25s	11	89	36	44	55	67	76
5	.20s	9	91	30	39	50	63	71
10	.10s	5	95	17	18	34	48	62

Figure 8.5d A comparison of the internal fragmentation and the efficiency

If the average segment size is small (size $s \leq 1024$), it is difficult to balance the two efficiencies. A page size $= 256$ seems adequate in that case. A larger page size would push the internal fragmentation over 20% and a smaller page size (for example, $p = 128$) would affect the swapping efficiency to the extent that it drops under half of its potential rate.

If the segment sizes average between 2048 and 4096 storage units, the proper page size seems to be $p = 512$. The internal fragmentation will be less than 10% and the swapping efficiency will not drop below two-thirds of its potential rate.

If the average of the segment sizes is very large ($s > 8192$), $p = 1024$ is an adequate choice for the page size. The internal fragmentation will be less than 6% and the swapping efficiency will be ⅔.

Comparing external fragmentation and internal fragmentation, it seems that the waste of storage may be as high as between 10% and 20% in either case. This figure depends in the case of segmentation on the relative hole size and, if the holes are approximately equal in size to the used storage blocks, the external fragmentation may reach the 30% mark. The internal fragmentation can also be that high, particularly if the average segment size is small (< 1024).

It is possible to avoid a fragmentation higher than 20%. The internal fragmentation can be diminished by packing segments together. This is a way of building artificially large segments so that the average segment size increases. The graph of figure 8.5c shows that then the page size can also be increased without losing too much space efficiency, but gaining a fair amount of swapping efficiency. If the average segment size can be pushed to slightly over 2000 storage units, a page size $p = 512$ limits the internal fragmentation to approximately 10% and increases the swapping efficiency to 55%. Though both techniques, paging and segmentation, are bound to waste some fraction of storage, it seems that limiting the amount of waste can be better controlled in a paging system than in a segmentation system.

PROBLEMS

1. Let the number of cells per drum track be equal to 2t (for example, let $t = 512$). Information is stored on the drum in units of pages. The page size p equals t/k, where k is an integer number. The response time is the time that elapses from the time of a page request until the page has arrived. Prove that the average minimum response time is equal to $p + t$.

2. Suppose that measuring the sizes of a large set of N segments showed that the sizes were normally distributed with average size s and a standard deviation d such that $s = 4d$. If the segments are stored in pages of size $p = k_d$, the average amount of space allocated to a segment (asas) depends

on k. For instance, if $k = 4$, half of the segments fit in one page and segments in the other half of the set fit in two pages. Therefore, $asas(4) = p/2 + 2p/2 = 6d$ in this case. Compute the value of asas(k) for $k = 1, 2, \ldots, 8$. Check how well this result fits in the graph of figure 8.5a.

3. The use of a paging drum improves the performance of the page traffic so that the overhead per page is equal to $f(p)*t$ instead of t. Let $f(p) = c+(1-c)p/2t$, where c is a constant in the range (0:1], 2t is the length of one drum track and $0 < p \leq 2t$. The factor f(p) is chosen such that $f(p=2t) = 1$ and $f(p \rightarrow 0) \rightarrow c$. This means that the overhead per page transfer is at least $c*t$, no matter how small the page size. Investigate the effect of this correction on the swapping efficiency. Is the effect significant enough that we want to lower the page sizes which were chosen for $t = 512$?

4. The interval fragmentation is defined as the wasted fraction of the total storage allocated to a large set of N segments. Only a small part of this information is actually in the main store; most of it is on backing store. The price of a storage cell in Ms is much higher than that of a cell in Bs. Therefore, we correct the definition of internal fragmentation to be the fraction of wasted space in the primary store, neglecting the waste on backing store entirely. Investigate whether this correction has a large impact on the value of the internal fragmentation as compared to the results obtained in this section. Redefine also the efficiencies and check the impact of the modification.

5. There is a curious phenomenon in figure 8.5c: All the graphs of the swapping efficiency pass through the value ⅔ (=67%) for $p = 1024$. This means that the swapping efficiency is independent of the segment size for this particular page size. Prove the statement that for given track size $= 2t$ the swapping efficiency is equal to ⅔ for $p = 2t$ independent of the average segment size. Prove also that the swapping efficiency increases with the segment size for $p > 2t$ and decreases with the segment size for $p < 2t$. If it is possible to assemble very large segments so that the average segment is much larger than t (for example, let $s = 16t$), then p can be chosen larger than 2t. The larger the average segment size, the higher both efficiencies will be.

READING LIST

The problem of finding an optimum segment size is discussed in [1]. Examples of modeling paging systems are found in [2, 3, 10]. The classic paper on the working set model is [4]. Hardware support for the working set model is discussed in [6]. Examples of performance analysis are found in

[5, 7, 9, 10]. One of the few papers on fragmentation is [8]. How much is to be gained by minimizing the latency time is shown in [11].

1. Batson, A., S. M., Jr., and D. C. Wood, "Measurements of Segment Size," *Comm. ACM* 13, 3 (March 1970).
2. Belady, L. A., R. A. Nielson, and G. S. Shedler, "An Anomaly in Space-Time Characteristics of Certain Programs Running in a Paging Machine," *Comm. ACM* 12, 6 (June 1969).
3. Courtois, P. J., "Decomposability, Instabilities, and Saturation in Multiprogramming Systems," *Comm. ACM* 18, 7 (July 1975).
4. Denning, P. J., "The Working Set Model for Program Behavior," *Comm. ACM* 11, 5 (May 1968).
5. Fuller, S. H., "Minimal-Total Processing Time Drum and Disk Scheduling Disciplines," *Comm. ACM* 17, 7 (July 1974).
6. Morris, J. B., "Demand Paging through Utilization of Working Sets on the MANIAC II," *Comm. ACM* 15, 10 (October 1972).
7. Oden, P. H., and G. S. Shedler, "A Model of Memory Contention in a Paging Machine," *Comm. ACM* 15, 8 (August 1972).
8. Randell, B., "A Note on Storage Fragmentation and Program Segmentation," *Comm. ACM* 12, 7 (July 1969).
9. Rodriguez-Rosell, J., "Empirical Working Set Behavior," *Comm. ACM* 16, 9 (September 1973).
10. Shedler, G. S., "A Queueing Model of a Multiprogrammed Computer with a Two-Level Storage System," *Comm. ACM* 16, 1 (January 1973).
11. Stone, H. S., and S. H. Fuller, "On the Near-Optimality of the Shortest-Latency-Time-First Drum Scheduling Discipline," *Comm. ACM* 16, 6 (June 1973).

9. Data Management

9.1 FILE STRUCTURES

9.1.1 In its early days the computer was, as its name indicates, primarily a tool to compute mathematical results by mechanical means. Now, the function of a computer as a device to store and manipulate large amounts of information is as important as its computational capabilities. With the aid of comparatively cheap bulk storage devices, a computer is capable of retaining a huge amount of coded information for long periods of time (months and years). A discussion of this machine function is appropriate here, because it is the task of an operating system to provide facilities to manage the retention of information over long periods.

The storage unit for a coherent piece of long-range information is a *file*. In this chapter first we discuss the internal organization of files and various accessing methods. Second, we discuss the facilities provided by the operating system to create, destroy and manipulate files. The next issue concerns the privacy and security of data with respect to unauthorized access attempts. The simplest protection rule either permits or totally denies a computation all access to an object. In recent years ideas have been developed on allowing the users to access each other's programs, files and data subject to a set of protection rules. If such rules are established, the operating system must be able to enforce them.

9.1.2 In this section we discuss the internal organization of files and the basic operations which allow users to retrieve information from files.

A file is a collection of data records assembled in a data structure so that information in the records is ordered and retrievable. The information in a record is often indicated by the unfortunate name "index." A record is the representation of a data object by means of a set of characteristic properties of the object in a given place in the store. That is, a record is a pair (index, address) where "index" describes the characteristic properties and "address" the place in the store. The index consists of a set of "keys." A key describes a characteristic property of a data object in the form of a pair ("attribute," "value"). For instance, consider the personnel of a company described in a file. Each record in the file represents an employee and lists attributes such as sex, date of birth, social security number, salary, date of joining the company, citizenship, etc. The records of a file usually have the same attributes, but they differ in the specific values assigned to these attributes. Some of the records will have the value "male" attached to the attribute "sex," others the value "female." Pairs, such as (sex, male), (date of birth, 510626), are possible keys of a record (see figure 9.1a).

The best way of structuring a file depends on various factors such as the frequency of adding or deleting records, the range of an attribute, the actual number of records as compared to the total number possible, etc. The fundamental question about structuring a file is whether the information about the connection of records is stable enough to justify its retention or changes are so frequent that information about classes of records should be reconstructed every time when needed. For instance, the value of the attribute "sex" does not change, so the class of records which possesses the key (sex, male) is very stable. In such a case it is useful to make this information part of the file structure, for instance by placing all records with the (sex, male) key at one end of the file and all the records with the key (sex, female) at the other end, or by linking all the records with the same key. On the other hand, because a key such as salary is less stable, it may not be appropriate to use it as the basis of the file structure.

12 96:

Name	: Doe
Initials	: J.F.
Sex	: male
Date of birth	: 51 06 26
Social security no.	: 152-3401-030
Salary	: $14,500
Starting date	: 74 09 01
Citizenship	: USA

Figure 9.1a Example of an employee record

We assume throughout the discussion that files are not constant, but change through occasional additions or deletions of records. It is therefore assumed that allocating space for new records and reclaiming the space of deleted records is part of a dynamic storage management scheme which serves the collection of all files. Such a dynamic storage management scheme must have the flexibility of assigning any piece of storage large enough to hold a record irrespective of its position in the store. That is to say, a structure which implements ordering of data objects must not rely upon the relative position of these objects in the store. Ordering of objects is implemented by pointers from one object to another.

9.1.3 The simplest implementation of a file structure is as a linked list of records. This implementation does not utilize any knowledge about the records in the file, and applies to all kinds of files. However, this structure displays the worst possible performance with respect to interrogation. If a subset of files with a given key or combination of keys is sought, the entire list must be searched. Information about the collection of records is dynamically constructed every time when needed and is lost after each use. We consider this too wasteful. Additional structure information will cost some extra space, but, since a file spends most of its lifetime on a relatively cheap storage medium, the space cost is less serious than the time cost.

Conceptually, a file is a Boolean matrix in which the columns represent the records and the rows the keys of the file. If the value of a matrix element is one then the corresponding record possesses the key; if zero, then it does not (see figure 9.1b).

A slightly different picture emerges if the rows represent the attributes instead of the keys. In that case the elements of the matrix indicate the attribute values.

	R_1	R_2		R_n
K_1	1	1		0
K_2	1	0		0
K_3	0	1		1
	⋮	⋮		⋮
K_m	1	0		1

Figure 9.1b The matrix representation of a file

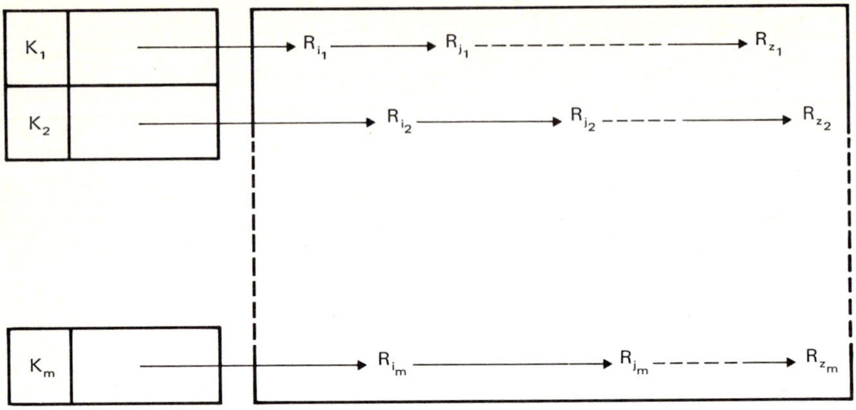

Figure 9.1c Structure of a multi-list file

9.1.4 The three major alternatives to the single list structure are the multi-list structure, the inverted file structure and the index sequential file structure. Other file structures are variations or hybrid combinations of these three basic types. The three structures differ in the amount of extra space needed, the retrieval time and the updating time overhead. Which structure is the best depends on the anticipated use of the file.

A record of a pure multi-list has a pointer field for every key it possesses. All the records which possess a given key are linked together through these pointer fields in a unique keylist. There are as many keylists as there are different keys. In addition to these link fields, the collection of records is extended with a list of pointers to the first elements of the keylists, one for every keylist. This list is called the directory of the file (see figure 9.1c).

Keylist K_q ($q \epsilon [1{:}m]$) links together all the records which have a one in the q-th row in the picture of figure 9.1b. Thus, the number of added pointer fields is equal to the number of ones in the Boolean matrix. The number of pointers in the directory is equal to the number of different keys.

In an inverted file a set of pointers to all the records that possess a given key is placed in the directory. The directory is divided in subsections, one for every key (see figure 9.1d). The extra space required for the pointers is the same as for a multilist. If the records are not large, the pointers can be replaced by the records themselves.

The structure of an inverted list is very suitable for interrogations concerning a given key. If a record is rarely added or deleted, a subsection can be implemented as a vector. Because machines are efficient at accessing consecutive storage cells, the collection of records which possess a given key can be traversed in minimal time. The term *inverted file* conveys the fact that addresses of records which possess a given key are collected through the key instead of through the records. In terms of the Boolean matrix of figure

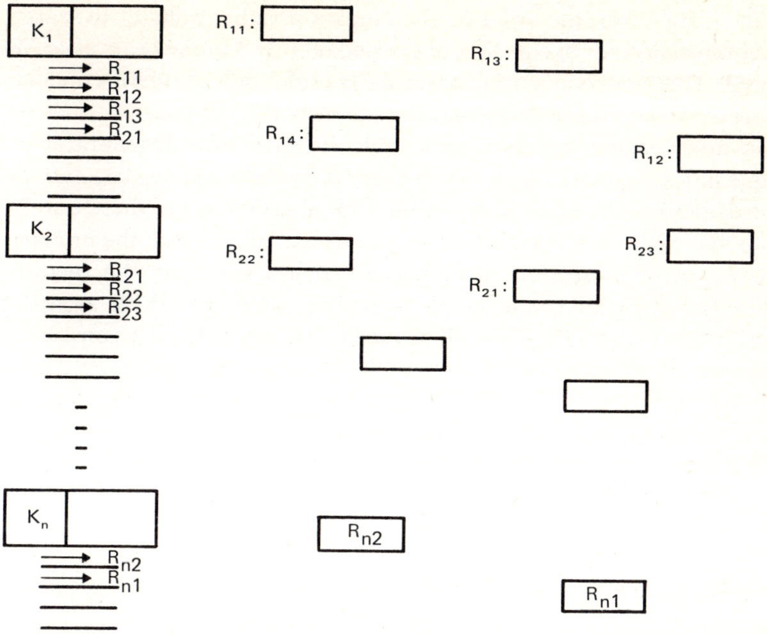

Figure 9.1d The directory of an inverted file

9.1b (see page 285), the matrix is searched by row rather than by column.

There is only a slight difference between the multi-list structure and the inverted file structure. There is primarily a difference in viewpoint. The pointers to the records that possess the same key are part of the directory of an inverted file, whereas these are distributed over the records of a multi-list file structure. Secondly, there is a possible difference in implementing the key information either as part of the records or as part of the directory. Finally, if it seems useful, the keywords of the records in an inverted file can also be extended with a link field so as to retain additional information which is useful to speed up file searches. For instance, if we want to search a personnel file for the male population earning more than $15,000 a year, the set of records that possesses the key (sex, male) can be split in two lists, one for the men earning more than $15,000 a year and one for those earning less.

An index sequential file is appropriate where use of the file indicates that keys will be interrogated in some priority order. If such an order is established, the records of the file can be listed in alphabetical order in one single list. For instance, a file describing information published in the New York *Times* may be ordered by date of issue, represented by the first three keys of every record in the order year, month, day. If the records are ordered by date, a query about a topic within a set of consecutive issues can easily be handled. However, the order by date makes it rather difficult to search the file, for instance, for events that happened on July 4 in the years after World War II. The index sequential structure is useful only if queries concerning consecutive days occur much more frequently than others.

An inverted file structure or a multi-list structure degenerates into a simple index sequential structure if every record has just one key and no two records possess the same key. Applied to an inverted file these conditions mean that each subsection has exactly one element and that the intersection of any pair of subsections is empty. In such a situation, the records are ordered in a linear sequence through the directory. With regard to a multi-list structure, the conditions mean that every keylist consists of exactly one element and that no two keylists contain the same record pointer. The link field attached to a record attribute is obviously redundant in this case, because its value would be *nil* anyway.

In principle it is always possible to structure a file as an index sequential file. This is obvious if we look once more at the Boolean matrix representation of figure 9.1a. A column of the matrix can be viewed as the unique binary representation of a record. A natural ordering is induced by the order in which the keys are assigned to the rows. The records of the file can be ordered by magnitude of their binary representation. However, it is questionable whether a sequential structure is desirable. It is, if there is an inclusion relation between the keys, that is, if we wish to interrogate for a given key all the records with a binary representation smaller than the given one. Otherwise we run into the difficulties pointed out in the New York *Times* example.

9.1.5 Search operations through a file are based on two primitive operations, searching through the directory, called directory search, and searching through the records, called file search. The purpose of the directory search is to produce a pointer to a keylist; the purpose of the file search is to step through a keylist.

The directory search is performed by the function "decode(K,x)", where K is a key of the file to which decode is applied. The directory contains an ordered set of elements $e_1(K), \ldots, e_n(K)$, each of which points to a K keylist. If the file has a multi-list structure, there is exactly one element e(K) for every key K. If it is an inverted file, the number of elements $e_i(K)$ is equal to the number of records which possess key K. The result of applying decode(K,x) depends on the value of x. If x = *nil*, decode returns $e_1(K)$, the first element of section(K) in the directory. If $x = e_n(k)$, where $e_n(K)$ is the last element of section(K), decode returns *nil*. If $x = e_i(K)$ and $i \neq n$ (that is, $e_i(K)$ is not the last element of section(K)), then decode returns $e_{i+1}(K)$, the next element of section(K). The parameter x is redundant for a file structured as a multi-list. For such files the result of decode(K) can be defined as the directory element e(K) which points to the unique K keylist.

The file is searched by the function "retrieve(k,x)", where k is a pointer to a keylist. The result of retrieve is a record address or *nil*, depending on the value of x. If x = *nil*, the result of retrieve(k,x) is the first record on keylist k. If x is the last record on keylist k, retrieve returns *nil* and if x is any record on keylist k excluding the last record, retrieve returns the address of the next record on the list. An inverted file has exactly one element on every keylist. For such files the parameter x in the function retrieve is redundant. The result of retrieve(k) can be defined as the address of the record to which k points.

The decode and retrieve algorithms are applicable to any generalized file structure which is created as a combination of the multi-list and inverted file structure. A procedure which outputs the addresses of all records possessing a given key K is

```
procedure SEARCH(K) =
begin local x = nil
   repeat x ← decode(K,x) until x = nil do
      begin local y = nil
         repeat y ← retrieve(x,y) until y = nil do OUTPUT(y) od
      end
   od
end
```

The function SEARCH can be modified into a general and powerful file operation by replacing the call on OUTPUT by any other operation which the user desires to apply to all records possessing key K. This can be done if SEARCH receives a second parameter which represents an operation on a record. The call SEARCH(K,f) applies function f to all records that possess key K.

Note that for a file structured as a multi-list the outer repetition loop is superfluous and for an inverted file the inner repetition loop is superfluous. Applied to the simple index sequential structure (one key per record, no two records having the same key), both the repetition loops are superfluous. Though it seems that a simple index sequential structure allows the simplest search, this is not really true, because the directory search procedure will be more complicated.

9.1.6 Most interrogations of files do not concern just one key but a combination of keys. A query is in fact a request for addresses of all the records that match a Boolean expression in which the operands are keys or relational expressions and the operators *and* and *or*. For example, one might ask for the records of all males born after 1950 and all females born after 1952.

We know from propositional calculus that a Boolean expression can be written in a unique (modulo commuting) canonical form from which all parentheses have been eliminated. For instance, the form (a *or* b) *and* c can be rewritten as a *and* c *or* b *and* c. We assume in the following discussion that input to a query is given as a Boolean expression in canonical form.

The query input is a disjunction of Boolean terms (that is, an expression of the form T_1 *or* T_2 *or* . . . *or* T_p). A Boolean term is a conjunction of Boolean factors (that is, an expression of the form F_1 *and* F_2 *and* . . . *and* F_q). Written in the canonical form, all the factors in a Boolean term are different and not all the factors in two Boolean terms are the same; if this were the case, the factor or term could be deleted from the expression.

The set of all records matching a given input is the union of the records that match the Boolean terms of the input. A record is selected by (or matches) a Boolean term if it is in the intersection of all the keylists specified by the Boolean factors of this term. So the task of analyzing the input can be split into two algorithms: ANDSEARCH, which determines the addresses of all records matching a single Boolean term, and ORSEARCH, which constructs the union of all those addresses found by the former algorithm.

A Boolean term of the input has the form K_1 *and* K_2 *and* . . . *and* K_n. The scanning procedure ANDSEARCH can be designed in one of two ways. Either we produce all the records of the keylists attached to $K_1, K_2, \ldots, K_n$ and take the intersection of those, or we step through just one keylist and scan every record so encountered for the presence of the other keys. We pursue here the second alternative.

Let A be an array in which a set of keys can be stored. A procedure TESTRECORD(y,A) scans the record, whose address is given by y, for the presence of the keys listed in A. If it finds all the keys in record y, it outputs y, otherwise *nil*. A program for procedure ANDSEARCH can now be constructed. Its body is the same as that of SEARCH except for the preparations of the array A at the beginning and the conditional statement which replaces the call OUTPUT(y) in the SEARCH program.

```
procedure ANDSEARCH(K1, K2, . . . , Kn) =
if n = 1 then SEARCH(K1)
else
   begin local x = nil; local A = (K2, K3, . . . , Kn)
     repeat x ← decode(K1,x) until x = nil do
       begin local y = nil
         repeat y ← retrieve(x,y) until y = nil do
           if TESTRECORD(y,A) ≠ nil then OUTPUT(y) fi
         od
       end
     od
   end
fi
```

A straightforward implementation of procedure ORSEARCH applies ANDSEARCH to every term. However, the result achieved this way may output some records several times, because a particular record may match more than one term. It should not be necessary to test the same record twice. Therefore, we construct a program for ORSEARCH which uses a slight variation of the program ANDSEARCH. It retains the produced record addresses in an output list and, in the modified version MANDSEARCH, a record is skipped if it already is in the output list. The latter test is performed by the procedure SELECTED.

```
SELECTED(y,L) =        $ y is a record address and L a list of record
                         addresses
begin local i = 0
  repeat i ← i+1 until i = length(L) or y = L_i
  SELECTED ← (y = L_i)
end
```

The procedure ORSEARCH starts with selecting a key in every term. Since factors within a conjunction may be commuted, we may assume without loss of generality that the first factor of every term has been selected. Let the selected keys be $K_{11}, K_{12}, \ldots, K_{1m}$, where m is the number of terms in the input expression. Procedure ORSEARCH steps through all the keylists of the selected keys and applies the modified MANDSEARCH to every term.

```
procedure ORSEARCH(T_1, T_2, . . . , T_m = keyterm) =
begin local outputlist = empty; outputlist_1 = nil
  local j = 0
  repeat j ← j+1 until j > m do MANDSEARCH(T_j) od
end
```

The program of MANDSEARCH differs from the regular ANDSEARCH mainly in the innermost loop of the program. It uses furthermore a modified version of SEARCH (in case a term consists of a single factor) in which the OUTPUT statement is replaced by a conditional output statement. Output is executed only if the record in question does not already appear in the output list. This modified version of SEARCH is not programmed here. We conclude with the program for MANDSEARCH.

```
procedure MANDSEARCH(K_1, K_2, . . . , K_n) =
if n = 1 then MODSEARCH
else
  begin local x = nil; local A = (K_2,K_3, . . . , K_n)
    repeat x ← decode(K_1,x) until x = nil do
      begin local y = nil
        repeat y ← retrieve(x,y) until y = nil do
          if not SELECTED(y) then if TESTRECORD(y,A) ≠ nil then
            OUTPUT(y) fi fi
        od
      end
    od
  end
fi
```

PROBLEMS

1. The directory of an inverted file may get very large, because it contains at least one pointer to each record. Therefore, it is built out of two layers. The first layer is a fixed array with one entry per key. The second layer consists of n variable size blocks, where n is the number of different keys. The key entries point to the beginning addresses of the blocks and an entry in a block points to a record. Program the procedure decode for this directory structure.

2. If an attribute has a large value range (for example, the attribute birthday), then it is not practical to list all the possible keys which can be generated with this attribute in the directory. Instead of the key, the attribute is listed. In such a case it makes sense to mix the multiple list structure and the inverted file structure. We divide the records carrying the attribute into several attribute lists (for example, one per decade) and place the pointers to these lists in the directory. Program a procedure SEARCH which extracts from the file all the records whose attribute values are within a given range.

3. A procedure which tests for a conjunction of keys in a multi-list file can be designed as an algorithm which determines the intersection of the keylists in question. Program such a procedure SECSEARCH. Compare this procedure with procedure ANDSEARCH in terms of expected number of simple actions such as comparison tests or assignments.

4. Procedure ANDSEARCH uses an arbitrary keylist as basis and tests the records of this list for the presence of the remaining keys in the conjunction. The procedure can possibly be refined if the length of each keylist is known. Let the operation length(K) return the number of records on a keylist in a multi-list file. Modify procedure ANDSEARCH such that the shortest keylist is chosen as basis. Is this modification useful in the sense that the number of simple operations such as comparisons and assignments decreases?

A similar refinement may be possible in procedure SELECTED, if the records carry a unique number and all the keylists are ordered using these numbers. It is not necessary for every record of a keylist to be checked against all the records in the output list. The extent of the comparison can be limited using the ordering numbers. Program a modified version of SELECTED which contains such a shortcut.

5. The union of a set of keylists can be constructed in a pseudo parallel manner. Let the records be numbered as described in the second half of problem 4. The addresses of records put out are also retained in an output list. A selected record should not be put out more than once. The record to

be put out is the one with the lowest number among all the first elements of the keylist. After putting out a record, the next record is the one with the lowest number among the first elements of the unscanned parts of the keylists. Program this pseudo parallel construction of the union of several keylists. Is it more or less efficient compared to the serial processing of the keylists?

9.2 FILE DIRECTORIES

9.2.1 If a large amount of information about records of a file is stored in a directory, the latter must be carefully structured to minimize the retrieval time of information kept in the file. In this section we discuss four basic ideas of directory accessing methods and related directory structures.

It is not uncommon for an attribute to have a large value range (the name or birthdate attribute of a personnel file, for instance). As a result, the file may have a large number of keys which have a common attribute but differ in attribute value. The problem is to find an efficient method for looking up a given key in the file directory.

It seems as if the problem can be avoided if the attributes are listed in the file directory instead of the keys. This is not so, because the problem merely shifts from the directory to the records. Instead of looking up a key in the directory, we now have to chase a list of records with the given attribute and pick out of the list the records which possess the matching key.

The problem of finding a given key in the directory is an instance of the general table look-up problem. Similar problems are encountered in other programming tasks. The lexical scan of a compiler is a well-known example. Every time a new symbol is read from the input string, this symbol must be matched with an entry in the symbol table (or a new entry must be created).

There is not one look-up algorithm which is better than any other. The feasibility and efficiency of a particular look-up method depends on the chosen table structure, its size and variability and the amount of extra space one is willing to allocate to speed up the look-up procedure. We discuss separately four basic methods, but the reader should bear in mind that practical implementations often are a mixture of several of these methods.

The simplest look-up method, which does not require any additional space, is the linear search. The entries in the directory are tested one by one until the matching key is found. We may expect that the average search time is proportional to half the table size, because, on the average, half of the table entries must be tested before the matching key is found.

The linear search is very slow, and it is therefore not recommended for large directories. It has the advantage of not requiring additional space or an elaborate initialization before the search can start. Therefore, the linear search method is appropriate for small subsections where the time or space investment of more elaborate methods does not pay off.

9.2.2 Another look-up method, which also does not require additional space in the directory, is known as *hash coding*. Hash coding is similar to the content addressable store which we find in an associative memory: given the contents or value of an object, the device produces its address. In the case of hash coding, the device is an algorithm implemented in software. The hash function h(K) takes a key as input, and it derives from the bit representation of this key a table address. Such a table address is constructed by selecting a bit pattern from the key representation, multiplying or dividing it by a constant or another bit pattern extracted from the key and taking the remainder of dividing by the table size. The hash function h(K) should be chosen such that the set of addresses generated by a random set of keys is uniformly distributed across the set of all possible table addresses. Such an ideal distribution is not obtainable in practice. But the actual distribution must not be too far from a uniform distribution or else there will be a serious clustering problem: the number of generated addresses will be greater in one area of the table than in other areas of equal length. In the neighborhood of a cluster it is more difficult to find empty space when a new key is entered in the table. Also, it may take several probes before a matching key is found.

Cluster or no cluster, there is always a chance that the hash function will compute the same address for two different keys: $h(K_1) = h(K_2) = \alpha$ where $K_1 \neq K_2$. At least one of the two keys will not match the contents of the table entry α, so for this key the search must be continued until a match is found. We prefer to generate subsequent addresses in the continued search by using an algorithm which is much simpler than the hash algorithm. At the same time we try to keep the number of iterations of the continued address calculation as small as possible. Let $h_i(K)$ be the address computed in the i-th step after the initial address calculation. We define

$$h_i(K) = h_0(K) + d_i \pmod{t} \qquad \text{for } i = 1, 2, \ldots$$

where $h_0(K) = h(K)$, t is the table size and d_i is the distance of the original hash address to the i-th hash address.

The address calculation can be continued in various ways after the initial hash computation if no immediate match is found. We can simply apply a linear search defining $d_j = i$ for all i. This method may be adequate if the distance between two unused entries in the table is rarely large, but it has the disadvantage that $h_{i+k}(K_1) = h_{j+k}(K_2)$ for all $k = 1, 2, \ldots$ if $h_i(K_1) = h_j(K_2)$. That is to say, if two different keys once produce the same address, then these keys will trace exactly the same address sequence in all successive probes.

A better result is obtained if a set of random numbers $\{r_1, r_2, \ldots, r_n\}$ is generated and $d_i = r_i$. Now the address traces of two different keys will be exactly the same only if the traces started at the same address, that is, only if $h_0(K_1) = h_0(K_2)$. So, the probability that two keys will produce the same address trace is much smaller than in the case of a linear search. However, this improvement is achieved at the price of extra space for a table of random numbers.

9.2.3 Better results are obtained with the so-called "quadratic hash" method. This time we define $d_i = c*i^2$

$$h_i(K) = h_0(K) + c*i^2 \pmod t$$

where t is the table size (a prime number) and c a constant ($c \neq 0$). The latter expression explains why the method is called the quadratic hash method, because the distance of the i-th address to the initial address is a function of i^2.

The two generated address sequences will be exactly the same again only if two keys start at the same initial address. If by coincidence $h_0(K_1) = h_j(K_2)$ for $j \neq 0 \pmod t$, the addresses generated by the two keys i steps later will not coincide again. That is to say, we can prove that now $h_i(K_1) \neq h_{j+i}(K_2)$ for $i = 1, 2, \ldots, t-1$. To show this, we write

$$\begin{aligned} h_i(K_1) &= h_0(K_1) + c*i^2 && \pmod t \\ h_{j+i}(K_2) &= h_j(K_2) + c*(j+i)^2 - c*j^2 && \pmod t \\ &= h_j(K_2) + c*i*(2j+i) && \pmod t \end{aligned}$$

The two expressions are equal if $i = 2j+i \pmod t$ or $2j = 0 \pmod t$. Since t is a prime number, the only solution of this equation is $j = 0$. But this value was excluded, so $h_0(K_1) = h_j(K_2)$ and $j \neq 0$ implies $h_i(K_1) \neq h_{j+i}(K_2)$ for all $i = 1, 2, \ldots, t-1$.

Unlike the random search, the quadratic hash does not need extra space for storing a table of constants. The quadratic hash can be further simplified if the constant c is chosen equal to one. This can be done without loss of generality, because there is nothing to be gained by using a constant $c > 1$. The quadratic hash method as presented here has one drawback in that it does not generate more than half of all the table addresses (see problem 1). A trivial modification of the step function assures that all the table addresses are generated before the search comes back to the original hash address (see problem 2.)

9.2.4 In some cases it is possible to arrange the keys in the directory in a linear order. If the ordered keys are stored in equidistant locations, a particular key can be retrieved by the binary search algorithm.

Let the keys in the directory be $K_0, K_1, K_2, \ldots, K_n$ ($n > 1$) and let the distance between two keys be d. If K_0 is in location L, K_1 is in location $L+d$ and K_i in location $L+i*d$, $i \in \{0, 1, \ldots, n\}$. A given key K is retrieved by the binary search algorithm in the following way (see figure 9.2a). The given key is first compared to both extremes; if it is equal to one of these, the address of that extreme is returned and the algorithm terminates.

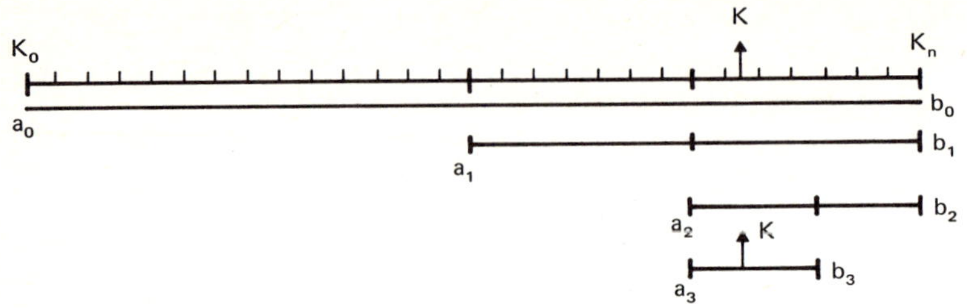

Figure 9.2a Retrieval by the binary search algorithm

Next the given key is compared to (one of) the key(s) in the middle between K_0 and K_n. If K is equal to this key, the address of that key is returned and the algorithm terminates. Otherwise, we conclude that K must be in the left half if K is less than the middle key or in the right half if K is greater than the middle key. Subsequently, K is compared to the middle key of that half in which K resides. This process of splitting the interval in half and comparing is continued until a match is found.

If the number of keys is not too small ($n > 6$), the binary search algorithm performs better than the linear search algorithm. On the average, the latter needs $n/2$ comparisons before a match is found. The number of comparisons made in the binary search is of the order $\log_2 n$, because the number of intervals which are inspected is equal to k where 2^k is the smallest power of two greater or equal to n. For $n = 16$ the two methods differ by a factor 2, but for $n = 1024$ the expected search time of the linear search is a factor 50 larger than that of the binary search.

All the possible paths the binary search algorithm can follow to all possible outcomes can be represented in a binary tree. The root of this tree is the entire interval. Each node represents a subsection of the interval such that the intervals of two brother nodes together form the interval of their parent. The binary search algorithm determines at each node whether the separation point of its offsprings is the requested element. If so, the algorithm terminates with this point as result; if not, the algorithm moves on to the offspring whose interval contains the requested element in one of its interior points (see figure 9.2b).

The binary search algorithm does not require that the actual data being represented have a tree structure which is maintained in between activations of the algorithm. The algorithm is able to create the path that it follows during execution. Some simple variables and simple operations on those variables suffice for creating the path, because the location of any interior point can easily be derived from the length of an interval and the locations of the end points. In this case there is no point in keeping the tree structure around, because as much work is involved in traversing an existing path in the tree as in creating the path that leads to the requested element.

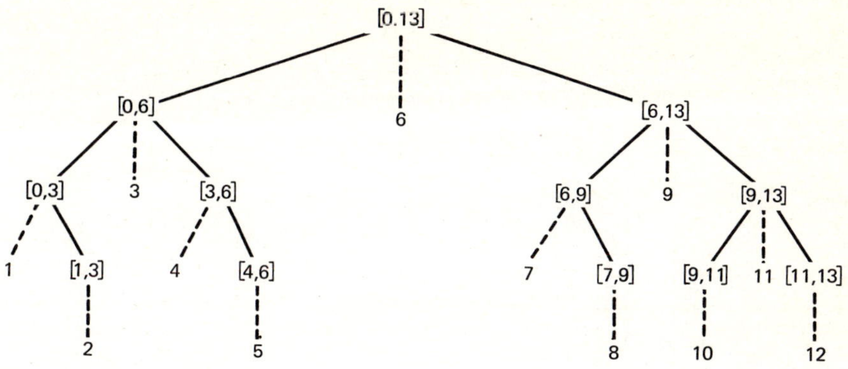

Figure 9.2b Example of a tree representing all possible paths of a binary search

9.2.5 If the distance between successive keys in the directory is not known, the binary search algorithm cannot be applied. In this case it is advantageous to maintain the tree containing all possible search paths. At the price of some space for storing the tree, a given key can be retrieved as efficiently as through a binary search. (If the paths are represented in a binary tree, the tree space is equal to the directory space.)

A tree-structured directory is particularly useful for a large file in which insertion and deletion of records is rare but interrogation and updating is common. A good example of a file having such characteristics is a library catalogue file. The records of this file describe the books of the library. Every book belongs to a particular category such as geography, fiction, politics, etc. The library is divided in sections, one section per category. Within a section, books are alphabetically ordered by author and title.

Title, author, or category is almost certainly part of the input to an interrogation of the file. The input is often a combination of those in addition to information such as its publisher. The purpose of an interrogation usually is to find out where a particular book is located in the library and whether or not it is available.

A record describing a book has eight fields: author, title, category, publisher, year of publication, name of borrower, catalogue number, and location in the library. It is very unlikely that a request for a book is solely based on knowledge about a combination of the last five attributes while information about the first three is entirely lacking. The directory is therefore organized as an inverted file based on the attributes title, author and category. In addition, all records are linked in order of catalogue number to respond to any odd request. A tree structure is added to the directory in order to enhance the efficiency of a search. The first level of the tree consists of three nodes, one for the attribute "title," onc for "author"

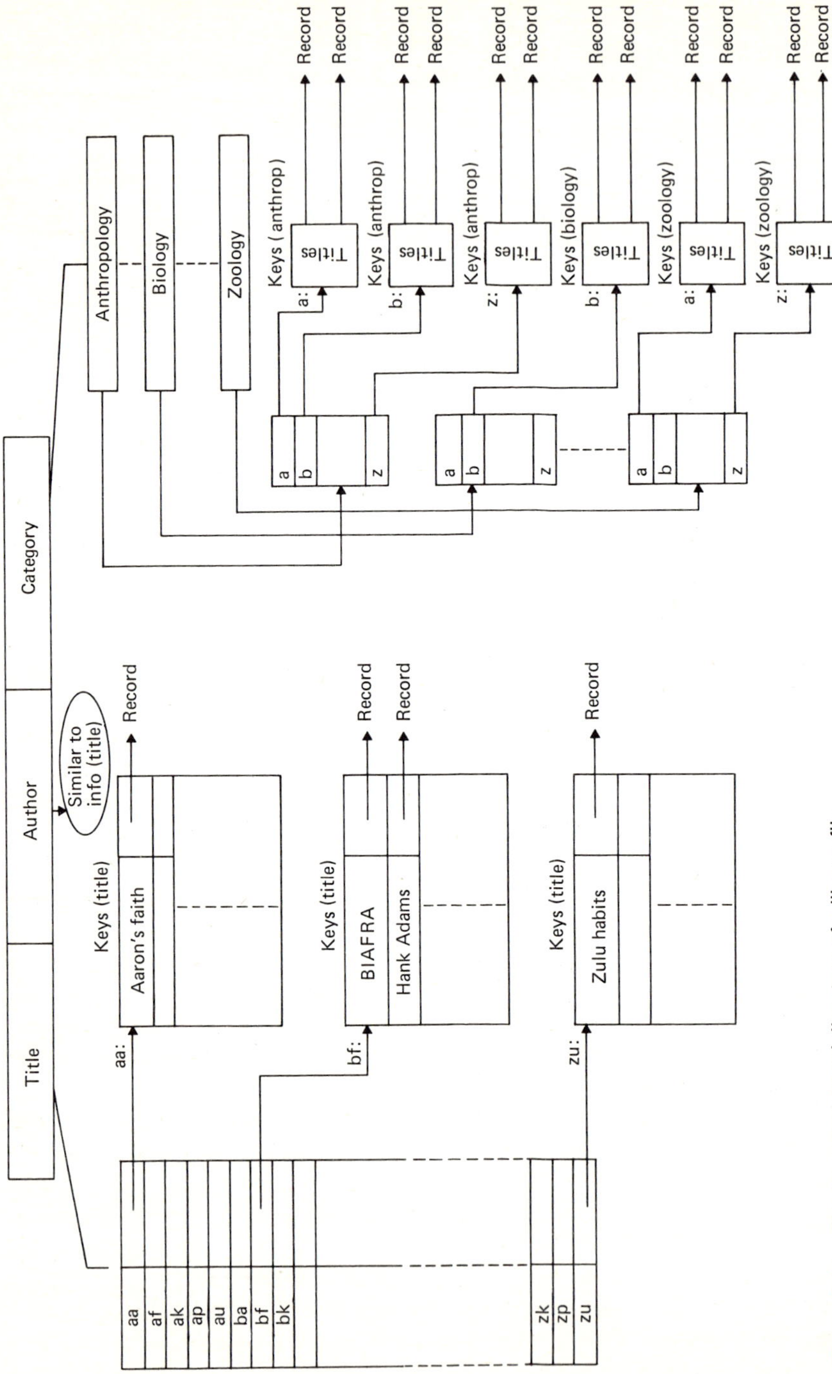

Figure 9.2c The tree-structured directory of a library file

and one for "category". The keys in the groups "title" and "author" are in alphabetic order. The keys in the group "category" are in alphabetic order of category and within one category in alphabetic order of title. The resulting directory looks like figure 9.2c.

PROBLEMS

1. A theorem of number theory states: if a and b are non-negative whole numbers and p is a prime number, then $a*b = 0 \pmod p$ implies $a = 0 \pmod p$ or $b = 0 \pmod p$. Let $R_0 = \{0, 1, 2, \ldots, p-1\}$ and $R_1 = \{1, 2, \ldots, p-1\}$. Prove that the set $U = \{i^2 | i \in R_0\}$ contains $(p+1)/2$ elements for $p > 2$. Hint: prove that there are exactly two different values $i,j \in R_1$ such that $i^2 = j^2 \pmod p$. The result implies that the presented quadratic hash generates only $(p+1)/2$ out of p available addresses.

2. A theorem of algebra states that for given integers a and b ($a \neq 0$) and given prime number p the equation $a*x = b \pmod p$ has a unique solution $x \in R_0$. Let $p > 2$ and let a be a number in $R_0 - U$ (that is, for all $j \in R_0$ $a \neq j^2 \pmod p$). Prove that the set $V = \{a*i^2 \mid i \in R_1\}$ contains $(p-1)/2$ elements and prove $U \cap V = \{\}$, $U \cup V = R_0$.

The quadratic hash function is now modified as follows. Choose an arbitrary element $a \in R_0 - U$. Define the step function such that

$$h_{2i} = h_0 + i^2 \pmod p,\ h_{2i+1} = h_0 + a*i^2 \pmod p \text{ for } i \in R_0$$

Show that all the addresses are generated exactly once if i steps through $\{0, 1, \ldots, (p-1)/2\}$.

If the table length p is chosen equal to a number $= -1 \pmod 4$, then $a = -1$ is an element of $R_0 - U$ (one can prove that $j^2 \neq -1 \pmod p$ for all j if $p = -1 \pmod 4$). In this case we simply have $h_{2i+1} = h_0 - i^2 \pmod p$.

3. Given the hash function $H(n) = 676*l_1 + 26*l_2 + l_3 \pmod t$ where $i = 31$ and l_i is the ordinal number of the i-th letter of name n in the alphabet (for example, $H(\text{begin}) = 676*2+26*5+7 \pmod{31} = 1$). Take a list of 31 names (for instance, the keywords of an Algol-like language extended with some names of standard functions such as SQRT, LOG, etc.). Insert the names in the table first with a linear hash, then with a quadratic hash. Count in both cases how many probes were necessary to find a match or an empty place in the table.

4. The bipartitioning in the binary search could be generalized into an n-partitioning in an n-ary search. The algorithm of the latter method partitions the interval in n pieces and compares the given key K with the keys at the $(n-1)$ separation points in the interior of the interval. Thus, the number of comparisons per loop execution increases with n, but the number of loop

executions is proportional to $\log_n l$, where l is the length of the directory measured in number of keys. So, the number of times the loop is executed decreases with increasing n.

a. Program an efficient n-ary search algorithm for n = 3.

b. Assume that the work in the loop of the n-ary search algorithm is proportional to $(n-1)*$[the number of comparisons]. Show that the expected total work of executing the loop until termination is the least of all for n = 2. This means that the binary search is, on the average, the most efficient algorithm of all possible n-ary search algorithms.

5. A given library file has a tree-structured directory (see figure 9.2c). Once the subset has been determined in which a given key resides, the key is located through a given hash function H. Program an algorithm which receives a title as input and returns the location of the book in the library or returns the indication that the book is not available. In which way should the program use additional information about author and/or category?

9.3 THE FILE SYSTEM

9.3.1 An important task of the operating system is the maintenance of the collection of all the user files. The data structure which is used by the system for the purpose of maintaining the user files is itself a file, often called the master file or system file. The records of the file describe the user files. In this section we discuss the structure of the master file and the information kept in the master file records. Furthermore, we discuss the facilities which the operating system must provide to a user for creating, destroying, modifying and using his files. The user communicates with the system through a predefined set of system commands. The collection of all these commands forms the user-system interface. It is often called the job control language of the system. There are as many job control languages as there are systems, so only the basic ideas are presented in this section.

9.3.2 A user is known to the operating system by a user identity number (ID). This number is written on the first card of the batch job (the job-control card) or transmitted as part of the LOGIN procedure of a timesharing session. Let us assume that an ID is a composition of two numbers, a group number (g) and an individual man number (m). A group consists, for instance, of some users who work together on a project or share an account number.

The structure of the master file directory is based on the user ID. This directory is structured as a three-level tree. The first level is a table of all groups. At the second level the users in each group are identified. At the third level appear the file names for each user (see figure 9.3a).

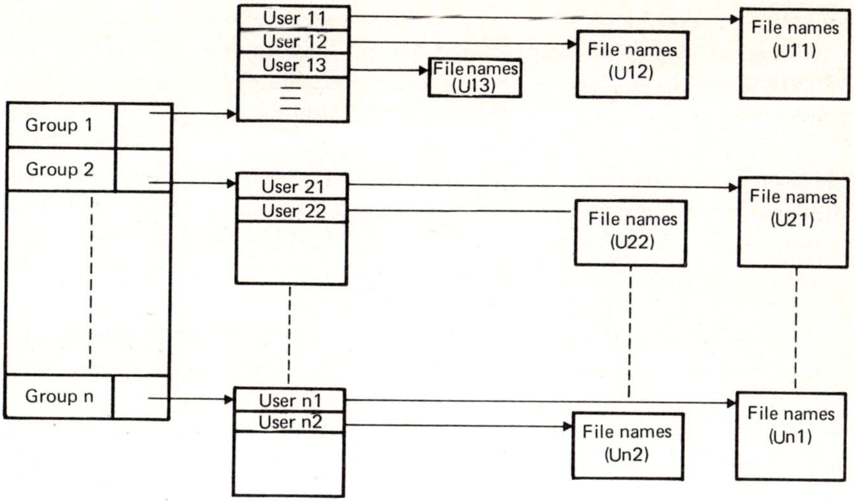

Figure 9.3a Tree-structured file system directory

The operating system provides the user a way to request access to a file. Given the master directory structure described above, a user file record is quickly located if the group number, the man number and the file name are known. Thus, in the general case a user gives these three quantities as input parameters of a file request. When a user requests access to one of his own files, it suffices to pass the file name as the only parameter, because the operating system can derive the two other parameters from the given user ID.

When not in use, a user file resides on a mass storage device. The file must be moved to the active store before its records can be accessed. There are valid reasons not to move a large file in one piece but in a number of fixed size chunks, often called blocks, sometimes called pages. (Although there is a similarity with the paging technique of primary and secondary storage, the term *page* is used here in the sense of line printer page.) One reason for subdividing files is that the user of the large file probably does not need the whole file at once, and can only operate on part of the information at a time. Another reason is that because the primary and secondary stores are shared by several users, no one of them should be permitted to deprive the others from also using storage space in these devices.

The block size must not be too small, because this would have an adverse effect on the performance of transferring files from passive to active storage and back. The argument is the same as that in favor of a large page size to obtain an acceptable ratio of transfer overhead (initiating and administrating the transfer) and transfer time. The counter argument of internal fragmentation is considered less serious in this case, because the file usually resides on a relatively cheap storage device. For example, a block size of 7200 bytes might be chosen because it accommodates the image of a line printer page: 60 lines with 120 characters per line.

9.3.3 It is very common for various files of a user to be related in some way. All the files which contain FORTRAN programs are related by the fact that these programs must be processed by the FORTRAN compiler. The result of compiling a program P is a file which contains program P in LOADable form. The result of modifying the original program may have the side effect that the old version is saved as a backup copy. It is very convenient if a user can express such a relationship in the file names. A file name is then composed of two parts, the subject name and the category name. For instance, SORT.ALG is the file name of an ALGOL program which sorts an array of integer numbers. The subject name describes the use or purpose of the file and the category name conveys the form in which the substance is represented. In due course the user also has the files SORT.BAC and SORT.OBJ with the backup version and the object code version.

The bulk of the information about a user file is in the user file record. Figure 9.3b lists the most important fields one may expect to find in a user file record. The attributes file name = (subject name, category) and owner ID = (group number, man number) are not represented as record fields, because their values are stored in the master directory. Moreover, these values are known in advance, because they are the input of a file access request and they are used to trace the path through the directory which leads to the requested user file record.

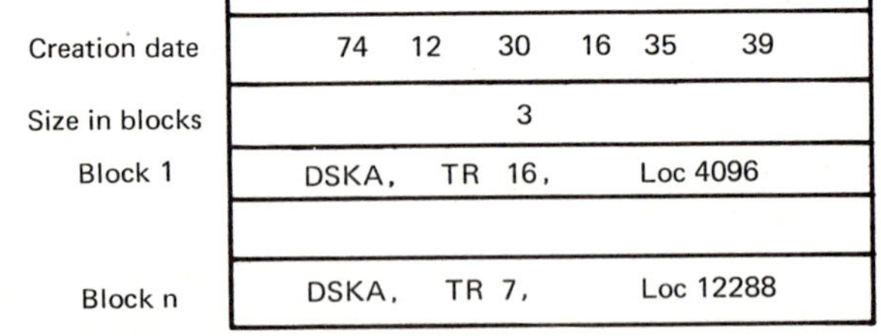

Figure 9.3b Record describing a user file

It is common for a password to be associated with a user ID. The user who logs into the system using a particular ID will be successful only if he knows the password associated with that ID. This prevents unauthorized use of a user ID and, among other things, it makes it impossible for a user to do whatever he likes with someone else's files (for instance, delete a file!). We come back to this point further on where the user privileges are discussed. Not many systems do provide a separate file password. If there is one, a request to access the file will be granted only if the user who requests access is able to produce the password. If there is no password, everybody has access to the file, but, in any case, what the user can do with the file depends on the user privileges (see below). The advantage of having a file password is that a file owner can make a selection of his files available to another user by telling that user only the passwords of the files in that selection. The file password feature can also be used by users who share a user ID to keep their files inaccessible to one another.

The field "user privileges" has six subfields.

d = delete	a = append
p = protect	r = read
w = write	e = execute

The owner of a file has at all times the right to change his privileges, no matter what the protect field indicates. (Here "owner" means the user who logs into the system with the user ID that corresponds to the (group,man) number pair of the file. If there is a file password, this must also have been produced to establish legitimate ownership.) Thus, the owner always has the right to delete the file (d), change the user privileges (p), modify the contents of the user file (w), append new information at the end of the file (a), read the contents of the file (r) or execute the file (e). The privileges are subdivided into two groups, the file control privileges (d,p,w) and the file use privileges (a,r,e). Users in the same group as the owner always have the file use privileges, no matter what the corresponding fields indicate. Their right to the file control privileges, however, depends on the given code. In the given example (see figure 9.3b), the users in the owner's group have the right to write into the file, but they cannot change the privileges or delete the file.

All users outside of the file owner's group lack any of the control privileges, no matter what the corresponding fields indicate. With respect to the use privileges, the outside users have the rights as indicated in the fields a, r and e. In the given example (see figure 9.3b) the outside users do have the right to read or execute the file, but cannot append new information to it. Thus, an outside user is able to copy the file, because he can read it. If he does so, he now owns a copy to which he can get all access privileges (for he will have created a new file in his own directory). But the outside user is not able to modify the original file or change its privilege code.

The meaning of the other fields of a user file record is obvious. The file status reflects which access privilege was granted to the current user. The next field conveys the identity of the current user. This information is, for instance, useful to prevent conflicting use of the file by several users. In the given example (see figure 9.3b), another user will not be permitted to start writing in the file while the current user is reading.

The file type field has either permanent or temporary value. The former is saved, but the latter is deleted when the owner logs off. The creation of a file is given in terms of the time of day when the file record was inserted in the master file. The size field is necessary to indicate how many block fields the record has. Each of the block fields points to the begin address of the storage area where the block is located.

9.3.4 There are three kinds of file operations: a) creation and deletion, b) activating files and c) operations on the contents of a file. We give some examples of each kind. Among the first kind we find operations such as

CREATE file name {⟨{type}{,privilege}⟩}
DELETE file name {[user ID]}
RENAME file name {⟨{type}{,privilege}⟩} = file name {[user ID]}
COPY file name {⟨{type}{,privilege}⟩} = file name {[user ID]}

The braces in the lines above mean that the part included between the braces is optional. Thus, the parameter of DELETE is either a file name or a file name followed by a user ID between square brackets. The file name parameter in CREATE is optionally followed by a type indication (temporary or permanent) or by a privilege code (a pattern of six bits) or both. If no type indication is given, the system assumes by default type "temporary". The default for the privilege code is all ones (if we want to be protective, we make the default case all zeros). The default for an ID-less parameter is the user ID of the caller.

CREATE starts by asking the user if he wishes to attach a password to the new file. The function of CREATE is to insert the input parameter name as a new file name in the file name list of the caller, to set up a pointer to a new file record, and to initialize that record. CREATE is unsuccessful if the input name already occurs in that file name list. The function of DELETE is almost the opposite of CREATE. Before starting the actual deletion of the file, it asks the caller to produce the password (if any). If this matches the contents of the password field, DELETE goes ahead, frees the space held by the file named as input parameter, and deletes the file name and its record from the master directory. DELETE fails if the caller does not have the right to delete the parameter file.

RENAME and COPY are operations on the file named on the righthand side of the equal sign. This file itself is not modified, but in case of RENAME, its descriptive data in the master directory is modified. If the righthand file requires a password, the user must know it or the operation is not executed. In case of RENAME, the existing file name named on the righthand side is overwritten by the file name used on the lefthand side. The type field and the privilege code in the file record are overwritten by the new type and code of the lefthand side. The function RENAME gives the user an opportunity to change a temporary file into a permanent file (and vice versa) and allows the user to change the access rights of other users. RENAME fails if the caller is an outside user. RENAME also fails if called by a user who does not have the protect privilege while a new privilege code is given on the lefthand side.

The operation COPY creates a new file which receives its name, type and code from the lefthand side and its file contents and part of the record from the righthand side. COPY called by an outside user fails if this user does not have the read privilege. COPY also fails if the file name used on the lefthand side already occurs in the user's file name list.

The operations in the second category apply to files which are executable programs. We find in this category operations such as

GET file name {[user ID]}
START
RUN file name {[user ID]}
SAVE filename {⟨{type}{,privilege code}⟩}

The operation GET creates an unnamed image of the executable file in the active store. We assume that a user can have only one executable program in the active store at a time. Owing to this assumption, the function START does not need a parameter, because the only program that can be started is the executable image. The operation RUN is a combination of GET and START. The purpose of having GET and START separately is that a program, once copied by GET, can be executed several times without having to copy the program file into the active store every time that START is called. The operations GET and RUN fail if the caller does not have at least one of the file use privileges: append, execute or read. START fails if there is no executable program in the user's area of the active store. GET and RUN do not create the image if the input file requires a password and the caller is not able to provide it.

The operation SAVE creates a new file corresponding to the given input parameter, and copies the executable program in the caller's area of the active store into this file. SAVE uses CREATE, so the caller has the option of setting a password. SAVE fails if the given file name already occurs in the caller's file name list. It also fails if there is no executable program in the caller's area of the active store. If the executable program was copied from a file, it inherits the privilege code of this file. This means that SAVE in this case also fails if the caller does not have the read privilege.

9.3.5 The third category consists of the operations in which the contents of the file are involved. We find in this category calls to editors, operations to compile, load and execute programs, and data transmission operations to control peripheral devices. Examples are:

EDIT file name {[user ID]}, INIT file name {⟨{type}{,privilege}⟩}
COMP,LOAD,EX file name {[user ID]}
TYPE,PRINT file name {[user ID]}

All operations in this category, except INIT, require that the caller give the password if the input file has one. EDIT is a call to an editing program which allows the user to change the contents of the file. (A discussion of the features of an editor falls outside the scope of this book.) Before the editing program is ready for the user, the operation EDIT deletes the backup version of the given file (if any), renames the given file as the backup version and creates a new file (initially empty) with the same name and characteristics as the given file. The new file is filled during the editing process. EDIT fails if the caller does not have the write privilege. The operation INIT is a combination of CREATE and EDIT, except for the fact that there is no backup version this time.

The COMP operation requires that there be a compilable program file with the given input file name and that the language in which the program is written can be derived from the file name (see 9.3.3). (The alternative is that the user calls RUN FORTRAN. Once this program has started, it asks for an input file whose name can be completely arbitrary.) The function of COMP is to compile the given file and place the resulting object code in a new file. It is convenient to give the new file the same subject name as the input file, and add a category name expressing the fact that this file contains object code (for example, OBJ). COMP fails if the caller does not have the execute privilege to the input file. The object file inherits the password and privilege code from the source file.

The operation LOAD requires that there be a compilable source file or an object file with the given input file name (otherwise the user should have called RUN LOADER). If LOAD finds an object file and a source file with the given name and if the creation of the object file is before the creation of the source file, then LOAD deletes this object file, because the object file has apparently been derived from an older version of the source file. If the source file is the most recently created, LOAD uses COMP in order to get a new object file. LOAD fails if the caller does not have the execute privilege. The result of LOAD is an anonymous executable program in the user's area of the active store. This program inherits the password and privilege code from the object file. The next thing the user can do is either START or SAVE this executable program. The operation EX is a combination of LOAD and START (similar to RUN).

The operation TYPE puts out the given input file on the user's terminal.

The operation PRINT prints the given input file on a line printer. Both operations require the caller to have the read privilege.

9.3.6 When a user calls one of the file operations, he is interacting directly with the operating system. At other times, for instance when a user is editing a file, he is interacting with a program. A question is how the operating system knows whether or not an incoming character is part of a system command. There are several ways to make this clear. We discuss three conventions which are widely used.

The first convention is the distinction between system command mode and program mode (similar to upper case/lower case on a typewriter). If the user is in system command mode, all the commands he types are processed by the operating system. Otherwise, the user's input is placed in the input buffer of the program he is running. The user starts in system command mode. The operating system switches the user to program mode when a command is executed and back to system command mode when the command is finished. Many operating systems make the current mode clear to the terminal user by printing a special character in the first character position of the new line. The system prints, for instance, a dollar sign on the next line on which the user can type a system command, and a star on the next line if the user is sending information to its running program.

An additional convention is that of the special escape character. The user starts in system command mode and the operating system changes the user to program mode when a system command has been accepted. Now the user forces the operating system to switch back to system command mode by placing a special character or character combination (unlikely to be used elsewhere) in the input. As soon as the character is received, the executing program is terminated (or suspended) and the user returns to system command mode. The system prints the system command mode character at the beginning of the next line so that the user knows that he is back in system command mode.

Yet another convention, which can be applied in addition to the other two or instead of them, reserves a special format for system commands. A system command is, for instance, defined as dollar sign followed by a name. This convention can be combined with the first method. In case the user is in system command mode, the system types the dollar sign at the beginning of the next line so that the user only has to type the command name. If in program mode, the user can still use a system command. A special case of this convention is the rub-out feature provided by most timesharing systems. No matter in which mode the user is, the rub-out character is always received by the operating system and interpreted as a system command. In this case the system responds by "forgetting" the last character typed by the user and not changing the mode which existed before the rub-out command.

The set of system commands is called the *job control language*, because it allows the user to operate on his programs and data. The set of commands presented here does not have enough structure to justify the predicate "language." However, there are job control languages which have block structure, as in ALGOL 60, and in which the user can build up strings of commands into a command program before execution of the commands starts. A discussion of structuring job control languages belongs to the language design area. This topic falls outside the scope of this book.

PROBLEMS

1. Given the master directory structure of section 9.3.2 (see figure 9.3a), write a program that lists the file type, privilege codes and creation of all the files of a user. The input to this program is the user's ID (by default).

2. a. The category to which a file belongs could be recorded in the file record instead of in the file name. Discuss whether or not there is a significant difference in these two ways of recording the file category.
   b. The files most frequently used are the files a user owns and the shared system files. A user can pass one of his own files as an input parameter to a system command without having to mention explicitly his user ID. It would be convenient if a user ID also could be omitted when a shared system file is used as input to a system command (for example, RUN FORTRAN, or RUN FORTRAN.SYS). This means that the default is not automatically the user ID of the caller. Devise an interpretation of a file name without user ID as input which allows the user to pass shared system files in this way.

3. It seems that the file operation RENAME is not strictly necessary (it certainly is convenient!). Looking at the definitions in section 9.3.4 it seems that RENAME can be implemented as a call to COPY followed by a DELETE. Investigate whether this is indeed true for all possible parameter combinations of RENAME.

4. Program the system command SAVE in some detail. System commands of the first category such as DELETE can be used in SAVE without being programmed in line. SAVE receives as parameter the name, type, and privilege code of the result file. If there already is a file by that name, that file must first be deleted. We assume that all files reside on disk. The space on the disk is described in a table with one entry per block. When space is freed or allocated, the entry in question must be updated. There is supposed to be sufficient space on the file disk. If not, then the result is disaster. An implicit parameter to the operation SAVE is the user control block. The latter points

to the first location of the executable program in the user's active store area and it reflects its length measured in machine words. The user control block also holds the privilege code and password which the active program inherited from the object program or source image. The result of SAVE must be (if it can be executed) that the user control block is updated, the new file record is initialized, the new file is on the disk and the disk space table is updated.

5. Check how each of the 15 system commands discussed in this section initializes or changes these four record fields in the file record: the creation, the file type, the privilege, and the password.

6. Design a file name lookup program that searches for a named file in the user's default directory and, if not found, in a special directory shared by all members of a group.

9.4 PROTECTION TECHNIQUES

9.4.1 The term *protection* is the technical term referring to all the mechanisms in an operating system which control the access of programs to shared objects in the system. In the early days, when users started to share system facilities and protection became an issue, their primary interest was protection against errors occurring in somebody else's program and serious degradation of service. First, a program of user A must not be able to generate an address (by accident or on purpose) in the storage area allocated to a program or data of user B. Second, the operating system must be so well designed that the user processes will not get into a deadlock state or in a state in which one of them is permanently blocked. Finally, if a user program makes an error (for example, in an infinite loop), this must not have a significant impact on the performance of the other programs. The erroneous program must not keep a CPU permanently busy or hold on to any other device for an indefinite period of time.

The next stage in the development of protection ideas came about when people started using a computer for storing and manipulating large amounts of data. Their privacy became an issue. A user should be able to keep his information secret from other users if he wishes. Not only should user A's information be protected against destruction by user B but user B should not be able to read or copy it unless user A grants explicit permission to do so.

In more recent days, the interest in protection has widened its horizon, mainly in two directions:

a. Proprietary programs: it may be very profitable if user A can make available some of its programs or data to user B. But user A must have the option of specifying what user B can do with A's information. If this can be done, there must be a protection enforcement mechanism which assures that user B accesses A's information in the permitted manner.

b. The principle of "need to know": at any moment a program should be able to access only those objects (programs and data) which it needs to run its current program section to completion. For instance, if parameters to a procedure are passed on top of a working space stack, the called procedure must not be able to access items further down in the stack. Another example: P and V access semaphore queues. The space reserved for these queues must be accessible to only the programs of P and V, not to the programs calling P or V. This form of protection prevents the wide propagation of an error. The effect of an error is restricted to the set of objects which are accessible at the time the error occurs.

In this section we first discuss briefly some of the protection techniques applied in conventional operating systems. Then protection is presented from a more general viewpoint, abstracted from the objects being protected. This general outlook enables us to find out what these seemingly different protection mechanisms have in common. A general approach also allows us to explore more elaborate protection mechanisms and extensions of the conventional techniques. Implementation issues will be discussed in section 9.5.

9.4.2 A wide variety of protection mechanisms has been implemented as part of conventional operating systems. The best-known examples are briefly discussed below.

a. The distinction of supervisor/user-mode: execution of some instructions (for example, data transmission commands to devices) is prohibited for programs in user mode. In some systems the user programs call certain system routines instead of these instructions; in other systems a user program is trapped if it attempts to execute one of the exceptional instructions. In any case, control passes to a supervisor program which has access to data which is hidden from the user programs. The exceptional instruction is executable in the privileged environment of the supervisor. The protection issue at hand is the fact that one user program cannot undertake certain actions which could have a disastrous effect on another program. The underlying assumption is that the supervisor program is more reliable than the user program!

b. A layer structured system: a layer L provides certain facilities to the layers above L. The outer layers do not have access to the local data of layer L or any of the inner layers, and have only restricted access to the functions provided by L. They can execute those functions, but they cannot read or modify them. The layer structure is in some sense an extension of the supervisor/user mode idea. Instead of just two layers, there is a larger number and every pair of layers has the relationship of user/supervisor.

c. Device allocation: every process should receive its fair share of the devices. This is guaranteed by programs especially designed to control a device or a pool of devices. These programs guarantee that the devices are properly used, by one user at a time if necessary. But these programs also make up a schedule of future users and enforce limitations on the length of time and number of resources a process can have.

d. The virtual memory system: such a system controls the allocation of storage space to programs and data. As a result of allocating space it generates very valuable information which can easily be checked at runtime. In a relocation system the lower and upper bounds of a user area are known. A simple hardware check assures that no addressing outside the allocated area can take place. In a paging or segmentation system the page table or segment table describes the space which a program can access. The hardware address map assures (by using the page or segment descriptors) that a program remains in its own realm. By this arrangement, one program cannot access (not even by mistake) the storage area of another program.

e. The file system: a user has the right to do with his own files as he pleases, but does not have this control over the files of others. If so desired, a user is able to obtain complete privacy, particularly if a password is attached to every file. The password and privilege code (see section 9.3.3) protect one user's files against unauthorized access by other users. This protection already provides the use of proprietary information, but all outside users have the same access privileges to the files of one user. Also, if the files have passwords, a user program cannot make a file available without human intervention. The programmer who created the file must give the password to the users who will be permitted to use the file.

9.4.3 In all the examples above, every program runs in an environment which permits the program to access some objects (storage areas, segments, local data, functions, devices, files, etc.), but denies the program access to other objects. An object is known by its name (the symbol table segment index, the stack pointer, a procedure name, a symbolic device name such as TTY1, a file name, etc.). We assume that for protection purposes an object has a unique name which never existed before and never will be created again. One way to achieve unique naming is to attach the time of creation to a name.

Every object has a specific set of operations which a program can perform on the object (for instance, insert, store, push, call, reserve, delete, etc.). The set of all operations that can be performed on an object determines the type of object. All objects which have exactly the same set of operations are said to be of the same type. For instance, the type of semaphore is determined by the P and V operations, which are the only operations that can be performed on semaphores. The type file is determined by the system commands discussed in the preceding section.

If a program is allowed to access a given object, its access rights are usually restricted to a subset of the possible operations which can be performed on the object. It makes sense to permit user programs to execute a compiler program, but the caller may not be allowed to read the compiler text; and it is very unlikely that he is allowed to change the compiler code.

An access right is a pair (object, operation) where the operation is one of the set of operations defined for this object type. In terms of access rights, an environment is a set of access rights. This set describes precisely those objects which a program running in that environment can access and the operations this program can perform on those objects. The concepts object, operation on an object, access right, and environment are the basic ingredients in terms of which a protection technique can be expressed. A particular protection mechanism is determined by the rules which govern these three aspects:

1. How the protection is enforced
2. How an environment can be modified
3. How a computation can migrate from one environment to another

A description of the five example protection mechanisms a) through e) illustrates the essential differences of these techniques

a. The distinction of user/supervisor mode
   Class of objects to be protected: subset S of the machine instructions
   Operations on these objects: execute
   User environment: lacks all rights in $R = \{r|r = (s,\text{execute}), s \in S\}$
   1. Enforcement: user is trapped if he attempts to use $r \in R$
   2. Modification: none
   3. Migration: computation moves from user environment to supervisor environment. The latter contains all $r \in R$.

b. The layer structured system
   The characterization of this technique is very similar to a). It is left to the reader (see problem 1).

c. Device allocation
Class of objects to be protected: device descriptors
Operations on those objects: request, release
User environment: contains either r_1 = (request,D) or r_2 = (release, D), but not both
1. Enforcement: error state if use of absent access right is attempted
2. Modification: *if* r_1 *then* remove (r_1); add (r_2)
else remove (r_2); add (r_1) *fi*
3. Migration: none

d. Use of pages or segments
Class of objects to be protected: pages
Operations on those objects: read, write, call, load, save
User environment: may contain for a particular page p no right at all, or r = (read,p), or w = (write,p) or c = (call,p) or any combination of those.
1. Enforcement: error state if use of absent right is attempted
2. Modification: none
3. Migration: possibly through call of system routine that operates in an environment containing the required right

e. The file system as described in section 9.3
Class of objects to be protected: user files
Basic operations on those objects: create, delete, write, protect, append, read, execute
Owner's environment: c = (create,f), d = (delete,f), w = (write,f), p = (protect,f), a = (append,f), r = (read,f), e = (execute,f)
Environment of user in owner's group: a, r, e and possibly a combination of d, w and p
Environment of outside user: a combination of a, r and e, or none
1. Enforcement: error state if use of absent right is attempted
2. Modification in owner's environment: none
Modification in group's environment: the rights d, w and p can be added or removed at any time if the privilege code is changed by a user who possesses right p.
Modification in outsider's environment: the rights a, r and e can be added or removed at any time if the privilege code is changed by a user who possesses right p.
3. Migration: possibly through call of system routine or execution of a program in someone else's environment

9.4.4 The descriptions above are models of protection techniques expressed in terms of our modeling tools: objects, operations, access rights and environments. The tools are general enough to allow modeling of all kinds of protection mechanisms. It is, for instance, not difficult to design a model for file protection in which a file owner (the user who creates the file) can determine for every user separately which access rights this user will have to the file. This file system will not use file passwords.

The set of all user files is partitioned in the sets $F_1, F_2, \ldots, F_n$ where n is the number of user IDs and F_i the set of files created by $user_i$ (that is, $\{1, \ldots, n\}$). The basic operations on a file are: create, delete, write, read, append and execute. (The files do not have a protection code, because the access rights are not fixed and uniform for all outside users.) The environment of $user_i$ contains all access rights to files $f \in F_i$ and those access rights (f,op), $f \in F_j \neq i$ which $user_j$ explicitly granted to $user_i$. This way the user who creates a file can choose how he wishes to share his file anywhere in between the two extremes of total privacy or granting all access rights to other users. Moreover, the access rights may be different from one user to another. Also, there is no need for human intervention when a user wishes to grant some access rights to another user. The file passwords are not necessary anymore.

The enforcement rule is simple; if a user attempts to operate on a file in a way he has no right to, access will be denied to him. Instead of being permitted to access the file, this user receives an error message.

The environment modification rule can be set in several ways. One way to state this rule is: access rights can be added to any environment but only at the time of creating a file. This excludes the possibility that a $user_j$ who received an access right from a $user_i$ ($i \neq j$) passes this right on to yet another $user_k$ ($k \neq i$, $k \neq j$). With regard to deletions the rule states: an access right is deleted if a user exercises the delete right or if a user attempts an access permitted to him, but the object does not exist any longer. This deletion rule would be very dangerous if names were not unique. If the same name can be used again for another object after deleting the object which earlier carried that name, an access right to the old object could be used to access the new object.

Another way to state the modification rule is: access rights can be added to an environment at all times and they will be removed from an environment when a user, who has the right to do so, deletes the file. With this rule a user can share any access right he possesses with any other user. The unique naming of objects is not so crucial in this case, because, when a file is deleted, all access rights to this file are at once removed from all environments. (Possible implementations are discussed in section 9.5.) Other modification rules can be constructed as a mixture of the two versions given here. It is also possible to construct a rule independent of the two presented here (see problem 3).

The migration rule is (as usual) governed by the access to executable files and system routines. If a $user_j$ has the right to call a file $f \in F_{i+j}$ and indeed calls f, $user_i$ migrates to the environment of file f. It is possible for this file to have access rights to files which $user_j$ does not possess in the environment where it called f. A similar migration may take place if $user_j$ calls a system routine.

9.4.5 Access rights and environments are also objects and need to be protected as such. The protection rules set for these objects have a great impact on the kind of protection mechanism we can model. We recognize remove, copy, and transfer as valid operations on an existing access right. Let these operations be applied to an access right r in environment E_k. Remove simply deletes right r from E_k. Copy and transfer have as a second parameter an environment. Both operations place a copy of right r in the environment named as second parameter. If there already is a copy in that environment, this copy is overwritten. In addition to this, transfer removes right r from E_k, the environment in which transfer was executed.

Any one of these three operations on access rights can be executed only if the environment in which the operation is attempted has the right to do so. Imagine that an access right is extended with a three bit field indicating which of the three operations on access rights can be performed in this environment. If, for instance, the copy bit is off, the environment cannot send a copy of this access right to another environment. An access right comes into existence when a user creates an object (other than an access right or environment). At that time, the environment of the creator receives all the access rights to the created object and all three bits of all these access rights are turned on. To complete the picture, we assume that copy and transfer have an optional third parameter which masks off the access right extension. An environment performing copy or transfer can in this way turn off any bits in the extension of the copied access right. Note that the bits can be turned off in copy or transfer, but not turned on! The receiver of an access right will not get more rights to this access right than the sender possesses.

Various policies of sharing information can be designed by setting rules for manipulating the access right extensions. Suppose the general policy is that copy always masks off the copy and transfer bits. This implies that access rights to an object can be received only from the creator of that object. No other user is able to pass an access right to that object on to yet another user. If, on the other hand, copy always turns off the copy bit, but not the transfer bit, the creator cannot prevent another user from passing on an access right to a third party, but he can be assured that the number of environments which possess the access right cannot increase without the creator himself causing the increase. If the creator also turns off the copy bit of an access right in his own environment, then we can be assured that there will never be more than one copy of that access right in the whole system.

Several paragraphs ago, a file environment modification rule was stated, saying: "access rights to a file can be added to other environments only at the time that this file is created." This rule meant to exclude the possibility that an access right could be passed on from one environment to another. The time restriction is superfluous if the access right extension is properly used. All that is needed is a version of copy which masks off copy and transfer. If the delete bit is also turned off, the creator can be assured that he keeps complete control of the file object.

The modeling tools used in this section allow us to create a conceptual picture of various protection techniques. The models show the relationship and differences of protection mechanisms and lay out the space in which all protection policies can be designed. The models are abstract in the sense that implementation issues have been totally ignored. If a specific protection policy is chosen, it is unlikely that it will be implemented with these general modeling tools. If, for instance, only the creator of a file is allowed to delete it and other environments can only transfer an access right to the file, there is no point in implementing the three extension bits. All the system has to know is in which environment the file was created. Thus, while the models are expressed in terms of a uniform set of concepts, the implementations of various protection techniques may be greatly different. Implementation issues are discussed in the next section.

PROBLEMS

1. Layer L_i of a layer structured system layer provides the functions $F_{i1}, \ldots, F_{im_i}$ for which the environments of all layers L_j for $j > i$ have the execute access right. The local data of layer L_i is indicated by D_i. Layer L_i has the right to read, write, delete or extend D_i, but other layers have no access right to D_i. Characterize the protection provided by the layer structure in terms of the modeling tools: object, operation, access right, environment and the three rules for protection enforcement, environment modification and migration from one environment to another.

2. A private semaphore, s, of a process, C, is a semaphore on which only C can perform a P operation. None of the other processes can perform P(s), but any process can perform V(s), including C. Devise and describe a protection technique for private semaphores.

3. If a user creates a file in environment E, this environment receives all access rights to this file and all manipulation rights to these access rights (delete, copy, transfer). An access right can be copied or transferred to another environment with only a subset of the manipulation rights. In this particular file system information can be appended to a file in any other environment, but all other access rights are the sole privilege of the creator environment. Also, it should not be possible that the right to append to a particular file is exercised in two different environments. Describe a model for a protection technique which satisfies the stated requirements.

4. The operations inspect (r,E) and extract (r,E), where r is an access right and E an environment, are the basic operations on environments. Inspect is a Boolean function which returns *true* if $r \in E$ and *false* otherwise. Extract is

the opposite of transfer; executed in environment E_k, it transfers right r from E to F_k if r $\in$ E before the action takes place; otherwise it does nothing. Would it be necessary to introduce a reverse copy (r,E), which, if executed in E_k, copies access right r from environment E? Or is reverse copy (r,E) superfluous, because it can be replaced by extract (r,E) followed by copy (r,E)? Would it be possible to delete the operations transfer and extract entirely and replace them by calls on copy, remove, inspect and reverse copy?

5. A block structured programming language provides some protection with respect to local data. Let B_{kj} represent the j-th lexicographical block at block depth k (for example, B_{13} means the third block, reading from left to right, encountered in the program which has one surrounding block). Let d_{ij} represent the local data declared in block B_{kj}. Describe a protection model of the block structure.

Even more interesting is what happens upon procedure entry when parameters are passed. Describe which rights are moved from the calling environment to the procedure body environment and back at the beginning and at the end of procedure execution. Do this for various parameter mechanisms: call by value, call by reference, call by copy, call by name. Are the rights and environments represented by real physical data?

9.5 IMPLEMENTATION OF PROTECTION TECHNIQUES

9.5.1 Implementation of a protection technique requires the encoding of special data structures and special programs. The data structures must realize the access rights and environments. The programs must implement the three rules: one for enforcing the protection, one for modifying environments, and one for process migration from one environment to another. In the preceding section we discovered that a particular protection technique can be encoded much more efficiently than the general model. In the file system of section 9.3, for instance, it is not necessary for every user process to have a separate set of file access rights, because the rights are the same for a large group of users.

In this section, we discuss some alternative ways in which a protection technique can be encoded. First, we look at the effect the encoding has on protection enforcement. Enforcement takes place along the path that leads from the name used in some environment to the object by that name. In some cases the protection check is nicely carried out at the beginning of this path; in other cases, it is better to check the access right at the end of this path. Next, we discuss some cases in which a static protection check suffices and some cases in which the protection must be checked dynamically. Finally, we discuss the activation of environments at procedure calls.

A procedure may be executed in an entirely different environment than the environment in which it is called (for example, a system routine). There is a question of how a protected object can be passed as a parameter across environment boundaries.

9.5.2 A program is allowed to apply access function f to a protected object s if and only if the access right (s,f) is in its environment E. It is the task of the mechanism protecting s to check that $(s,f) \in E$ before f is applied to s. How this is checked depends on the implementation of environments and access rights. When the program calls function f with parameter s, it uses the name of object s as it is known at the call site. When f is executed, the operation is performed on the object itself. The step from referring to the name to locating the actual object itself requires a name interpretation function. There are lots of name interpretation functions in an operating system. We list a few. A program uses an indexed address such as 3(R), where R is one of the fast registers. The name interpretation in this case is a simple addition of three to the contents of the R register. A Fortran program uses the name "eps" for one of its variables. The Fortran compiler translates this name into an offset from the program data base. A program running on a machine with paging refers to a location by a pair (p,w), where p is a page index and w a location in this page. The paging hardware interprets this "name" and maps it via the page descriptor indexed by p into a physical address in the store. Users, interacting with a timesharing system, apply system commands to file names. Such a name is interpreted by a lookup through the master directory.

There are basically two alternative ways of storing the access rights. The access rights can be stored at the site of the user of the rights or with the protected object (see figure 9.5a). These two alternative ways of storing the access rights are highly visible in a paging system and a file system as described in section 9.3. The objects to be protected in a paging system are the pages. Every process has a page table which describes all the pages this process can access. The page table is the page environment of the process. In many systems, a page descriptor contains a coding which indicates whether the process can read, write or execute the page. Thus, a page descriptor is equal to the set of access rights to the page.

The page tables are an example of storing the access rights at the site of the user. In this case the access rights are called the *capabilities* available to a program and the collection of all the access rights is called the capability list or C-list.

The file system described in section 9.3 is an example of the opposite implementation. There the access rights are given by the privilege code in the file record. The file environment of a program is known by the user ID it is running under. Depending on the correspondence of the user ID and the (group-,man-number) pair of a file, the program has all the access rights (the owner), or it has the file use rights and some of the file control rights

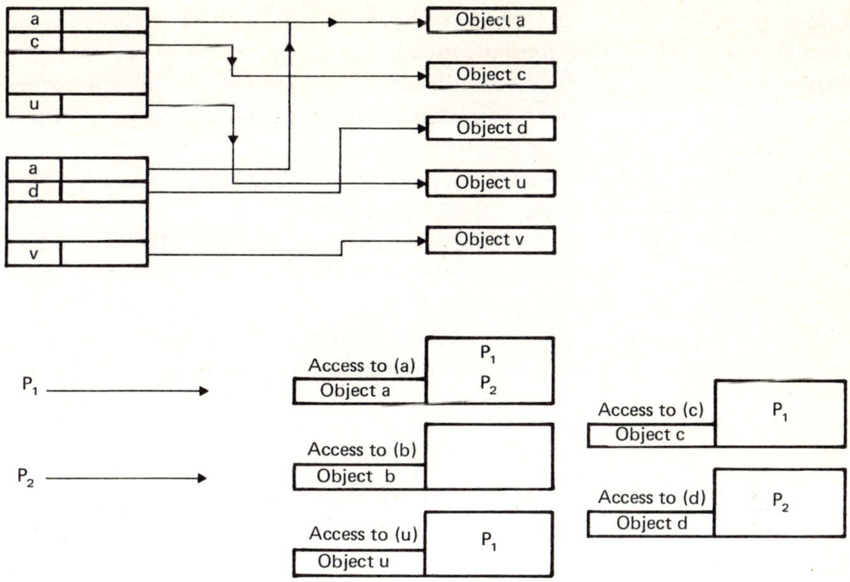

Figure 9.5a Access right stored with the user or with the objects

(users in the owner's group), or it has only some of the use rights (users outside the owner's group). This arrangement is clearly a case of storing the access rights with the objects (the files). In such a case an access right is often called an *access key* to the protected object.

Another example of storing the access rights with the objects is found in the compiler of a block structured language. The object names used in the program are stored in the symbol table with an indication of the block depth and lexicographical block number. The compiler maintains two global variables indicating the block depth and lexicographical block number of the block it is currently compiling. These two global variables determine the environment in which the compiler is currently working. The two numbers in a name descriptor of the symbol table represent the access key which determines whether or not the object name is presently accessible.

Storing the access rights as capabilities at the execution site has two major advantages. First, the protection check can be performed right at the beginning of the name interpretation, even without leaving the execution environment. Secondly, if a running program refers to the objects through the capability list, then it is impossible to name any objects to which the program has no access rights. For example, the page table describes all accessible pages and no more. It is impossible for a program to name any page outside its own page table.

A disadvantage of implementing capability lists is that because many lists may point to the same shared object, capability lists require some storage space. Also, some time overhead may go into loading and saving a capability list upon activation and deactivation. However, only the capability lists being used need be in active memory. The access keys stored with the objects may be less wasteful, particularly if many different environments have equal access rights to an object. A slight disadvantage of this method is that the protection check takes place at the end of the name interpretation, outside the execution environment and after the object has been located. Access lists have one more major advantage. If an access right to an object is deleted or added, the change is made in one central place, and goes into effect for all users at the same time. This is hard to achieve if an access right must be removed from several capability lists (see problem 4).

9.5.3 Protection checking is most expensive if it has to be done at execution time, every time a protected object is referenced. If this is necessary, it is important to make the protection check simple. A good example of simplicity is the check which is incorporated in the page mapping. Another way of cutting down on the time needed to perform runtime protection checks is to make the check once before a sequence of references to the same object as is commonly done in file systems. Let us say that a program is allowed to use one file for output and one file for input simultaneously. Before the program can read from the input file or write onto the output file, the program must open the file. This operation traces the path that leads through the master directory to the file record. Next, it checks whether the file can be used and whether the calling program has the file access key. If not, an error message results. Otherwise, the file status is set and the user ID is placed in the file record. Finally, the base address which gives access to the file is placed in a special location in the data area of the program (one for an input file and one for an output file).

After the file has been opened, the program can read from the input file and write onto the output file without naming the particular file again. All access is indirect through the two special data locations. This means that no further checking is necessary in successive read and write operations. This makes the runtime protection check far less expensive. (After completing all the read or write operations, the file is closed and another file can be opened.)

In some cases the protection check can be performed at compile time. An example is the local data of a block in a block structured language. If the operating system is written in a structured language, the protection of system layers can be checked at compile time. This results in significant savings when the system is running. (See also section 10.2).

9.5.4 A process migrates from one environment to another if it calls a procedure which uses a different set of access rights than the ones present in the calling environment. This is the case if a user program calls a system routine. For example, a program performs a P or V operation on a semaphore. This operation is executed in an environment which contains access rights to the ready list and the semaphore waiting queue. It does not need any of the rights in the calling environment and the calling environment does not have access rights to the ready list or semaphore queues. When a program calls "openfile", all this procedure needs from the calling environment in addition to the file name is the user ID in order to check the access key. When a program runs into a page fault, a system routine by that name is activated. The environment of this routine consists of all the page information. None of the access rights in this environment are present in the environment which ran into the page fault.

Let p(x) be a procedure which operates in an environment different from the calling environment. The object named by the parameter x resides either in the environment of the procedure, E_p, or in the calling environment, E_c. We explore the implications of both. First, let the object belong to E_p. In that case, E_c has a name for the object, but it has access to the object itself only through a procedure call. To clarify the point, there could be an environment E_p which contains all semaphores with their waiting queues and the ready list. Among the procedures operating in this environment are P and V. Suppose, for simplicity, that the number of semaphores is fixed and all semaphores are elements of an array S[1:n] in E_p. The outside environments are able to distinguish semaphores by index without having access to array S. In other words, the name by which a semaphore is known in E_c is just an integer number in the range [1:n]. Such a number is passed as a semaphore name in a P or V operation.

The weak point of this arrangement is the fact that the procedures operating in E_p have access to all the protected objects all the time. The programs must be very trustworthy to be sure that they will never make mistakes which could affect semaphores or waiting queues not passed as a parameter. In particular, the procedures in E_p must correctly interpret the parameters. The problem is not how to make sure that the caller passes the right semaphore index. The use of the semaphore depends on the calling environment and it is up to the processes using semaphores to make sure that the right semaphore is used. The procedures in E_p must correctly execute the P or V operation, correctly interpret the parameter and update the correct semaphore waiting list. The ideal situation is the one where the procedures in E_p do have access to the ready list and only one semaphore with attached waiting list at a time. The accessible semaphore is the one corresponding to the parameter passed by the caller.

In such an arrangement, environment E_p is better restricted to the necessary set of access rights, but E_p is not constant in time. In fact, there is a set of environments $E_{p1}, E_{p2}, \ldots, E_{pn}$ where n is the number of semaphores. Every time a P or V operation is called, one of these environments is activated. Working with the n different environments responds better to the "need to know" principle than working in the single environment E_p. On the other hand, there is, of course, a cost factor involved. Implementation of the set $E_{p1}, \ldots, E_{pn}$ requires extra space or runtime overhead. We pay in extra space if the n environments exist all the time or we pay in runtime overhead if an environment E_{pi} must be created upon procedure call and deleted when the procedure returns.

The file system is an example of an implementation with a single environment E_p, and the paging system is an example of an implementation with a set of different environments. The file name interpretation function has access to all the files through the master directory. The page mapping has access only to the page table of one user at a time. The page table base of the running program determines which environment E_{pi} is currently active.

An alternative technique is the one in which the protected object is placed in the calling environment E_c. Now the procedure environment E_p must receive access rights to the protected object from the calling environment E_c. However, the called procedure is likely to need an access right which is not present in E_c. For instance, if a semaphore is kept in E_c, this environment will not have the right to add or subtract from the semaphore. But the P or V operation must have that right, so it must be present in E_p when the P or V operation is executed. This technique is known as access right amplification.

PROBLEMS

1. A given system S has exactly n different access rights. An environment E either possesses access right r_i or it does not. How many different environments can exist at most? Let $n > 2$. Suppose that every pair of environments E_i, E_j has the property that there is exactly one access right $r \in E_i$ which is not in E_j and exactly one access right $s \in E_j$ which is not in E_i. What is the maximal and what the minimal number of environments that can exist if each access right occurs in one environment at least? Discuss which representation of environments is the most efficient in both cases.

2. The access rule for *own* variables in ALGOL 60 is that such a variable is accessible in the block B in which it is declared and its inner blocks (except for the inner blocks in which the name is redeclared) and the *own* variable retains its value in between activations of block B. An *own* variable cannot be implemented as a variable declared in a surrounding block of B, because there would be a possible name conflict or the surrounding block would have access to the *own* variable, which it should not. Also, one must be careful that an *own* variable declared at block depth k is not accessible to all blocks at depths equal or greater than k. Devise a protection model for *own* variables.

3. The function "openreading(x)", where x is a file name with an optional user ID, performs the protection check and opens the file for reading by the caller, if possible. The procedure places the pointer to the first block of the file in a location RFILE. Write a program for "openreading" that could be used in the file system described in section 9.3.

4. Let the page replacement algorithm select a page to be removed from $user_i$'s page table if $user_i$ needs another page. The selected page could be a page shared with other users. Compare how adequate the following implementations of sharing pages are with regard to replacement. a) Every user of a shared page has a descriptor which points to the location of that page. b) Every user of a shared page has a descriptor which points to an entry in a shared page table. The entry in this table points to the location of the shared page.

5. Instead of having several descriptors in different page tables point to a shared page or a descriptor of a shared page, there could be one single shared page table accessible to all processes. Now a process has access to two page tables; to its own, and to the shared page table. This method has the obvious advantage that the space is saved of all the descriptors of shared pages in the private page tables. How does this method compare to the two schemes of problem four with respect to the protection of pages? What impact would this implementation have on the replacement algorithm?

READING LIST

Data base management is nowadays a topic in its own right. One gets some idea of what this term covers by reading [1]. Protection based on capabilities is discussed in [3, 5]. Reading of [2] is recommended for understanding the distinction between protection and security. Implementation of protection is discussed in [5, 6].

1. CODASYL Systems Committee, "Introduction to Feature Analysis of Generalized Data Base Management Systems," *Comm. ACM* 14, 5 (May 1971).

2. Conway, R. W., W. L. Maxwell, and H. L. Morgan, "On the Implementation of Security Measures in Information Systems," *Comm. ACM* 15, 4 (April 1972).

3. Fabry, F. S., "Capability-Based Addressing," *Comm. ACM* 17, 7 (July 1974).

4. Ritchie, D. M., and K. Thompson, "The UNIX Time Sharing System," *Comm. ACM* 17, 7 (July 1974).

5. Saltzer, J. H., "Protection and Control of Information Sharing in Multics," *Comm. ACM* 17, 7 (July 1974).

6. Wulf, W. A., et al., "HYDRA the Kernel of a Multiprocessor Operating System," *Comm. ACM* 17, 6 (June 1974).

10. System Design Issues

10.1 DEADLOCK AVOIDANCE

10.1.1 A deadlock occurs if processes are waiting for resources which will not be released. In its simplest form, a process P_1 is holding a resource A and waits for a resource B, while a process P_2 is holding resource B and waits for resource A. In section 3.5 we saw how two processes can get themselves in such a state if P_1 executes in succession the P operations P(A); P(B) and process P_2 P(B); P(A), where the semaphores A and B have the initial value one. In the general deadlock state, every process of a group is waiting for a resource which is in use by one of the other processes in the group.

The danger of deadlock states is primarily present in the allocation of nonpreemptible resources. But we may also find allocation states of preemptible resources which are almost equivalent to deadlock states. A preemptible resource has the nice property that it can be taken away from its user, if need be. However, if the price of preempting a resource is high, we cannot afford to preempt resources too frequently. Primary storage is an example of this situation. A page frame is preempted at the price of saving a page and loading one. If too many processes share the primary store, each process has available only a small fraction of the pages it needs. As a result, preempting occurs very frequently and the paging system starts thrashing. This state is not any better than a deadlock state.

In this section we discuss how deadlocks in resource allocation states can be avoided if some minimal information is available about the possible needs of a process. We discuss the case of a number of resources of one uniform type and the case of different types of resources. The objective of a deadlock avoidance strategy is to utilize the resources better than would otherwise be possible.

10.1.2 Let user processes $U_1, U_2, \ldots, U_m$ compete for the resources $R_1, R_2, \ldots, R_n$. The resources are identical, so any one of the resources can be allocated if a user process requests one. We assume that the maximum number of resources a process needs at some time is known. This number is called its claim. For instance, a process uses three resources for a long time; then it needs five resources for a while; next it releases three resources and uses two for another period of time; finally the process releases both resources. The claim of this process, for the time beginning at the moment it requests the first resource up to the moment it releases the last resource, is five, the maximum number of resources it ever needs during this period. In some cases the claim is precisely known in advance (for example, the use of peripheral devices); in other cases the maximum number of resources needed is not precisely known in advance, but can be estimated reasonably well (for example, the number of pages needed to work smoothly). Further on we will see that it does not matter much if the estimate is somewhat too high.

The allocation state is determined by the claims of the user processes and the number of resources allocated to each of them. Four allocation states are plotted in figure 10.1a for $m = 3$, $n = 12$.

In all the allocation states of figure 10.1a, the processes together have in use 10 resources, so two resources remain free. The starting point of a user in the pictures above indicates the user's claim. The position of the arrowhead determines how many resources a process needs to reach its claim. This is the distance from the arrowhead to point zero.

We assume that the resource allocation is subject to these two rules: a) a

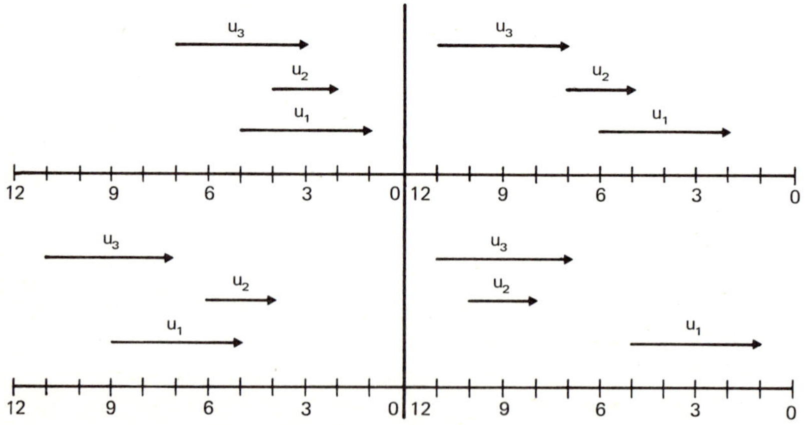

Figure 10.1a Some allocation states with three users and 12 resources

user process will not request more resources than it claimed; b) if a process has in use as many resources as it claimed, it will release all the resources in due time.

The four pictures of figure 10.1a are said to represent realizable allocation states because they satisfy these three conditions:

a. No process claimed more resources than available in the system
b. No process uses more resources than it claimed
c. The number of allocated resources is less than (or equal to) the total number of available resources.

If c_i represents the claim of user $process_i$, a_i the number of resources presently allocated to user $process_i$, n the total number of available resources, and rem the number of unallocated resources, a realizable state is characterized by

$$\text{a,b)}\quad 0 \leq a_i \leq c_i \leq n \qquad \text{for } i \in \{1, 2, \ldots, m\}$$

$$\text{c)}\quad \sum_{i=1}^{m} a_i \leq n \qquad \text{or} \qquad rem = n - \sum_{i=1}^{m} a_i \geq 0$$

The first line corresponds to conditions a) and b) and the second line corresponds to condition c).

10.1.3 Although the four allocation states of the pictures in figure 10.1a are realizable states, the second pair may lead to a deadlock state whereas the first pair is entirely safe. It is obvious what is wrong with the third picture. No matter to which user the remaining resources are allocated, no user will have in use as many resources as it claimed. Thus, all three users may request more resources before releasing any, leading to a deadlock. The allocation state of the third picture is therefore called unsafe. The trouble with the fourth picture is less obvious. It seems that everything is all right, because the two remaining resources can be allocated to U_1. This user then has all the resources it needs, so it is able to run to completion and release the resources (we assumed that it would do so). By that time the number of free resources has been increased to six. However, this number is not enough to satisfy either U_2 or U_3, because they may request seven or eight more resources. Thus, the allocation state of the fourth picture may also lead to a deadlock and is therefore unsafe.

The allocation states of the first and second picture are safe. This means we can show that all users can request as many resources as they claimed and the requested number will be allocated to these users at some time. In the first picture, allocating the two resources to U_1 or U_2 satisfies that user completely. After one of these has finished there will be at least four free resources. This number is sufficient for either one of the two remaining users. The users in the first picture can be serviced in the order U_1, U_2, U_3 or U_1, U_3, U_2 or U_2, U_1, U_3 or U_2, U_3, U_1. We can easily show that the second picture also represents a safe state. The users in that picture can be serviced in the order U_1, U_2, U_3, but in no other order.

So we see that some realizable states are safe and others are not. There is a condition which precisely determines whether a given realizable allocation state is safe or not. This condition can be expressed in terms of a picture as in figure 10.1a. We proceed as follows. Draw the allocation segments of all user processes and draw a vertical line l_x through the coordinate x. Some of the allocation segments are entirely to the left of l_x, others are entirely to the right of l_x, and some are intersected by l_x (see figure 10.1b).

The fact that we deal with realizable states means that all the allocation segments are contained in the total segment and that the sum of all the allocation segments is not greater than the total segment. In addition to the characteristics of a realizable state, the safety condition states:

> A realizable state is safe if and only if for all $x \in \{0, 1, \ldots, n\}$ the sum of the segment parts to the left of the vertical through x is less or equal to the part of the total segment to the left of x.

The safety test applied to a realizable state is obviously satisfied for $x = 0$ and $x = n$. In $x = 0$, all allocation segments are to the left of l_x and the total segment is also entirely to the left of l_0. Thus, for $x = 0$ the test amounts to checking $\sum_{i=1}^{m} a_i \leq n$, which is true in a realizable state. The test is satisfactory for $x = n$, because there are no segments which start to the left of l_n, so the sum of all the parts left of l_n is zero.

The safety condition applied to figure 10.1b shows that that state is safe. The critical point is $x = 3$, where the sum of the allocation segment left ends is equal to 17 and the length of the left part of the total segment is also

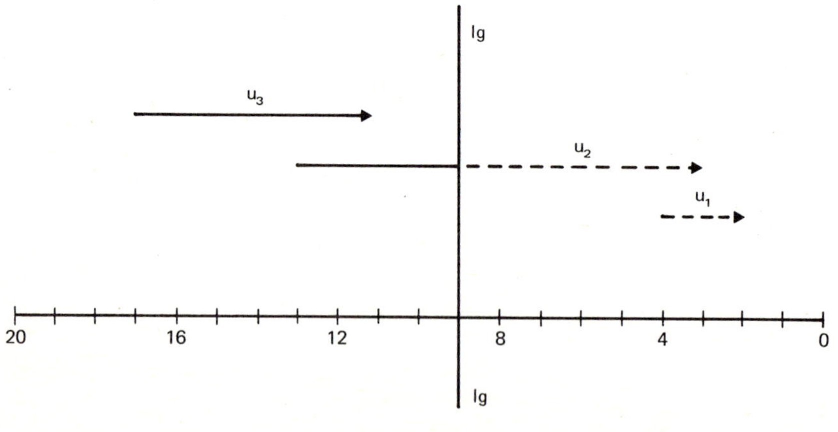

Figure 10.1b Graphical representation of the safety condition

equal to 17. It turns out that there are two free resources; the users can be serviced in the order (U_1, U_2, U_3) and no other.

Applied to the four pictures of figure 10.1a, the safety condition shows that the first two pictures are safe (the critical points are $x = 2$ and $x = 5$), but the third and fourth are not, because the safety condition fails for both pictures in $x = 7$ and other points.

In order to show that the safety condition is necessary and sufficient, we denote the sum of the allocation segment parts to the left of l_x by left(x) and to the right by right(x). The part of the total segment to the left of l_x has the length $n-x$. Thus the safety condition is left(x) $\leq n-x$.

Suppose there is a coordinate $x \in \{0, 1, \ldots, n\}$ for which

$$\text{left}(x) > n-x$$

The equation

$$\text{left}(x)+\text{right}(x)+\text{rem} = n$$

is valid for all x in the interval. Combining these two yields

$$n-(\text{right}(x)+\text{rem}) > n-x \qquad \text{or} \qquad \text{right}(x)+\text{rem} < x.$$

This says that the sum of all the right parts, even if all the remaining resources were allocated, is always less than x. This implies that none of the left parts can be extended with a right part of length x. But a right part of that length is needed to reach $x = 0$. Therefore, the state is not safe.

To prove that the condition is sufficient, assume that the state is not safe, but left(x) $\leq n-x$ for all $x \in \{0, 1, \ldots, n\}$. Now there are allocation segments which can never be extended up to $x = 0$. Of those segments take the one with the rightmost arrowhead (in case of a tie, it does not matter which one). Let this arrowhead be $x = x'$. Since left(x') $\leq n-x'$, right(x')+rem $\geq x'$. If right(x') > 0, then there are arrowheads to the right of x'. These belong to allocation segments which can be extended to $x = 0$, so in due time at least an amount equal to right(x') will be returned. By that time rem $\geq x'$, so there are then enough resources to extend the allocation segment with its arrowhead in x'. This is in contradiction to the initial assumption. Thus, if the state is not safe, it is not possible that left(x) $\leq n-x$ for all $x \in \{0, 1, \ldots, n\}$.

10.1.4 With regard to an implementation, it is better to keep a record of the position of a user process than of the number of resources allocated to it. The claim, allocation and position are related by $c_i - a_i = p_i$. Since a test for (non) negative is cheap in every machine, we define $s(x) = n-x-\text{left}(x)$ for all $x \in \{0, 1, \ldots, n\}$. The numbers s(x) can be recorded in an array $S[0{:}n-1]$, where S_k is initialized to $n-k$. When a user moves from position $p+1$ to position p, element S_k must be decremented by one for all k in $[0{:}p]$. If a user process releases a resource and moves from position p to position $p+1$, all elements S_k are incremented by one for k in $[0{:}p]$.

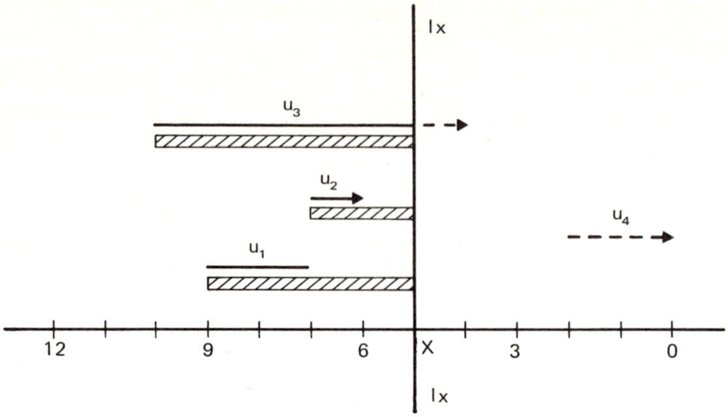

Figure 10.1c Graphical representation of max(x) = MAX(left(x))

Deadlocks can be avoided if the allocation state is always safe. An algorithm that checks the safety simply tests whether all elements $s_k \geq 0$. If so, the state is safe; otherwise it is not. It is normally not necessary to check all n elements of array S. The safety test is applied when a user process requests another resource. We then wish to know whether the new state, after allocating the resource, will be safe. If the allocation brings the requesting user in position p, the elements with index k in [0:p] are decremented by one; but the others remain unchanged. It is therefore not necessary to test the elements $S_{p+1}, S_{p+2}, \ldots, S_n$.

If n is not very small ($n > 5$), the test can be further simplified or deliberately shortened without losing much in effectiveness. With this goal in mind, we introduce the function max(x) which is equal to the maximum value that can be reached by left(x) (see figure 10.1c).

The maximum value which left(x) can assume for a given set of user processes is determined by the coordinate x and the claims of the processes. For a given x, only claims $c_i > x$ count, because others do not have a part left of the vertical l_x. The contribution to max(x) of a user_i with claim $c_i > x$ is $(c_i - x)$, so $\max(x) = \sum (c_i - x)$ for all $i \in \{1, \ldots, m\}$ for which $c_i > x$. Naturally, $\text{left}(x) \leq \max(x)$.

If there is (for a given allocation state) a coordinate x′ in [0:n] for which $\max(x') \leq n - x$, then it turns out that $\max(x) \leq n - x$ for all x in [x′:n]. This is shown by mathematical induction. Given that the relation holds for $x = x'$, assume it holds for $x = y$, where $x' \leq y < n$. Let q be the number of allocation segments which start to the left of l_y (that is, the number of claims c_i for which $c_i > y$). The relation $\max(y+1) = \max(y) - q$ is always true. If $q = 0$, then $\max(y+1) = \max(y) = 0$, so in this case $\max(y+1) \leq n-(y+1)$ is true, because $y < n$. If $q > 0$,

$$\max(y+1) \leq \max(y)-q \leq \max(y)-1 \leq n-y-1 \leq n-(y+1)$$

Thus, if the relation is true for $x = y$, it is also true for $x = y+1$. The induction principle states that $\max(x) \leq n-x$ is then true for all x in $[x':n]$.

The combination of $\text{left}(x) \leq \max(x)$ for all x in $[0:n]$ and a given $x = x'$ for which $\max(x') \leq n-x'$ leads to the important conclusion that, in that case, $\text{left}(x) \leq \max(x) \leq n-x$ for all x in $[x':n]$. That is to say, with the relation given for x', it is not necessary to test any of the elements $S_x, \ldots, S_{n-1}$, because the relation guarantees that these elements are not negative! (Remember that $S_k = n-k-\text{left}(k)$.)

With regard to an implementation, it is more convenient to replace max(x) by a variable which can be submitted to a less-than-zero test. Therefore, let array $M[0:n-1]$, where $M_k = n-k-\max(k)$, be initialized at the same value as array $S[0:n-1]$ (i.e. $M_k := S_k := n-k$). When a new user process with a claim $= c$ is admitted to the group of competitors for the resources, all the elements M_k for which $k \leq c$ are decremented by $c-k$. When a process with claim $= c$ leaves, the same elements are incremented by $c-k$.

Working with array M has a great advantage over working with array S, because M solely depends on the claims which means that M does not change when a resource is allocated or released! Array M changes only when a user process enters or leaves the group. Array M has therefore a more static character than array S, which must be updated every time a resource is allocated or released.

It is useful to implement both arrays as part of a deadlock avoidance scheme. Array M is updated when a process enters or leaves, and array S is updated when a resource is allocated or returned. At all times we retain the smallest index k for which $M_k \geq 0$ (this index may get larger when a process enters or it may get smaller when a process leaves). This index k determines how many elements of array S must be tested. If a resource is requested which would bring the requesting user process to position p, the elements $S_0, \ldots, S_m$ must be tested where $m = \text{MIN}(k-1,p)$. The resource can be allocated safely if all these elements are greater than zero, because subtracting in that case one does not create a negative element.

A program which controls the admission of user programs uses the global variable "minindex" in which it retains the minimum index k for which $M_k \geq 0$.

```
enter(c = claim) =
begin local k = c
   for k in−[0:c] do M_k ← M_k − c + k
      if M_k ≥ 0 then minindex ← k fi
   od
   claim_i ← position_i ← c
end
```

The index i identifies the process which enters the group of competitors. The minus sign indicates that the variable k steps through the range from right to left (from c to 0). This explains the name "minindex".

The safety test uses minindex to see how far array S must be scanned. The test is applied every time a $user_i$ requests a resource. The resource is allocated if the state after allocation is safe.

request =
begin local m = MIN(minindex,$position_i$)$-$1; *local* k
  if some k *in* [0:m] *sat* $S_k = 0$ *then*
    REPORT("resource cannot be allocated")
  else $position_i \leftarrow position_i - 1$; assign free resource to user(i)
      for k *in* [0:$position_i$] *do* $S_k \leftarrow S_k - 1$ *od*
  fi
end

10.1.5 The case of resources of various types is more complicated. A simple example shows that it is not enough to apply a deadlock avoidance discipline separately to each type of resource. Let there be three resources of type T_1 and three of type T_2. User U_1 needs three resources of type T_1 and two of type T_2; user U_2 needs two resources of type T_1 and three of type T_2. All users are holding one resource of each type. The allocation state is shown in figure 10.1d.

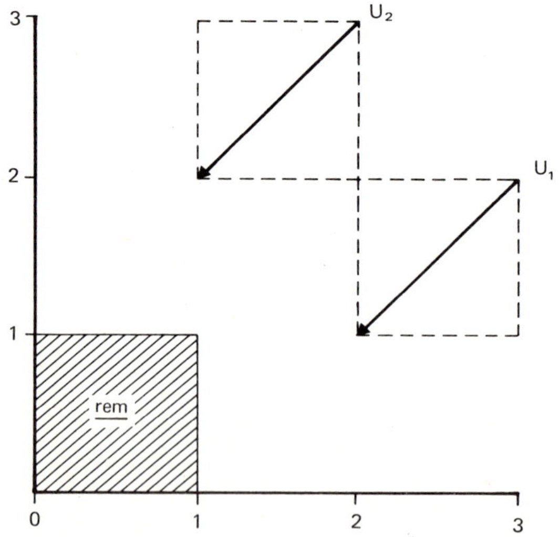

Figure 10.1d Allocation state after allocating one resource of each type to U1 and U2

In this state user U_1 can request two more resources of type T_1, and user U_2 can request one more. Looking at type T_1 alone, the allocation state is safe, because the remaining resource of type T_1 can be allocated to U_2, and when U_2returns its resources, U_1 can get two more resources of type T_1. The allocation state for type T_2 is also safe. However, the combined allocation state is not safe, because U_1 may request two T_1 resources before releasing a T_2 resource and U_2, in turn, may request two T_2 resources before it releases its type T_1 resource. Thus the system can be deadlocked in a way which cannot be derived from the state of each resource type separately.

Analogous to the one type resource case, we call an allocation state safe if it would be possible to service the competing processes in some order when all processes request what they claimed. The claim of a process is now a vector $e_i = (c_1, c_2, \ldots, c_t)$ with an element for each resource type. The allocation of a process is a vector of $a_i = (a_1, a_2, \ldots, a_t)$, which changes when process$_i$ gets a resource or releases one.

Among the competing processes there must be at least one user process which needs of every resource type not more than the number of resources that remain of that type. This means in terms of figure 10.1d that there must be at least one process whose rectangle intersects or touches the rectangle representing the remaining resources. Otherwise every process can request of at least one type more resources than remain before releasing any. That would be a deadlock state. Assume there is a user process as described above and let this user be U_1. The vector *rem* represents the number of remaining resources of each type; the vector $rank_k := c_k - a_k$ specifies how many resources of each type process P_k may request before it is satisfied. The relation

$$c_1 - a_1 \leq rem \qquad \text{or} \qquad rank_1 \leq rem$$

must be true or else the allocation may get into a deadlock. User process U_1 is able to get all the resources it needs, so it will return all the resources it now uses in due time. By that time $rem' = rem + a_1$, because U_1 presently has a_1 resources in use. If the state is safe, there must be another user process, U_2, for which that number of resources is sufficient to get all it needs. Thus, there must be a user process U_2 for which

$$c_2 - a_2 \leq rem' = rem + a_1 \qquad \text{or} \qquad rank_2 \leq rem + a_1$$

Extending this reasoning for all user processes, we find that it must be possible to number the user processes such that the set of relations

$$c_i - a_i \leq rem + \sum_{k<i} a_k \qquad \text{or} \qquad rank_i \leq rem + \sum_{k<i} a_k$$

is true for i = 1, 2, . . . , m. It is obvious that this safety condition is also sufficient, because, if such a set of relations holds, the processes could be serviced in the order of the numbering. As long as the allocation state is safe, it cannot lead to a deadlock. Therefore, a resource request should be granted if and only if the set of relations still holds after allocation.

It seems that this safety condition can be checked only by a backtracking algorithm which scans all m! possible ways of numbering the m user processes. Assume that k ($k < m$) processes have been found which satisfy the first k relations. If the algorithm cannot find a $(k+1)$st process among the $(n-k)$ remaining processes such that the $(k+1)$st relation is satisfied, it seems that the algorithm must backtrack, remove the k-th process and try another in its place. Fortunately, it can be proved that backtracking is not necessary. It can be shown that, if a $(k+1)$st process cannot be found to satisfy the $(k+1)$st relation, the allocation state is not safe. This implies that, if the state is safe, a numbering which has been successful up to k can be extended to include all user processes.

Assume that a subset K of k user processes has been found such that the first k relations are satisfied. Assume that a $(k+1)$st cannot be found among the $(m-k)$ remaining processes such that the $(k+1)$st relation is satisfied. If the allocation state is nevertheless safe, there exists at least one numbering such that all m relations are satisfied. Although we don't know this numbering, the users in K occur somewhere in it (see figure 10.1e).

Look at user process U_q, which is the first in the existing numbered sequence that does not belong to subset K. (There is such a q because $k < m$.) This user process U_q satisfies

$$rank_q \leq rem + \sum_{k \epsilon K} a_k$$

where the numbering refers to the existing sequence. The last term consists entirely of allocations to elements of subset K. U_q can be used as U_{k+1} to extend the attempted numbering, because it also satisfies the relation

$$rank_k + 1 \leq rem + \sum_{l \epsilon K} a_l$$

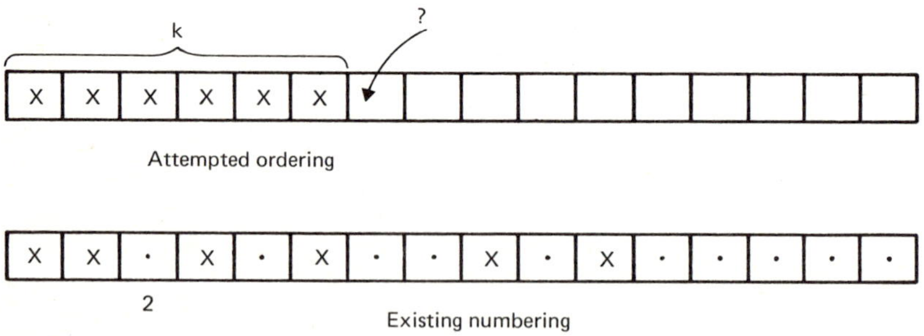

Figure 10.1e An attempt to number the user processes

in which the last term contains the allocations to all elcments of subset K. However, this is in conflict with the assumption that there is no user process among the (m − k) remaining processes which can be used as (k + 1)st process in the row. Thus, there exists no numbering such that all m relations are satisfied, and the state is unsafe. This implies at the same time that there is no need to backtrack, because if the attempted numbering cannot be extended, none can.

An algorithm which checks a given allocation state for safety in the multi-type resource case attempts to find a way of numbering the user processes such that the m relations are satisfied. The algorithm starts out with all the processes in the set NS (here represented by an array) and tries to remove all elements from this set, satisfying the relations one by one.

```
safetytest = Boolean
begin local NS[1:m] = {1, 2, 3, . . . , m}      $ m is the number of competitors
  local q = m; local i, k; local y = r
  repeat k ← 0
  for i in [1:q] do
     if rank[NS_i] ≤ y then y ← y + a[NS_i]
     else k ← k + 1; NS_k ← NS_i fi
  od
  until q = k or k = 0 do q ← k od
  safetytest ← (k = 0)
end
```

Every element of NS is tried. If it cannot be used for the next relation, it is returned to a used place in Ns. If it satisfies the next relation, its allocation is added to vector y which includes *rem* and the sigma term of the last relation. If no elements are returned to NS (k = 0) the algorithm reports a safe state. If all the elements are returned to NS (k = q) the algorithm reports that the state is not safe.

This algorithm is straightforward, but not very fast for large m. It has a *for* loop within a *repeat* statement, both of which are executed a number of times proportional to m. We say that the algorithm is executed in $O(m^2)$ time (because of the nesting). There are algorithms which test for safety in $O(m \log_2 m)$ time. (The savings come from a better method for sorting NS, for instance, by a heapsort; see section 6.5.) The faster safety check algorithms are described in the literature.

PROBLEMS

1. An allocation state in which resources have been allocated to two or more user processes which claim all the resources is always an unsafe state.

Let U_1 and U_2 both have a claim $= n$ (the number of resources) and assume that both have in use one resource. The safety condition for a single type of resource says that left(x) $\leq n-x$ for all x in [0:n]. In the given situation, we have left$(n-1) = 2$ and this is greater than $n-(n-1) = 1$. Thus, this state is unsafe. Prove that the following general statement is true: the allocation state is unsafe if resources are allocated to more than k user processes which each have claim $> n-k$. This means that a safe state can contain more user processes with a small claim than with a large claim.

2. Give a safe allocation state for a single type of resource. Prove that there is at least one user process which needs, in addition to what it already has, not more than the number of remaining resources. Next, show that the state is again safe if a resource is allocated to any one of the user processes which needs no more resources than remain.

3. The safety test for a single type of resource is implemented by testing $S_k \geq 0$ where $S_k = n-k-$left(k). The test can be terminated if, in addition to S, array M[0:n−1] records the maximum value which left(x) can assume. If k is the smallest index such that $M_k \geq 0$, the S test can be stopped at index $(k-1)$. Write a program which updates array S when a resource is released and a program which updates array M when a process leaves the competing group. Also, prove that a safe state is transformed into another safe state when a resource is released.

4. The smallest index k for which $M_k \geq 0$ could be fixed instead of having it float with process arrival and departure. Fixing k means that an arriving process is submitted to an admission test. A process is not admitted if the result would be that $M_k < 0$. Is it still necessary to record $M_0, \ldots, M_k$? If not, is it useful to do so? The advantage of fixing the smallest index k is in the fact that now the elements $M_{k+1}, \ldots, M_n$ and $S_k, \ldots, S_n$ are entirely superfluous, so there is not even space needed for these elements. It seems that this pushes the idea too far. Show that then the total claim is less than the available number of resources. This leads to a waste of resource capacity if the user processes use only a fraction of what they claim.

5. More interesting than the general test for safety is the test which assures that a transition from a safe state leads again to a safe state. Let a safe allocation state be given for a set of resources of various types. Let user process U_k request some resources (not more than one of each type). Prove that the safety test applied to the new allocation state can be terminated as soon as U_k can be used to satisfy the next relation in the general safety condition. Modify the given program for the general safety test to exploit this possible short cut.

10.2 MODULARITY

10.2.1 Modularity is one of those words frequently used without a precise meaning. Put in the most general terms, it expresses that a program or a system is constructed in parts. Partitioning a program or a system is an important design issue. The partitioning helps the designer to concentrate on particular aspects and it allows him to abstract from irrelevant detail. Moreover, suitable partitioning facilitates verification and debugging of the code. Finally, a well-partitioned system is easier to modify, because it is possible to understand a small part without having to comprehend the entire system.

The term modularity lacks a fixed interpretation, because there are many ways in which a system or a program can be partitioned. The way in which it is split in parts primarily depends on the modularization principle applied by the designers. It is necessary to adopt such a principle, because the designer must decide how the system is going to be structured *before* it is designed! More than a decade ago it was thought that a very simple partitioning would suffice. On the grounds that user programs are not allowed to execute some machine instructions, the system was split in two parts distinguished by the terms user mode and supervisor mode. It was soon recognized that such a bipartitioning is insufficient. A monolithic supervisor does not simplify the task of the designer; it is hard to debug, it proved to be far from flawless, and modifications are very hard to implement because of unknown effects on other parts of the system. Designing a layer structured system is more than a mere extension of the supervisor/user idea. Here we find a partitioning in which each piece is distinctly smaller in terms of design effort and size of code than the system as a whole. If the layers are properly designed, there is a fundamental protection of one layer against malfunctioning of another layer. The interaction of layers is restricted to a well-defined interface. This makes it easier to test a layer or verify that it operates as it should. Also, the effect of modifying the code is restricted to one layer in a well-designed layered system.

The major subject of this section is a particular modularization principle which seems promising for future system design. It is based on some recent ideas which developed in the programming language design area and attempts to satisfy the fundamental criteria for a good modularization principle. These criteria are discussed below.

10.2.2 The usefulness of a modularization principle is judged by two criteria:

a. Does it help the designer to separate logic from implementation?
b. Does it minimize the interconnections between modules?

Normal interdependence of modules is described in terms of the service which one module can acquire from another. If module M_1 provides service s to module M_2, the latter must know how to use this service. For instance, a user has the right to open or close a file. All the user has to know about an operation is its name, effect and the actual parameter format. It is of no concern to the user how these operations search the master directory or even how the directory is structured. In general terms: user module M_2 must have a precise specification of service s, but the implementation of service s in service module M_1 should be entirely hidden from M_2.

A clear and accurate specification is of the utmost importance for the documentation of a system. It is a particularly bad practice to describe a program or system in terms of its implementation. It is, for instance, hard to derive the semantics of a demand paging system by reading the programs for page fault handling and page transfer. The idea is much better explained in terms of frames, page tables, page descriptors and the possible absence of a page.

Interconnections between modules are mainly defined by the specified services provided by one module to another module. If specification and implementation are separated, a modification in the coding, or even representation of the data structures involved, has no effect on other modules. A change in the specification effects, of course, all modules which make use of the service. For instance, the implementation of semaphore waiting lists could be changed from a linked list to an array structure. Such a change has a great impact on the waiting list operations which insert or delete elements into or from a waiting list. However, its logic or the way a P or V is called is not affected by the radical change in representation.

Some other interconnections are there by convention, for example, function call and parameter mechanism. It is general practice to describe the actual parameters in locations immediately following a procedure call. The procedure entry code makes use of this knowledge when it decodes the descriptors one by one and initializes the function parameters. A change in this protocol has a profound effect on all programs if all the calling sequences must be changed. The designer is fortunate if a compiler is available which can generate the calling sequences. The modification can then be restricted to two places in the compiler: one change in the program which generates the calling sequence and another change in the program for procedure entry.

Interconnections which are generally bad are of the kind where one module has direct access to the internal structure of another module. These are the interconnections of the kind where module M_1 happens to know the meaning of bit i in word w of module M's page p and uses this knowledge in its own program. Such interconnections cause the bugs to be hard to find and make it extremely difficult to trace all places affected by a modification in the implementation. Therefore, interconnections between modules based on knowledge about internal coding or data representation must be avoided. Interaction between modules must be arranged through shared data which is explicitly created for that purpose.

D. L. Parnas proposed to use the need-to-know principle which in the military determines a person's clearance status. A module must know how to use a service; therefore it needs a precise specification. This is what it needs to know. However, it must not have direct access to the implementation of that service. This is what the user module should not know. Restricting the knowledge which one module has about another module to what it needs to know helps to avoid troublesome interconnections.

10.2.3 Programming languages have long provided means to separate application from implementation. The feature that provides this is the procedure or function mechanism. At the call site the programmer must understand what effect a particular function call has on its context. He must know the type of parameter that can be passed and must know about possible side effects caused by the function call. All this information is part of the specification of the function. However, at the call site the implementation of the function is not relevant. The implementation is defined separately in a function declaration. Changes in the coding of the function which do not affect the specification also do not affect the function calls. The function mechanism is therefore a suitable example of a feature which satisfies the two modularization criteria.

A more recent development in programming language design is the definition of data types (called "mode" in ALGOL68, "type" in PASCAL(1970) and "class" in SIMULA67). This feature allows the programmer to define the internal structure of objects of his choice.

The data type facility is even more powerful if the programmer can also name the operations which can be performed on the objects of the defined type. This facility is provided up to a certain extent in ALGOL68, but it is fully present in SIMULA67. A class in SIMULA67 has various "fields"; some of these fields represent data, but others name a function which can be performed on an object of that type. In the spirit of the class concept in SIMULA67 we could define

```
type complex =
  fields re, im = real
  let x, y = real, u, v = complex in
    proc com(x, y) = complex; begin com.re ← x; com.im ← y end
    proc inprod(u, v) = real; inprod ← u.re*v.re+u.im*v.im
    proc cadd(u, v) = complex
      begin cadd.re ← u.re+v.re; cadd.im ← u.im+v.im end
    proc cmul(u, v) = complex
      begin emul.re ← u.re*v.re−u.im*v.im;
        cmul.im ← u.re*v.im+u.im*v.re end
end
```

The type definition specifies that objects of type complex have the internal structure of a real number pair. The procedures declared in the type definition determine the set of operations which can be performed on objects of this type. We may find, for instance, the statement z ← com(p,q) in a program in which p and q have been declared as real variables (or constants) and z as a complex variable. All the operations listed in this type are procedures which return a value as result. The type of this value is indicated following the equal sign on the first procedure declaration line. The name of the operation is used in the body of the procedure to name the result. The dot notation represents the field selection.

The need-to-know principle is strongly enforced if we set as a rule that the internal structure of a typed object is not accessible outside the type definition. (This rule is indeed provided in SIMULA67, though not by default.) This rule assures that application and implementation are strictly separated. The internal structure is not accessible at the call site, so the latter is independent of the implementation. If, for instance, the representation of complex numbers in Cartesian coordinates is replaced by a representation in polar coordinates the calling sequences remain unaltered. All changes are concentrated in one place, the type definition. Also, the fact that the type definition precisely describes what a programmer can do with an object of type complex protects the programmer against incorrect or tricky operations on the internal structure of complex objects. Typed objects present themselves as atomic to every context outside the type definition. In many programming languages the types integer and real are treated exactly this way. Objects of these types are known by the operations which can be performed on them, but their internal structure is hidden from the programmer. (We do not change a bit in the exponent part of a real number!)

In the remainder of this section we explore how data type definitions can be used as a modularization principle. Applying this principle, a module corresponds to a data type or a set of data types sharing a common data structure. Data type definitions are used to describe part of a paging system for a hypothetical 16 bit machine, HM, which looks somewhat like a PDP-11.

The CPU of HM is equipped with a set of eight working page registers, WP[0:7]. A loaded working page register points to a main store frame (an area in locations [512∗m:512∗m+511] in the main store, where m is 128 or 256 or 512, depending on the size of the main store. The working page register has a two bit access code and a two bit protection field. The access field contains the used and dirty bit; the protection field has room for four protection codes.

All store locations are accessed through a working page register. An address is a pair (p,w), where p indicates a working page register and w a word location in the frame pointed at by WP[p]. The address mapping

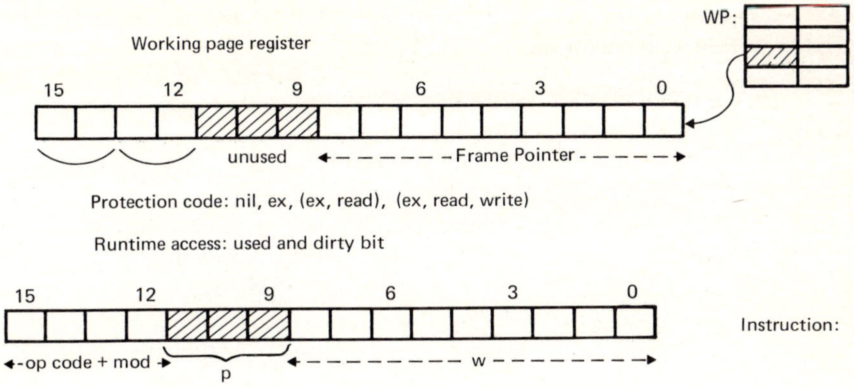

Figure 10.2a Working page register format and address format

hardware interprets the field [9:11] of an instruction as the p index and the field [0:8] as the word index. The physical location is found by the rule

$$\text{location} = 512 * \text{WP}[p] + w$$

HM has a nice short address field of only 12 bits. Even more important is the fact that the paging hardware does not need to check whether or not the references page is present! The paging hardware applies the same quasi-static checking technique as provided by the open file) feature. The presence of a page must be checked at the time that a working register is loaded in one of the working page registers. However, there is no check every time this register is accessed in the address map.

The protection code determines the way in which the frame can be accessed. Depending on the protection code, certain operations cannot be performed on the page in that frame. The protection code provides read, write and execute protection. The bits u, d are set by the hardware when a WP is accessed. Bit u is always set, bit d set only if the access results in storing information in the frame.

A small subset of the HM instruction set applies to working page registers. The applicable commands are: load, copy, and clear. The latter sets the protection code to zero so that the working page register then points to a totally inaccessible page. The copy instruction allows the running program to read out a working page register. The value read can be placed in a CPU register or a storage cell that is accessible to the running program. The load instruction copies the contents of a CPU register or a main store location into a working page register.

So much for the hardware of HM. Now we describe a paging system for HM which provides the necessary privacy but also the ability to share pages.

First we define a data type page descriptor and then build a paging module based on this type definition.

```
type page descriptor = machine word
                                    $ a machine word is a 16-bit array
  field page state = page descriptor[14:15]
  field page protection = page descriptor[12:13]
  field frame ref = page descriptor[0:11]
  let w = page descriptor, m = main store address in
    proc clear(w) = begin w.protection ← (0,0) end
    proc reset state(w) = begin w.state ← (0,0) end
    proc pstate(w) = integer; begin pstate ← w//2^14 end
    proc protection code(w) = integer
         begin protection code ← (w//2^12)%4 end
    proc frame(w) = integer; begin frame ← w%2^12 end
    comment the symbol % represents the remainder function;
    proc load(w,m) = begin w ← Main store[m] end
end
```

This type definition describes commands which can easily be constructed using the hardware instructions that apply to working page registers. Assuming that HM has eight working page registers, the paging module declares WP = *array*[10:7] *of* page descriptor. As it stands, WP can be loaded from any store location by any running program. The paging module will make this impossible. In addition to WP, the paging module declares three arrays: the page table PT = array[0:4095] *of* page descriptor, the frame table FT = array[0:511] *of* integer, and the table of duplicates DT = array [0:511] *of* integer. Array PT is the universal page table in which all existing pages are described. We use the page state of a descriptor to distinguish four cases: empty = (0,0) if the descriptor does not point to a frame, absent = (0,1) if it points to a frame in the secondary store, unique = (1,0) if it points to a frame in the main store, and double = (1,1) if it points to a frame in the main store which has an exact copy in the secondary store. Array FT is the mapping table of main store frames onto page descriptors. If page p is in frame f, then FT[f] = p. This table is used in order to find the page descriptor attached to a particular WP register. Array DT mainly serves as a backup for the secondary frame references. For instance, if page descriptor p is a double and its page is in main store frame f, the page descriptor then points to f, FT_f = p and DT_f = secondary frame reference.

The page table is chosen so large that we may assume that all page descriptors are permanently stored in the main store (we make this assumption so as to avoid irrelevant complexity of the example). The table is subdivided into 16 sections of half a page each. (The number 16 is chosen arbitrarily.) At any moment there are two sections active, section 0 and section i, where the value i is recorded in the local variable active section. A running program has access to these two sections. A primary frame ref in a working page register less than 256 (bit[8] = 0) refers to section zero; values in the range [256:511] refer to section i. The variable active section serves as the page table base of the running program.

The 16 sections of page descriptors form one shared and 15 separate paging environments, PE_0, PE_1, PE_2, . . . , PE_{15}. Environment PE_1 is reserved for the paging module itself. The first eight pages of PE_1 are permanently reserved for the page table, the ninth for the frame table and the tenth for the duplicate table. The first 10 elements of FT are permanently reserved for pointers to the first 10 PE_1 pages. The first 10 elements of DT are unused. The page descriptors of PE_1 are located in PT[256:511].

The first 10 elements of DT remain void, because there is no backup version of the tables in the secondary store. The first 10 descriptors of PE_1 are initialized at: page state = unique, page protection = (1,1) (so the page module can write into that page), and frame ref = i, where i ranges from zero through 10 for the 10 descriptors (see figure 10.2b).

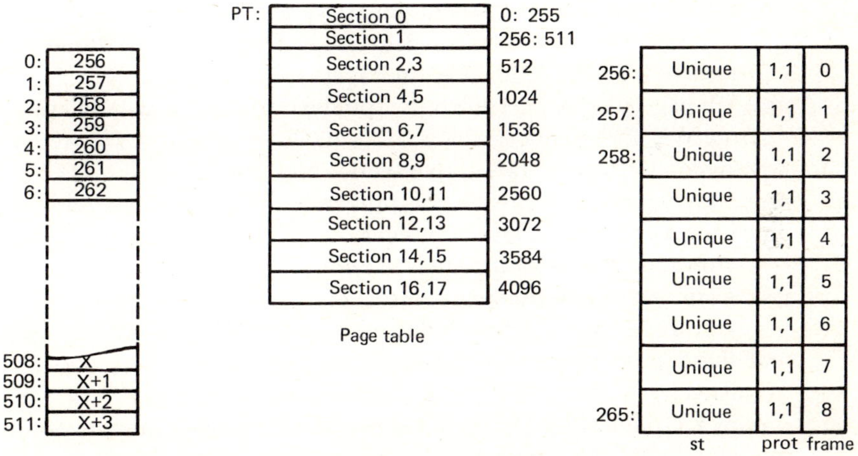

Figure 10.2b Initialization of frame table and page table

The tables and the variable active section are locally defined in the paging module. Thus, these data structures are accessible only in the way defined by the paging module. The operations defined by the paging module are listed in a short module description below.

```
paging module =
let local WP = array[0:7] of page descriptor
    local FT, DT = array [0:511] of integer
    local PT = array [0:4095] of page descriptor
    local active section = oneof [0:15]
    local SECFT = array[0:4095] of bit
      $ SECFT is a bit array, stored in 256 contiguous locations,
        describing the free secondary frames
      $ the initialization has been omitted from this outline
    constant empty = 0, absent = 1, unique = 2, double = 3;
    pindex, wpindex, protection code, findex, i = integer
  in
    proc state(pindex) = integer; begin state ← pstate(PT[pindex]) end
    proc activate (pindex in wpindex) =
        ⟨transfer PT[pindex] to WP[wpindex]⟩
    proc deactivate(wpindex) =
        ⟨remove descriptor from WP[wpindex] and clear it⟩
    proc get shared page(pindex in wpindex) =
        ⟨transfer PT[pindex%256] to WP[wpindex]⟩
    proc create page(protection code) = pindex
        ⟨find a free element PT[x] in the active section and
        initialize PT[x] as an empty page, find a free secondary frame,
        reserve it and store its index in PT[x]⟩
    proc kill page(pindex) = ⟨delete PT[pindex], free the space, delete
       from WP, if present⟩
    proc switch to PE(i) = ⟨set active section to i⟩
    proc copy(wpindex) = integer; begin copy ← WP[wpindex] end
    proc primary frame(pindex) = integer
        ⟨return frame index if page is in main store⟩
    proc secondary frame(pindex) = integer
        ⟨return secondary frame index⟩
    proc share (pindex, protection code) = oneof[0:255]
      ⟨take a free descriptor PT[x] in section zero,
      copy PT[pindex] into PT[x], fill in the protection code and return x⟩
    proc attach(findex to pindex) =
      ⟨store secondary frame reference in DT[findex],
      set PT[pindex] to findex and update both descriptors⟩
    proc detach(pindex) =
      ⟨release frame(PT[pindex]), set frame ref to DT[PT[pindex]],
        remove copy from WP (if any) and update the descriptor states⟩
end
```

Four operations are programmed below so as to demonstrate the use of the type definition and the data structures of the paging module.

```
proc activate (pindex in wpindex) =
begin
   local p = pindex+if pindex < 256 then 0 else 256*(active section-1) fi
   $ this procedure expects a descriptor pointing to a main store frame
   load (WP[wpindex], protection code(PT[pindex])*2^12 frame(PT[pindex]))
end
```

Page faults are not handled in the activate operation. Demand paging can be implemented in a demand paging module. This module provides another version of activate in which the state of the page is inspected. If it is empty or absent, a frame in the main store is selected, and possibly cleared, and the page is fetched through a transfer command. A page replacement algorithm belongs to the internal activities of that module.

```
proc create page(protection code) = pindex
begin local base = 256*active section
   if some k in [base:base+255] sat protection code(PT[k]) = 0 then
      if some j in [0:4095] sat SECF[j] = 0 then
         SECFT[j] ← 1; create page ← k
         load(PT[k], 2^14*empty+(protection code%4)*2^12+j)
      else REPORT("secondary store full") fi
   else REPORT("section full") fi
end

proc attach(findex to pindex) =
begin local p = pindex+if p < 256 then 0 else 256*(active section-1) fi
   $ this procedure expects pstate = empty or absent
   DT[findex] ← frame(PT[p]); FT[findex] ← p
   load(PT[p], (PT[p]-frame(PT[p])+2^15+f))
   $ adding 2^15 changes empty into unique and absent into double
end

proc detach(pindex) =
begin local p = pindex+if p < 256 then 0 else 256*(active section-1) fi
   local k = frame(PT[p])
   $ this procedure expects pstate = unique or double
   if some j in [0:7] sat frame(WP[j]) = k then
      $ if working page register dirty, then pstate must be set to unique
      if pstate(WP[j]) = 3 then load(PT[p], PT[p]-pstate(PT[p]+unique)
         fi
      clear(WP[j])
   fi
   load(PT[p], PT[p]-k-2^15+DT[k])
   $ subtracting 2^15 changes unique into empty and double into absent
   FT[k] ← DT[k] ← 0
end
```

The paging module hides all the details of implementation from the users of this module. Users do not have access to the page table and do not even know about the frame table. It is as if a user has an array of 512 page descriptors, of which he shares the first 256 with all other users. The users are aware of the function of the eight working page registers. The paging module makes the meaning clear by providing the activate and deactivate operations.

This descriptive method applied to a paging module is rather static compared to the earlier descriptors of page fault handling in chapter 7. Here the description centers around the data structures involved, whereas earlier descriptions showed primarily the flow of control from one process to another or from one execution environment to another. It seems that both methods have their merits, but the control flow description has been emphasized too much in the past. One important issue has not been brought up in the data structure description. Although the description specifies all the operations which can be applied to objects of a particular type, the timing constraints are not expressed anywhere. It is evident that, for instance, several executions of share or fetch should not be interleaved. The necessary synchronization can be implemented by P or V operations, or the paging module can be promoted to a true monitoring process. In the latter case, all operations provided by the paging monitor become monitor requests. A slightly different approach is discussed in the next section. It does not create the need for a monitor process with its preferential status and also makes it unnecessary to write calls to P and V in the programs.

PROBLEMS

1. The dimension of a linear vector is the number of elements it contains. Operations on linear vectors are addition, subtraction, multiplication with a scalar, taking the inner product, and computing the length (or modulus) of a vector. The length of a vector is the square root of the sum of the squares of all elements. Write a type definition for linear vectors with elements of type real. The dimension is given as a parameter of the type definition: *type* real vector(n = integer).

2. A machine M has an associative memory of 12 registers. Each register can hold a segment number and the associated segment descriptor in which are stored a protection code, a base address, and the segment length. A virtual address is a pair(s,w), where s is a number in the range [0:255] and w a number in the range [0:segment length − 1]. The hardware decodes a virtual address through the associative memory. If the given segment descriptor number is not in the associative memory, an address exception interrupt occurs (see chapter 7). Design a module which defines a fixed set of segment environments. This module does not have to take care of loading and storing segments.

3. On top of the paging environments designed for machine HM, we plan a system layer in which processes and semaphores are implemented. Assume that the number of processes is fixed. The number of semaphores is also fixed. The set of semaphores includes a private semaphore for each process. Design a semaphore module which defines the P and V. Determine what kind of operations on processes must be available to the semaphore module. (Note that the semaphore module should not know more about the operations on processes than their specification.)

4. In the paging module described in this section several operations have been listed with a short explanation of their functions. Program some of these in more detail particularly: deactivate, kill page and share.

10.3 VERIFICATION

10.3.1 In the Fifties and early Sixties efficiency was considered the most important issue in programmer pragmatics. A programmer was proud of a concise program which performed a computation in a minimum amount of CPU time and a small amount of space. In the late Sixties and early Seventies programmers learned that the attitude of emphasizing efficiency at the cost of transparent structure and documentation is penny-wise and pound-foolish. On the one hand the programmers today can afford to pay somewhat less tribute to efficiency, because the machines are so much faster and larger while the computing cost is much lower than 15 years ago. On the other hand, many programs and systems are so large that it is not possible to understand them as a monolithic object. Partitioning becomes a necessity to be able to manage the design, the testing, and the modifications.

Now, transparent structure is given the highest priority and efficiency comes second. This is not to say that efficiency is unimportant. On the contrary, the interest in efficiency is shown by the many studies on system performance and scheduling disciplines. The ranking of structuring and efficiency means that the programmer should not trade good structure for the sake of saving a bit or a microsecond of CPU time. However, given a well-structured design, it should be implemented as efficiently as possible. A transparent structure is in the long run more efficient, because it may save dear manhours of debugging and finding the places where the code must be changed.

The task of verifying that the design of a system and its implementation are correct has been approached in several ways. Special systems have been developed to prove the correctness of programs. Theorists have classified program structures of which the correctness can be formally proved. Another school of thought advocates the idea that the correctness must be an inherent part of the design. This means that the designer must construct his system so that he can prove that it is correct. This constructive approach to the verification task now seems the most promising, particularly for a system in which several computations run in parallel.

This section shows some examples of the constructive verification approach. The verification is greatly enhanced if a system is composed of constructs with provable properties. (It is like the chess player who is able to evaluate a board position by virtue of the strict rules by which the pieces can move.) A particular construct, called a path expression, is presented in this section to demonstrate how the correctness of synchronization relationships can be verified.

10.3.2 The design language in which a system is described can be a great help to verify simple properties of the system. For instance, if the language provides a *while* statement, the sequence of statements, *while* BE *do* S_1 *od*; S_2, has the property that, when (and if) statement S_2 begins executing, the value of BE is false, because this is the condition which terminates the while statement. Not only does the explicit control structure facilitate the verification, but concepts such as block structure or a procedure mechanism can also be of assistance. Block structure as defined in ALGOL60 may be somewhat inadequate to express context rules for operating systems, but related concepts can be used to great advantage. An example of such a related concept is that of the type definition which hides the internal structure of typed objects from the environment in which these objects are used.

Language constructs may also be useful in implementing certain rules of system behavior. One of the rules involves the collection of all waiting lists. We wish to make certain that a process can be in only one waiting list at a time. If every process has a single link field, then it is sufficient to show that no two processes have the same offspring or parent. Without the help of language constructs, we must show that every assignment to link fields obeys this rule. The proof can be given more rigorously if the rule is implemented through a description language concept. Keeping this purpose in mind, we define

```
type process =
   field priority = integer
   field STATE = oneof (blocked, ready, running)
   field psem = semaphore
   field link = ref self
   field saved stack pointer = machine address
 ____

 ____

   let p,q = process in
      ____
      exchlink(p,q) = begin local x = p.link; p.link ← q.link; q.link ← x end
      ____
      ____
end
```

This sketchy type definition for processes has a field "link" which can reference a process. The link field is initialized when a process is declared and is set to point to the declared process itself. The type definition provides exactly one operation on link fields, "exchlink". The two link fields of a pair of processes are interchanged when exchlink is applied. Thus, changes in the set of link values are caused by application of exchlink or by creating or killing a process. Exchlink splits a circular list in two if it is applied to two elements of one list, and concatenates two lists if applied to two elements in two distinct lists (see figure 10.3a).

When a process is created, a new circular list is introduced consisting of the process pointing at itself. When a process p is killed, the rule is that exchlink is applied to p and all the processes whose link fields point to p. It can easily be shown that these rules assure that a process cannot be in more than one list at a time. A given state S_1 is transformed into state S_2 by applying exchlink into S'_2 if a new process is created and into S''_2 if a process is killed. Assume that state S_1 has the desired property. State S_2 also has the desired property because exchlink adds one more list or concaternates two lists. State S'_2 has the desired property, because a new list is added consisting of the newly declared process pointing to itself. State S''_2 has the desired property, because there is only one process in state S_1 pointing to the process to be killed and exchlink leaves that property invariant. Since the initial state has the desired property, the induction principle states that all states have the property that a process cannot be in more than one list.

Sometimes a pseudo variable may help to verify a program. A pseudo variable is a variable which is not necessary for the execution of the program. It is added for verification purposes and can be removed from the program when it actually runs. In section 5.1 we discussed the communication of a group of senders with a group of receivers via a finite message buffer of n equal-size slots. Since a message fits in any slot, the slots will be used in a circular fashion. That is, after filling slot i, the next slot to be filled is slot (i+1) mod(n). Likewise, after taking a message from slot j, the next will be taken from slot (j+1) mod(n). The positions of the slots last filled and emptied are recorded in the pointers "front" and "rear" (see figure 10.3b).

A modified version of the last program in 5.1 implements the circular use of the buffer slots (⊕ represents addition modulo the buffer size).

```
proc deposit(m = message) =          proc remove(m = message) =
  begin                                begin'
    P(slotnum)                           P(mesnum)
      P(sender)                            P(receiver)
        S:front ← front ⊕ 1                  R:rear ← rear ⊕ 1
        BUF[front] ← m                       m ← BUF[rear]
      V(sender)                            V(receiver)
    V(mesnum)                            V(slotnum)
  end                                  end
```

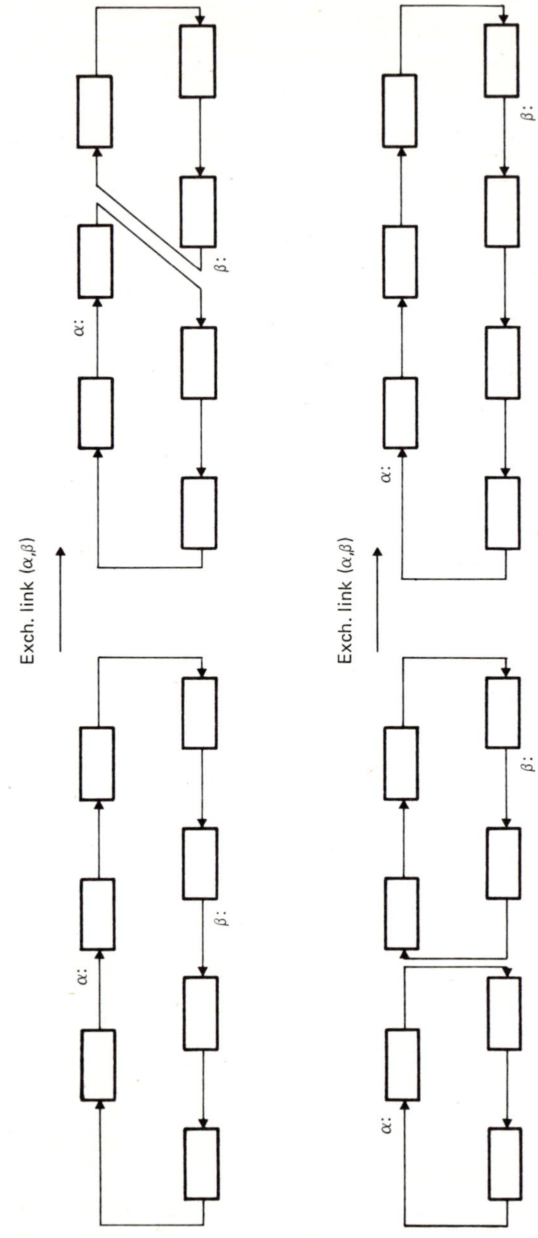

Figure 10.3a Breaking and merging circular lists by exchanging links

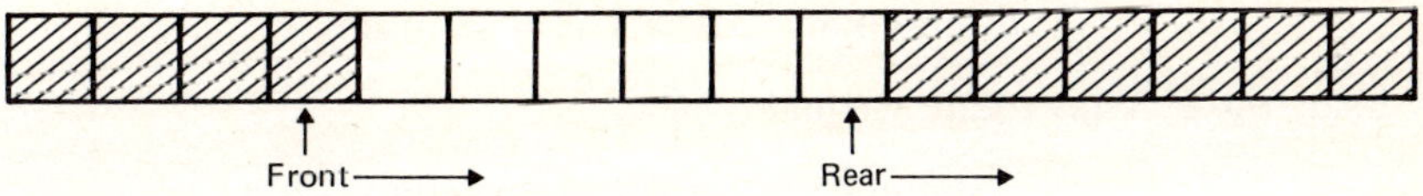

Figure 10.3b N-slot communication buffer

Semaphore “sender” is a critical section semaphore to make sure that only one sender at a time can place a message in the buffer. Likewise, the semaphore “receiver” allows only one receiver at a time to take a message out of the buffer. These semaphores are initialized to one. Semaphore “slotnum” is initialized to n becausc it indicates the number of free slots in the buffer. Semaphore mesnum indicates the number of messages placed but not taken out. It is initialized to zero, because the buffer is empty to begin with. The pointers rear and front are initially equal to zero.

We must prove that the buffer will not overflow or underflow. This would be the case if the front pointer overtakes the rear pointer or vice versa. More interesting is the proof that a sender and a receiver can be allowed to operate on the buffer at the same time. We can prove that a sender and a receiver cannot simultaneously operate on the same slot! This is the reason why it is not necessary to use one critical section semaphore for both senders and receivers.

The proof is given by using two pseudo variables and by using the properties of P and V. We assume that the semaphores in the deposit and remove programs are not used in other programs. On the line labeled S: we add the statement $F \leftarrow F+1$ and on the line labeled R: we add $R \leftarrow R+1$. These two pseudo variables are initialized to zero, like the front and rear pointer, but F and R count on instead of returning to 1 when $n+1$ is reached.

P and V have the property that the number of times that a semaphore sem is decremented in a P operation is never greater than the initial value of sem + the number of times that sem is incremented in a V operation. In other words, the P and V leave the relation

$$\text{DECR(sem)} \leq \text{INIT(sem)} + \text{INCR(sem)}$$

invariant. This relation applies to all semaphores in the programs for deposit and remove.

The statement sequence of deposit reveals that by the time a sender places a message in the buffer,

$$\text{DECR(slotmum)} \geq F > \text{INCR(mesnum)}$$

and the sequence of statements in remove implies that by the time a receiver removes a message from the buffer,

$$\text{DECR(mesnum)} \geq \text{R} > \text{INCR(slotnum)}$$

Using the P, V invariant, we find

$$\text{F} \leq \text{DECR(slotnum)} \leq \text{n}+\text{INCR(slotnum)} < \text{n}+\text{R}$$

and

$$\text{R} \leq \text{DECR(mesnum)} \leq \text{INCR(mesnum)} < \text{F}$$

The two relations combined state that by the time a sender places a message while at the same time a receiver removes a message

$$0 < \text{F}-\text{R} < \text{n}$$

Since front = F mod(n) and rear = R mod(n), this relation implies that the front and rear pointer do not point to the same slot if a sender and a receiver operate on the buffer at the same time.

10.3.3 Concurrency is the major phenomenon which makes designing an operating system different from designing large sequential programs. Up to this point the necessary synchronization has been implemented by placing a call to a P or V in the program text where needed. However, placing these calls in the text is really not any better than programming an iterative statement by a pair of goto statements at the beginning and end of a loop, instead of using a *for* or *while* or *repeat* statement. These beautiful language constructs have primarily been developed for writing sequential programs. The type definitions discussed in the preceding section define the internal structure of typed objects and the set of operations which can be applied to these objects, but nothing is said about timing constraints. Particularly with respect to concurrency, a type definition should also define the order in which the listed operations can be applied. This feature is provided by *path expressions*. The use of path expressions is shown by applying it to the buffer communication example. It is another demonstration of facilitating the verification through powerful description constructs. The proof given by using the P, V invariant becomes entirely superfluous.

First we define a type "*oneslot buffer*" and then a type "*ring buffer*."

```
type oneslot buffer =
  field slot = message
  path write; read end
  let m = message, s = oneslot buffer in
    write(m in s) = begin s.slot ← m end
    read(m from s) = begin m ← s.slot end
end
```

The path expression *path* write; read *end* expresses that writing and reading a oneslot buffer must occur in this order. In other words, between two successive write operations exactly one read operation must take place and between two successive read operations one write operation must take place. (The path expression is equivalent to the regular expression (write; read)*.) Note that the path expression is part of the internal structure of a oneslot buffer; every oneslot buffer has its own path, because the prescribed sequence of operations must be enforced for every oneslot buffer separately. The mechanism of the path expression works as follows. If two programs P_1 and P_2 attempt to write into one and the same oneslot buffer s, only one program (P_1, say) will be enabled to write in s, the other program must wait. When P_1 is done writing, P_2 cannot write, and P_1 can't write again. If a program P_3 attempts to read while P_1 is writing, P_3 is also delayed. As soon as P_1 has finished writing, P_3 is enabled to read and when P_3 has finished reading, P_2 can write.

Next we define the type ring buffer which corresponds to the n-slot buffer whose slots were used round robin.

```
type ring buffer(n = integer) =
   field ring = array[0:n−1] of oneslot buffer
   fields front, rear = integer(0)
   path advance front; copy front end
   path advance rear; copy rear end
let m = message, r = ring buffer in
      hidden proc advance front(r) = begin r.front ← r.front ⊕ 1 end
      hidden proc advance rear(r) = begin r.rear ← r.rear ⊕ 1 end
      hidden proc copy front(r) = integer; begin copy front ← r.front end
      hidden proc copy rear(r) = integer; begin copy rear ← r.rear end
      proc deposit(m in r) =
      begin advance front(r); write(r.ring[copy front(r)]) end
      proc remove(m from r) =
      begin advance rear(r); read(r.ring[copy rear(r)]) end
end
```

The path expression *path* advance front; copy front *end* assures that the front pointer is incremented exactly once before its value is used. (The prefix *hidden* means that these procedures are not exported outside the type definition.) It seems possible that depositing messages can indefinitely continue while no messages are taken out. The path expression which enforces the order of executing advance front and copy front does not forbid this at all. However, by the time the front pointer has overtaken the rear pointer, the senders will stop. At that time the earlier type definition for a oneslot buffer determines what happens next. In this situation the slot pointed at by the rear pointer can still be filled, because the last operation performed on it was read. But the next slot is disabled for writing for the path expression for a oneslot buffer because a read has not yet taken place after the last write.

The proof that a sender cannot deposit a message in a slot from which, at the same time, a receiver is removing a message is now trivial. It is based on the write, read path defined in the oneslot buffer type.

The operator + is used in path expressions to indicate selective execution. Critical sections are programmed with this operator. For instance, *path* a; b+c; d *end* means that first operation a must be executed, then either operation b or operation c and finally operation d; thereafter operation a may go again. We can also allow repetition within paths, indicated by the operator * (the Kleene star). For instance, *path* open; (read+write)*; close *end* describes the ordering of operations on a file. First the file must be opened, then an arbitrary number (zero is also allowed) of read and write operations follow and finally the file is closed. The read and write operations are here defined as mutually critical sections. It seems that reading could be allowed to go on in parallel. Concurrent execution is indicated by a brace pair { }. For instance, *path* {read}+write *end* means that either an arbitrary number of read operations may overlap in time, or one single write operation can be performed at a time.

Path expressions constructed with the operators ; + *, and in which no function name occurs more than once and a repeated element only occurs in a sequence preceded and followed by a nonrepeated element, are known as simple path expressions. The adjective *simple* is justified by the fact that these path expressions can be implemented by ordinary P, V operations (see problem 4).

The expressive power of simple path expressions is far greater than that of P and V. It is therefore questionable whether there is a need for more elaborate operators in path expressions. Anyway, the purpose of presenting the path expressions here is primarily to demonstrate the usefulness of a powerful description language. Modularity is an absolute necessity to make the verification task tractable. But well chosen features in a design or implementation language makes it possible to incorporate the verification in the design.

PROBLEMS

1. This problem is an exercise in utilizing a language feature to facilitate program verification. The problem is to write a program which outputs the postfix form of an infix expression involving operands, parentheses, and the operator +, for example, a+b+(c+d+(e+f)+g. The evaluation rule for these expressions is from left to right, but parentheses overrule the order of evaluation. Thus the postfix form of the given example is

ab+cd+ef+++g+

We assume that the input string is correctly structured. Given is

```
proc NEXT = lexeme
begin local lex = READ
   if lex ϵ operand then
      PRINT(lex); lex ← READ
   fi
end
```

A lexeme is a description of an input character. If lex is a lexeme, the next operator or parenthesis is placed in lex by the statement lex ← NEXT. It is legitimate to ask lex = '+' or lex = '(', etc. It is also possible to detect the end of the input by asking lex = eof, where eof stands for "end of file".

First write an iterative program, and then write a program which uses two recursive procedures, one for the operator +, and one for the parentheses. The plus procedure calls the parenthesis procedure when it finds an open parenthesis and processes the input until it finds a closed parenthesis or eof. The parenthesis procedure calls the plus procedure when it finds a + and it continues processing the input until it finds the matching closed parenthesis or eof.

Comparing the two programs, it will be evident that a stack mechanism had to be implemented in the iterative program but not in the recursive program.

2. A single receiver removes messages from a buffer with message slots of various sizes. There are exactly n senders and the buffer has n slots of every size, or a sender can always find a slot for his message assuming that a sender does not send another message until the preceding one has been received. Inspection and placing or taking a message is safeguarded by the critical section semaphore "mutex" (initial value one). The number of messages placed but not yet received is recorded in a shared variable n. Compare the following two versions of a receiver program.

```
Receiver (version 1):
repeat  P(mutex)
        if n > 0 then select message from buffer; n ← n−1 fi
        V(mutex)
until Receiver halt

Receiver (version 2):
repeat local condition
   P(mutex)
      if (condition ← n) > 0 then
         select message from buffer; n ← n−1 fi
   V(mutex)
until condition do P(buffernotempty) od
```

Semaphore buffernotempty is initialized to zero. Write two matching versions of a sender program. Show that the first version has a starvation problem (it could happen that the receiver is very active but a sender will never get a chance to deposit a message). Use the P, V invariant to show that there is no starvation in the second version.

3. The senders in the given P, V program for deposit search for an empty slot and place the message immediately in that slot before another sender is permitted to deposit a message. The P, V program for remove has a similar characteristic. Rewrite these programs so that a sender reserves a slot in which it is going to place a message, but before it actually deposits a message, another sender may already reserve another slot; likewise, for the receivers. These modified programs do not require that the buffer slots be subject to a round robin discipline.

4. The simple path expression *path* a; b+c; d *end* could be implemented by P, V operations on three semaphores s_1, s_2 and s_3. Define A = $P(s_1)$; a; $V(s_2)$, B = $P(s_2)$; b; $V(s_3)$, C = $P(s_2)$; c; $V(s_3)$ and D = $P(s_3)$; d; $V(s_1)$. These functions accomplish the same thing as a, b, c and d with the path expression if s_1 is initially one and the other semaphores zero. Initially, A is the only function that can be executed. When it finishes it enables either B or C and after that D is enabled. When D completes, the initial state is reached again. Describe an algorithm that parses a simple path expression without braces, but with parentheses and repetition. The algorithm may create as many semaphores as needed. The output of the algorithm must be a modified set of functions starting with a P and ending with a V such that the modified functions are equivalent to the given path expression.

5. The use of the concurrency operator assigns a priority to the concurrently executed function. If reading is going on and given is the path expression *path*{READ}+WRITE *end*, reading continues as long as new readers arrive. Writing cannot start until all reading has subsided. Show that priority is given to the writers by the combination of paths

path readrequest+{start writing; stop writing} *end*
path {read}+write *end*

where *proc* READ = *begin* readrequest; read *end* and
proc WRITE = *begin* start writing; write; stop writing *end*.

Try to construct a selfish scheme where each group has an equal chance to start, but once a group is busy, it won't give up until no one in that group shows further interest.

10.4 DOCUMENTATION

10.4.1 Writing an operating system consists of three major tasks:

1. Design and coding
2. Performance analysis and debugging
3. Description and documentation

These three tasks have often been treated as subsequent phases, even carried out by different groups of people. The arguments in favor of having separate groups working on the three tasks are rather negative in nature. The supervisors and sponsors of the project assume that the designers have a biased view on their work and therefore, so the reasoning goes, cannot be trusted to analyze it. People working on tasks 1 or 2 are supposed to lack writing skills or lack the ability to communicate with the user, so a third group of system promotors comes into being. One might think that, having the separate groups, each group is forced to describe precisely what it has accomplished. However, practice has shown misconceptions, misunderstandings, and frustrations among all the people involved.

In the preceding section it was argued that the verification must be incorporated into the design in the sense that the designer builds into the system the means to verify its correctness. The three tasks of design, analysis and documentation should likewise be integrated into one production effort. The three tasks should be seen as three different aspects of the total work instead of as three separate phases. In this section we discuss the nature of such an integrated design.

10.4.2 Famous among APL programmers are the magic one line programs which perform the most fantastic computations. Would you believe that

$$[1] \rightarrow y \neq x+y \leftarrow 0-(x \leftarrow x\lceil y)-z \leftarrow x\lfloor y$$

places the greatest common divisor of two positive numbers x and y in z? Programs written in such a concise notation are hard to read if the reader does not know what the program is supposed to do. The absence of meaningful control structures makes it very hard to analyze programs, particularly large programs. This is a well-known problem with programs written in assembly code. On the other hand, it is an illusion to think that other programming languages are any better in conveying what a program does. The primary purpose of the programming language is to write a program in an executable form. This places certain constraints on the language and its use to describe a design plan. On the one hand, the language is too restrictive and, on the other hand, too demanding. It is too restrictive, because the designer will inevitably come across some data structure or other concept which cannot easily be expressed in the language. The language is too demanding, because it requires that everything be spelled out in detail, making it hard on the designer to abstract from irrelevant matters at various stages of the design.

It is unfair to show a program to somebody and ask him what it does. This is not unlike telling a suspect to prove that he is innocent. A program does not convey what it does but how it is done. It describes the implementation in terms of control flow and data structures. Though rather elaborate data structures can be created in modern programming languages, a representation of how it is done is never going to tell you what it is supposed to do or how well it does it. Therefore, we must see an executable program as a particular piece in the design plan. However, it is only part of the total product; it must not exist on its own without a proper explanation and justification.

Once we have come this far, we see that good documentation is indispensible. In fact the text of the executable programs is only a part of the total design plan description. The documentation will not only describe how the system is implemented, but it also states the objectives of the system, the major design decisions, its overall structure, and other specifications such as figures for the maximum number of users, available equipment, performance, etc. Here in this section we restrict our discussion to the documentation related to the design.

Designers can make two major mistakes in adopting a method for documenting their system. The first mistake is to interpret the notion "documentation" to mean extensive commenting of the code. This leads to useless repetition of the code itself as in

```
ADDI   R, 1      $ add one to register R
```

This sort of comment is another form of implementation description and is therefore inadequate to convey the design plan. The other major mistake designers can make is to describe everything in the same degree of detail. This leads to the useless complete description which tells the reader so much more than he wishes to know or needs to know that he cannot find out what he wants to know or ought to know. These mistakes can be avoided if some thought is given as to how the documentation is going to be organized. In the remainder of this section we present a possible method for creating useful documentation.

10.4.3 The principle of this method is that the documentation is described in parts, called segments, each of which consists of four sections. The first section is an optional introduction describing terminology or relationships to other parts. The second section is a design specification which describes and explains the semantics of this part. This description is not bound to a particular programming language. It may contain abstractions and unspecified objects which are explained elsewhere. The description is often in terms of fundamental control flow expressions, data representations and short phrases in English. Most descriptions in this book are in that style.

The third section lists the important decisions the designers are aware of. It is often very hard and time-consuming to reconstruct a decision and its motivation if it has not been documented, but must be derived from the final programs. This is particularly difficult for the people responsible for maintaining a system if they did not participate in the design. On the other hand, the designer does not always realize the importance of a decision until later. Therefore, the section on design decisions must be open-ended. By the time the significance of certain decisions becomes clear, new descriptions must be added and old ones modified or deleted.

The fourth section is an analysis of the design and the performance of this part. In the beginning it will contain mostly conjectures about the behavior of this part of the system and means to test, verify and measure it. Later, when related parts have been designed and tested, the analysis section may contain test results and suggestions for improvement. The analysis section must obviously also be open-ended.

It seems as if one kind of section is missing, because coding was not listed. There is, however, no need for such a section. The documentation describes the system concepts in various degrees of detail. Therefore, for every documentation segment S which contains uncoded objects, there will be other segments which describe these uncoded objects in more detail. We plan to structure the documentation such that the segments can be ordered by "more or less detail". If segments S_2 and S_3 describe objects of segment S_1 in more detail, then S_1 is before S_2 and S_3. If S_2 is before S_4, then also S_1 is said to be before S_4. We try to structure the documentation such that S_i before S_j implies that S_j is not before S_i. (We try to structure the documentation such that the relation "before" is transitive and irreversible.)

We do not rule out the possibility that there are pairs of documentation segments for which the relation "before" is undefined. The relation is like a family relationship based on "offspring of." It is not even necessary for the documentation to have a tree structure where every node has exactly one parent. The structure is that of a directed graph where the terminal nodes are the code segments.

This method of documentation does not require a top-down approach to the design. It is likely that a segment S_1 is initialized before segment S_2 if S_1 is before S_2. But we may continue the design for a while descending into more detail and then come back and start at an unrelated segment. The way the decision section and the analysis sections are set up makes the design process more iterative than top-down. The possible modifications of the decision sections and analysis sections make it difficult to show the documentation method here on paper, because the aspect of a developing system design cannot easily be represented. Another difficulty is the size of a real system. All we can present here is the very first steps of documenting a system. An example of the first steps is given in the remainder of this section.

10.4.4 Here follows a sketch of the initial documentation of a layer structured timesharing system.

Segment 0. System Outline
preceded by: none; succeeded by: 1, –
Specs: ⟨this segment begins with a listing of the equipment, the size and speed of various devices⟩

The timesharing operating system, LTS, consists of eight layers.

1. Fixed page environments
2. Processes
3. Demand paging
4. File system
5. Peripheral devices
6. Operator console
7. Compilers, loaders
8. User terminals

The ordering implies that data and code of layers 1, 2 and 3 must remain permanently in the mainstore, because the information flow between the two storage levels is controlled by layer 3.

Decs: 1. The file system is placed as low as possible so that the peripheral devices can also transfer information as files. 2. Compilers, etc. are placed above layer 6 so that malfunctioning or lack of input data can be signalled to the human operator.

An: 1. Would it be better to reverse the order of layers 4 and 5? If peripheral devices create files, it is necessary for files to be expandable, because input files can be of unknown length. 2. How many users can the system support? (Plot number of users against response time.) 3. Is the secondary store large enough to keep a reasonable number of user files around? (Give average size of user area measured in pages and frequency of disk overflow.)

Segment 1. Paging Environments
preceded by: 0; succeeded by: –.
Specs: ⟨here follows a description of the paging hardware⟩

The specifications of this section could be those of the paging environments for HM as discussed in section 10.2. First a definition of page descriptor is given; subsequently the data structures and operations on paging environments are described. The level of detail is also the same as in section 10.1.

Decs: 1. Pagefault handling is excluded from this layer, because it involves rather slow data transmissions which causes in turn a need for suspending processes in order to avoid wasting CPU time. But the lowest layer does not know about processes. 2. The states "absent" and "double" are defined here in order to avoid a duplication of all page information in layer 3.

An: 1. The page table is divided into 16 areas. Would it be better to split it into more areas of smaller size?

2. Would it be better to reverse the order of layers 1 and 2? In the given order we need a primitive synchronization tool such as LOCK/UNLOCK for certain operations on page descriptors (for example, share). The other way around we must devise special instructions for the lowest layer to fill working page registers. The chosen order seems preferable for two reasons: a) paging environments are not tied to processes; b) since a process can be transferred from one paging environment to another, there will be less need to create a special process for every function in the operating system. Most of the work can be done through system functions working in their own environment.

3. What is the best way to implement the access restrictions determined by the type and module definitions? It is possible to force every user to generate his machine code through a modified assembler which generates the appropriate calling sequences. The environment transition can be implemented through an interrupt. This interrupt activates the lowest layer which in turn changes the page table base.

The next documentation segment may describe the operations on page descriptors in more detail. It might also contain the programs for these operations written in an implementation language. Instead of going down the path of the first layer, we could first write a segment of another layer. The order in which the segments are initialized is not prescribed. Needless to say, every segment must be expandable, because information will be added as the design progresses.

We conclude the documentation here. The example is not so much presented to describe the LTS operating system as to exemplify how the documentation is set up. Moreover, we stated earlier that the documentation is by no means static, but grows and changes with the system. Documentation is a highly dynamic matter which must be treated as an integral part of the design effort. The worst we can do is not document at all, but almost as bad is a documentation produced as an afterthought separated in time from the design, and written by people who did not participate in the design.

PROBLEMS

1. This documentation method is very close to the methods which have been advocated for program decomposition. The documentation segments correspond to various abstractions which the programmer wishes to think through separately. Apply the documentation/decomposition method to the problem below.

Every user has a fixed set of page descriptors. Pages can be created and deleted. A pointer indicates the last allocated page descriptor. When a page is created, the pointer is moved upwards until a free descriptor is found. When the pointer reaches the upperbound, it is reset to the beginning of the table. When a page is deleted, the descriptor is marked "free". Write documentation on the construction of a program which finds a free descriptor and assigns it to a new (empty) page.

2. A more elaborate exercise in documenting a system is an application of the described method to the simple batch system described in chapter 2. The structure of the system is still so simple that the documentation can be produced in a couple of days. It is not necessary to go into the coding details; programs written in FORTRAN or an ALGOL-like language should be the terminal segments of the documentation. The specifications of the system are found in section 2.2.

3. Another documentation exercise is the description of the file system described in sections 9.4 and 9.5. This exercise shows that it is not necessary to apply a top-down design method. It may be necessary to make assumptions about the service provided by parts of the system that remain unspecified. In that case a documentation segment should be created in which this assumption is recorded.

4. The outline of the LTS operating system (section 10.4.4) specifies a separate layer for the operator console. Investigate why it is not desirable to place the operator console in the same layer as the user terminals. Also consider the consequences of exchanging the file system layer and the operator control layer. In section 5.2 we discussed the functional hierarchy implemented by the layers. Indicate for the LTS layer structure the connections of each layer with the other layers. Is the hierarchy of the layer structure also present in the documentation?

READING LIST

Two new approaches to system construction are [1, 4]. The various aspects of system deadlocks are reviewed in [2]. Deadlock avoidance by stating claims is discussed in [3, 5]. The issue of deriving information from observed events is discussed in [6]. Fundamental ideas on design methodology are presented in [7, 8, 9].

1. Campbell, R., and A. N. Habermann, "Specification of Process Synchronization by Path Expressions," *Lecture Notes in Computer Science*, Springer Verlag (1974).

2. Coffman, E. G., Jr., M. J. Elphick, and A. Shoshani, "System Deadlocks," *Computing Surveys* 3, 2 (June 1971).

3. Habermann, A. N., "Prevention of System Deadlocks," *Comm. ACM* 12, 7 (July 1969).

4. Hoare, C. A. R., "Monitors: An Operating System Structuring Concept," *Comm. ACM* 17, 10 (October 1974); see also Erratum: *Comm. ACM* 18, 2 (February 1975).

5. Holt, R. C., "Some Deadlock Properties of Computer Systems," *Computing Surveys*, 4, 3 (September 1972).

6. Lampson, B., "A Note on the Confinement Problem," *Comm. ACM* 16, 10 (October 1973).

7. Liskov, B., "A Design Methodology for Reliable Software Systems," *Proceedings of the AFIPS FJCC* 41 (December 1972).

8. Parnas, D. L., "A Technique for Software Module Specification with Examples," *Comm. ACM* 15, 5 (May 1972).

9. Parnas, D. L., "On the Criteria to Be Used in Decomposing Systems into Modules," *Comm. ACM* 15, 12 (December 1972).

INDEX

6789/4321